Enactments

EDITED BY RICHARD SCHECHNER

To perform is to imagine, represent, live and enact present circumstances, past events and future possibilities. Performance takes place across a very broad range of venues from city streets to the countryside, in theatres and in offices, on battlefields and in hospital operating rooms. The genres of performance are many, from the arts to the myriad performances of everyday life, from courtrooms to legislative chambers, from theatres to wars to circuses.

ENACTMENTS will encompass performance in as many of its aspects and realities as there are authors able to write about them.

ENACTMENTS will include active scholarship, readable thought and engaged analysis across the broad spectrum of performance studies.

on the edge of utopia

performance and ritual at burning man

RACHEL BOWDITCH

Seagull Books
LONDON NEW YORK CALCUTTA

Seagull Books 2010

ISBN-13 978 1 9064 9 725 5
ISSN 1751 0864

British Library Cataloguing-in-Publication Data

A catalogue record for this book is available from the British Library

Typeset by Seagull Books, Calcutta, India

Printed and bound by Leelabati Printers, Calcutta, India

To Sophie, John, Bruce, Mark and Kirsten,
to my parents and to all my teachers.

Imagine you are put upon a desert plain, a space which is so vast and blank that only your initiative can make of it a place. Imagine it is swept by fearsome winds and scorching temperatures, and only by your effort can you make of it a home. Imagine you're surrounded by thousands of other people, that together you form a city, and that within this teeming city there is nothing that's for sale. The Black Rock Desert is an empty void. Not a bird or bush or bump disturb its surface. It is a place that is no place at all apart from what we choose to make of it. The *playa* is like an enormous blank canvas. The desert is a blank slate. It is empty when Burning Man begins and it is cleaned up, it is empty again at the end, as if it never happened.

—Harvey (2000a)

CONTENTS

ACKNOWLEDGEMENTS

I am grateful to my mentors Kevin Burns, Gautam Dasgupta, RoseLee Goldberg and Richard Schechner who taught me the value of the experimental and the avant-garde. I would like to thank Barbara Kirshenblatt-Gimblett for all the research skills and tools she has taught me; André Lepecki for his encouragement and wisdom; Deborah Kapchan for her insights and perspective; RoseLee Goldberg for her mentorship and support; and Richard Schechner who believed in this project from the beginning and provided invaluable editing advice. New York University and the Department of Performance Studies in Tisch School of the Arts offered extensive resources in the early phases of my research, especially the faculty: Diana Taylor, Ann Pellegrini, Karen Shimakawa, Allen Weiss, Anna Deavere Smith, José Muñoz, Tavia Nyong'o and Barbara Browning. This book would not have been possible without the support of Richard Schechner, editor of the Enactments Series, the insight and expertise of Mariellen Sandford, and my publisher Naveen Kishore at Seagull Books.

Thanks to the incredible support from the Burning Man community who gave of their time and knowledge in many interviews: Larry Harvey, Crimson Rose, Will Roger, Marian Goodell, Harley K. Dubois, and especially Michael Mikel who worked closely with me in the final months of editing, generously offering time, historical context and advice. Also thanks to Andie Grace, Christine Kristen aka Lady Bee, Kelly Anders, Terry Schoop aka Retro, David Best, Adrian Roberts, Jim Glaser, Shawna Hofmann, Malakai, Matty Dowlen, Chris Sia, Neal Everett, Suzanne Bernel, Kevin Bourque, Eric Newton, Richard 'Spark' Szpigiel, Raquel Reyna, Paradox Pollack, Carmenchu, Reggie Ballard, Lea Bender, Paul D. Miller, Mark van Proyen and Al Ridenour; Jen Colasuonno and the Merry-Go-Round for hosting me while conducting research in San Francisco; Daniel Pinchbeck, John Rinaldi aka Chicken John, Cassandra Marshall, Robert Heacock aka Captain Bob, Tedward, Colinne Hemrich, Michele Steele, Camp Hex, Kostume Kult, the Red Nose District, Jessie Kile and all the performers and participants who allowed me to interview them. A special thanks to all the Burning Man photographers who gave me permission to use their images in this book: Bill Tonnesen, John Romero, Scott London, Gabe Kirchheimer, Joshua Brott, Stewart Harvey, Rick Egan, Gregory Zabilski, Pixie, Sharlene Stephens and others. Burning Man scholars Brian Doherty, Catherine Chen, Sarah Pike, Mark van Proyen, Lee Gilmore and Wendy Clupper provided insight and perspective.

Presenting my research at conferences and publishing parts of it as I went along provided a forum for developing and editing my work. Thank you to John Bell for publishing my article 'Dancing with Fire: The Ultimate Effigy' in *Puppetry International* 22 (2007); and Debra Bruch at the *Journal of Religion and Theatre* 6(2) (2007) for publishing 'Temple of Tears: Revitalizing and Inventing Ritual in the Burning Man Community in the Black Rock Desert, Nevada'. I presented aspects of this research at the following conferences: the 10th Annual Conference on Holidays, Ritual, Festival, Celebration, and Public Display, Willamette University, Salem, Oregon, 2006; American Society for Theatre Research (ASTR) Escaping America seminar, Phoenix, 2007; the Mid-Atlantic Popular Culture Conference on Fantastical Cities, Philadelphia, 2007; the Association of Theatre in Higher Education (ATHE) Religion and Theatre focus group, New Orleans, 2007; and the Hemispheric Institute Encuentro, Buenos Aires, Argentina, 2007, and Bogota, Colombia, 2009. Dialogue with and critiques from scholars in a variety of disciplines—Paolo Vignolo, Milla Riggio, Zeca Ligiero, Lance Gharavi, John Sebastian, Jack Santino, Elaine Aston, Leslie Durham, Erith Jaffe-Berg, Silvija Jestrovic and Blagovesta Momchedjikova—have served to further develop the work.

And finally, thanks to Linda Essig, my colleagues and my students at the School of Theatre and Film at Arizona State University for their encouragement and inspiration in my final stages of writing and editing, especially Kathy Nigh for a fresh set of eyes; my mom, dad, Mimi, Bruce, Kirsten, Mark and his family, John's family and all of my friends, who have given me support throughout this entire process; and most of all to my incredible research assistant and photographer, my husband, John Tzelepis, for his patience and love.

LIST OF FIGURES

PREFACE

I first learned about Burning Man in 1998 on the banks of the Seine River in Paris. I was in Paris studying physical theatre at Ecole de Jacques Lecoq when a visiting friend from the San Francisco Art Institute, Scott Newell, asked me if I had ever heard of Burning Man. I said no. He told me about this event full of interactive performances, rituals, costumes, masking and art installations. My friend was earning academic credit at the San Francisco Art Institute by building large-scale installations at Burning Man. This work was coordinated by his professor, Mark van Proyen, the coeditor of *After Burn*: *Reflections on Burning Man* (2005).

When I returned to the United States in 1999, Lea Bender, one of my closest friends and cofounder of our theatre company *Vessel,* told me about her experience of attending Burning Man for the first time. She had moved south to San Francisco after our summer internships at the Dell'Arte School of Physical Theatre in Blue Lake, California, where I first encountered fire performance. In San Francisco she met a troupe of circus performers who invited her to join them at Burning Man. Her experience was transformative. I decided I needed to go to Burning Man and finally found my way there in 2001.

The experience did indeed change my life, although not in the ways I expected. The person I went with was not enjoying the experience and was critical of everything. His relentless negative commentary forced me to be outside as well as inside Burning Man. I had an illuminating if ambivalent first experience. I detected a parallel ambivalence throughout the community. As I sat at Nine and Oblivion, our playa address, gazing at the vast desert landscape, I realized how privileged I was, as an American, to 'play at survival' in the desert. As I sat in the desert in a tipi complete with a faux lawn, Christmas lights and cushions, suddenly, a dust storm hit and whited everything out. Everyone rushed to put on goggles, dust masks and bandanas to protect themselves against the suffocating billows of fine white dust. This was Tuesday, 4 September 2001. Seven days later I was in New York City observing a similar cloud of billowing white plumes and crowds of real survivors donning dust masks. It was 9/11, a significant historical turning point for the United States and the world, and there were repercussions even at Burning Man. Most significantly, there was a shift towards political art and performance that reflected the political climate in the US; that is not to say political performance did not occur before 2001 but its presence was more acute post-9/11, as Chapter 3 will reveal.

While the event began in 1986, the Burning Man phenomenon has gained the increasing attention of scholars from a variety of disciplines: anthropology, sociological, theology, ritual studies and performance studies. By 2005, the first two critical books on Burning Man had been published: *This is Burning Man: The Rise of a New American Underground* (2004) by Brian Doherty; and *AfterBurn: Reflections on Burning Man* (2005), a compilation of essays on Burning Man edited by Lee Gilmore and Mark van Proyen. There have been numerous dissertations on Burning Man, including my own, and many more are currently in progress both nationally and internationally, indicating the growing interest in Burning Man as a site of scholarly inquiry.[1] Doherty's book, geared to a popular audience, focuses on the early history and development of the event and has been invaluable in my understanding of Burning Man's earliest presence on Baker Beach in San Francisco and how this evolved into Black Rock City in the desert of Nevada.

My fieldwork took place from 2001 to 2008 and required a critical rethinking of methodological approaches towards the archive and how we document the ephemeral, especially art predicated on disappearance—art that is constructed to be destroyed. I frame my analysis diachronically and synchronically on how ritual and performance have evolved within this eight-year span. Each year's theme—'The Seven Ages of Man' (2001), 'Floating World' (2002), 'Beyond Belief' (2003), 'Vault of Heaven' (2004), 'Psyche' (2005), 'Hope and Fear' (2006), 'Green Man' (2007) and 'The American Dream' (2008)—is determined by Burning Man founder Larry Harvey and dictates the overall concept that governs the aesthetics and content of the art as well as the street names and the design of the Man, which changes each year.

Through interviews and detailed participant-observation, I have gained a close-up, in-depth understanding of the Burning Man Organization and how it functions; how the city is created; how the population has grown and evolved; how art, performance, and ritual are integrated into the community; and how Burning Man has profoundly transformed the lives of many of its participants. Merging participant-observation, interviews, and photographic and video documentation with archival research (documents, newspaper articles, photographs, and digital archival resources) I fuse quantitative and qualitative methods to analyse the event. In addition to fieldwork, I engage with discourses on counterculture, utopia, secular pilgrimage, the new American alternative circus, and secular ritual practices. Using these discourses, I place Burning Man in relationship to ritual, play and performance; the archive and the repertoire; ephemerality and disappearance; the performance of everyday life; and liveness and performativity.[2]

Burning Man is a predominantly 'white'/middle-class US event, even though some diversity does exist. I share similar demographic characteristics with a majority of the Burning Man population being 'white' and 'middle class'. Although I have an American passport and two 'white' American parents, I was born in Rome, Italy, and spent the first 18 years of my life overseas: Italy; Addis Abba, Ethiopia; Jakarta, Indonesia; Singapore; and Tel Aviv, Israel. Since then I have lived in Saratoga Springs, New York; London; Paris, France; New York City; and most recently Phoenix, Arizona. Technically, I am 'American' but I see the United States through a 'nomadic' lens. I remain a mosaic of all the cultures I have met, lived in and with, and embraced, and this inevitably influences my perspective and scholarship.

As a performance studies scholar, theatre director, teacher and performer, my perspective merges theory and practice, drawing on my embodied understanding of performance as well as theoretical and historical approaches. My own theatre training—at Skidmore College (1994–8), the British American Drama Academy (BADA) in London (1996), Suzuki and Viewpoint training with Anne Bogart and the SITI company (1996), Dell'Arte School of Physical Theatre in Blue Lake, California (1998), Ecole de Jacques Lecoq in Paris, France (1998–9), and in the Department of Performance Studies at New York University (2003–06)—has served as a starting point for understanding myself as a reflexive subject moving through Black Rock City and responding somatically to the rhythms and choreography of the temporary community. Through an artistic and theatrical sensibility, I found a way to begin effectively communicating with a community that was unfamiliar to me. While I do not consider myself a 'Burner', I do feel connected to the community and its ideals of artistic experimentation and risk taking. However, I also feel a critical distance, which has allowed me to navigate the complex event from a variety of vantage points, both as an insider and outsider.

As I began my fieldwork, several questions emerged, the first being: what can the lens of Performance Studies as an analytical tool offer ethnographic participant-observation methodology? I approached my subjects from the perspective of an artist/director/performance studies scholar as well as from the perspective of an ethnographer. Many of my 'subjects' related to me on an artist-to-artist level and spoke with me about technique and method in a language we had in common. The relationship was artist to artist as well as ethnographer to subject. In critically rethinking the traditional role of ethnographer and the technique of participant-observation, I am inspired by Deidre Sklar's somatic, reflexive approach in *Dancing with the Virgin: Body and Faith in the Fiesta of Tortugas, New Mexico* (2001). Adopting Sklar's approach, I recorded sights, sounds, smells, gestures and everyday movements as a way of understanding the preparations for and the experience of Burning Man.

Through my senses, I gained an in-depth embodied knowledge of the festival and its meaning within the community. It is in the ritualized details of preparation and participation that the meaning of the festival is unearthed. In order to convey this experience, I juxtapose my perceptions and experiences of moving through Black Rock City with direct citations from my field notes and participants' narratives about their Burning Man experience. Fusing Michel de Certeau's ideas of 'walking the city' with

Mike Pearson and Michael Shanks's notion of 'desire mapping', I chart my path through the playa, tracing my movements on a map. Part of my somatic approach incorporates daily recordings of how my body moved through the city each day and how this mapping can be a way of embodied learning about the community. Finally, the inherent ephemerality of the event—created to be destroyed—challenges how I navigate the detritus of the event, the archive and the embodied memories of affective experiences, the repertoire (see Taylor 2003).

The book follows the arc of my experiences at Burning Man in order to give the reader a glimpse into what it is like to attend the event. I trace the process from preparing for the journey to the desert and the pilgrimage to Black Rock City, to moving through the city and navigating its complex culture, and then on to the preparations for the burn, the burn itself, the cool down, the aftermath and the Burning Man diaspora.[3] Tracing the history of the event from its inception in 1986 through 2008, I lay the historical foundations for understanding the growth and evolution of the event, from a personal healing ritual into an ephemeral city. Turning to the spatial configuration of Black Rock City, I analyse Burning Man as a rehearsal for utopia, one full of ambiguity and contradictions, in which participants negotiate a delicate balance between freedom and surveillance, the 'gift economy' and consumerism.

The spectrum of performance practices within Black Rock City ranges from performances of the everyday to highly structured and rehearsed spectacles. I consider the everyday performances at Burning Man, the blurring of art and life, and the performance and play of self in relation to the carnivalesque. Countercultures characteristically exhibit utopian undertones of a deliberate, conscious and organized effort to construct a more satisfying culture and society. Burning Man, like carnival or the Saturnalia, also functions as a social pressure valve: by constructing what Mikhail Bakhtin calls a 'second world' (1984), participants temporarily turn the world upside down. This inversion leads to the desire to invent new rituals and belief systems. Through a small sampling of professional performance groups within the Burning Man community—The Burning Man Opera, AWD, Xeno, El Circo, and Cirque Berzerk—I situate their work within the context of the 'new American alternative circus' and explore the important role Burning Man continues to play in the development of this genre.

The four central rituals at Burning Man—the Lamplighters, the ephemeral temples created by artist David Best, the Fire Conclave and the burning of the Man—serve as the community's connective tissue and create meaning for the participants. The book concludes with 'Beyond Black Rock City', which focuses on the transformation of the seven-day event into an ongoing virtual community and the elaborate Burning Man Regional Network of actual communities, which extends the Burning Man ethos and aesthetic into communities across the United States and around the world.

Notes

The spelling and grammar in the book follow British Standard English according to the Oxford Editor's Dictionary.

1 Recent Ph.D. dissertations on Burning Man include: Rachel Bowditch, 'Fire, Ritual, Play, and Profit: Rehearsing Utopian Performance at Burning Man' (2007, New York University); Wendy Clupper, 'The Performance Culture of Burning Man' (2007, University of Maryland); Lee Gilmore, 'Theatre in Crowded Fire: Spirituality, Ritualization and Cultural Performativity at the Burning Man Festival' (2005, Graduate Theological Union); Katherine Chen, 'The Burning Man Organization Grows Up: Blending Bureaucratic and Alternative Structures' (2004, Harvard University; now published); Jeremy Hockett, 'Reckoning Ritual and Counter-culture in the Burning Man Community: Communication, Ethnography, and the Self in Reflexive Modernism' (2004, University of New Mexico); Richard Stevens, 'Burning for the Other: Semiotics of a Levinasian Theological Aesthetics in the Light of Burning Man' (2003, Graduate Theological Union).

2 Beginning my research while I was a Masters student in Performance Studies, I have conducted four summers of fieldwork at the Burning Man event in the Black Rock Desert of Nevada (2001, 2004, 2005 and 2008) and have attended many Burning Man regional performances and events, mostly in New York City. I conducted over a hundred interviews with key Burning Man personnel including: Burning Man founder Larry Harvey; Burning Man Limited Liability Company members Michael Mikel, Crimson Rose, Harley K. Dubois, Marian Goodell and Will Roger; as well as participants, performers and artists who play a significant role in the artistic community of Burning Man. Working with my husband and research assistant, John Tzelepis, we shot over 2,000 full colour

images and approximately 15 hours of digital video footage of the event from 2004, 2005 and 2008. Many of the images from earlier years are archival images created by various Burning Man participants who have given me permission to include them.

3 Richard Schechner proposes a performance sequence of preparation, rehearsal, warm-up, performance, cool-down and aftermath (1988: 281). I use this sequence as a way to understand the various phases of Burning Man as a large-scale performance.

INTRODUCTION

> There is a yet unnamed art movement that may prove to be of some significance, and Burning Man is close to its center. It often manifests itself as circus, ritual, and spectacle. [. . .] It is a movement away from static gallery art and formal theater and towards site-specific, time-specific installation and performance. [. . .] It is profoundly democratic. It is radically inclusive, it is a difficult challenge, and it is beckoning (Kristen 2003: 343).

Burning Man is as epic as the Ramlila of Ramnagar,[1] as flamboyant as New Orleans' Mardi Gras and Brazilian carnival, and as spontaneous as a Rainbow Gathering. Imagine the wildest circus in the world and magnify that a hundredfold. But it has not always been so enormous or wild. Steadily, since its beginnings in 1986, Burning Man has evolved from Larry Harvey's personal healing ritual into a contemporary cultural phenomenon where ritual, religion, visual art and performance collide on an epic scale. During the week before Labour Day, approximately 49,000 people gravitate towards the ancient lakebed of Lake Lahontan in the Black Rock Desert of northwest Nevada to build their own separate world: 'Black Rock City'. This 'playa', or beach, entirely devoid of vegetation, is one of the largest in the United States. As it was in 2008—and has been for a number of years prior—Black Rock City is a simulation of a real city, replete with street signs, roads, theme camps, art villages, hundreds of huge interactive art installations, a temple, hundreds of 'art cars', a post office, a daily newspaper, an airport and hundreds of planned and spontaneous performances. A 40-foot wooden effigy of a Man stands on an altar at the centre of Black Rock City as the *axis mundi* of the Burning Man community, around which art, performance and community revolve. The Man stands at the end of a monumental avenue lined with wooden spires, like a Neolithic temple complex, its linear streets evenly dividing the semicircular array of civic architecture, arranged from 2 o'clock to 10 o'clock around the figure, replicating the shape of an enormous sundial. The entire event culminates on Saturday night in the ritual burning of the 40-foot wooden effigy of a Man, followed on Sunday night by the burning of a wooden temple.

Just as abruptly as it appears, with a lifespan of one very intense week, Black Rock City vanishes. An important coda to the festival is the total cleaning and restoration of the desert, erasing all evidence of the City's evanescent presence. Black Rock City remains only as a trace in photographs, videos, writings, oral histories and memories. During the months of Black Rock City's nonexistence, the Burning Man community continues to exist across the US and the world via an elaborate network called the 'Burning Man Regional Network'.

Historically, avant-garde artists have taken an oppositional stance to established mainstream culture, challenging and subverting the conventional practices and boundaries of all of the arts, from writing to painting to performance. While evincing creative tensions between individual invention and collective artistic creative processes, Burning Man revives avant-garde ideals of the 1960s and 1970s: ideals of community, democracy and collaborative creation. But Burning Man reinvents these goals and processes, fusing them with a savvy twenty-first century technological edge. Burning Man continues, yet profoundly revises and challenges, the narrative and historical continuum of the practices pioneered by Black Mountain College, Fluxus, Happenings, Environmental Theatre, Land Art and the Judson Dance Theatre. As a social experiment in community, Burning Man forges new directions for performance and interactive installation art, pushing the limits of what is possible in terms of scale, scope, ambition, participation, and innovation. Burning Man is a 'performance of great magnitude' (see Schechner 1988: 251).

At one level, Burning Man is a meeting of many artists from different disciplines—a kind of arts festival.[2] But at another, Burning Man practises the blurring of art and life advocated by Allan Kaprow and others. For the week of Burning Man, arts of all kinds are practised 'as life' in a temporary community created to foster precisely this kind of conflation. Although the Burning Man Organization (BMO) charges a steep admission fee to enter Black Rock City, it is different from many corporate festivals around the United States. What makes Burning Man an anomaly is that the BMO does not accept any corporate sponsorship, nor does it apply for grants or any outside funding—the entire event is generated by ticket sales marketed through word-of-mouth and viral marketing. In the current climate of ubiquitous corporate sponsorship, with arts festivals branded by AT&T, American Express, Coca-Cola and other corporations, it is rare to find a large-scale festival that does not have at least some form of corporate backing. However, Burning Man has an ambivalent relationship with economics and commerce, as this book will reveal.

Culture Jamming: The Myth of Counterculture

Cultural rebellion is not a new phenomenon and has existed in almost every phase of history. The first major US countercultural movement, which emerged after World War II as a result of the Vietnam War and the national draft, was signified by shared beliefs, values and behaviours that exhibited a lifestyle significantly different from the dominant culture. The term 'generation x', coined by Robert Capa in the early 1950s, became a catch-all phrase that captured the identity of youth culture after World War II. According to John M. Ulrich and Andrea L. Harris, since the 1960s the term has always signified a group of young people seemingly without individual identity and who face an uncertain and hostile future (2003: 3). Their use of the term 'generation x' does not signify a chronological age but a way of seeing the world that blurs the boundaries between the subculture and the mainstream. It is precisely this blankness or lack of identity that paved the way for recycling culture through pastiche, collage and assemblage—what is known as 'culture jamming'—a process coterminous with the postmodern cultural landscape (ibid.: 10).

The process of culture jamming lays the groundwork for the emergence of Burning Man. As Chapter 1 explores, the culture jamming entity called the Cacophony Society is largely responsible for what Burning Man is today.

As a countercultural phenomenon, Burning Man is a generative space for the rehearsal of alternative lifestyles and identities; at the same time, it rearticulates and redefines the relationship between the alternative and the mainstream. The term 'counterculture' is unstable, requiring explanation. 'Counterculture' as a concept was first introduced in 1969 by Theodore Roszak in *The Making of a Counter Culture: Reflections on the Technocratic Society and Its Youthful Opposition*. Counterculture is both against the dominant culture and an active alternative to it. As Keith Melville noted in *Communes in the Counter Culture: Origins, Theories, Styles of Life* (1972), small pockets have for some time been forging a new mode of existence outside of Guy Debord's 'society of the spectacle' (1977), a trend that indicates a desire to move towards simplification and decommodification.

As J. Milton Yinger notes, 'Today's counterculturalists can be thought of as the shamans of urban society, dreaming new dreams, formulating new myths, forging alternative paradigms' (1982: 9). He points out that a society without countercultures is a vulnerable society, unable to deal with rapidly changing social conditions (ibid.: 15). Countercultural movements form a set of values and beliefs that comprise a reaction against the dominant culture and, in doing so, develop significant innovations and social forms that eventually get folded back into the mainstream way of life. These transformations and innovations form what Louis A. Zurcher calls 'cultural lead' (in ibid.: 51). Countercultural movements, as forces for social change on the frontiers of society, have the power to make real changes into the established way of life. As sociologist Seymour Leventman notes, 'It is this experience of excitation, even exultation, that pushed people beyond the pale of ordinary existence where they seemingly reconstruct their lives and, by so doing, change society' (1982: 11). Supporting this claim, Emile Durkheim points out, 'The ideal society is not outside of real society; it is a part of it' (1996: 422).

However, in a *Nation of Rebels: Why Counterculture Became Consumer Culture*, Joseph Heath and Andrew Potter (2004) put forward the compelling argument that there is no such thing as counterculture. They argue that counterculture is a myth, that as a concept it offers the illusion of an opportunity or possibility for subverting or being outside the mainstream. Their argument suggests that there is no such thing as 'outside'; that a counterculture fits comfortably within the constructs of mainstream capitalism and is actually supported by it.[3] Heath and Potter suggest that the idea of counterculture is so deeply embedded that it influences every aspect of social and political life: 'if counter-culture is a myth, then it is one that has misled an enormous number of people, with untold political consequences' (ibid.: 16). This complicated, contradictory relationship between counterculture and the mainstream is at play in the Burning Man phenomenon, which raises such issues as the negotiation between capitalism and the gift economy, freedom and surveillance, commerce and decommodification.

Burning Man, as a reaction against mainstream values and beliefs, could be seen as the beginning of a countercultural movement, one in the process of development. While not yet a movement to the same degree as the 1960s cultural rebellion, Burning Man is planting the seeds of an alternative way of living in the world. The process of building towards a movement, as Yinger suggests, begins with deviant behaviour that forges a growing community and enacts a set of common values and beliefs (1982: 24). Gaining national and international attention from both the media and participants, Burning Man is no longer under the radar but has seeped into mainstream consciousness. A significant departure from the 1960s counterculture, Burning Man participants adhere to no one political dogma, set of religious values or lifestyle. As a conglomerate of subcultures within the larger construct of the counterculture, Burning Man celebrates an array of lifestyles. The Burning Man phrase 'radical self-expression' encourages participants to practise a myriad of lifestyles within the confines of a shared system of values, which include engaging in the 'gift economy', adhering to the 'leave no trace' philosophy of environmental conservation, and practising 'radical self-reliance' which is required for surviving the harsh desert conditions. It is through the acceptance of these core values and of all varieties of lifestyles that a sense of community and belonging emerges.

Over the past two decades, these values have seeped beyond the desert and into everyday life with the emergence of the Burning Man

Regional Network. This network of people, consisting of those who attend Burning Man and then return to their hometowns, transplant the values established by the desert event and bring them into new communities. The seeds planted in communities around the US and the world have the potential for social transformation and change. However, this process is just beginning to take root and has not fully flourished into a large-scale countercultural movement. So, while I resist calling Burning Man a countercultural movement at this point in time, the process has begun.

In *America*, Jean Baudrillard names the desert as the quintessentially postmodern space and a metaphor for America itself: 'For us, the whole of America is a desert' (1988: 99). Baudrillard's postmodern desert is not an endpoint, but a beginning space where a new narrative can begin. The desert allows for a playful space of freedom on the margins of everyday life creating a constantly shifting boundary between the marginal and the mainstream. Burning Man is literally situated in Baudrillard's ideal postmodern desert, offering a space of possibility for the creation of new modes of expression, new or 'alternative' lifestyles, as well as for recycling and reassembling culture. As Baudrillard poignantly writes, 'American culture is heir to the deserts. [. . .] They denote the emptiness, the radical nudity that is the background to every human institution. At the same time, they designate human institutions as a metaphor of that emptiness and the work of man as the continuity of the desert, culture as a mirage' (ibid.: 63). Black Rock City is a detailed and complex simulation of a real city—one on the cusp of perpetual disappearance. It manifests for a week, and then transfers into an online virtual community via e-mail, blogs, websites, chat rooms, and Second Life known as 'Burning Life' where participants recreate Black Rock City in virtual reality.

Situating Burning Man within the framework of what Michael Hardt and Antonio Negri call 'Empire' (2000), Burning Man could be seen as a rehearsal for a utopian, counter-Empire performance. Hardt and Negri suggest that a new global order and a new form of sovereignty are materializing before our very eyes. They label this emergent global power 'Empire'. Resisting the growing monopoly of Empire is what Hardt and Negri call 'counter-Empire' or 'counter-globalization' (ibid.: 207). The forces of the multitude that sustain Empire are also capable of autonomously constructing a counter-Empire, though a new and necessary cartography of these alternative political structures remains to be drawn. Hardt and Negri state, 'The counter-Empire must also be a new global vision, a new way of living in the world' (ibid.). While Burning Man is creating new paradigms for performance, installation art, community and ritual, it is also a radical, creative resistance to the pressures of a capitalist, consumer society, however futile. Burning Man creates an oasis challenging capitalism, but this challenge is, finally, ambiguous and impossible.

Burning Man is a ritual, festival, performance and playground serving as a unique site through which people can choose to make and remake their worlds. As a 'cultural performance',[4] Burning Man produces and reproduces culture, moulding and shaping tradition as well as inventing it.[5] As a festival, Burning Man serves as a powerful vehicle for reinforcing and affirming identity as well as for forging new social realities. Burning Man is a complete symbolic system, temporally bound, spatially separated from the everyday: repetitive, adaptive and performative. Using Richard Schechner's distinction between 'as performance' and 'is performance' (see Schechner 1985: 104), Burning Man can be seen 'as' a performance of everyday life, behaviour that Erving Goffman locates in *The Presentation of Self in Everyday Life* (1959). In the case of Burning Man, I extend the notion of 'as performance' to include secular pilgrimage, secular ritual and utopian paradigms. Burning Man also 'is performance', that is, a series of spontaneous and improvised as well as rehearsed and staged live performances from amateur to professional. Weaving together the 'as' and 'is' modes of understanding performance reveals the deep structures driving the complex social and cultural phenomenon of Burning Man.

The Convergence of Ritual and Performance at Burning Man

Two main discourses run throughout this consideration of Burning Man: ritual and performance. Both are infused with a sense of play and the carnivalesque. These two operate as a Mobius strip, twisting performance and ritual in such ways that one cannot say which is 'dominant'. Schechner's theory is that the relation of ritual to entertainment is a polarity with efficacy/ritual and entertainment/art at opposites ends of the helix-continuum he calls 'performance' (1988: 142). The final act of burning the Man combines ritual and entertainment; the entire event negotiates a delicate balance between these two extreme ends of the continuum. While the conflagration is a massively entertaining spectacle, it is also a ritual that inspires real life changes and transformations with some participants changing their careers, their locations, their relationships, even their names. The convergence of invented rituals and everyday performance at Burning Man lays the foundation for community-making, revitalizing American avant-garde ideals, which once included community-making as a major component, especially in the 1960s.

Here is how I first experienced the powerful convergence of ritual and performance. One evening around dusk in 2001, I was sitting in Center Camp Café—Black Rock City's social nucleus—when I heard a Tibetan prayer gong. A crowd began to gather. I rushed out to see over 100 people marching in a solemn procession, carrying long poles with lanterns; the people were clad in floor-length white robes painted at the edges with flames. A hushed crowd watched the spectacular procession pass. The salmon-coloured sky lit the scene with a rosy pink hue. I later learned that these were Black Rock City's Lamplighters (whom I discuss further in Chapter 5). Suddenly, breaking the trance-like silence, was the thumping beat of techno music in the distance, steadily growing louder and louder as it approached Center Camp. Along with the music came an energetic mob of about 200 dressed in shades of pink. On one side the Lamplighters observed their solemn ritual; on the other, the playful Pink Parade approached: a collision seemed inevitable. But, seamlessly, the 200 pink people danced through the Lamplighters, fusing the sacred with the profane. Tibetan gongs blurred with techno, ancient with postmodern.

The two processions passed. The Lamplighters continued along their path lighting the city and the Pink Parade seized Center Camp. Soon, the entire place was a thumping dance party. The Pink King and Queen made their grand entrance, followed by the Pink Paparazzi. People of all shapes and sizes clad in every shade of pink imaginable shook and rattled in all directions. This momentary collision sparked my realization that very disparate worlds could coexist for one week every year in Black Rock City. For seven days, participants remove themselves from their everyday lives and enter into the harsh desert landscape, bringing what they need to survive in order to create a replica of a city filled with art and performance. I wondered at how we, as Americans, have the luxury of spending a week of leisure in the desert, building an imaginary city full of excessive abundance, a symptom of American capitalism and consumerism. I began to understand Burning Man as a convergence of ritual and performance on an enormous scale—and as an event that is inherently political, in which participants create an alternative world. Burning Man is a political intervention as well as a ritual and artistic enterprise. Burning Man is in the process of becoming an artistic, social and cultural movement of some significance that is creating new paradigms for social interaction and art-making practices in the United States.

Notes

1 The Ramlila in Ramnagar, India, is an annual 30-day epic festival retelling the Ramayana and the story of Rama and Sita, where thousands gather around multiple stages throughout the city.

2 The etymology of the term 'festival' derives from the Latin *festum*, denoting public joy and merriment (Falassi 1987: 1).

3 Joseph Heath and Andrew Potter give two poignant examples: the sale of 'subversive' running shoes sold by the 'counterculture/culture jamming' magazine *Adbusters*; and the evolution of hippies into yuppies. As Heath and Potter note regarding the sale of sneakers by *Adbusters*, 'After that day [that shoes were sold by *Adbusters*], no rational person could possibly believe that there is any tension between "mainstream" and "alternative" culture. After that day, it became obvious to everyone that cultural rebellion, of the type epitomized by *Adbusters* magazine, is not a threat to the system—it is the system' (2004: 3). The hippie culture of the 1960s violated all the dress codes of the 1950s by growing long hair, refusing to wear suits and ties, wearing beads and colourful clothing. But soon love beads and peace signs were available for purchase almost everywhere, demonstrating how the system rapidly appropriates symbols of resistance, quelling their revolutionary status, and returns them back to the masses as commodities. And, as Heath and Potter ironically illustrate, hippies were just consumers in a different guise: 'Nothing symbolized their rejection of "consumerism" more than love beads, Birkenstocks, and the VW Beetle. [. . .] Then the hippies became yuppies. [. . .] So how does one get from a VW Beetle to a Ford Explorer? It turns out not to be so difficult. Hippie ideology and yuppie ideology are one and the same' (ibid.: 3, 4).

4 'Cultural performance' is a term Milton Singer introduced in the 1950s to describe ritual and artistic activities in southern India, and applied to a range of clearly framed occasions such as weddings, festivals, dances, concerts and recitations (1972: 78). As performative, active agencies of change, cultural performances not only transmit traditional knowledge, but also assist in the discovery and invention of new knowledge.

5 Theodore Jennings believes adaptation is the decisive clue to understanding the nature of cultural performances (1996: 327).

PART ONE

BLUEPRINT OF BLACK ROCK CITY

Aerial view of Black Rock City, 2003.
Photograph by Gabe Kirchheimer.

CHAPTER 1
SEEDS OF A MOVEMENT: FROM CHAOS TO ORDER

> The idea of a journey out of the normal parameters of life, the entry into a different, other world, the search for something new, the multiple motives of participants, ranging from homage and veneration to simple impulses of curiosity—are extremely common, if not always universal, denominators of pilgrimage (Reader and Walter 1993: 8).

Secular Pilgrimage: Getting to Black Rock City

I made my first pilgrimage to Burning Man in the Black Rock Desert of Nevada in 2001, then again in 2004, 2005 and 2008. My 2004 journey was typical of these ventures. On 30 August that year, I left Phoenix, Arizona, at 5.30 a.m., before sunrise, and set out on a 14-hour drive to Black Rock City. I headed towards Las Vegas on Route 60 to Route 93, my car packed with sleeping bags, a tent, a Coleman stove, two bins full of dry and canned food, batteries, flashlights, a first aid-kit, ChapStick, dust masks, goggles, sunblock, warm clothing, costumes, garbage bags, earplugs, handy wipes, duct tape, a spray bottle and 20 gallons of water.

The sun rose at 6 a.m., casting long shadows across the desert and the Joshua Tree Forest. The journey from Phoenix to Fallon, Nevada, passed through Las Vegas, the Hoover Dam, Tonopah and Hawthorne. I spent the night in Fallon, famous for nuclear testing and military bases. On Monday morning, I woke at 6 a.m. and did my final packing preparations. My last stop in the 'default' world (as it is called by the Burning Man community) before heading towards the Black Rock Desert was the Safeway grocery store to pick up a few last minute items: ice, a sewing kit, granola bars and a few more gallons of water. The store was unusually busy for 7.30 a.m., and the Burners stood out amid the bustling shoppers, their colourful and creative clothing screaming, 'I'm going to Burning Man!'

The shelves were quite sparse for an American supermarket chain, and it was easy to see that most of the products had sold out. The aisles were crowded with people readying themselves for their pilgrimage to the desert in a silent atmosphere of preparation, anticipation and excitement. The shelves of water were nearly empty—I bought the last five-gallon jug—and the piles of fruit were severely depleted as the Burners hoarded supplies for the next seven days. After Fallon, the only place to get rations before entering Black Rock Desert territory is the small general store in Empire.

From Fallon, I drove down Alternate Route 50 to Route 447 towards Pyramid Lake, Empire and Gerlach. The single-lane highway was packed bumper-to-bumper with RVs, cars and buses inching along towards the entrance to Black Rock City, which is exactly nine miles from Gerlach, on Route 34. On the left are the mountains and on the right, the Black Rock Desert playa. Expanding northeasterly from Gerlach, the playa is the flat, ancient lakebed of Lake Lahontan, almost entirely devoid of vegetation. Shaped like a lopsided 'Y', this part of the desert is often described as having a stem and two arms, a west arm and an east arm. The playa, one of the largest in the US, occupies much of the stem and the west arm. Extending from Gerlach north to the Double Hot Springs, the playa is about 27 miles long and 12 miles wide, bordered on the west by the Calico Mountains and on the east by the Black Rock Range, with elevations from 4,800 to 8,400 feet. The entire Black Rock Desert and its associated wilderness areas encompass 1,857 square miles in which there are no paved roads; it is surrounded by Washoe County, Pershing County and Humboldt County (Bureau of Land Management, BLM 2000).[1]

Desolate, yes, but far from devoid of people. Humans have been present for 12,000 years; this area is part of the Paiute tribal homeland[2] and Paiute reservations in the area include: to the north, the Summit Lake

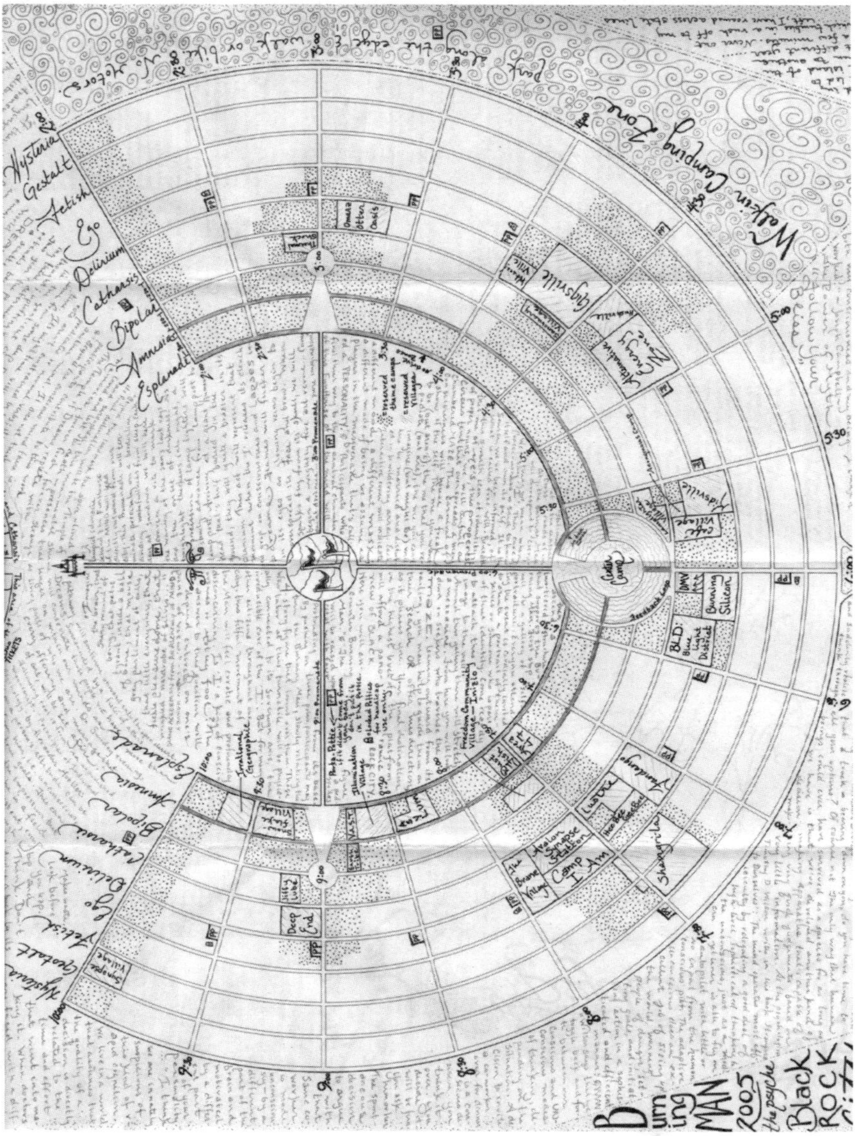

FIGURE 1.1. Black Rock City map, 'Psyche', 2005.
Courtesy of the Burning Man Organization.

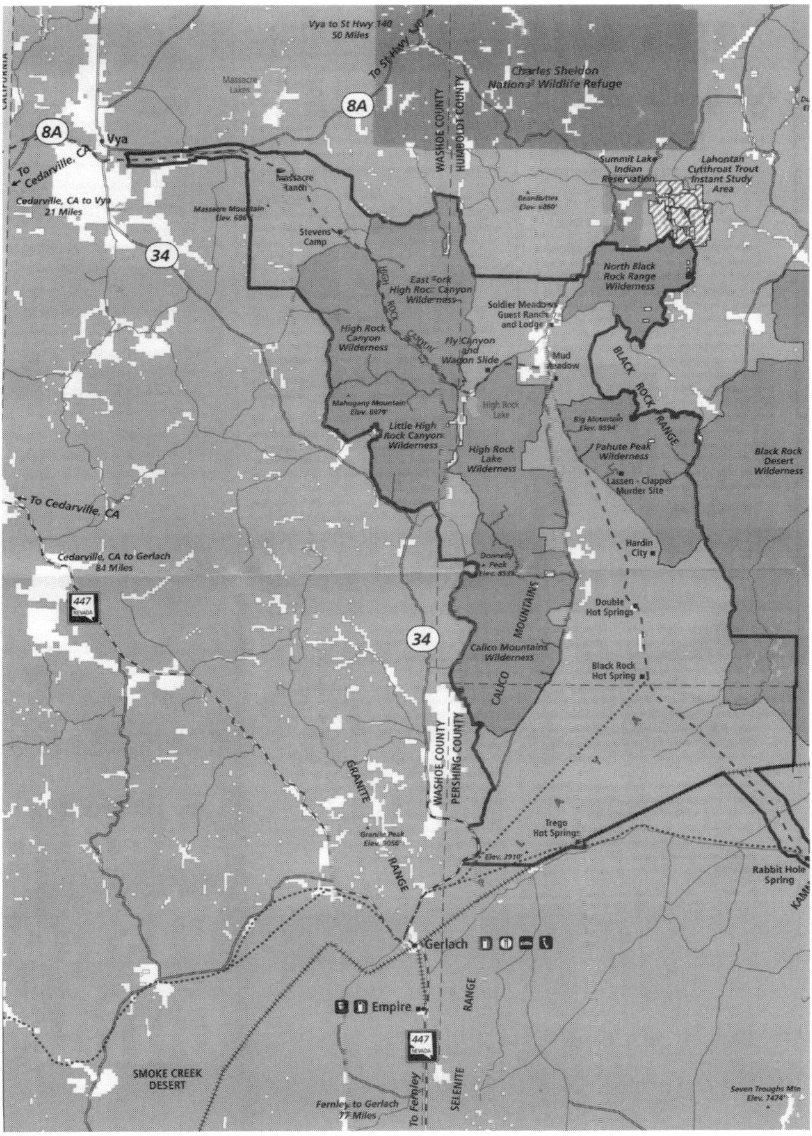

FIGURE 1.2. Map of the Black Rock Desert.
Courtesy of the Bureau of Land Management, Nevada.

Reservation; to the northeast, the Fort McDermitt Reservation; and to the southwest, the Pyramid Lake Reservation (ibid.). The area also contains palaeontological and archaeological resources of national importance—the remains of woolly mammoths, sabre-tooth tigers and other Pleistocene animals that were trapped there along the marshy shores of ancient Lake Lahontan. At present, the alkali left in the soil after the lake dried up prevents anything from growing. Sometimes, you find seashells as a reminder of the distant past, or a scorpion scurrying about, but not much else. It is in this desolate, harsh landscape that a temporary swarm of humanity, 49,000-strong, comes to create Black Rock City and to celebrate, around Labour Day, the annual burning of a 40-foot effigy of a Man.

The Black Rock Desert is a national conservation area managed by the Nevada Bureau of Land Management (BLM) and the US Department of the Interior. The Nevada BLM oversees over 1 million acres of public land in this desert. For the duration of Burning Man, the 100 people in the regional BLM office in Winnemucca are paid by the BMO to monitor the event. Laura M. Levy, a BLM ranger from the Winnemucca Field Office, told me that Burning Man 'gives us something to do!' When I asked her why all these people would want to come here, she replied not without irony, 'To get away from it all with 35,000 of your best friends' (2004). The scale of Burning Man requires the BLM to draw law enforcement from all over Nevada to police the seven-day event.

Each year, the BMO needs a permit from the BLM to use the land. In 2001, the Black Rock Desert was declared a national conservation area and the BMO successfully lobbied in Washington to amend the by-laws that allow large commercial events to take place on the land. According to Burning Man Law-Enforcement Liaison Tom Price, who worked in Washington, on Capitol Hill, for 10 years, Burning Man is the largest user of public land in the country. At Black Rock City's annual 'Media Mecca' panel in 2004, Price stated that the permit granted to the BMO generates more revenue for the government than the next 15,000 permits combined (see Harvey 2005). In 2004, the BLM issued the BMO a two-year permit; in 2006, for the first time in the history of the event, the BLM issued the BMO a five-year permit. The BLM charges Burning Man four dollars per day per participant, which comes to about $850,000 for one week (in 2006). This fee is rolled into the ever-escalating admission price.

FIGURE 1.3. The empty Black Rock Desert, 2004.
Photograph by Austin Granger.

In 1996, tickets were $20 in advance and $40 at the gate. In 13 years, they have steadily increased in price to over $295. In a tiered pricing scale, the first 10,000 tickets that went on sale on 18 January 2008 cost $210; the next 10,000 cost $225; and the rest $295. That year, the first 10,000 tickets were sold out within the first few hours, generating revenue of 2.1 million dollars in less than 24 hours. Scholarship tickets for $95 and artist tickets for $145 are available but require a detailed application process. In 2008, for the first time, no tickets were sold at the event in order for the organizers to fully prepare for the incoming population.

The BLM permit obligates the BMO to 'leave no trace', an environmental policy it is required to implement in order to hold the event on protected public land.[3] For the final burning of the effigy, and all other fires, fire blankets are used to protect the playa from burn scars. Each year, the land is inspected before and after the event. Surveying the Black Rock City site and setting up its boundary fence takes place a month beforehand and is coordinated by Burning Man's Department of Public Works (DPW). Once the event is over, it usually takes the DPW a month to clean the desert. In the early days, unprotected fires baked the playa, leaving giant scars on its immaculate white surface. To remove the scars, the DPW had to dig the playa up and turn over the soil. Each year, six months after the event, the BLM checks the playa to verify that no damage has been done. Burning Man passes the BLM inspection every year and serves as a role model for other large-scale events, but not without the help of the Burning Man community whose motto is 'Pack it in, Pack it out.'

The packing is a large part of the experience. Just as was true for nineteenth-century travellers, participants need to be well prepared before venturing off the pavement into Black Rock country. They spend from one month to a year getting ready for the pilgrimage to the desert. The Burning Man *Survival Guide* is available on the Burning Man website and distributed to everyone entering Black Rock City. Participants are informed that everyone must comply with the requirements set forth by the BLM. Each individual is responsible for following the 'leave no trace' edict, properly disposing of dirty water, known as 'grey water,' coming with enough food and water (one gallon per day per person), planning every meal, using proper gear for the harsh conditions and protecting the playa from fire scars and burns (Burning Man Organization, BMO 2004d).

Feathers, glass containers, loose glitter and anything else that might break or blow away—creating what is known as Matter Out of Place (MOOP)—is strictly prohibited. The gale force winds that sweep through the City take with them anything that is not securely anchored down. Steel rebar stakes (used in construction) and heavy-duty tarps are required to sustain structures in such unpredictable weather. Goggles and dust masks are a prerequisite as dust storms sweep Black Rock City almost daily. When these whiteouts descend on the City, movement comes to a halt: one can barely see a foot ahead. These storms give Black Rock citizens a white, luminescent glow as the fine dust covers each person like a second skin.

Fully packed and prepared, Burning Man pilgrims approach their destination. Heading towards the southern entrance to the Black Rock Desert, the closest town is Gerlach, established in 1906. In 1909, the Western Pacific Railroad built a major train depot and a large roundhouse there. A wooden water tower near the town's centre, which is listed on the National Register of Historic Places, is the only vestige of early railroading. Each year, a kiosk is placed near the tower to collect donations from Burning Man participants to protect it and ensure its continuing survival. Gerlach's only amenities are a gas station, a car-repair and towing service, Bruno's restaurant and Burning Man's roadside office.

Empire, just south of Gerlach, has the only general store for hundreds of miles. Established in 1922, Empire was a company town for the Pacific Portland Cement Company which mines gypsum in the nearby mountains. Finished gypsum products are still produced and shipped to Gerlach on the shortest operating railroad in Nevada (BLM 2000). The total population of Empire and Gerlach is approximately 500; hence, the influx of 49,000 people is, on the one hand, a source of tremendous revenue, and on the other hand, a threat to the delicate desert ecosystem and scarce resources of the towns.

In the *Survival Guide*, the BMO urges participants not to use any of the water from these towns nor deposit any garbage in them. It also asks that participants display respect and courtesy towards the residents of the towns and the adjacent Paiute reservation by dressing decently and refraining from creating a 'party atmosphere'. The BMO has gone to great lengths to establish a good relationship with these towns by becoming actively involved with the community all year round, attending town meetings and donating money to local schools and charities.

A resident, who works for the road department and has lived in Gerlach his entire life, seemed mildly amused by the costumes of the Burning Man crowd. In 2004, he attended Burning Man once during the week to see the art and was impressed by it. He explained that, at first, the gas stations and small businesses such as Bruno's were overwhelmed by the sudden influx of people, but now each town prepares in advance to be able to meet the demands of the Burning Man community. 'We see more of the Burning Man people, now they are here all year round. Gerlach prepares ahead of time. Bruno's and the Empire store do pretty well,' he told me (Gerlach Resident 2004). Sherry, a waitress at Bruno's, has lived in Gerlach for four years. She loves Burning Man because of the excitement it provides, the interesting people it attracts and for the economic boost it brings to the town (2004). Over the years, Empire and Gerlach have come to depend upon Burning Man's business.

Arriving at Black Rock City

In the distance I discern the vague outline of a city, looming in the desert like a mirage. Coming up on the right is a handmade sign: 'Burning Man: Vault of Heaven'. I turn off the paved highway onto a dirt road full of jagged rocks and craters. About a mile later, I arrive at the gate; it is around noon, the hottest part of the day. The road is marked off with barriers and a small side road for 'will-call' where one can pick up or purchase tickets. I had already bought mine the day they went on sale in January for $165.

At the first checkpoint, I am met by a large topless man in a black skirt. His job is to search the car for anyone trying to sneak into the event. Once the car is thoroughly checked, I am given the rundown of Burning Man policies such as 'leave no trace', 'pack it in, pack it out', 'no MOOP in the poop'[4] and 'drive 5 miles an hour'. Then, I am greeted by a second man; wearing a magenta fairy dress. He hands me my ticket—emblazoned across it in capital letters is 'PARTICIPATE!'—and says, 'Welcome Home!'

I progress to the second checkpoint where I am approached by a third greeter, a woman in a fuchsia dress with black hair, now grey from the playa dust. She asks if I am a Burning Man virgin and I happily say 'No.' (My first year at Burning Man I had said, 'Yes' and was asked to get out of the car and do a dance. Burning Man virgins are required to perform a number of initiation tasks at the discretion of the greeter.) Then she demands, 'What do you have for me?' I was prepared for this, and I hand her a fruit roll-up which she gratefully accepts. These gate volunteers are called 'greeters' and it is customary to give them treats for their thankless labour. She proudly tells me that this is her first year as a greeter, then hands me a map of Black Rock City and a 'What, When, Where' programme of events, offering, like the other greeters, a hearty 'Welcome Home!' This is the procedure each person entering Black Rock City must go through.

Ahead, I see the Man looming on the horizon. The road is roped off with signs that read '5 miles an hour'. Crawling along at the prescribed speed so as not to kick up the fine playa dust, I reach a fork, the road on the left bypassing the City from 6 to 10 o'clock, the other to the right from 6 to 2 o'clock. I turn left onto Sedna, the furthest circle of this city of semicircles. Finally, I reach 7 o'clock where I make a right and head down to Mercury. I enter a sea of tents, caravans, tipis, geodesic domes, rental trucks and makeshift structures. There is a frenzied energy as everyone is busy setting up the theme camps and villages. I arrive at Asylum Village, located at 7 o'clock and Esplanade, one of the New York City villages at Burning Man with over 150 members. I have arrived in Black Rock City.

A City of Pilgrims

The journey through the desert of Nevada to Black Rock City is one aspect of Burning Man that is shared by all those participants who make the secular pilgrimage.[5] Religious pilgrimage centres, both ancient and contemporary, continue to exert a powerful pull on believers. Pilgrimage is a panhuman phenomenon found in the religious traditions of Islam, Christianity, Judaism, Buddhism and Hinduism. Jews and Christians gravitate towards the Holy Land, Hindus towards the 'four Dhams' and Muslims towards Mecca.

In *Image and Pilgrimage in Christian Culture: Anthropological Perspectives* (1978), Victor Turner and Edith Turner provocatively suggest that a tourist is half a pilgrim and a pilgrim is half a tourist. This poignant remark signifies an important transition in pilgrimage discourse to include travel to secular destinations. Secular pilgrimage sites such as Burning Man create a temporary transient community of pilgrims who enter into a liminal state of spontaneous bonding, what Victor Turner called *spontaneous communitas*.[6] Through the journey to a distant place, the pilgrim is separated from everyday social life, temporarily becoming geographically and socially marginal.[7] Black Rock City itself is spatially liminal, existing on the margins, far away from any town, city or centre of political and economic influence.

A central aspect of pilgrimage is the idea of the quest, of seeking something that lies outside of everyday life.[8] While the idea of the quest is linked to the desire for permanent personal transformation, pilgrims often form only temporary physical communities. As in the case of Burning Man, this community actually becomes permanent only after it physically disperses.[9] Creeping down the highway towards Black Rock City, one is struck by the sheer number of Burners on the road, each one preparing for a 'unique' experience; one of the draws of Burning Man is the freedom to shape and create one's own experience with no preconceived scenario or mould into which you are required to fit. Burning Man is an organic, living organism in a continuous process of transformation and evolution; each individual's motivation and vision plays a part in this transformation, forming what Ian Reader and Tony Walter call a 'pilgrimage network' that affects both individuals and the collective (1993). Each individual desire and fantasy is given the opportunity to be tested and tried out, ultimately shaping the entire community from year to year.

What are the primary motivations drawing 49,000 people to the desert annually—and who are these pilgrims? The annual census of the Black Rock City population conducted by the BMO began in 2001, and the data has remained remarkably consistent over the years. While Figures 1.4a–f—using data from the 2004 Census—represent only 13 per cent of the population, they paint a rough portrait of the demographics of the Burning Man community. After months of preparation, individuals and groups from around the country and the world are drawn to Burning Man. When asked why, 37 per cent of those surveyed by the BMO responded 'fire' (see Chapter 6), 23 per cent responded 'community' and 13 per cent responded 'personal quest'. Their motives are frequently mixed: personal transformation, the desire to build community, to party like never before, and, even, to watch others perform and party.

Pilgrim, partier or spectator—at Burning Man, the line between 'pilgrim' and 'tourist' is indeed blurred. Those who volunteer and actively participate in activities such as building a theme camp or an art installation, those dedicated to the vision and ethos of the community, could be viewed as pilgrims or Burners; those who attend mostly to 'see'—identified by Burners as 'tourists'—are looked down upon and stigmatized. However, it is not always easy to distinguish the two and both groups comprise a certain socio-economic range. The Census results indicated that 57 per cent were male, 41 per cent female and 1 per cent transgender. The largest age group was between 31 and 40, with the second largest being the 21–30 year olds. Only 4 per cent were under 21 and 2 per cent over 60. The population was (and continues to be) a kaleidoscope of subcultures[10] from hippie, punk, hardcore grunge, techno-raver, techno pagan, information technology geeks, circus performers to fire performers, as well as intellectuals and journalists to name a few.

The Census data indicated that the event was predominantly heterosexual (70 per cent), with 18 per cent bisexual and 8 per cent homosexual. The majority of those attending the event were from urban areas, followed by suburban residents; only 15 per cent were from rural areas. The Census also indicated that 40 per cent had a college degree and 16 per cent a graduate-level degree. Only 3 per cent had not graduated from high school. In 2004, 40 per cent of the participants were single, 17 per cent were married and 17 per cent were in a serious relationship. Twenty-four per cent of the population earned between $25,000 and $50,000; the rest were equally distributed between $15,000 to over $100,000. It is interesting to note that the Census did not include a racial demographic. Without collecting questionnaires and data, one can deduce at a glance that Burning Man was/is a predominantly white, middle-class event. While Latinos, African Americans, Native Americans and Asian Americans are present, they represent a minority of the population.

How did this teeming city of pilgrims and Burners evolve from founder Larry Harvey's personal healing ritual on Baker Beach in San Francisco into an ephemeral city brimming over with art, ritual and performance in the Black Rock Desert of Nevada? How did Harvey's personal experience transform over two decades into a complex communal pilgrimage? I trace the year-to-year evolution of the event until 2008, the

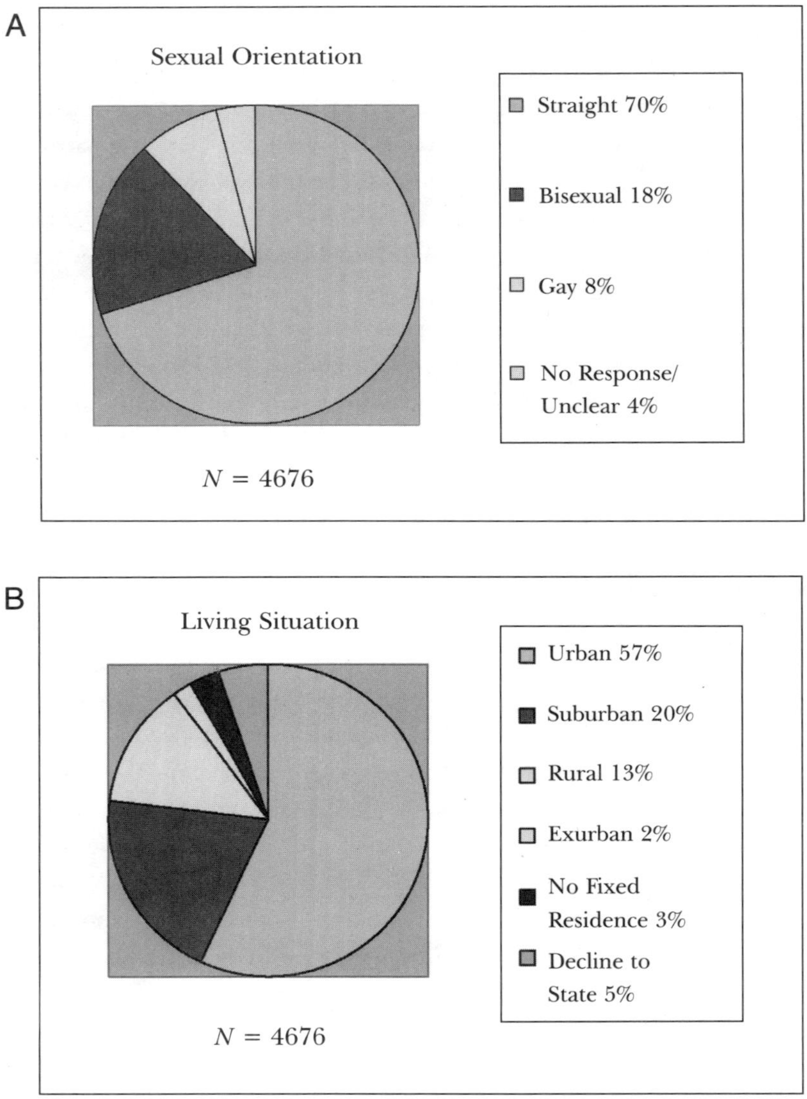

FIGURE 1.4 (ABOVE, FACING PAGE AND FOLLOWING PAGE). A sample of the Black Rock City Census conducted by Burning Man Organization in 2004 surveyed 4,676 participants of the 35,400, representing 13 per cent of the population. Courtesy of the Burning Man Organization.

C

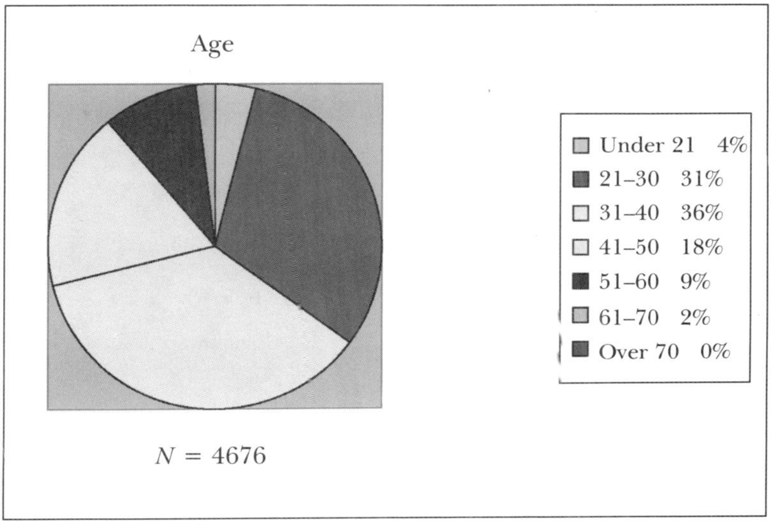
Age
Under 21 4%
21–30 31%
31–40 36%
41–50 18%
51–60 9%
61–70 2%
Over 70 0%
N = 4676

D

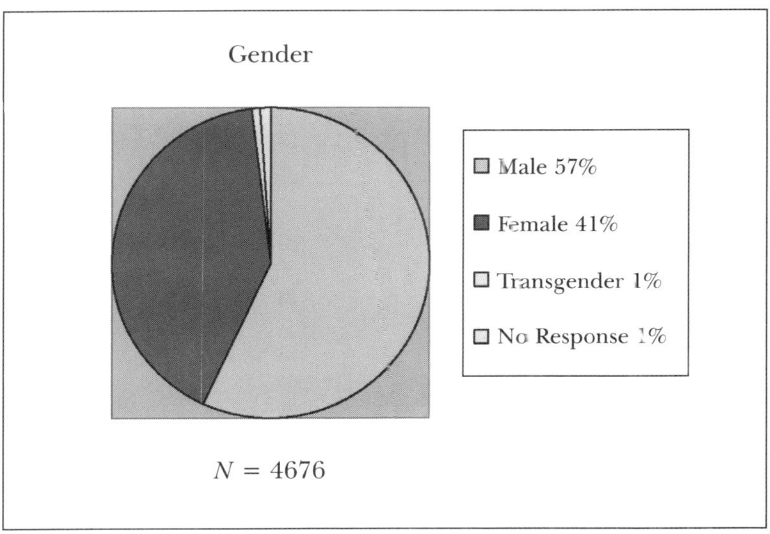
Gender
Male 57%
Female 41%
Transgender 1%
No Response 1%
N = 4676

E

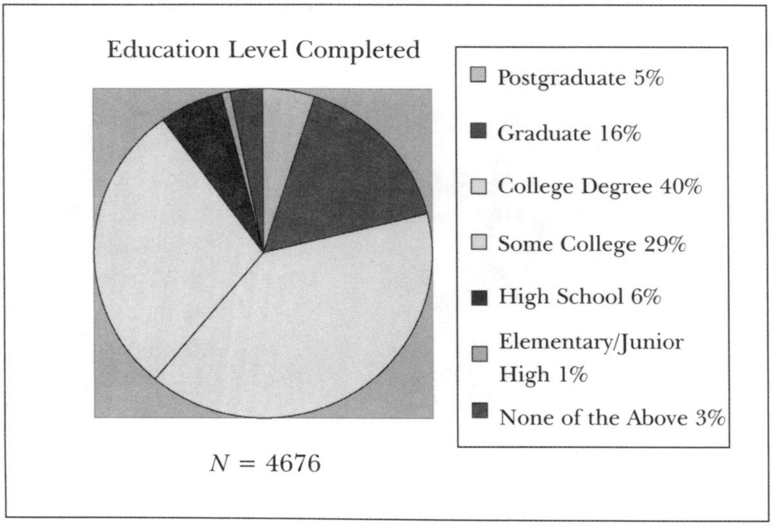
Education Level Completed
Postgraduate 5%
Graduate 16%
College Degree 40%
Some College 29%
High School 6%
Elementary/Junior High 1%
None of the Above 3%
N = 4676

F

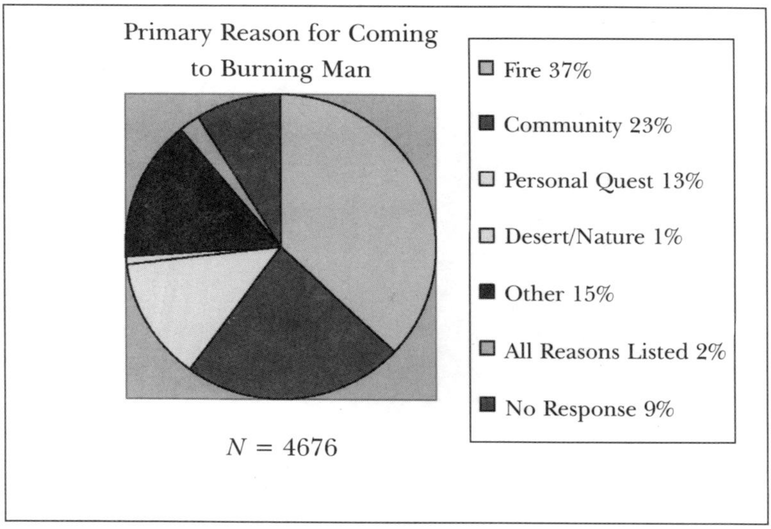
Primary Reason for Coming to Burning Man
Fire 37%
Community 23%
Personal Quest 13%
Desert/Nature 1%
Other 15%
All Reasons Listed 2%
No Response 9%
N = 4676

emergence of the Black Rock City Limited Liability Company (LLC), and the design of Black Rock City to offer one perspective of Burning Man's history—along with a counter-narrative. These two perspectives set the stage for an analysis of performance and ritual within Black Rock City.[11]

The Burning Man Legend

The story of Burning Man begins with a legend that may help explain how a spontaneous personal ritual was transformed into an ephemeral city of art and performance with 49,000 citizens. The first fire on Baker Beach in San Francisco in 1986 may have been unplanned, but there were many ideas and influences that fed into that original act. Harvey sees Burning Man as the convergence of all the fragments of his life—they coalesced to create the firm foundation on which Burning Man stands today. He also credits as an important source of inspiration the sculptor Mary Graubarger; he talks about her in his early recollections of the origins of Burning Man. Harvey met Graubarger, host of the early Beach Burns, in the mid-1970s through ex-girlfriend Janet Lohr (in Doherty 2004: 26). As Graubarger recounts, 'I was a sculptor and I'd get bored sitting around the studio, so I'd pick up stuff washed up on shore and build sculptures. We'd stay 'til the evening and cook, and then it seemed natural to torch the sculptures. It was a personal thing, for fun' (in ibid.: 27). About Harvey, who attended these Beach Burns, Graubarger recalled, 'It hit him that you could be free and not have an institution and create this incredible art and burn it. The burning part, it really affects people. Some of us would burn everything we had—blankets, clothes [. . .]. It's more beautiful to have people experience it and then it's gone' (in ibid.).[12] As Harvey remembers, these spontaneous events would be going on up and down Baker Beach, a cove near the Golden Gate Bridge.

On 21 June 1985, at the height of his relationship, Larry Harvey, his girlfriend and her son went to Graubarger's summer solstice celebration on Baker Beach. Harvey fondly remembers that, 'It was nominally pagan, although with a San Francisco twist' (1997b). Graubarger had a small boom box with an electronic drum track emitting soulless mechanical thuds while they tossed a few mannequins dressed in polyester and a couch into a fire they had built on the beach. Harvey realized that, 'This is my kind of solstice celebration!' (ibid.). His girlfriend's son saturated the sand with gaso-

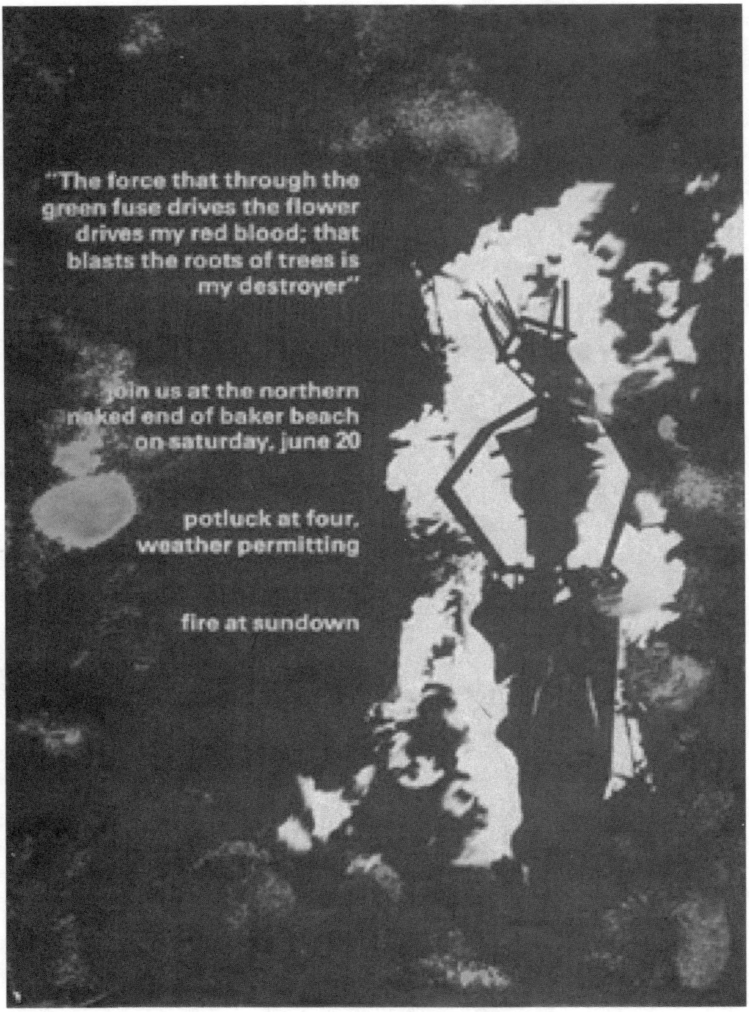

FIGURE 1.5. Burning Man flyer, 1987, featuring a quote from the Dylan Thomas poem 'The Force that Through the Green Fuse Drives the Flower' (1934). Courtesy of the Burning Man Organization.

line, then began to write in fire with a burning stick. The couple joined the boy, and Harvey describes the moment as 'supremely romantic' (ibid.).

The relationship did not last. Here is how Harvey, in a speech to the citizens of Black Rock City on the Hualapai playa in 1997, described what happened: 'I had heartbreak. I had a mid-life crisis that lasted two years. [. . .] If you've ever had a heartbreak you know it's the anniversaries that kill you' (ibid.). After thinking about that night on the beach for a year after the breakup, Harvey woke up on the solstice and thought, 'I'm tired of this' (ibid.). Graubarger was no longer holding her summer solstice event, so Harvey called up his friend Jerry James and said, 'Let's burn a man, Jerry.' The original man was eight feet tall and built out of scrap lumber in a basement in Noe Valley. Harvey and James called a few of their close friends to help them haul the man to Baker Beach; Harvey recalls that there were 12 of them. They soaked the man with gasoline and set him on fire. As soon as it was lit, Harvey remembers:

> It was like a second sun brought down to this earth. [. . .] It transfixed us. That's where the story begins, in fact, because the moment it was lit, everybody on that beach, north and south, came running. That beach was a little like our city now, with its two embracing arms around the void of the playa here. And suddenly our numbers tripled. [. . .] A man on a guitar started singing, and we all sang along. [. . .] This became the first interactive performance (ibid.).

As Harvey noted, choosing to enact the ritual in a public environment was an important decision that turned the personal into the transpersonal. 'People are fascinated by fire, and when you combine fire with the human form, I think it has a certain significance that certainly transcended our intent. So, we just came back and did it the next year' (in Nash 1995). By burning the 'Man', Harvey and James engaged in what Harvey calls the first recorded act of 'radical self-expression', a possibility already embedded in the bohemian culture of San Francisco: that you could manifest your spirit by acting on a creative impulse (see Doherty 2004: 29). They asked no one's permission and they recruited friends to help them; thus, they had spontaneously and unconsciously invented a ritual.

Harvey regrets telling the break-up story because it has been repeated endlessly in the media. But however much Harvey now wants to disavow the heartbreak origin story, some old Burning Man associates swear that it was Harvey's official line for many years in the early 1990s. When I interviewed Harvey in 2004, he said, 'Well, that's how the story goes. It's close enough. But of course it's either under- or over-determined depending on how you look at it. But, yeah, it had some emotional resonance for me among other things. [. . .] The story protects the legend' (2004a). Michael Mikel, Burning Man board member, claims he started the myth:

> I was basically Larry's PR guy. It was a great idea. There was a break up about that time, I knew about that. It tied in very well, whether true or not. It is great for mythmaking and legends. Likewise, I am the person who told Larry to always wear a white hat and that became legend in itself. Iconic. In order for a movement to occur you need a leader, a figurehead and Larry was a good front man. He reads a lot. He is an intellectual and very good with speeches. I coaxed him into that position. I am always in the background. I fed him material. I fed him ideas for his speeches and expressions. He used those very effectively. I don't need to be in the spotlight (2008).

When I asked Burning Man board member Will Roger why Harvey had burned the first Man, he replied:

> I think it was because it was something fun to do. People I think look for a lot of reasons because it has grown to be such an important thing. I think originally there wasn't a whole lot of reason. There were things going on in his life, you can talk to him about that, the relationship thing; he had a kid. [. . .] If you are looking for some religious or mystical or artistic reason, there wasn't anything like that (2005).

The exact origin of the event is impossible to pinpoint, impossible to explain with one unequivocal moment in time—which is in part why the story has taken on mythic proportions. Many forces contributed to what Burning Man is today.

Harvey does not like to discuss his past but the few known autobiographical facts help to paint the portrait of the man who founded Burning Man. Larry Harvey was born in 1948 and grew up on a small farm on the outskirts of Portland, Oregon, where his parents had lived all their lives.[13] Harvey's father was a carpenter and mason, a self-made man. Larry and his brother Stewart were adopted, which made Harvey feel like an outsider, isolated from the rest of the world. He left his parents' home to serve briefly in the army in the late 1960s, and attended Portland State University on the GI Bill but felt his professors limited his thoughts and ideas. Dropping out of college, Harvey moved to San Francisco in 1978

FIGURE 1.6. Beach Burn, 1987. Photographer unknown.
Courtesy of the Burning Man Organization.

with girlfriend, Janet Lohr, and soon discovered the city's thriving underground art scene. Lohr was an elementary-school teacher and supported Harvey financially until their romance ended (in ibid.: 22). Then, in the early 1980s, Harvey married Patricia Johnson, a Jamaican woman. The relationship did not last but they had a son, Tristan.

Throughout the 1980s, Harvey held random jobs, including bike messengering, driving a cab and running his own landscaping business (called Paradise Regained), but none of them proved to be satisfying. He wasn't interested in decorative gardening; he just wanted to build things: 'Just adorning plants, who cares? I didn't want to create a comfy, cozy space. I wanted to create Mars' (in Doherty 2004: 23). Jerry James, who worked with Harvey in landscaping, quickly became his best friend, and the rest is Burning Man history. In the cultural flux of San Francisco in the late 1980s, Harvey's personal healing ritual sparked an energy that would ignite a fascinating cultural phenomenon that is emblematic of the late twentieth and early twenty-first centuries.

Early Days At Baker Beach: The Cacophony Society Finds Burning Man

For the first few years, the ritual remained nameless. It was not 'Burning Man' until 1988—the name came to Harvey while he was obsessively watching a video of an early Beach Burn (ibid.: 32). The first year, 1986, the Man was eight feet tall and crudely constructed out of scrap wood. By the following year, he had grown to 20 feet and took a couple of weekends to build. The first burns were promoted by word of mouth and handmade flyers. James revealed, 'I was a trained builder; he [Harvey] wasn't. While it was his concept and idea to do this thing, I was really the one who built it. He helped. The design motif was really his, but when it came to creating a figure out of lumber, I was the person who could bring that off in practical terms' (in ibid.: 33). James describes the first Burn as a family picnic with 20 people and the second one as a larger family picnic attended by 80—but still a picnic (ibid.).

In 1988, the Man grew to 30 feet tall and approximately 200 people attended the Beach Burn. It was a pivotal year: the Cacophony Society discovered Burning Man on Baker Beach and Harvey met Cacophony's central organizers, John Law and Michael Mikel (aka Michael Michael or

Danger Ranger), two men who would shape the future of Burning Man and steer it in a new direction. After finding the 1988 Burning Man ritual on the beach, the Cacophony Society publicized the 1989 Beach Burn in their newsletter, *The Rough Draft*, increasing attendance to 300 plus, attracting the attention of a local TV station. By 1989, the Man had grown to its current height of 40 feet.[14]

Burning Man would not be what it is today without the intervention of the Cacophony Society, which is largely responsible for the carnivalesque, neo-Dada atmosphere that has developed around the main event. Cacophony introduced the idea of 'culture jamming', an aesthetic that has shaped the development of Burning Man from a ritual into an arts festival. The Cacophony Society, founded by Lance Alexander, Jean Moshofsky and Jason Wechter, was a direct descendent of an underground secret society known as the Suicide Club, begun in 1977 as a course taught by Gary Warne at the Communiversity at San Francisco State University. One of its mantras was to live each day as if it were your last. In an interview, Burning Man veteran John Rinaldi (aka Chicken John), pointedly told me:

> Gary Warne is the reason why we are here. Without Gary, there would be no Burning Man, no Cacophony. There would be no Madagascar Institute,[15] no Survival Research Laboratories,[16] because all these things feed upon each other. [. . .] Gary did this thing where you would write him a question and he would write you the answer back. For him, that was the biggest way to jam culture—to provide unlimited information to the people. He preceded the Internet (2006).

When the Suicide Club sputtered out in 1982 after Warne died, Suicide Club alumni eventually formed a new group called the Cacophony Society in 1986, the same year that Burning Man started, and both were outgrowths of mid-1980s San Francisco culture. The ethos of the Cacophony Society was inspired by the playful and subversive anti-art aesthetic of Dada[17] and the Surrealists. The Cacophonists called themselves 'a randomly gathered network of free spirits united in the pursuit of experiences beyond the pale of mainstream society' (Cacophony Society 2008: 1). They not only recycled culture, they precycled it—that is, they would grab anything that wasn't nailed down, combing through the industrial detritus of society, recycling it as art and investing it with new meaning. Chicken John, a former Cacophony member, explained that Cacophony allowed you to become a general for a day with everyone else as your army. Part of the goal was to generate urban legends and modern myths that would circulate through the collective unconscious. One of the main tenets of the Society, also borrowed by Burning Man, was that each person *is* the entertainment, *is* the show (see Chapter 3).

Michael Mikel, central to the historical convergence of the Cacophony Society and Burning Man, grew up in Texas and served in the US Navy for six years, touring all over the Middle East and Asia, and arrived in San Francisco at the tail end of the Haight-Ashbury scene. With a background in electro-mechanical engineering, he left the service and started a career in Silicon Valley in the early 1970s—the beginning of the personal computer boom—working at Fairchild Semiconductor as a technician researching and developing assembly machines that built integrated circuits. (His boss left the company to found Intel.) After his stint at Fairchild, Mikel started a consulting company, Cimbotics Engineering, which developed the first robotic assembly line for Apple. Mikel first heard about the Suicide Club in 1978, a clandestine group infamous for climbing the Golden Gate Bridge at midnight and holding parties in abandoned buildings, but they were so far underground that he had no way to find them (Mikel 2008).

It was not until 10 years later that he discovered the first Cacophony Society newsletter, *Rough Draft*, in Rainbow grocery in San Francisco, created by three members of the old Suicide Club. He immediately connected with the Cacophony organizers and began researching and collecting everything he could from the Club. The Club's main flaw was that it was a very insular and isolated group; no new ideas were coming in. In order for Cacophony to survive and grow, it needed to be more open. From the very beginning, Mikel decided to make Cacophony radically inclusive; as its manifesto states, 'You may already be a member' (Cacophony Society 2008: 1). The expression created by Mikel was first used on the masthead of *Rough Draft* in February 1990.

Mikel became a central Cacophony organizer and began the process of cross-fertilization—connecting with other groups and co-listing events in the monthly newsletter. This proved to be very effective and the Cacophony Society grew every year until 2000. Though there were 600 people on the mailing list by then, a core group of 40 or 50 people were doing 90 per cent of the events. In its heyday, between 1986 and 1996, the Cacophony Society organized over 200 mischievous events, including guerrilla theatre, themed parties, public spectacles, pranks, hoaxes, billboard alterations and 'zone trips'.

The first event Mikel organized was *Cyber Punk at Sector 4*. He was working in Silicon Valley, in a company that bought and recycled computer parts; thus, he had access to a warehouse of junk computer parts. One night, he decided to host a treasure hunt in the warehouse. Participants wandered into a space that was plunged in darkness, then through a labyrinth of used computer parts while they sought hidden clues with their flashlights. Meanwhile, a group of volunteers plagued them with tricks, including emptying a 55-gallon drum of plastic computer keys on them. Mikel remembers it being a bizarre, theatrical environment (2008).

The second event Mikel organized was the *Oliver North Shredding Party*. North was going to give a lecture at Shore Line Amphitheatre in Redwood City and the 'shredding party'—literally, a party where secret documents were to be shredded—was organized for the night before. Mikel got an RV full of seven or eight friends to ceremonially shred secret documents as North had previously done. Then Mikel passed out several hundred computer chips and told participants that they were 'super listening devices' to track North's every move. The party stuck these devices with double-sided tape all over the outside of the amphitheatre. Around midnight, everyone left—that was the end of the party. The next day, the news headlines screamed 'Bomb Scare at Shore Line Amphitheatre. We Do Not Know What These Are but We Are Going to Find Out' (ibid.). Mikel chuckles recalling how their simple act caused such a media uproar.

Cacophony did three events called *Atomic Café*, during which they would blindfold people and take them into abandoned buildings. Not knowing where they were, the participants were dependent upon each other and the organizers. The first *Atomic Café* took place on 7 October 1989 at an underground bunker at Fort Mason. Participants had to enter through a little hatch. Working with a group of art students, the organizers had painted the inside of the bunker with post-apocalyptic scenes. A generator, a porta-potty, chairs and tables with red-checkered tablecloths had been placed inside. During the event, 1950s civil defence training films were projected on the walls. Only 25 people attended the first event and 75 the second one, held on 2 June 1990, at a government building south of Market Street, four storeys tall and with a basement. The 75 blindfolded participants were brought to the venue in a rented 18-foot U-Haul truck.

Once inside, there was a live band, laser lights, performances and a party atmosphere. According to Mikel, 'We created experience' (2008).

The third *Atomic Café* was attended by more than 130 people, on 8 February 1992, in an abandoned toothpaste factory in Berkeley. The premise of the event was that the last remaining members of a post-nuclear explosion world were trapped in the bunker. The bunker was surrounded by radiation; therefore, participants had to bring survival food such as canned or dried goods which later turned into a buffet. Everyone played a role in the fictive narrative. Harvey fondly remembers the event:

> It was quite illegal and subversive. It required a tunnel to get into it. It was a wonderfully theatrical setting. It was participatory theatre. It was genius. I loved the transgressive aspect of it. I played an android figure, nine feet tall, covered with antique computer parts and with these waffle stilts. I wore a wonderful black-and-white mask. There were people repelling down from different levels, and the evening concluded with the nightclub at the end of universe in which a replica of the atom bomb was recreated, filled with toy soldiers. Like a piñata, people were blindfolded to strike the 'bomb'. It was amusing to see blind men trying to hit the bomb. It took a lot of blows before it exploded (2008b).

From 1977 until 1993, when security cameras were installed, the Cacophony Society held an annual formal dinner party on the Golden Gate Bridge on the last Saturday in February. In 1997, on Bastille Day, they did an event called *Let Them Eat Cake* as a political protest of sorts—members dressed as French aristocrats and gave out cake to homeless people in front of City Hall. A mock guillotine was used to behead a couple of dummies resembling local politicians (Mikel 2008). Two national Cacophony events that continue to this day are *Santacon*, where participants dress up as Santa and parade the streets, and the *Brides of March*, started by Mikel, where participants parade around San Francisco in bridal attire. The event is held concurrently in Seattle, Portland and Reno.

Costuming has always been an important part of the Suicide Club and the Cacophony Society. Part of Mikel's archive includes the Suicide Club costume closet from the earliest events, featuring clown outfits, gorilla suits and other colourful attire. For Mikel, costuming 'has been largely used as a tool to break people's patterns and barriers. It is out of the ordinary' (ibid.). The idea of an alias evolved out of Cacophony where you would play a role or develop a new persona depending on the event. As

Mikel remembers, 'During the Cacophony era, many of those involved had many different aliases depending on the type of event they were doing. Having a new personality and being reborn with a playa alias at Burning Man is a tradition that came directly from Cacophony' (ibid.). Mikel's Cacophony aliases included Sergeant JFO (Just Following Orders), Maxwell Maud, and his preferred playa alias, Danger Ranger. As the primary editor of *Rough Draft* in 1994, his pen name was Genevieve J. Petrone, given to him by the previous editor, Carrie Gailbraith (aka Ethel Keytone), who found the unusual alias carved on a World War I monument hidden away in Golden Gate Park.

The idea of pilgrimage began with Cacophony: the idea of going into another space. The first 'zone trip' was started by two Cacophony members, Phil Bewley and Carrie Gailbraith. Inspired by Andrei Tarkovsky's 1979 film *Stalker*, a 'zone trip' was entering a 'post-apocalyptic world, a strange place where things change when you are not looking at them. At the center of this zone is a little room where all your dreams become real. There is this quest that people go through to get there' (ibid.). Some 'zone trips' were held in abandoned houses, warehouses or in an unusual neighbourhood. Bewley and Gailbraith discovered that they grew up in the same small town of Covina, California, and they thought it would be interesting to plan an expedition to the town. The first 'zone trip' was designed as a scientific research project and all the participants wore lab coats. At 3 a.m., as several cars caravanned to Covina, Mikel realized they needed a ritual crossing over into the 'zone':

> I had everybody pull off at this little rest stop and we did this symbolic crossing of the line. I said, 'We are now going into another world.' And sure enough, as much as the mental jump that we took but also the effects of sleep deprivation and whatever drugs people were on, the world did look different. We saw things with new eyes. We saw things we hadn't noticed before—sometimes very subtle. And we were therefore transformed (ibid.).

This 'zone trip' to Covina is where Mikel met John Law for the first time, and all of these events form the history that grew into Burning Man. The 'zone trip' is where the relationship between Cacophony and Burning Man begins, forever changing the history of both. From the start, the concept of 'leave no trace' was one of the core principles. Cacophonists would go into a space and be very careful not to destroy anything, and that idea preceded the desert event. Cacophonists poured time, money and energy into building Burning Man rather than on other Cacophony events, and the rapid growth of Burning Man ultimately resulted in Cacophony's demise; it now exists primarily as a website maintained by Scott Beale of Laughing Squid.

1990: The Cacophony Society and the Zone Trip to Black Rock Desert

Thanks to word of mouth and viral marketing by the Cacophony Society, the 1990 crowd of about 800 was so huge that many had to crawl along the bluff in order to see the spectacle. Harvey remembers that, in order to avoid the crowds at the main entrance, a crew slowly lowered the 40-foot Man down the side of a cliff onto the beach. The authorities intervened and told them to stop but the Man was so heavy that he couldn't be hoisted back up; so they continued to lower him all the way to the beach (Harvey 2004a). On the night of 21 June 1990, the authorities gave Harvey permission to raise the Man but not to burn him. This agreement, arrived at through on-site negotiations, signalled Harvey's willingness to cooperate with government officials and the law and has ensured the survival of the event. But that night the crowd wasn't interested in the future; it wanted action and grew agitated waiting for the Man to burn. According to one account, the crowd began to shout, 'Burn him! Burn him!' The mob got uglier and someone tried to strangle Harvey in a fit of anger (BMO 2006d). The Man did not burn that night on Baker Beach; he was dismantled, removed from the beach and stored in an empty parking lot. The angry crowd eventually dissipated.

Several weeks later, at a meeting at the Golden Gate House, then a centre of underground culture, organizers set about deciding what to do. Mikel, Harvey and Law, along with other Cacophony members, happened to watch a video of a strange giant croquette game in the Black Rock Desert with 8-foot croquette balls and pickup trucks for mallets—a larger-than-life game created by a group of ex-Berkeley residents who moved to Gerlach, Nevada, in the late 1970s. Mikel, Harvey and Law thought, 'This is the place where we could do Burning Man' (Mikel 2008). Law and a group of Cacophonists had celebrated Labour Day there the previous year and Law, with Kevin Evans, had made plans for a return 'zone trip' in 1990. Three weeks before Labour Day, Harvey found his Man torn to pieces and completely destroyed by a new tenant who had occupied the property where the figure was being stored. Frantically, Harvey procured a loan to purchase new materials, and volunteers worked day and night to rebuild the Man from start to finish. On 1 September 1990, with 20 minutes remaining before the Ryder rental truck arrived, the reconstructed figure was ready to be hauled away to the desert to be burned (BMO 2006d).

On the day of departure to the desert, about 80 people arrived at Golden Gate Park with all sorts of luggage, camping gear, coolers, suitcases and duffel bags. There was tremendous excitement and electricity in the air as they loaded their belongings into the rental truck alongside the Man. As Louis M. Brill recalls:

> I was struck by the enormity of the moment. We were packing up, getting ready to leave the city to do what? It didn't matter. It was the big A—an adventure into the unknown. [. . .] Suddenly 80 people had become 80 friends who cared for each other, had made a commitment to follow this strange wooden statue to the desert and live with it till its last moments when wood was to become ash and smoke. Did we know what we were doing? Probably not. Did we care? Yeah! We knew that whatever we were doing, it would be different. If only for that weekend, we were going to put some meaning into a special experience, recreating an ancient pagan ritual that was actually thousands of years old (2006).

Cacophony Zone Trip Flyer

Bad Day at Black Rock (Zone Trip #4)

When: Labor Day weekend, September 1–3 [1990].

Where: Black Rock Desert, Nevada

RSVP: [. . .]

An established Cacophony tradition, the Zone Trip is an extended event that takes us outside our local area of time and place. On this particular expedition, we shall travel to a vast, desolate, white expanse stretching onward to the horizon in all directions . . . A place where you could gain nothing or lose everything and no one would ever know. A place well beyond that which you think you understand. We will be accompanied by the Burning Man, a 40-foot-tall wooden icon which will travel with us into the Zone and there meet with destiny. This excursion is an opportunity to leave your old self and be reborn through the cleansing fires of the trackless, pure desert.

Activities Include:

1. The en-route ceremony of the caravan crossing into the Zone boundary. Bring with you something of symbolic value.
2. Campsite erection in the tradition of modern Dadaistic nomadic Gypsies.
3. The construction of a brick oven for the baking of bread.
4. A group ritual requiring your participation to raise and immolate the Burning Man.
5. Night-time viewing of relevant desert videos on a big screen.
6. Semi-formal evening cocktail party with music. Bring your favorite CDs.
7. Visit to a natural local hot springs.
8. Other activities as we make them up.

This event is co-hosted by the Cacophony Society, [*the*] *Burning Man Committee, and the Black Rock Desert Rangers. Special thanks to Dogedoo Productions.*

This first *Rough Draft* introduces the groups' identification with the Dadaesque aesthetic that pervades Burning Man, especially the instruction to wear semi-formal cocktail attire to celebrate the burning. By 1990, the fusion of ritual and performance had crystallized and has since informed the ethos and aesthetic of Burning Man culture.

Driving through the night, the loose caravan descended upon the small town of Gerlach, Nevada, at sunrise. The caravanners ate breakfast at Bruno's, the only restaurant in town. Then they drove along the road leading to the desert and, about six miles later, went off it and directly onto Black Rock Desert, initiating the first pilgrimage onto the playa. The caravan stopped 100 feet later, everyone got out of their cars and Mikel drew a long line into the desert floor known as a 'zone gateway'. As Brill recounts, 'We crossed the line and knew we were definitely not in Kansas anymore' (2006). After a few minutes, they all returned to their cars and proceeded deeper into the desert to find a place to set up camp. The first order of business was to raise the Man—the entire entourage had to use thick rope and their combined body weight to hoist him to an upright position. Once the Man was elevated, Brill recalls, 'It was the most mag-

FIGURE 1.7 (FACING PAGE). Cacophony *Rough Draft* (September 1990). Courtesy of Michael Mikel.

ROUGH DRAFT

ISSUE #48
SEPTEMBER 1990

The Official Organ of the SF Cacophony Society

The Cacophony Society is a randomly gathered network of free spirits united in the pursuit of experiences beyond the pale of mainstream society. We are the Merry Pranksters of the 90's, traveling through the social landscape, dispensing a variety of mind challenging activities to everyone. You may already be a member!

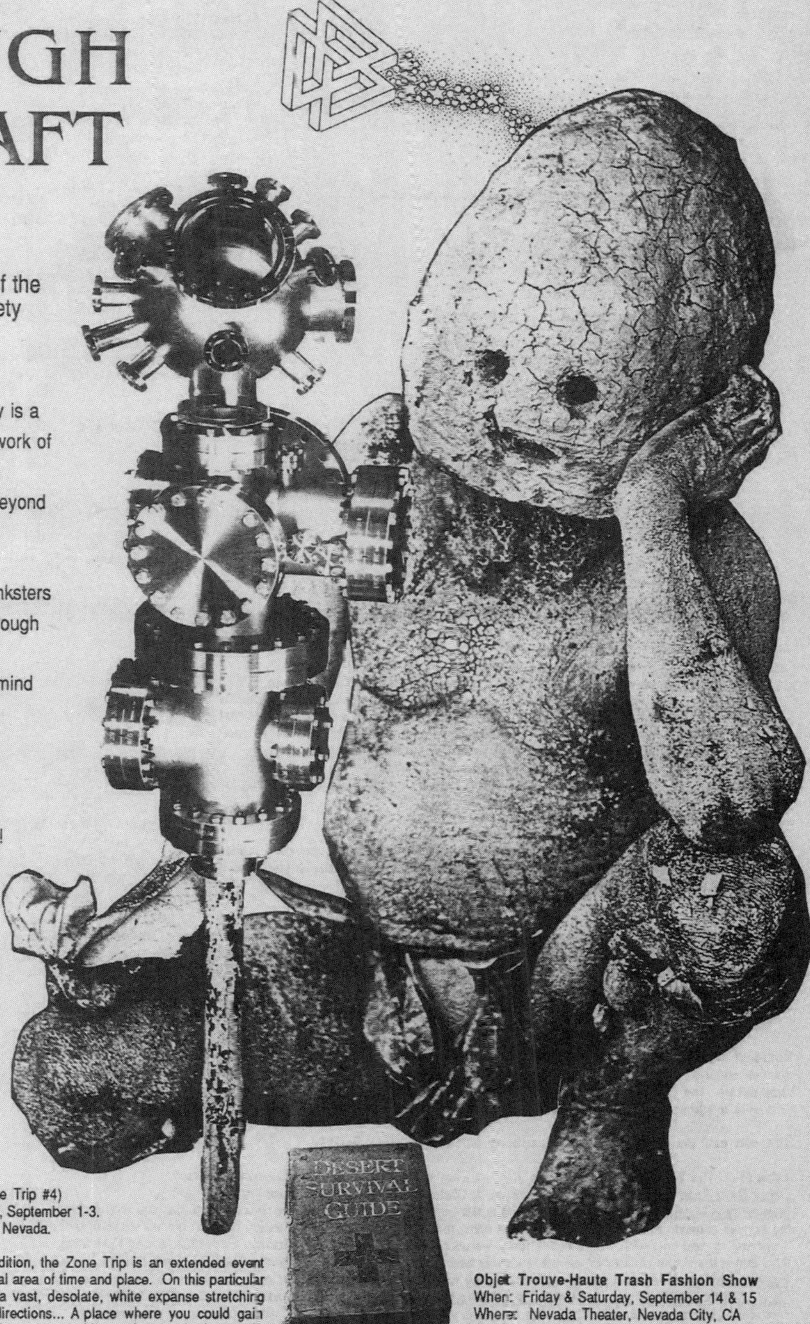

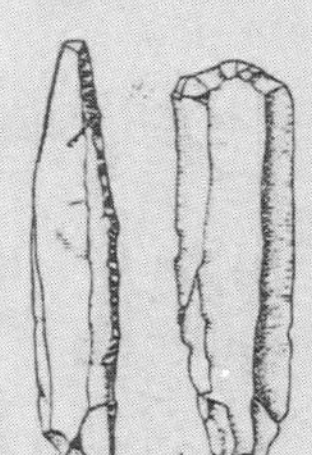

Bad Day At Black Rock (Zone Trip #4)
When: Labor day weekend, September 1-3.
Where: Black Rock Desert, Nevada.
RSVP: 415/665-0351

An established Cacophony tradition, the Zone Trip is an extended event that takes us outside of our local area of time and place. On this particular expedition, we shall travel to a vast, desolate, white expanse stretching onward to the horizon in all directions... A place where you could gain nothing or lose everything and no one would ever know. A place well beyond that which you think you understand. We will be accompanied by the Burning Man, a 40 foot tall wooden icon which will travel with us into the Zone and there meet with destiny. This excursion is an opportunity to leave your old self and be be reborn through the cleansing fires of the trackless, pure desert.

Activities include:
- The en-route ceremony of the caravan crossing into the Zone boundary. Bring with you something of strong symbolic value.
- Campsite erection in the tradition of modern dadastic nomadic Gypsies.
- The construction of a brick oven for the baking of bread.
- A group ritual requiring your participation to raise and immolate the Burning Man.
- Night-time viewing of relevant desert videos on a big screen.
- Semi-formal evening cocktail party with music. Bring your favorite CDs.
- Visit to a natural local hot springs.
- Other activities as we make them up.

This event is co-hosted by the Cacophony Society, Burning Man Committee, and the Black Rock Desert Rangers.
Special thanks to Dogedoo Productions.

Objet Trouve-Haute Trash Fashion Show
When: Friday & Saturday, September 14 & 15
Where: Nevada Theater, Nevada City, CA

Another long distance event in September? YES! This event has been going on for 7 years up in Nevada City and is a fashion show in which all the modeled clothing has been constructed from materials scavenged from the local dumpsites, and designed and assembled by people with names such as: Prima Debris, Disposabelle, House of Original Sin, Rayona Visqueen, Polly Ethylena, Recyclarella and Venus de Mylar. This may be the last year this show is held so we think it is important to make this important cultural journey. If you intend to go, it is important to get your tickets in advance, because they always sell out. You can can purchase your tickets from Synergy II Bookstore, 315D Spring Street, Nevada City, CA 95959, phone 916/265-3813.
Tickets are $8 per one night or $15 for a 2-night pass.

Cacophony-like Minds
When: Monday, September 17th, 7:30 pm.
Where: Sacred Grounds Coffeeshop, 2095 Hayes at Cole, SF.

Everyone is welcome at the monthly "meeting" of the Cacophony Society, when we sit around remembering past events and thinking of new hare-brained schemes for the future.

nificent sight, the Man towering into the sky, surrounded by the beauty of the Black Rock's barren landscape and a big, beautiful, cloudy blue sky' (ibid.).

A circle of tents was formed to create what is now considered the first village, and a central tent made from a pole and a single parachute became a communal hang-out area, the prototype of what is now called 'Center Camp'. There was no formal organization of tents, nor were there any porta-potties. They had no permits from the BLM and the authorities were unaware of the event—the location of the camp was deep in the desert and not visible from the main road. The Man was placed at a distance from the camp, so that people had to go on yet another pilgrimage to visit him. On the night of this first desert Burn, some pilgrims brought tokens of personal significance to sacrifice; others simply watched. A fellow Cacophonist, David Warren, had the honour of igniting the Man by breathing fire onto him. In Cacophony tradition and style, as the Man went up in flames, the group, dressed in party finery, celebrated with a formal cocktail party. As Brill recalls, 'women in elegant gowns, men in tuxedos, others in bizarre costumes. Drinks were hoisted, people were toasted, there was joy in the air' (ibid.). These participants brought with them the ethos of the San Francisco underground bohemian culture that was to shape the culture of Black Rock City. From this first 'zone trip' to the desert, two important seeds were planted: invented ritual practices and Dadaesque performance. This fusion with Cacophony shaped the unique artistic and carnivalesque Burning Man world that developed over the next two decades.

Building a Desert Civilization

In 1991, by word of mouth, the group more than tripled in size to 250 people. It essentially remained an intimate ritual within a tight circle of friends and friends of friends. The camp this time was crescent shaped, set up spontaneously—unplanned and unmapped. In 1991, the first Desert Survival Guide was written to prepare participants for the harsh conditions, and fire performer Crimson Rose lit the Man (see Figure 1.8). Burning Man board member Harley K. Dubois remembers the first theme camp being a perfect square house with a pitched roof built by Jerry James in 1991. Another early theme camp Dubois remembers was a man in a military hat who would pull out a full china and silver tea set and

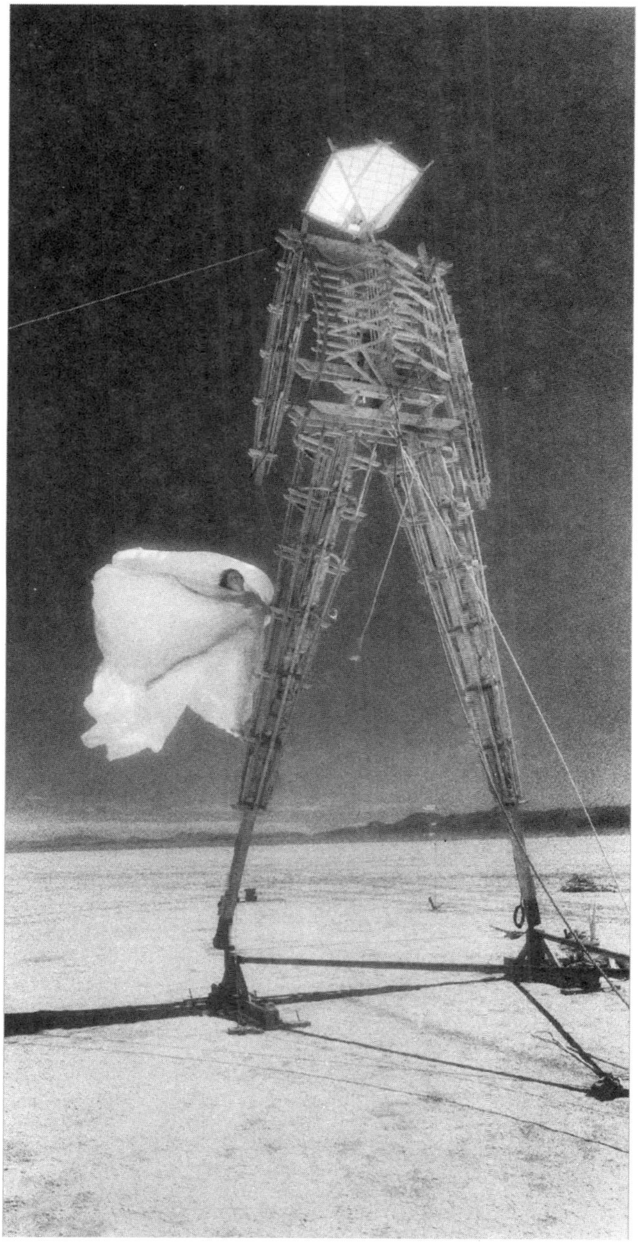

FIGURE 1.8. Crimson Rose, with wings, on the Man, 1990. Photograph by Stewart Harvey.

serve tea at random hours. There was also a lingerie golf course which required participants to be in fancy underwear. Dubois remembers the early days of the event as more spontaneous and wild-looking, 'You just did whatever you wanted' (2008).

Dubois never attended a Beach Burn but she helped set up the after-parties at Burning Man veteran, P. Segal's 1907 Golden Gate Avenue residence. She was also a member of the Cacophony Society and attended many of their events. Dubois attended Burning Man for the first time in 1991 with Segal, who liked to stay up all night and sleep until 4 p.m.; Dubois on the other hand liked to wake up with the sun and make coffee. Discovering that she was the only one on the playa with coffee at that hour, she served everyone coffee—that is how she met everyone and became involved. First friends with Law, she soon met Mikel and Harvey. The first major acquisition she oversaw was a $400 espresso-maker. Dubois wanted to volunteer and so her first job at Burning Man was running volunteerism for the organization (ibid.).

After the espresso machine, she acquired a radio to keep track of everybody. Dubois remembers that it was the self-motivated participants who quickly filled organizational positions. At this point, everything was volunteer-based and no one received a salary including Harvey. The marketing at the time was very basic and she would pick up the phone and call people to ask whether they were coming back the next year. Dubois doesn't believe that, 'Larry had the skill sets to be able to take it from the inception stage to critical mass stage. And he needed help and he needed my help' (ibid.). Dubois was instrumental in the organization, management and growth of the event. She was responsible for writing thank-you cards to people who helped out by donating resources and time. Since 1991, Dubois has been a major player behind the scenes and managing people. She was the person who would walk into a crowd and say, 'I need three people right now to go to the gate' (ibid.). Since the beginning, Dubois has been largely responsible for creating the infrastructure of the BMO and that continues to be her role to this day.

The word had got out and was spreading fast. The event continued to grow exponentially, with over 600 drawn to the desert in 1992. For the first time, a $25-admission fee was charged, but the gate was strictly conceptual—no borders or fence, just a single wooden doorway in the middle of the vast desert landscape, more an art installation than a barrier.

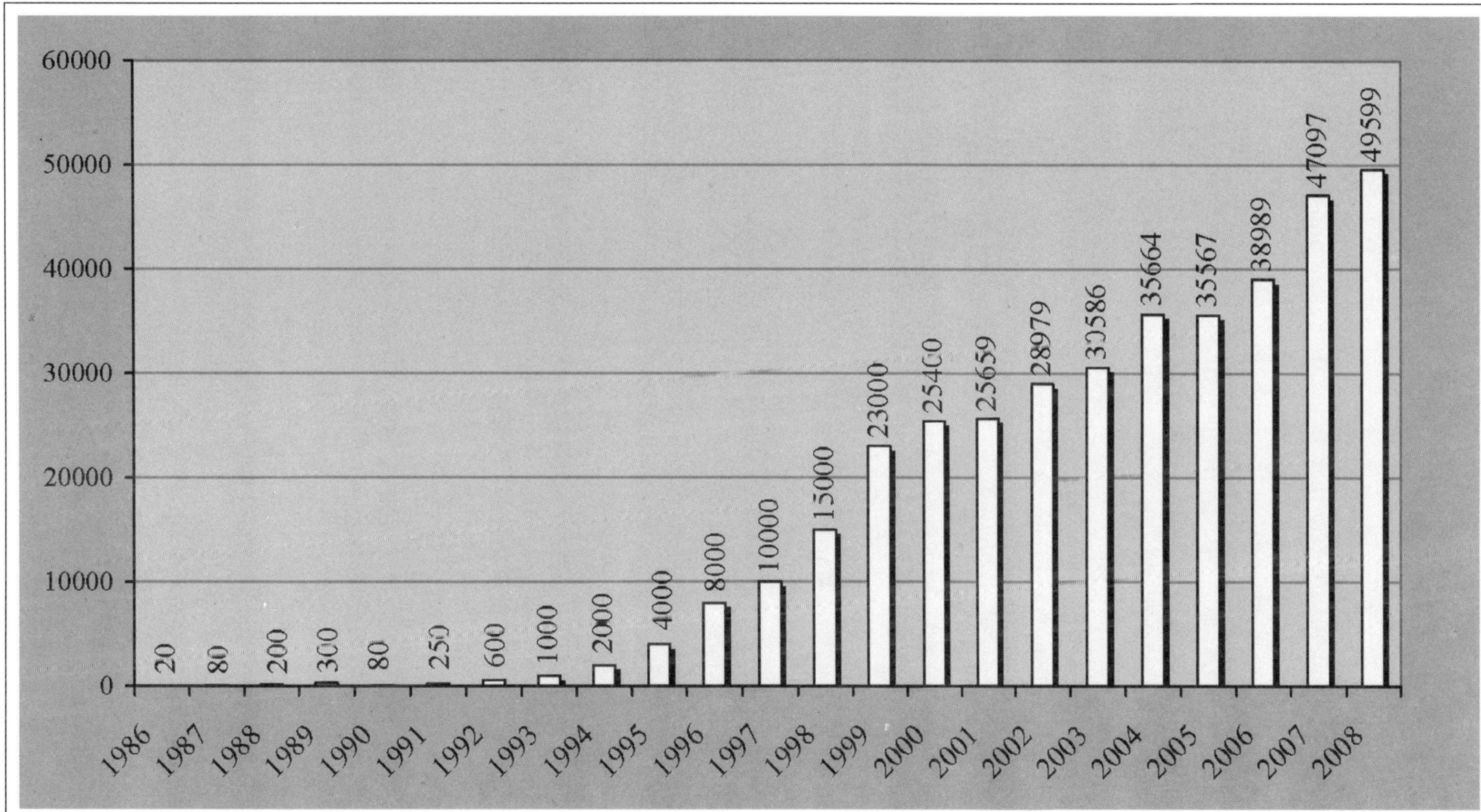

FIGURE 1.9. Population of Burning Man from 1986 to 2008, from *Afterburn Reports*. Created by author.

Paying admission was based on the honour system; many participants found the encampment before they found the 'gate', and few actually paid. The event was located further north in the deeper space of the desert than it is today, and it was not easy to find. People could buy tickets in advance via mail and receive directions and coordinates to the desert location. Long-time Burner and editor of Burning Man's alternative daily newspaper, *Piss Clear*,[18] Adrian Roberts, recalls receiving directions such as, 'Drive for exactly five miles north, then turn at a 90-degree angle and drive for five more miles' (2007b). He remembers it being a miracle that he found the camp; it would have been easy to get disoriented and end up at the other end of the desert.

In 1992, Mikel created the first edition of the *Black Rock Gazette*, Burning Man's daily newspaper, and founded the Black Rock Rangers, the peacekeeping entity of the event. The first playa wedding and the first techno rave camp were also in 1992.[19] And, in 1992, Harvey dubbed the gathering 'the Black Rock Arts Festival', although it would be several years before the event lived up to its title.

By 1993, the encampment had grown to 1,000 participants and subgroups began to form. Cacophonist Peter Doty created 'Christmas camp', an early theme camp done up with Christmas decorations; Doty blasted Christmas carols and served eggnog and fruitcake and the white playa dust gave his camp an appropriate 'white Christmas' look:

> I even staged a dysfunctional family freak-out because after all that's what Christmas is really all about. I started screaming, 'Why can't we for once just go out to the desert and have a perfect Christmas? Is that really asking too much? I hate all of you: I wish you were all dead!' Then, I'd run sobbing into my tent, which gave me cover to change into the Santa outfit (in Doherty 2004: 62).

Even as separate theme camps multiplied over the years, the population remained a community. The idea of the encampment as a city was in Harvey's mind early on, and, in 1994, he designed lamps that were placed to lead up to the Man, defining the area as civic space. The lighting of the lanterns became a civic tradition, complete with designated 'Lamplighters'; by 2006, there were several hundreds of them (see Chapter 5). Harvey noticed from the very beginning that once you put surveying stripes on the ground—or, in this case, marked off an area with lanterns—people filled the space and created a civic architecture and a world. That same year, Harvey

FIGURE 1.10. PlayaPost stamp, 2003.
Photograph by author.

FIGURE 1.11. Dr MegaVolt, created and performed by Austin Richards, 2002. Photograph by Gabe Kirchheimer.

made a makeshift sign that read, 'Black Rock City'; thereafter sprouted a series of tongue-in-cheek civic organizations. At first, the civic architecture and organizations were a joke to many, and some were clearly a satiric commentary on real-world organizations (such as Fedex, which became Pedex (pedestrian mail), and the Department of Motor Vehicles, which became the Department of Mutant Vehicles). At the Black Rock post office, you can have mail sent to any address on the playa as well as send mail from Burning Man with a Black Rock City postmark (see Figure 1.10)—for five days each year, Black Rock City has its own registered US postmark. The post office is complete with disgruntled uniformed post-office workers who harass you and make you fill out laborious faux bureaucratic forms in exchange for free postage and delivery, all done in the spirit of Dada.

While all these organizations started as faux establishments, ironic gestures along the lines of the escapades of the Dadaists and absurdists, over time they have evolved into lasting civic organizations and now make up the fabric of Black Rock City. As Harvey remembers, 'It was purely an ironic gesture to me. It was funny. [. . .] But at the heart of it, I was serious. And gradually, as more responsibility fell on people, we really began to recognize that and take this seriously' (2004a). Step-by-step, a civic structure developed around the Man, but until 1997 it was still essentially unstructured and somewhat chaotic.

In 1994, the numbers doubled to 2,000. Burning Man acquired a web presence when the Internet was still relatively unknown and an email list was established. In 1995, the population doubled once again to 4,000 and the encampment was officially called Black Rock City. Both the media and the authorities began to take notice—CNN became one of the first to cover the event. In 1994, Mikel and Law approached Harvey with the idea of forming a tripartite partnership to legally own and operate the event. Harvey, Mikel and Law became Burning Man's primary organizers, with Harvey as the general planner and conceptualizer, Mikel handling the books and organizing the Rangers, and Law in charge of logistics, transportation and camp setup. What started as a ritual and a neo-Dada art festival had grown into a business, although not one that made them any money at this point—they struggled to make ends meet and barely covered their expenses. A company was formed to serve as Burning Man's legal face to the world. Mikel and Law's attention was now focused on Burning Man rather than the Cacophony Society, contributing to the latter's demise.

The Social Drama of 1996: The Last Year of Anarchy

By 1996, the free-for-all anarchy of the early days was spiralling out of control. Bruce Sterling's article about Burning Man, featured in a 1996 issue of *Wired Magazine* and entitled 'Greetings from Burning Man! The New American Holiday', drew even more attention from the budding tech industry. With the advent of the Internet, Burning Man started attracting participants worldwide. As virtual-reality programming pioneer Mark Pesce notes, the playa is a real-world physical analogue to virtual space and the Internet. The Silicon Valley's dot-com millionaires had discovered Burning Man, and they poured money and resources into building elaborate theme camps and innovative art installations, often incorporating new technology such as lasers and Tesla coils, pushing the work to a new level of ambition and scale. One of the most spectacular and technologically elaborate performances was Dr MegaVolt, performed by Dr Austin Richards, who holds a Ph.D. in particle physics from the University of California, Berkeley (see Figure 1.11). Richards has been building Tesla coils since 1981 and performing his Dr MegaVolt character since 1997. He performed for the first time at Burning Man in 1998 and every year after that, taking a few years off in between.

A counterpoint to this artistic boom was a darker, more apocalyptic edge of a society spinning out of control. Without rules or regulations imposed on participants, the City sprawled like an amoeba without definition or shape. Participants played with guns in drive-by shooting ranges and drove rental cars at high speeds across the playa, often using them as bumper cars, and totalling vehicles, having paid for full insurance coverage. It was an arts festival but it was also a city of decadence and indulgence.

The 1996 theme was fitting: 'The Inferno' narrative centred around a fictional mega corporation, Helco, run by Papa Satan, which was trying to buy Burning Man. *Black Rock Gazette* covered this mock 'impending merger' daily, even as Harvey firmly stated, 'Burning Man is Not For Sale!' (Wooldridge 1996). The staged tension of the drama about the impending sale of Burning Man to fictional corporate conglomerates was echoed by real tension that simmered between Harvey and Law. As one Burning Man artist remembers, 'That was an apocalyptic event. Things were going wrong. It felt like we were at war' (in Doherty 2004: 105).

A major event threatened to shut Burning Man down: the tragic death of Michael Fury and the social drama[20] surrounding the tragedy. Fury was a veteran Burner who played in the punk-polka act Polkacide and was known for his wild, reckless behaviour. The first phase of the social drama, the breach, came before the event opened. According to Chicken John, there were approximately 13 people in the desert helping set up the site. Fury had gone drinking in the nearby town of Gerlach. Returning to the desert on his motorcycle, Fury saw Law's truck driving in the distance, driven by Burning Man old timers SteveCo and his friend Mark Perez. Fury was playing chicken with the truck, dodging in and out, driving full speed towards it. The accident occurred when, in a too-close pass, Fury's head collided with the truck's driver-side mirror. As Chicken John recalls, 'His head was over there and his body was over here. It was horrifying' (Rinaldi 2006). The organizers feared that this incident would shut down the event for good. Harvey claimed no responsibility for the accident. According to Doherty, when Harvey arrived on the scene, he said, 'There is no blood on our hands,' which upset a few people, namely Law whose truck was involved (in Doherty 2004: 84).

The fatal collision was only the beginning. A second crisis occurred late Sunday night or early Monday morning during the event itself, when an apparently drugged-out man driving recklessly cruised out near the rave camp and ran over a woman and then into a tent where two people were sleeping. Everyone survived but the three people were seriously injured, one permanently. Doherty remembers Law staggering into his camp with a bewildered look on his face and saying to everyone, 'I hope you enjoyed this 'cause it ain't ever happening again' (in ibid.: 108). The tragedies of 1996 deeply affected Law who felt he couldn't control the rising level of destructiveness at Burning Man.

Law, coming from the Suicide Club mentality of exclusivity, did not want the event to get any bigger; however, Harvey and Mikel both realized that the event had the potential to grow and, in order to do that, safety structures had to be implemented. Mikel wanted participants to become active agents in creating their own experience and world as well as take full responsibility for their actions. It was after the 1996 incident that Mikel added the terminology on the back of the ticket that reads, 'You accept the responsibility for serious injury or death by attending this event.' It became like a contract—a shared sense of participation but also a shared responsibility. After a huge falling out with Harvey, Law walked away and didn't look back (in ibid.: 116). Harvey reportedly then asked Mikel if he was still on board; he was. The three former partners established PaperMan LLC in 1997 so that the Burning Man Project could continue without Law. Law left, but kept his ownership in the trademark. Harvey and Mikel, along with four others, eventually created the Black Rock City LLC, the organization that has produced the Burning Man event since 1997. Over the course of 20 years, the impromptu, chaotic Beach Burn has evolved into a highly structured 'for-profit' organization that continues to expand and become more sophisticated each year.

The Black Rock City Limited Liability Company and the Burning Man Organization

The formation of the Black Rock City Limited Liability Company (LLC) was part of the effort to manage the increasingly complex event. Originally, the LLC had nine board members but, in 1999, a permanent board of six was formed, with Larry Harvey as the Executive Director and Michael Mikel, Nanci Elliot (aka Crimson Rose), William Peterson (aka Will Roger), Harley K. Dubois and Marian Goodell. This board continues to govern the Burning Man Organization as of 2009. Seen by some as a concession to the establishment, Harvey defended the choice to become an LLC as necessary for sustaining the event by paying the main organizers who had dedicated their lives to the project. Harvey maintains that, 'None of us have been particularly financially enriched by this enterprise' (BMO 2005a). The Black Rock City LLC was formed as a partnership of managers that maintains the status of a corporation. The members of the board are co-owners of the Burning Man enterprise; as a private company —unlike a not-for-profit—this entity pays taxes and is afforded legal rights and protections. The Black Rock City LLC is the entity that rents portable toilets, applies for permits, signs contracts with businesses, maintains a bank account and is represented by lawyers (BMO 2006i).

Each of the six LLC board members is given a specific role, and Harvey's is to come up with the annual theme. When I asked him what his inspiration is, he responded, 'I make them up. It depends what is happening in my life, mostly' (2004a). When I asked Will Roger about

Harvey's role, he replied, 'He's our spiritual and creative leader. He has to do that, that's his job. He's the thinker of the group, the philosopher. He always comes up with an idea that he can write about, that he can lure people into sharing the creative part of it' (2005). Mikel has been instrumental in the growth and organization of Burning Man since 1990. His current role is as a visionary, archivist and shaman of sorts, looking into the future and prophesizing what the event could become:

> My role is primarily that of catalyst and idea-generator. I have always looked towards the future and tried to put myself where I think I need to be and I often find myself waiting for my fellow LLC members and the rest of the organization to catch up. My part in management is usually in the early formative period of an idea that grows to become an independent group or department on its own. The Rangers and Gate are a couple of examples. Tools and technology are another area where my ideas have taken root. Long ago, I pioneered the use of night-vision and radar for the perimeter defence of Black Rock City. It took 2 years for me to convince the other LLC members to allocate funding for radar technology. When finally placed in use during the 2001 event, the radar system paid for itself by the 4th day of operation. Another idea that has had an impact is in the area of logistics. In 1997, I was laughed at when I purchased the first shipping container to be used for storage and transportation. There are now 97 shipping containers in our transportation fleet. [. . .] While I do not appear to be much involved with the management of this thing, my hand functions at a higher level. I am involved with overall budget and long-range planning. I also serve to maintain a balance of power that is often needed in the boardroom (2008).

The authentic Cacophony and Burning Man archive is not at the Burning Man headquarters in San Francisco where you might expect, but in Mikel's attic. Filing cabinet after filing cabinet is filled with treasure troves of this countercultural history which Mikel has been avidly collecting over the years.

Will Roger is the Director of Nevada Relations and Special Projects and established the first Burning Man office in Gerlach, Nevada, in a former jail. Roger manages the building of the City, the Man, the base of the Man, as well as the Black Rock City Airport operations where over 90 planes land during the event. Roger attends daily meetings with all of the medical personnel, emergency services, law enforcement and the BLM during the festival. He surveys the daily growth of the City from a small airplane to determine how the City is filling out day to day. He is also responsible for building 'First Camp', historically the first and last settlement in Black Rock City and home to five of the six LLC board members and their significant others, located in the heart of Black Rock City at 6 o'clock and Esplanade. Equipped with an office trailer, it is the nexus of decision-making for the services and agencies required to make the City function. This camp also serves as a place for welcoming public officials to Black Rock City and as the venue for daily agency meetings. In order to enter First Camp, guests are screened and must have an appointment. Mikel, however, chooses not to live at First Camp and sets up home on the last row of the City in the walk-in camping:

> I have always felt that First Camp is too pretentious and separate from the rest of the community. First Camp has become an ivory tower. There is way too much money and infrastructure support provided to it. [. . .] At First Camp, you need an appointment to get past the guard. Anyone can walk into my camp and talk to me. I really feel that I am more accessible and closer to the community where I camp out on the edge of Black Rock City (ibid.).

Harley K. Dubois, as Director of Community Services and the Playa Safety Council, is responsible for managing the events infrastructure. She oversees all the services, including the placement of Black Rock City and the perimeter; the commissary that feeds the Burning Man staff; Gate Keepers and Greeters; Black Rock Rangers; Lamplighters; the placement of the theme camps and villages; the Playa Information Services; the Department of Mutant Vehicles (DMV); Earth Guardians; recycling; and all the volunteers. Since 2007, Terry Schoop has taken over managing Community Services from Dubois who oversees him. In the last five years, Dubois developed an extensive training programme from first aid to self-development and communication style. Dubois said, 'We are implementing, it sounds really corporate, a manner of vocabulary and manner of speaking, a manner of expectations of behaviours for all of the staff members so that we can operate faster, better, and more effectively and efficiently as well as maintaining a happy, fun, creative working environment' (2008). Dubois had no previous experience in corporate management—guided by instinct, she saw what needed to get done and did it.

Marian Goodell (aka Maid Marian) holds a BFA in creative writing from Goucher College in Baltimore and an MFA in photography from the

Academy of Art University in San Francisco. She first attended Burning Man in 1995 as a participant and met Harvey, whom she dated for five-and-a-half years. At the time, she was working for a web design firm and she put her advertising, design and computer skills to work for the BMO. She managed the mailing list and media relations as well as established the first website; it was one of the first online communities and was only text-based. Goodell oversees the DPW set-up and clean up of Black Rock City, accounting, legal, budget processes, public relations, media communications, the web design team, community outreach, the Regional Network, Burners Without Borders and Black Rock Solar. She produces *Jackrabbit Speaks*, an Internet newsletter with 70,000 subscribers; the *Burning Man Journal*, the *Survival Guide* and the 'What? When? Where?' on-site events guide (Goodell 2008).

Crimson Rose, attending since 1991, is Managing Art Director in charge of the Fire Conclave, the 650 fire performers who surround the Man on the Saturday night of the event (see Chapter 6). As Administrative Director, she oversees registration, ticket sales, online merchandise sales (such as Burning Man calendars, T-shirts and DVDs, none of which is sold on site) and office management (Rose 2008). Dubois and Goodell share the administrative oversight of the San Francisco Burning Man headquarters to ensure everything runs smoothly. Dubois, Goodell and Rose meet with people on a daily basis and have all the staff members reporting to them. It is clear from interviewing the Black Rock City LLC board members that the women micromanage the event and run the Organization.

According to Goodell, Harvey:

> [Is the] elder statesman but is not involved in the day-to-day management of the office or the event. He comes up with the theme. He travels and gives speeches about Burning Man. That is his work. He is very valuable. A figurehead that is somewhat active. Michael is recognized in the community and that is useful. If the executives are never out there, then the people feel separate. Michael goes to all these events.
>
> [. . .]
>
> I love to come to work! We have created our own little world. It is extremely challenging and extremely emotional. Our friendships and relationships, all my boyfriends for the past ten years, have been a part of this community. They have all been employees of mine, which is

> extremely hard. It is very intimate and very hard to do it that way. I have had to learn a lot about myself in order to have those relationships be successful from a business standpoint. I have gotten a lot from it (2008).

The board, which meets every other week, supervises salaries, hiring and firing, and undertakes all financial and policy decisions that affect the survival and the long-term goals of Burning Man. Burning Man grew out of a community where decisions were made by consensus, and the LLC board still functions according to this model. Supporting the six board members are 24 senior staff members and numerous paid contractors who function as leaders in various aspects of the organization.[21] In 2007, senior staff members Andie Grace and Ray Allen joined the board as advisors; they are, however, not owners in the LLC. In order to receive health insurance, staff members must work for the BMO for more than six months consecutively.

The basic organization has been extremely stable, and Roger explained why: 'The six of us have been pretty solid all along the way. It's a different kind of company because it is based on friendship. We are all good friends. And I think because of that we have been extremely tolerant of each other. There have been the normal ups and downs as in any relationship but nothing that has been a deal breaker' (2005). In its hierarchical structure, the LLC resembles a typical corporate top-to-bottom paradigm controlled by the original board of six LLC members, with Harvey serving as Executive Director/CEO of Burning Man. The interest of all owners of the LLC is valued at $20,000 plus 10 per cent a year after 2000 (BMO 2006i). Harvey states clearly in the *Afterburn Report* in 2005 that should any member of the LLC choose to depart, he or she will receive as sole compensation for his or her many years of service what he ironically calls a 'golden parachute' of $20,000, and their share will then revert back to the group (see BMO 2005a). They intend to recruit new board members over time from among trusted colleagues within the organization.

The LLC is not a 'tontine', a form of partnership in which all assets can revert to a surviving member; the aim is for property of the Black Rock City LLC to belong to the culture of Burning Man and not to one sole individual. Harvey is proud of his colleagues for agreeing to this form of partnership because he feels it demonstrates a basic principle:

> We have never imagined that Burning Man is or should be property in any ordinary sense of the term. Everyone feels that the Project should not be treated as a commodity. The idea that any one of us might possess the right to transfer these assets onto the market felt aberrant. We've labored so long in the radically de-commodified world of Burning Man that this agreement represents a form of common sense. Millions of dollars may stream into Burning Man each year, and millions may flow out, but Burning Man is not for sale (ibid.).

As an example of how commercialization has been resisted, Harvey proudly recalls how the BMO sued MTV for an attempt at airing unauthorized footage of the event. MTV had already started running promos that read, 'Secret Rites of Burning Man!' focusing on the more Dionysian aspects—the sex, drugs and alcohol. The BMO felt MTV was trying to exploit the event and turn it into a mainstream product, violating the integrity and spirit of the event. The filmmaker had signed a media release form that legally prevented MTV from using the footage. The case was settled out of court and the footage never aired (Harvey 2004a).

While this view seems idealistic and utopian, it represents a radical departure from most corporate models that are structured on profit-making. The BMO is 100 per cent dependent on ticket sales; it has never applied for any grants or sought private investments or commercial sponsorship; and it does not permit any vending on site apart from Center Camp Café and Camp Arctica, which sells ice. Harvey boasts: 'If anything, we joke; we are more aptly termed a "no-profit".' Harvey is proud of the fact that they have never had investors or commercial sponsorships, the typical sources of income and funding that ensure the potential for turning a profit in a 'regular' business (BMO 2005a).

The Black Rock City LLC is paradoxically a for-profit corporation with a solely cultural mission—to produce the event known as Burning Man. Its goals are to guide, nurture and protect the permanent community created by its culture, which is most evident through the Burning Man Regional Network. Adopting the Cacophony mantra, the mission statement says that Burning Man is radically inclusive, and it is accessible to anyone who can purchase an entrance ticket. The guiding principles of Burning Man culture are outlined in its mission statement: 'immediacy: experience before theory, moral relationships before politics, survival before services, roles before jobs, embodied ritual before symbolism, work before vested interest, participant support before sponsorship [. . .] We will always burn the Man' (BMO 2006e).

In 2007, John Law filed a lawsuit against Harvey and Mikel to cancel the Burning Man trademark owned by PaperMan LLC, which was formed in 1997 when Law was no longer involved with Burning Man. Legally, PaperMan LLC owned the trademark and Black Rock City LLC produced the event and Harvey and Mikel are on the boards of both organizations. All the other Black Rock City LLC board members had no ownership stake in the Burning Man trademark. The litigation ended with a confidential settlement between all three men, whereby the Black Rock City LLC purchased the Burning Man trademark from PaperMan LLC in exchange for Law dropping his charges (BMO 2007a).

Black Rock Arts Foundation

While the Black Rock City LLC continues to run the Burning Man event, a not-for-profit organization was formed in 2001 by five members of the LLC board (not including Mikel). A firewall exists between the organizations to keep them legally separate. The Black Rock Arts Foundation (BRAF) was created to support Burning Man artists outside of Black Rock City as a way to promote interactive, community-based art and installations. Most of the installation art created at Burning Man is interactive and designed to be touched, handled, played with and moved through. It is art that demands a collaborative response and intentionally blurs the distinction between 'audience and art form, professional and amateur, spectator and participant' (Black Rock Arts Foundation, BRAF 2008). BRAF's goal is to help artists whose work exists outside the scope of mainstream galleries, museums and marketplaces to reclaim art as a medium of personal, social and civic transformation.

BRAF's 12-person board of directors includes four LLC members, as well as a 21-member advisory board that includes Peter Schurman (executive director of MoveOn.org); Mark Pincus (founder of Tribe.net); John Perry Barlow (songwriter for the Grateful Dead); and Leo Villareal (visual artist and a founder of the New York theme camp, Disorient) among other notable members. In 2003, BRAF gave out $5,000 in grants, increasing in size to $11,400 in 2004, $16,130 in 2005, $20,000 in 2006 and $37,000 in 2007 (ibid.). These grants given by the not-for-profit BRAF are solely for

FIGURE 1.12. Pepe Ozan's *Dreamer* in Black Rock City, 2005. Photograph by John Tzelepis.

projects outside of Black Rock City and should not to be confused with the $437,973 (in 2005) in grants given to fund projects on the playa by the for-profit BMO (BMO 2005a). Most grants given by BRAF range from $1,000 to $5,000 and are given to between four and eight people depending on the year. In 2004, Reverend Billy and the Church of Stop Shopping received a $6,000 BRAF grant to take their show on the road. Other projects supported by BRAF to take art created for Burning Man to other venues are David Best's *Hayes Green Temple Project* (2005); Michael Christian's sculpture *Flock* (2001), which moved to San Francisco's Civic Center Plaza in front of City Hall; and Pepe Ozan's *Dreamer* (2005), installed in San Francisco's Golden Gate Park (see Figure 1.12) (BRAF 2008).

Emergence of Black Rock City: 1997–2008

Due to problems acquiring land permits from the Nevada BLM, the site of the Burn in 1997 was on private land. The tract, owned by John Casey, was called the Hualapai Playa (pronounced 'wall-a-pie'), named after a vanished Native American tribe whose name means 'people of the pines'. It was not until 1997, when they were able to seal the event with a natural boundary, that the planners could be sure that everyone in attendance had bought a ticket, which they styled as a tax to their 'citizens' (Harvey 2004a). The money collected was used to pay for porta-potties, mailings and Harvey's rent back in San Francisco. A single point of entry was set up and, for the first time in Burning Man's history, everyone was charged admission. The ticket price more than doubled from $20 in 1996 to $50 in 1997 ($75 at the gate). Washoe County required that Burning Man pay a land-use fee and, because it didn't trust the Burning Man organizers to pay up, the Washoe County Sheriff's Department placed law-enforcement officers at the gate to collect the admission money. The county took the entire earnings—over $350,000. In a moment of panic, Harvey turned to the community for help and received $50,000 in on-site donations, which went towards expenses. Up until this point, 10 years after the first event, none of the organizers had ever been paid for their work. Later, Washoe County Sheriff's Department returned $50,000, after realizing it had taken everything.

The 1997 theme was 'Mysteria', which in Latin means 'mystery'. Attendance had grown to a staggering 10,000 participants. After the 1996 tragedies, the organizers realized they needed to implement safety rules.

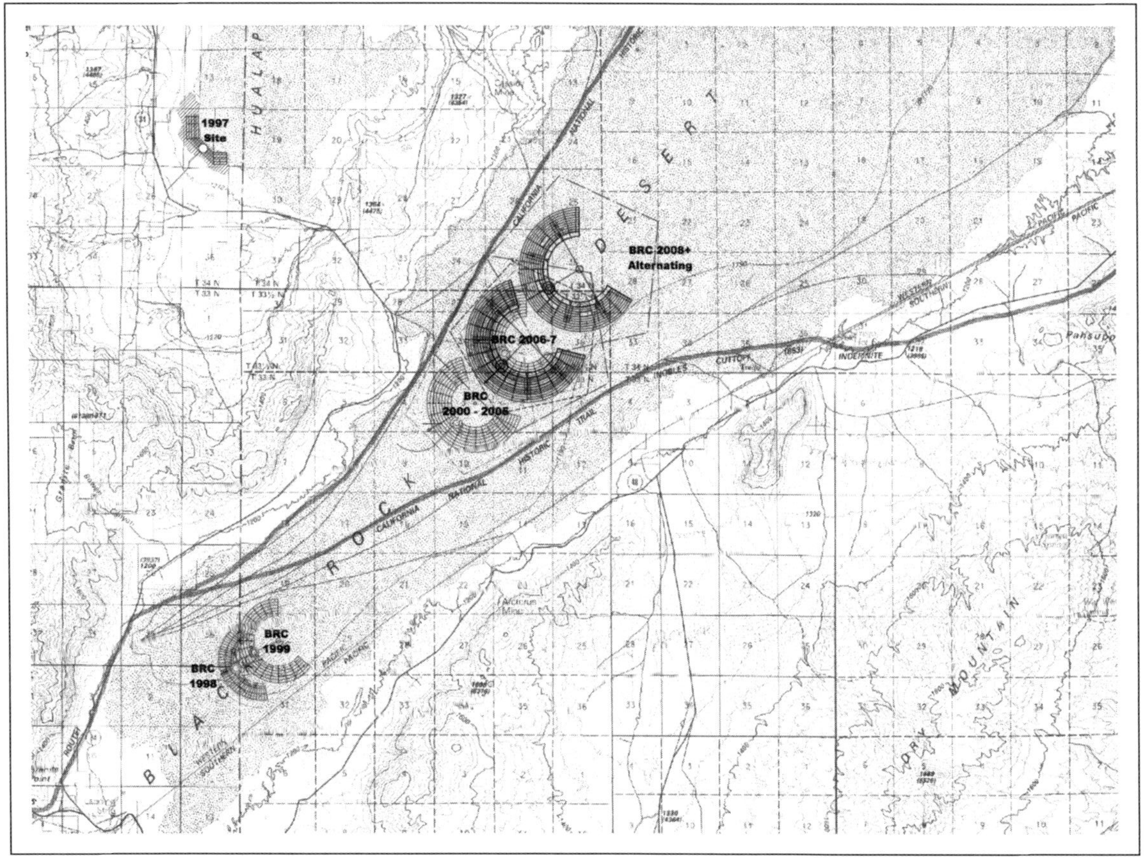

FIGURE 1.13. Site location map of Black Rock City, 1997–2008.

Courtesy of the Burning Man Organization.

In order to operate as a legitimate business that deals with insurance companies, law enforcement and lawyers, the BMO had to establish and enforce safety regulations. However, they have to this day resisted making rules that regulate behaviour—no matter how outrageous—as long as it does not harm anyone or the land. Some old-timers continue to complain that these regulations have crushed the original spirit of Burning Man, but, in order to operate as a legal entity, these procedures were necessary for the continuation of the event. No driving on the playa and no guns were the first two rules. Black Rock City was transformed into a pedestrian city with an enforced speed limit of five miles an hour. Participants were requested to drive to their campsites and park their cars for the duration of the event, a rule strictly enforced to this day.

The authorities of Washoe County imposed its own regulations, requiring that the sprawling campground be easily navigable in case of an emergency. As in most towns and cities, addresses and coordinates are used by emergency services to pinpoint the location of an incident. With safety in mind, the BMO brainstormed about how to create a city with avenues and streets while still maintaining its organic, artistic quality. The BMO invited architect Rod Garrett to design the first blueprint of Black Rock City. The centre of the City was determined by the location of the Man, which functioned like the fixed point of a drawing compass. From this spot, the builders surveyed the arc that defined the curve of Black Rock's concentric streets. The half circle was divided into blocks by a series of radial streets, like spokes projecting outward from the hub of an enormous wheel. The Man could be seen from every part of the City and served as a point of navigation; Black Rock City was in orbit around him.[22] This began the two-year process of developing the basic scheme from which the present City has grown. The design had to provide for basic emergency services and needed to be easy to navigate for participants, who in years past had easily become disoriented amidst the chaotic arrangement of bodies and vehicles. There was no book or manual for creating Black Rock City. As Roger recalls, it was an exciting moment in Burning Man's history because they were able to literally design a city around the idea of art and community (2005).

The Department of Public Works

To help build the City in 1997, Will Roger and Rod Garrett gathered a group of people to form the DPW. To this day, DPW is the first group of volunteers to arrive in the desert, approximately one month before Labour Day, and is the last to leave. This group of several hundred volunteers plans, surveys and builds the basic infrastructure of the City. Their responsibilities include demarcating more than 38 miles of road with flags; making and placing more than 2,000 signs; establishing the gate; building Center Camp Café, which covers nearly half an acre; building and placing lantern spires and City lighting; maintaining potable water systems; building functional and safe shade structures; maintaining a depot for material storage; building the Man; constructing border fencing; and setting up the small-plane airport and runway (BMO 2006a).

Will Roger, the head of DPW, remembers his first crew, a collection of circus people, punks and vagabonds—including Justin Atwood and the Minneapolis Hard Times Bike Club crew—who were penniless and stranded on the Hualapai Playa in 1997. They formed the nucleus of what became the DPW—volunteers willing for whatever reason to spend months in the hateful desert setting up and cleaning up Black Rock City for no more than food, beer and enough cash to catch a bus back to wherever they started. These DPW vagabonds formed 'Pedal Camp' and, over the years, have earned the reputation for being rough and rowdy.

Up until 1997, the event had lasted for three days but Roger pushed hard to make it a weeklong event—he felt that the amount of time and energy required to build Black Rock City demanded a bigger payoff for the volunteer crew. There were other innovations that year. For the first time, the City was coherently zoned by theme camps, and special areas were designated for walk-in camping, law-enforcement headquarters, large-scale sound installations and villages. The new civic design was largely determined by health and safety concerns. In the early 1990s, the encampment was deliberately hidden in the desert from the authorities but, with an increase in scale and population and for safety reasons, the event needed to be easy to find and accessible. In 1997, the City was designed with five concentric rings to accommodate 10,000 participants and grew to 10 rings in 2003 to accommodate 30,000 participants (BMO 2006b).

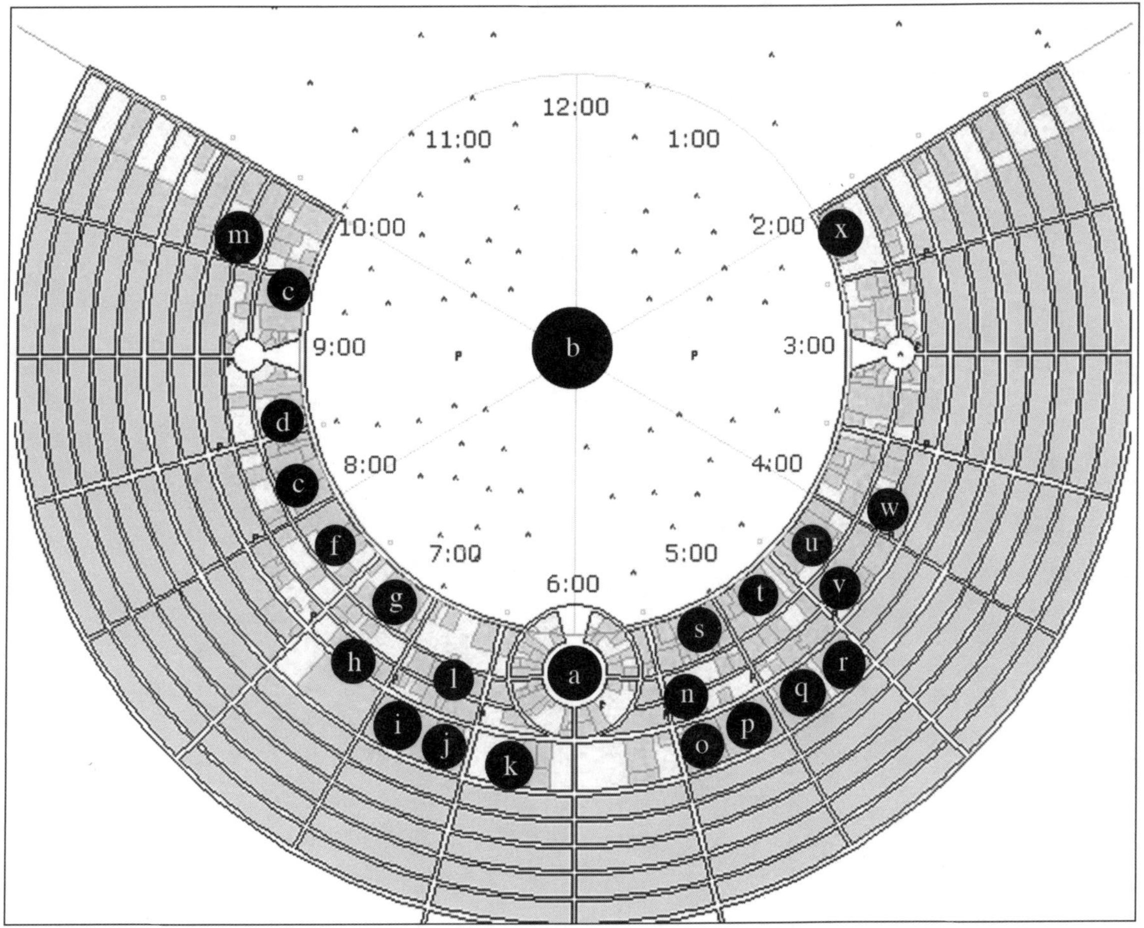

Map of Villages in Black Rock City (2004)

a. Center Camp Café
b. The Man
c. Area 47
d. Snowflake Village
e. Irrational Geographic Society
f. The Illumination Village
g. Asylum Village
h. Woonami Village
i. The Brane
j. Avalon Space Salon
k. Fandango
l. Shangri-La Village
m. Re-evolution Village
n. Lamplighter Village
o. Kidsville
p. Alternative Energy Zone
q. Hushville
r. Infinite Oasis
s. Conglomerate Village
t. The Embassy
u. Sanctuary Village
v. Gigsville
w. Wheeeeeville

FIGURE 1.14. Map of Villages, Black Rock City, 2004. Created by the author.

Theme Camps and Villages

Early on, participants began transforming their camps into interactive environments, what Harvey calls 'acts of radical self-expression'. The concept of 'villages' within Black Rock City spontaneously emerged from participants forming groups of campsites. A village is a cluster of camps within the larger community of Burning Man. As Roger remembers:

> Our first large villages were in 1997. Before that theme camps just naturally came out of the original people that camped at Burning Man. One camp would show up and put pink flamingos in front of their tent and it would become 'Pink Flamingo Camp'. And back then you probably needed two flamingos to make a theme. Now you would need a hundred (2005).

The distinction between a village and a theme camp is size: a village has more than 150 people while a theme camp has fewer. The requirement for a theme camp is that it should create a visual presence and in some way provide a communal space or activity. Those wanting to create a theme camp must register on the Burning Man website, filling out an extensive questionnaire due by the end of June each year. The questionnaire asks the name of the theme camp, a diagram of the camp's layout and a detailed plan for interactivity, such as hosting workshops or events that are open to the entire community. One can request an ideal location within Black Rock City but to be considered for the Esplanade, the City's main thoroughfare, the camp needs to have a completely conceived visual scheme. Theme camps are also required to submit their date of arrival, number of vehicles and generators, number of art installations, as well as clean up and fire-safety plans (BMO 2006g). Once registered, the camp is given its place on the City map. Loud sound camps are placed at the edges of the City and family-oriented camps are kept separate from adult-themed camps.

The application to become a village is similar to that for a theme camp but additionally requires a village mission-statement, identification of core members and a mayor or contact person to serve as liaison between the BMO and the village. Over the years, theme camps and villages have become increasingly ambitious. In 2005, there were 31 registered villages and over 500 theme camps. Some villages have been in Black Rock City for years, such as 'Kidsville' (started in 1997), 'Illumination Village' (1998), 'Irrational Geographic Society' (1998), 'Gigsville (1998), 'Area 47'

(2000), 'Snowflake Village' (2000), 'Asylum Village' (2001), 'Hushville' (2001) and 'Jiffylube Penetration Village' (2002) (BMO 2006g).[23]

Plans moved forward to shift the event from the private Hualapai Playa back to the public Black Rock Playa managed by the Nevada BLM. The Black Rock City LLC applied for a permit to use the public land but the BLM would not consider the application. After waiting 28 days, the BLM permit application was returned unprocessed (BMO 2006h). There was a serious concern in the Burning Man community that the 1998 event was not going to happen. Christina Harbridge, a volunteer and an expert in negotiations with government, believed that in 1997 Burning Man had been taken advantage of by the Washoe officials. She told the Burning Man organizers that because they were generating significant income for the county—they had power and leverage (Doherty 2004: 128). The BMO realized it needed someone to interface with the local authorities, so Marian Goodell, LLC board member and then Harvey's girlfriend, took on that role. She attended local Gerlach and Empire town hall meetings and showed up at the BLM offices to fight for a public land-use permit. After eight weeks of letters from the Burning Man community, the district manager of the Winnemucca office began to process their permit application. After a 10-week wait, in mid-June, the Burning Man LLC received the land permit. While it might seem that such cooperation with authorities is against the Burning Man philosophy, Harvey maintains that it is the only reason Burning Man continues—and he has no problem playing by the rules.

When Burning Man returned to the Black Rock playa in 1998 with permission from the Nevada BLM, the population grew to 15,000 and the event lasted a week. The map of the City stretched from 1st to 20th Street North and 1st to 20th Street South, intersected by five radial streets named Outer Avenue, Baltic Avenue, Atlantic Avenue, Village Way and Esplanade; the latter is Black Rock City's main boulevard. The 1998 theme was 'Nebulous Entity', an outer-space theme that reflected the vast open space of the playa. It was also in 1998 that the Earth Guardians were formed to help the BLM manage the desert and protect it from damage.

The most prominent villages and theme camps were Infinity Village, Drano Village, Illumination Village, Bleu Light District, Gigsville, Irrational Geographic Society and Spiral Oasis. Tickets were $65 in

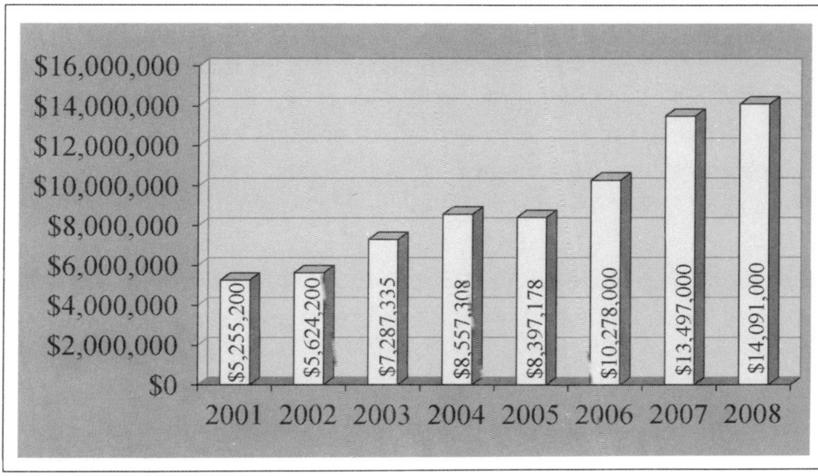

FIGURE 1.15. Burning Man Annual Operating Budget, from *Afterburn Reports* 2001–08. Created by author.

advance and $100 at the gate. Learning from previous years, the DPW erected a boundary fence, enclosing the City to ensure that each participant paid to enter. And for the first time in Burning Man history, Harvey got paid a full-time salary of $30,000 and the BMO made a profit (Harvey 2000a). The City experienced a steady growth each year and performances and art installations reflecting the designated theme became more and more elaborate.

Financial Overview: 2001–08

In 2001, the BMO generated $5,255,200 in ticket sales and in 2008 $14,091,000—an increase of $8,835,800 in less than eight years. In 2008, it spent approximately $1,108,000 for the rental of the Black Rock Desert from the BLM; $329,000 on local agencies such as law enforcement and highway patrol; $287,000 on medical units and supplies; $231,737 on liability insurance and workman's comp; $771,000 on portable toilets; $337,000 on taxes; and $631,000 on acquiring assets like heavy machinery, furniture, computers, portable buildings and trailers. In 2001, payroll was $607,000 and has grown to $3,134,000 in 2008, indicating a $2,503,000 increase in salaries (BMO 2008f). The paid number of employees has also expanded over this five-year period and is in a constant state of flux.

By 2000, however, it became apparent that if Burning Man was to survive, the LLC would need to acquire property. Rented equipment, for example, costs much more over time than goods that are purchased. In 2001, it acquired property on which to permanently locate the workshops, housing and storage facilities needed by the BMO. In the spring of 2001, it purchased $72,000 worth of real estate in Nevada; in 2004, it acquired several properties in Nevada for $247,103 and spent $656,142 on land and building improvements to them (BMO 2004b). These properties were the Black Rock Station, an 80-acre work ranch with over 50 containers, office buildings, semi-trailers, travel trailers, pallets of fence stakes, spires, burn platforms and vehicles used in the production of Burning Man. The second property, Bruno's Trailer Park, known to DPW crews as 'Gerlach Estates', houses workers before and after the event, roughly 175 at its maximum. The third is the Black Rock Saloon, used as a recreation area for the DPW workers, with a pool table and a bar. The LLC also has a Reno office outfitted with computers and fax machines, typically staffed three days per week from May to August leading up to the event. And finally, it purchased a house in Gerlach, which functions as a meeting space and temporary housing for personnel spending a few days in the area (ibid.). In 2003, the Black Rock City LLC moved into a new 10,000-square-foot office space located at 1900 3rd Street in San Francisco to serve as Burning Man's headquarters, which it rented for $259,223 a year. In 2009, the BMO moved to a new temporary office space and intends to purchase office space to build permanent headquarters. The BMO has invested nearly a million dollars in building its infrastructure and accumulating assets (BMO 2003a).

In 2001, the Black Rock City LLC distributed 32 arts grants totalling $270,000; in 2008, it increased the amount to $521,000, becoming one of the largest arts funding organizations in California (BMO 2001). Each year, artists must compete for grants to fund interactive art installations on the playa by submitting an extensive application with sketches, drawings, budget and project personnel. The first year of the art grant programme in 1999 saw a vast improvement in quality, scale, scope and ambition. Ten dollars of every ticket goes towards the art funding. As Burning Man art curator Christine Kristen (aka Lady Bee) remarks:

> It is not our goal to be taken seriously by the art world. However, we would like Burning Man to be recognized as a legitimate arts venue. The artists

> range from amateurs to professionals—previous experience is not necessary and few artists make a living as artists outside of Burning Man. There is a space for artists to create work outside of the art world that is valid and not only valid but timely and might change the future of art-making. We will never replace the gallery system but there are other ways to make and experience art. We believe that Burning Man is on the forefront of some kind of new art-making that we are hoping will become more important than it is at this point. We are an incubator for artists to develop work that they can bring back to the 'default' world. Burning Man is becoming a desirable venue for artists to showcase their work (2005).

Grants range from $5,000 to $60,000 depending on the scale and scope of the project, its relation to the year's given theme and its interactive potential. Grants are not given for theme camps or solo projects.

Harvey insists that the LLC still struggles to make ends meet from year to year. Due to the restraints it has placed on itself by refusing corporate sponsorship, the LLC has never earned a significant profit. Each year's ticket sales generate just about enough income to fund its operation. Its long-term goal is to create a capital fund derived from the profit as a source of emergency funds. As of the 2005 annual *Afterburn Report*, it has not been able to achieve this. Nonetheless, while the organization is unable to invest in capital funds, its financial reports indicate an end-of-year cash reserve of $100,000 in 2001, $444,571 in 2004, $234,000 in 2005 and $855,000 in 2006 (BMO 2006c). Salaries are going up, attendance is rising, property is being bought, and money is being saved, indicating the growing profitability and stability of the event as a business.

An Alternative History

That is one version of Burning Man's history; here is an alternative one. In order to hear a different perspective, I interviewed a Burning Man old-timer. For John Rinaldi (aka Chicken John), doing interviews on Burning Man is like a part-time job. He is regularly contacted for interviews regarding Burning Man, as he was involved early on in several aspects of the organization, primarily the DPW. Chicken John attended Burning Man in 1994 but returned in full force in 1995 with his first circus, Circus Redickuless. After a badly planned tour on the road, he dragged the tattered remnants of the circus with him to Burning Man (Rinaldi 2006).

Chicken John ran the now defunct underground San Francisco venue, The Odeon, located at 3223 Mission Street and home to a variety of performance and musical acts. Operational until May 2005, it hosted many Burning Man-related events, including weekly 'Anti-Burning Man' nights. The logo was the face of the Man with a line through it. Chicken John, still a die-hard culture jammer, continues to host Cacophony-style 'zone trips', and recounts one in 2006 that he took with 35 people—from San Francisco to Death Valley to visit a woman who has been performing for an empty house for 40 years: 'She painted an audience on the walls so she could perform to a packed house every night. She's 87. She fell, so now she can't dance any more so she sits on the stage and tells stories. It was mindblowing' (ibid.).

As the godfather of John Law's child, Chicken John regards Law as a dear friend and mentor. Having witnessed all the stages of Burning Man's growth, Chicken John has a rather cynical perspective when it comes to Harvey and offers an alternative narrative. While Law left the organization voluntarily, he has continued to watch the event flourish from a distance. Chicken John remarks, 'It is so distasteful to him. It was his event. Larry has nothing to do with Burning Man, at all. He created a stick figure, that's it. The idea of a theme camp and the gift economy: that was all John Law, you understand that. You understand that it is a Cacophony event' (ibid.).

As Burning Man grew more popular, money was poured into creating Black Rock City rather than other Cacophony events. Chicken John and Law remain bitter about the fact that Burning Man organizers are making money off of the event, which goes against Cacophony ideals. After Law left, Chicken John took over many of his responsibilities and served as a stage/production manager for the event. He reflects on what Burning Man was when he first encountered it: 'When I found Burning Man, Burning Man was a very, very teeny tiny itsy bitsy almost inconsequential part of the Cacophony Society. [. . .] When I went to Burning Man the first time, I thought, here was this great community of people, and here is one of the things that they do. Boy was I wrong' (ibid.). Darryl Van Rhey, as Chicken John refers to Harvey (it's an anagram of sorts), was just a regular guy, and the woman, Mary Graubarger, hosted Beach Burns on the solstice. One of the sculptures was the figure of a man. For some reason, one year she was unable to do it and Harvey agreed to instead:

> So, this story about a broken heart is just a bunch of crap. It's just someone else's idea. Larry has successfully appropriated other people's ideas and stumbled into this great thing. [. . .] But then, when we [Cacophony] lost control of it and Larry regained control. He took a Cacophony event and bastardized it and prostituted it and turned it into a money-making machine using all the Cacophony ideas and therefore ruining the Cacophony Society. [. . .] You have to stop having this event because this event is killing all other Cacophony events. And the reason that the San Francisco and Los Angeles art scenes didn't rise up to become powerful constituencies in the political arena, is because Burning Man took everybody's time, energy and money. Hundreds of millions. Now let's add some compound interest to that, now it's tens of billions (ibid.).

While Chicken John despises what Burning Man has become, he still attends the event—he feels it is the only place left for people to express 'unbridled generosity' (ibid.). He critiques Burning Man's catchphrase of being 'radically inclusive'—according to him, its inner circle is radically exclusive. Chicken John believes that Harvey not only considers himself an intellectual but intellectual property. In 2005, Chicken John challenged the BMO's curatorial practices and grant distribution process, claiming that it was undemocratic. He felt that the grant decisions should be made by a rotating curator from within the Burning Man community rather than by Harvey and Burning Man curator Christine Kristen (aka Lady Bee). In protest, he created 'Borg2' and made a bet with Harvey that if he could raise $250,000 that Harvey would change Burning Man's curatorial policies; if he failed, he would sit in the dunk pool at the San Francisco Burning Man decompression party. 'Borg2' raised only $25,000 and failed to reach their goal—so Chicken John sat in the dunk pool. In an interview with Kristen in 2005 about Borg2 and a rotating curatorial process, she said:

> Burning Man, to be honest, has never been a democracy. We work in cooperation with the community—however, it is not a democracy. The tricky thing is that Burning Man is entirely funded by ticket sales, so participants feel a certain ownership about how the event is run. It is their money that is making the event possible, which is true, however, they are not in the office working five days a week all year round (2005).

This incident highlighted the ongoing tension within the organization. Despite being staged as a radically inclusive democratic event, the organization holds all the decision-making power within the community. In several of my interviews with Burning Man participants, they were under the illusion that the event was a not-for-profit; they were surprised to find out it was a for-profit LLC. While the hierarchy of the event runs like clockwork behind the scenes, at the actual event there is the impression that no one is in charge and it is a free-for-all. While Burning Man's 10 guiding principles include radical inclusion, self-reliance, self-expression, communal effort, civic responsibility, leaving no trace and participation, they also include notions of gifting, decommodification and immediacy (BMO 2006f). Tension exists between the idealistic, utopian notion of Burning Man as a solely cultural, social event and the reality of the flourishing for-profit business (see Chapter 2). This history and counter-history of Burning Man over the last 20 years, as it has grown from a personal healing ritual into a bustling city, sets the stage for understanding the formation of the Burning Man community and its culture, its invented rituals and performances. From the preparation for and journey to the desert to participants' yearnings for a new way of being in the world, Burning Man is a utopian experiment, one that is inherently ambiguous and complicated.

Notes

1 According to the Bureau of Land Management (BLM), three historic trails traverse the playa and traces of these crossings have been found from wagon wheel ruts, historic carvings and axle-grease markings on rocks. The most famous being the 1848 California gold rush, which saw a surge of pioneers trekking through the brutal desert to discover their fortunes on the West Coast (BLM 2000). In the summer, the playa consists of fine clay silt that is a smooth surface to drive on; in 1997, the official land speed record of 763 mph was set on the Black Rock playa by the British SSC Thrust jet car. In winter, the playa is wet and largely impassable.

2 Today, the Paiute live on reservations in Arizona, California, Nevada and Oregon. In a 2000 Census, the Pyramid Lake Paiute tribe had a population of 1,734 (Paiute Tribe 2008).

3 'Leave No Trace' has become a Burning Man catchphrase. In 1994, the US Forest Service teamed with the National Outdoor Leadership School and the BLM to establish a not-for-profit organization, Leave No Trace Inc., to protect the Black Rock Desert and other wilderness areas. The Leave No Trace educational programme promotes skills and ethics to support the sustainable use of all wild lands and natural areas. The con-

cept originated as a way to help minimize public impact while allowing citizens to enjoy the outdoors (Leave No Trace Inc. 2001).

4 Matter Out of Place. The porta-pottie company that services Burning Man has threatened to quit because people throw more than just bodily waste into the containers—shoes, food, tampons and other items making the cleaning process almost impossible and time-consuming. It has become a major concern for the organizers (BMO 2004b).

5 The term 'secular pilgrimage' can be used to describe such sites as Princess Diana's crash site; the World Trade Center site; Glastonbury in England; and Elvis Presley's Graceland home. These and other sites draw seekers, mourners and fans from around the world. Extending the notion of secular pilgrimage further, Alexander Moore argues that Disney World in Florida is a pilgrimage site where an amusement park is transformed into a sacred place (in Reader and Walter 1993: 1–6).

6 The Turners argued that pilgrimages, because they are antistructural, encourage spontaneity, consequently engendering *communitas* among participants. *Communitas* is the Latin term for community and can be grasped only in relation to structure (Turner 1969: 96). *Communitas* can be divided into three categories: spontaneous, normative or ideological (ibid.: 137). *Existential* or *spontaneous communitas* may arise unpredictably between individuals when a shared experience is encountered:

> This modality of relationship appears to flourish best in spontaneously liminal situations—phases betwixt and between states where social- structural role-playing is dominant, and especially between equals. [. . .] What they seek is a transformative experience that goes to the root of each person's being and finds in that root something profoundly communal and shared. [. . .] Spontaneous communitas is a phase, a moment, not a permanent condition' (ibid.: 138–40).

Normative communitas is the expected forging of community in deliberate communal situations such as a birthday party or the 4th of July (ibid.: 132). *Ideological communitas* applies to utopian ideals of society, an ideal vision of how we would like society to be. At Burning Man, *spontaneous* and *ideological* communitas is most commonly experienced.

7 As pilgrimage scholars William H. Swatos and Luigi Tomasi (2002), Ian Reader and Tony Walter (1993), and J. G. Davies (1988) note, the desire to travel and the journey itself are the essence of pilgrimage. It is the experience of travel that distinguishes pilgrimage from other forms of ritual practices.

8 In *The Modern Pilgrim: Multidisciplinary Explorations of Christian Pilgrimage* (1998), Paulus Post and others call this motivational behaviour 'quest patterns' which guide and shape each pilgrim's unique experience (et al.: 26).

9 Reader and Walter suggest that these temporary encounters serve as the gel for the creation of permanent communities. Pilgrimage is a process that reaffirms the existing social order, welding communities together and creating or reiterating a sense of group consciousness (1993: 11).

10 Among sociologists and anthropologists, the term 'subculture' is a contested term. Sociologist Mike Brake gives a clear definition: 'Subcultures exist where there is some form of organized and recognized constellation of values, behavior and action which are responded to as different from the prevailing set of norms' (1985: 8–9).

11 For a thorough examination and explanation of the origins and early days of Burning Man, see Brian Doherty's *This is Burning Man: The Rise of A New American Underground* (2004). Doherty's book is the first comprehensive history on the origins of Burning Man and he does extensive interviews with all the people involved. I do not repeat his research here. To trace a history of this ephemeral event, I conducted interviews with Burning Man organizers and participants and drew upon archival newspaper resources. Here, I have attempted as best as I can to create a linear narrative that will give a sense of progression and evolution rather than attempt to give a comprehensive encyclopaedia of every event and detail.

12 In Chapter 2, I discuss the parallels and differences between Burning Man and the Northwest Coast Native American potlatches where people burned their belongings to show off their status and wealth.

13 All biographical information regarding Harvey is taken from Doherty's *This is Burning Man* (2004) and my interviews with Harvey, unless otherwise noted.

14 In 1990, Harvey drafted the blueprints for the Man that are still used today, and Dan Miller became the chief engineer in charge of construction and erection of the figure. The building of the Man in 1990 took place in a large parking lot near 11th Street and Folsom (Harvey 2004a).

15 The Madagascar Institute, founded in 1999, is a Brooklyn-based art institute whose slogan is 'Fear is never boring'. It specializes in large-scale sculptures, live performances and guerrilla art events in the spirit of Cacophony. Its large-scale events, that often take place in empty warehouse spaces, evoke a Burning Man vibe of costuming, load music, and interactive art sculptures (Madagascar Institute 2008).

16 The Survival Research Laboratories (SRL), a San Francisco-based organization, was founded by Mark Pauline in 1978 as an organization of 'cre-

ative technicians dedicated to re-directing the techniques, tools, and tenets of industry, science, and the military away from their typical manifestations' (Pauline 2008). Since its founding, SRL has staged over 45 mechanized performances in the US and Europe. Pauline notes, 'Each performance consists of a unique set of ritualized interactions between machines, robots, and special effects devices, employed in developing themes of socio-political satire. Humans are present only as audience or operators' (ibid.). They have brought their work to Burning Man over the years, and many of these sculptures have involved fire.

17 Dada was an artistic movement that began in Zürich, Switzerland, during World War I and was most active from 1916 to 1920. Embracing the principle of 'anti-art', the movement influenced later styles, movements and groups including Surrealism, Pop Art and Fluxus (Richter 1965: 11–23). Dadaist Hans Arp, tearing up a drawing he was frustrated with, let the pieces of the drawing flutter to the floor. He noticed that the pieces formed an interesting pattern, an expression that he had not created intentionally. What Arp had discovered was how to create art devoid of the artist's intention. Chance techniques were elaborated upon by Tristan Tzara and André Breton to create 'automatic poetry'. This forged a new direction in art-making: free association, fragmentary trains of thought, and unexpected juxtapositions of words, sounds, actions or images. These ideas led from Dada to Surrealism and was later important to the work of John Cage, Allan Kaprow and the Fluxus artists (among others). Cage, who knew Asian philosophy, saw connections between Dada's chance techniques and the ancient Chinese I-Ching. Cage used chance to create musical compositions and writing. All these experiments with chance come to play in an environment such as Black Rock City.

18 *Piss Clear*, Black Rock City's alternative newspaper, was founded in 1995 by Adrian Roberts as an alternative voice to the official *Black Rock Gazette*. Roberts, who has attended the event since 1993, supports the entire cost of the newspaper without the help of the BMO or fundraisers. Publishing three issues during each Burning Man, Roberts sends the issue via the internet at Center Camp to a printer in Reno, who then delivers 10,000 copies of the paper to Black Rock City. In my interview with Roberts, he announced that 2007 was the last year of *Piss Clear*, making it 13 years on the playa (Roberts 2007b).

19 A rave camp is one that has a sound system, DJs and plays loud techno drawing large crowds of 'ravers'. Dancing usually lasts until dawn.

20 The term social drama is developed by Victor Turner and divided into four phases: (1) breach, (2) crisis (3) redressive action and (4) reintegration or schism (see Turner 1969)

21 Staff information as of 2008: Christine Kristen (aka Lady Bee) was Burning Man's art curator from 1998 to 2008 and managed the Artery, the art management camp in Black Rock City where all artists must sign in and register their work. Kristen wrote art content for the Burning Man website, managed the event archives and lectured about the art of Burning Man. Tony Perez is in charge of the Department of Public Works, managing the building and striking of Black Rock City. He started working with Burning Man in 1996. Wally Bomgaars (aka Odwally) manages the Department of Mutant Vehicles (DMV) and is the Exodus Manager. Terry Schoop is Black Rock City Community Services Department Manager. Bex Workman is Regional Network Coordinator. Dave Pedroli (aka Superdave) is Nevada Properties Manager, responsible for the maintenance, development and acquisition of the Black Rock City LLC properties in Nevada: Black Rock Station, Gerlach Office, Gerlach showers, Black Rock Social Club, Bruno's Trailer Park and the Reno office. Dave Thornton is the accounting/finance person. Duane Hoover is Team Manager for the Law Enforcement and Agency Liaison (LEAL). Erin MacCool (aka Playground) is Project Manager/Labour Coordinator for the Department of Public Works (DPW). Greg Miller (aka Seadog) is head of the Black Rock Rangers. Heather Gallagher manages the Burning Man technology department. Joseph Pred is the Emergency Services Operations chief. Mark Bucky Evan Oliver II (aka Spiderman) is Black Rock City's perimeter patroller. Matt Morgan (aka HazMatt) is DPW Superintendent, managing the Purchasing Department, which handles supplies for DPW. Ray Allen is Executive Project Manager handling legal matters, government and media relations, insurance issues and human resources. In the weeks leading up to the Burning Man event, Allen ensures that Black Rock City is in compliance with government requirements. Finally, special staff member Rod Garrett has been Black Rock City's chief designer since 1997 (see BMO 2008c).

22 Harvey noticed that the civic shape emulated the shape around his and Jerry James' burning figure on the beach, a natural half circle (2004a).

23 Other villages in 2005 were: Alternative Energy Zone Village, Thermal Shock, Lamplighter Village, Shangri-La Village, Earth Tribe, The Deep End, VAST, Lustre, Otter Oasis, Sanctuary Village, Wheeee!ville, Fandango, Freedom Community Village, The Blue Light District, Avalon Synapse Village, Burning Silicon Collective Camp, Camp I Am, Dust Fish, The Brane Village and Free Photography Zone Village (see BMO 2005a).

CHAPTER 2
REHEARSING UTOPIA

> A map of the world that does not include Utopia is not worth glancing at, for it leaves out the one country at which Humanity is always landing. And when Humanity lands there, it looks out, and seeing a better country, sets sail (Oscar Wilde, in Parrington 1964: viii).

> Planning a better world has always been a pleasant occupation (in ibid.: 3).

> Live performance provides a place where people come together, embodied and passionate, to share experiences of meaning making and imagination that can describe or capture fleeting intimations of a better world (Dolan 2005: 2).

Historically, utopias have been inherently ambiguous, impossible to achieve, impractical and unrealistic. While Burning Man is not a utopia per se, it does rehearse a utopian ideology. By analysing Burning Man's financial reports, its gift economy and its ethos of volunteerism, we come up with an understanding of the event as a staged rehearsal of a consumer-free society; as an alternative way of living. American literary historian Vernon Louis Parrington points out that many of the men who have been called 'utopians' might more accurately be called social planners (1964: 4–5).

According to Parrington's definition, Harvey could be considered a social planner, a community architect with a vision of a new model for society and community living. For Harvey, Burning Man is a model of civilization, 'It is hopeful but particularly utopian' (2004a). He wants participants to return home with the confidence that they can radically change the 'real' world by extending the Burning Man ethos into the everyday.

The term 'utopia' was coined in 1516 by Sir Thomas More in *Utopia*, blending two Greek words: *topos* or place, and *u* that means 'no' or 'not'. Thus, *utopia* can be translated as 'noplace' or 'nowhere'. The first model for utopia is laid out in Plato's *Republic*, written between 390 and 370 BCE. Plato set the stage for many utopian experiments appearing in a myriad of forms and styles including St Augustine's *City of God* (426), More's *Utopia* (1516), Johann Valentin Andreae's *Christianopolis* (1619), Tommaso Campanella's *City of the Sun* (1623), Francis Bacon's *New Atlantis* (1626–27) and Karl Marx's Socialist utopia in *Das Kapital* (1867). More's *Utopia*, a commentary on the social ills of sixteenth-century England, was published only 24 years after Columbus 'discovered' America. Parrington writes that 'from the very beginning, Americans have dreamt of a different, and usually of a better world. America is a Utopia' (1964: vii). As Archibald MacLeish similarly wrote, 'America was built on promises [. . .] From the first voyage and the first ship there were promises' (1939: vvi). Since the 1680s, the United States has been the site for the founding of hundreds of utopian communities, both religious and secular. Popular US utopian experiments include: Brook Farm (1841–7), Joyful (1880–90), Winters Island (1890–1900), Fountain Grove (1875–1900), Little Landers (1900–15), Fellowship Farm (1915–25), Llano (1910–20), Holy City (1920–50) and Tuolumne Farms (1945–50) (Hine 1966: 132–57).

Even before California was 'discovered', it existed as a utopian concept. The 'island of California' was imagined in the writings of Garcia Ordonez de Montalvo, which he described as a 'terrestrial paradise' (in ibid.: ix).[1] Indeed, California since the 1850s has been the US hub for utopian colonies and settlements that experimented with new cooperative forms of living. Robert V. Hine defines such communities: 'A utopian colony, thus, consists of a group of people who are attempting to establish a new social pattern based upon a vision of the ideal society and who have withdrawn themselves from the community at large to embody that vision in experimental form' (ibid.: 5). Burning Man, born out of San Francisco bohemian values, is a quintessential example of a Californian utopian community.

Utopias have been considered 'decisive social bombs of revolutionary changes' and as 'signs' or 'signals' of evolutionary developments in society, providing a liminal space where new forms of economic and political possibilities are enacted and rehearsed (Morris 1890: 27, 91). For historian Lyman Tower Sargent, utopia is a mirror held up to the present that shows the faults of contemporary society; utopia rightly upsets people because it constantly suggests that the life we lead, the society we have built, is 'inadequate, incomplete, and sick' (2000). As writers such as Ernst Bloch have noted, utopia can be defined as anticipation of the 'not-yet-conscious' (2000: 191). Utopia is the representation of a necessary yet impossible society.

The formation of a temporary festival community like Burning Man becomes a fertile site for the occurrence of what Jill Dolan calls 'utopian performatives' (2005: 2).[2] Utopian performatives, according to Dolan, are small but profound moments that occur during a performance when the audience is lifted out of and above everyday life and experiences the emotionally charged sensation of a better world (ibid.: 5). All that comprises Burning Man is one epic performance in which participants are both performers and spectators, and as such their chances of experiencing a performative utopian moment are increased significantly. These utopian moments promote a sense of *communitas*, civic participation and emotional well-being, which together create an opportunity for imagining new models of how the world could be (ibid.: 10). It is in these charged moments of performative encounters that the possibility of a better world takes place. As Dolan notes, like the performance itself, these moments are fleeting, ephemeral, unpredictable and spontaneous (ibid.: 5). A ticket to attend Burning Man includes a certain promise of a utopian performative—one of collective transformation.

While utopia at Burning Man exists as momentary flashes collectively experienced, Black Rock City, for one week each year, is a physical plan for a utopian community that occurs in real space and real time. Suspended between an imaginary no place (utopia) in a vast, open expanse of desert, and a 'someplace' that is a juxtaposition of multiple spaces, lifestyles, social groups and patterns, Burning Man is what Michel

Foucault calls a 'heterotopia'.[3] Heterotopias juxtapose in a 'single real place several spaces, several sites that are in themselves incompatible' (Foucault 1986: 24); the term best describes the multiple lifestyles and subcultural worlds that coexist, side by side, within Black Rock City. Festivals, according to Foucault, are temporal heterotopias in that they are a break from traditional time and place, simultaneously representing, contesting and inverting the everyday. Like Burning Man, heterotopic sites are not easily accessible and crossing the threshold into them is like a rite of passage.[4]

Utopic Space: The Ideal City

The concept of the 'ideal city' has been a part of utopian thought since Plato's *Republic*. Sargent notes that concrete plans for ideal cities have existed from the Middle Ages to the present. In the twentieth century, architects and visionaries such as Charles Edouard Jeanneret-Gris (Le Corbusier), Frank Lloyd Wright, Buckminister Fuller and Paolo Soleri thought of themselves as utopians. (Soleri is still at work on a community in Arizona called Arcosanti.) But while many architects produce utopian plans, few are actually built. Black Rock City is a rare exception.

The shape of Black Rock City echoes several well-known utopian as well as sacred architectural patterns, including a mandala (the Sanskrit word for circle), Stonehenge, a Greek amphitheatre and the *Memory Theatre* of Giulio Camillo (1480–1544). Ancient Greek amphitheatres, such as those in Athens and Epidaurus, were set into natural landscapes, enabling spectators to see the world of the stage as well as the terrain beyond. At Black Rock City, the desert landscape surrounds the entire spectacle. The concentric rings of audience seats in the ancient amphitheatres are mirrored in the arc of the streets of Black Rock City where the Burning Man participants reside. The circle is completed by the performance space, with the Man as its focal point.

Circular and semicircular urban architecture can also be found in the utopian ideal cities of Hygeia (Tod and Wheeler 1978: 124), Ebenezer Howard's Garden City (1902) and Leonard A. Cooke's 1915 plan for the city of Llano (Hayden 1976: 298). Even the legendary city of Atlantis was supposedly composed of quadrilaterals and concentric circles (Pradeau 2000: 87). In Campanella's *City of the Sun*, the city was 'divided into seven huge rings or circles named for the seven planets, and each is connected with the next by four streets passing through four gates facing the four points of the compass' (Negley and Patrick 1971: 318). The blueprint of Black Rock City echoes the concentric ring layout, and, although not explicitly or intentionally, also reflects the configuration of Stonehenge (2100–2000 BCE): geometrically arranged in successive rings of stones, the central group being the U-shaped ring, oriented so it serves as a lunar–solar observatory and calendar. According to Anthony Lawlor, the megaliths of Stonehenge are thought to have acted as a huge cosmological 'clock' for sighting and predicting solstices, equinoxes and eclipses of both sun and moon, the most notable event being the sunrise of the summer solstice (1994: 122). Black Rock City first took the gigantic clock-face shape to correspond to the 1999 theme, 'Wheel of Time'. As already described, the linear streets were modelled after a clock—from 2 to 10, and the radial streets after the planets, replicating the shape of an enormous sundial. The design has been used repeatedly since then.[5]

The shape of Black Rock City also invokes a Tibetan half-circle mandala:

> [A] symbolic replica of the world, a geometric projection of it reduced to an essential pattern. In its geometry, it acts like a spiritual or psychological wheel of many spokes, each interacting with the center. By extension, it represents the center of the universe, because the mandala, being the center, is connected to the Cosmic Center or world axis (Mann 1993: 98).

The shape of Black Rock City also mirrors two other historic architectural models: Thomas More's utopian island Abraxa (1516) and Jeremy Bentham's Panopticon (1787) (see Figures 2.1–2.3). Comparing Black Rock City with Abraxa and Bentham's notorious Panopticon for the prison system, where a single guard, in a centrally elevated tower, can keep the prisoners, occupying cells facing the tower in a semi-circle, under perpetual surveillance, reveals the range and degree of freedom allowed within the City from total utopian freedom to unfettered surveillance. On the one hand, Burning Man is a second world of unlicensed freedoms, much like the apparent free-for-all world of carnival. On the other hand, it is a highly monitored site, with multiple levels of surveillance from its own peace-keeping entity, The Black Rock Rangers, to the Pershing County Sheriff. Thus, the symbolic design of Black Rock City is suspended between these two conflicting ideas, at once set up to facilitate both utopian ideals of freedom and perpetual surveillance.

In *Utopia*, More describes Abraxa as a circular island shaped like a crescent moon (see Figure 2.2). As Louis Marin notes, Abraxa is a complete city, with 'streets, recreational areas, squares, and esplanades. They are arranged from the perspective of seeing all possible routes and circuits at once. [. . .] It is everywhere and nowhere simultaneously' (1984: 103, 104, 207). Marin's description of Abraxa described, almost word for word, the map and layout of Black Rock City. If one places More's 1516 sketch of Abraxa next to the 2001 blueprint of Black Rock City, one can see that the two are practically interchangeable.

Most participants may be under the illusion that by entering Black Rock City they are stepping into a realm exempt from the rules and regulations that govern everyday life, a utopian space of unbridled freedom and excess. However, participants do not escape surveillance nor state and federal laws. Before entering Black Rock City, each person is given a list of rules and regulations, printed on the back of the ticket. By purchasing a nonrefundable ticket, you voluntarily assume the risk of serious injury, even death, and release the BMO from any claim arising from this risk. You are advised to bring enough food, water, shelter and first aid to survive for one week in the harsh desert conditions, and commercial vending of any kind, as well as the use of firearms or explosives, is prohibited. The ticket is a legally binding contract between the buyer and the BMO, and the use of the ticket is in essence your signature. You enter Black Rock City at your own risk and cannot legally hold the BMO responsible for anything that occurs within City limits.

Six concentric rings of surveillance hover imperceptibly around Black Rock City at various distances. The inner ring comprises the Black Rock Rangers, a group of several hundred Burning Man volunteers trained to serve as the peacekeepers of Black Rock City. The Rangers are the first to respond to any emergency or incident. The second ring is made up of the undercover and plain-clothed police officers embedded within the City. Approximately 20 undercover cops were roaming the City in 2005. The third ring is the local Washoe County and the Pershing County Sheriff's Office. It has free range of the event but does not interfere unless the Black Rock Rangers ask for assistance. Rarely do you see a uniformed

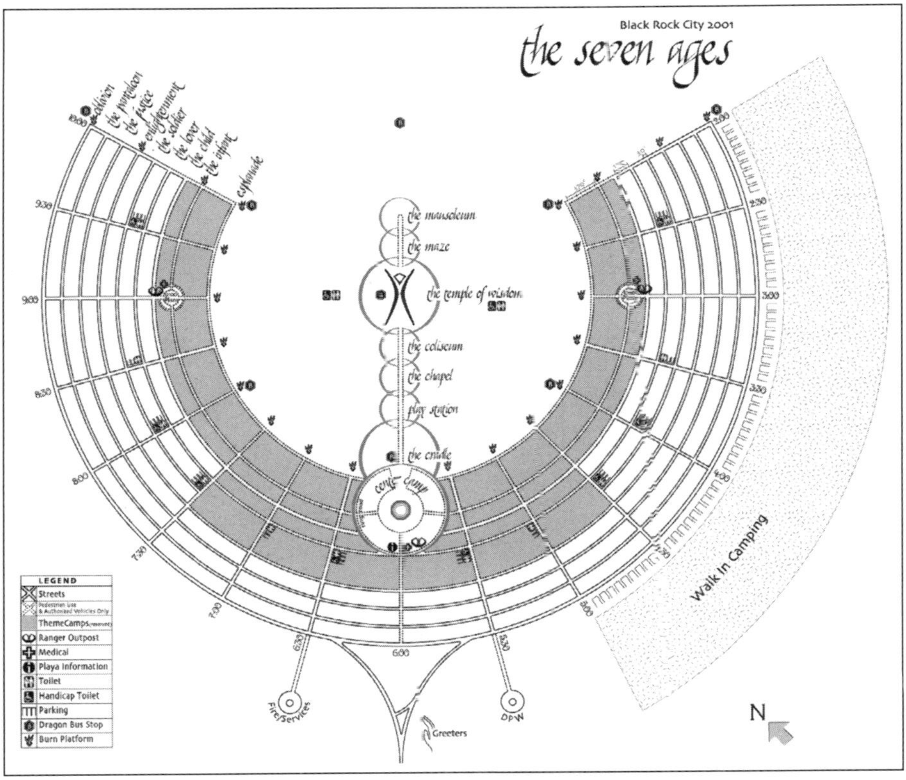

FIGURE 2.1 (ABOVE). Diagram of Thomas More's Utopian island Abraxa. Created by author.

FIGURE 2.2 (BELOW). Blueprint of Black Rock City, 2001. Courtesy of the Burning Man Organization.

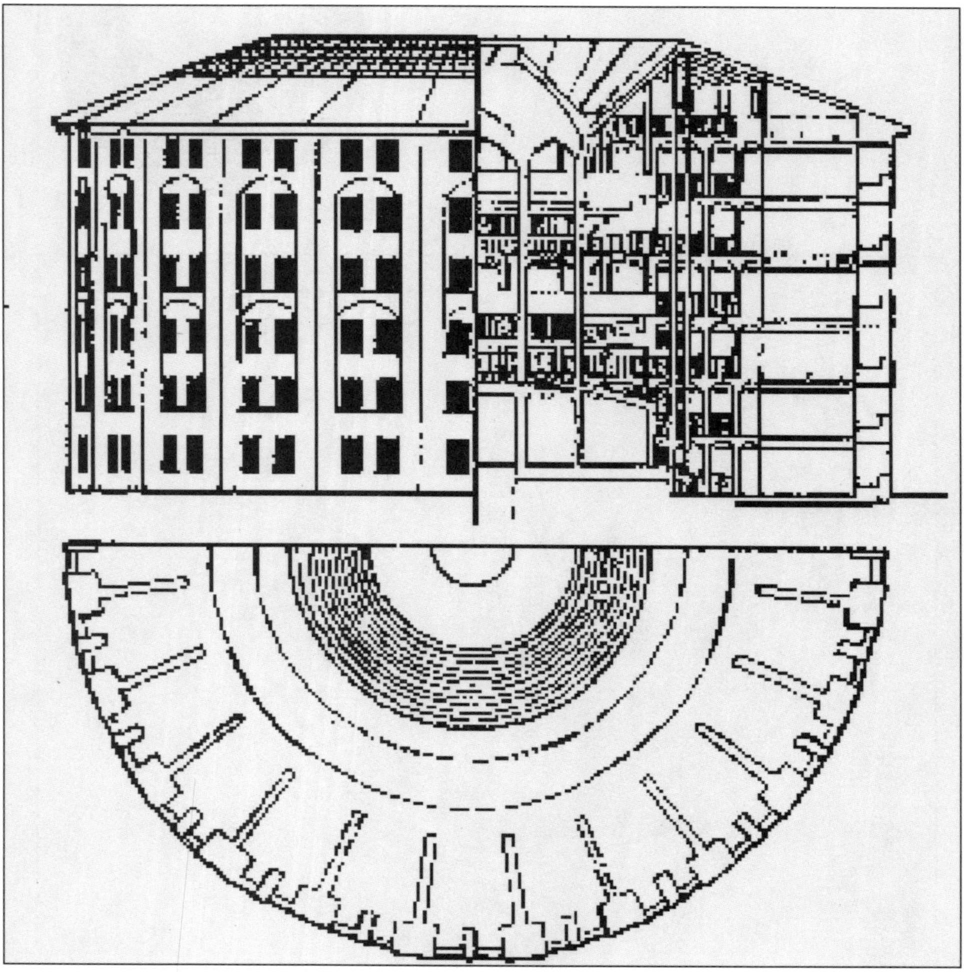

FIGURE 2.3. Blueprint of Jeremy Bentham's Panopticon, 1787 [1791]. Public domain.

policeman wandering the streets of Black Rock City. The fourth ring is the BLM Rangers, monitoring the event for environmental damage or misconduct—camps spilling 'grey' water or building open fires directly on the playa surface. The BLM will notify the Black Rock Rangers if they see a violation and the Rangers will then approach the violator. The fifth ring is the state police cars monitoring from the five-mile periphery, occasionally a police helicopter. The state police do not interfere unless there is a major emergency. It is mandatory that these agencies are present and the BMO pays approximately $329,000 (in 2008) a year for their services at the event (BMO 2006c). The sixth ring is the media eye on Burning Man.

Burning Man and the Law

The early days of Burning Man could be billed as what anarchist writer Hakim Bey calls a Temporary Autonomous Zone (TAZ)—a spontaneous yet intentional community (or festival) living outside the boundaries of everyday life. Operating clandestinely, beneath the law, for brief moments in time, a TAZ, according to Bey, 'is like an uprising which does not engage directly with the State, a guerilla operation which liberates an area (of land, of time, of imagination) and then dissolves itself to re-form elsewhere before the State can crush it' (1991: 3). While Burning Man began as a TAZ, there has been an increased presence of police and surveillance over time. In order for the event to survive, the BMO needed to comply with the authorities and the law, forever changing what was originally a true anarchist TAZ. In an article in the *Black Rock Gazette*, the BMO defends the presence of these agencies, stating that its mission is not to police participants' lifestyles or inhibit self-expression but to promote safety and assist in convictions if the occasion arises (Reid 2003).

The BMO knows that cooperation with the authorities is the only way the event will legally take place; therefore, it makes a concerted effort to maintain good relations. The authorities have the power to shut down the event at any minute if things get out of hand. What are the rules and regulations imposed on the community? In the Burning Man *Survival Guide*, there are two pages dedicated to 'Law Enforcement at Burning Man', specifying the laws, limits and rights of participants in great detail. Like in any city, there are rules of conduct that apply to all Black Rock citizens. An act of assault or theft; the use and possession of illegal drugs and drug paraphernalia with the intent to distribute; the possession of unauthorized fireworks or firearms; and unauthorized burning are violations of the law and are subject to prosecution. Other limitations and regulations stated in Burning Man's 'Ten Commandments' specify no driving on the playa after arrival; no commercial vending; no dogs and no high sound levels from loud rave/techno camps (BMO 2004b). With all these rules, what are the rights of Black Rock City citizens?

According to the *Survival Guide*, citizens have the right to privacy and freedom of speech. Police and government employees must have a search warrant to enter your camp or any enclosed private area. It also recommends, 'The more steps you take to make your vehicle and tent private, the more expectation of privacy you will have against unwarranted search. On the other hand, if your tent has no walls, or your vehicle doors are always open, then your right to privacy is diminished and police may search without a warrant' (BMO 2004d). With regard to the law, the public/private distinction within the boundaries of the City are upheld and enforced; however, the distinctions between what is private and what is public are sometimes unclear. What you do in your tent and your private space is your business; as soon as they are brought into a public space—Center Camp, the Esplanade or theme camps with public/shared space—the same activities, such as drug use and public sex, are punishable by law.

In the article 'Playa Community Policing' in the *Black Rock Gazette* in 2003, Terry Reid, Winnemucca District Manager for the BLM, states that the primary goal of the organizers and the BLM is to make the event safe for all participants and protect the delicate ecosystem of the desert (2003). According to Reid, the BLM has received criticism from several local citizens for allowing Burning Man to take place on public land. In order to meet this challenge, the BLM and the BMO have established Burning Man as what Reid calls a 'community policing event' that involves law-enforcement officers from Pershing County, the Washoe County Sheriff, Nevada Highway Patrol, Elko County Sheriff, Nevada Department of Health, Regional Medical Services Authority (REMSA) and the Black Rock Rangers (ibid.). The event is monitored by bicycles, golf carts, patrol vehicles and helicopters, which patrol and maintain order in the City (ibid.).

In 2002, the Law Enforcement and Agency Liaison (LEAL) was established as a mediating agency between law enforcement and the BMO. Agency meetings chaired by the LEAL team manager are held daily at

4.15 p.m. at First Camp and are attended by Will Roger, BLM staff, Pershing County and Washoe County law-enforcement representatives, Nevada Highway Patrol, REMSA and the Health Department. In a continual process of self-reflexivity and on-site daily meetings to monitor the progress of the week, these gatherings cite policy improvements for the next year (Roger 2005). After each Burning Man event, all departments are required to submit what are known as 'Ember Reports', written by managers from each department, detailing every success and failure as well as a candid assessment of that year's outcome. In the 2004 report submitted by LEAL Team Manager Duane Hoover, he stated that citations were given for unsafe driving on the perimeter, fence-crashing, waste, illegal drug use and water-dumping on the playa (BMO 2004b). Many people feel that they have stepped into a world where laws do not apply once they enter the City's gate. However, law-enforcement agencies consider Black Rock City a 'target rich environment' with people being more careless than they would be elsewhere with the display and use of illegal substances and drug paraphernalia and public sex acts (ibid.).

In 2003, *Piss Clear*, established in 1995 by Adrian Roberts as an alternative to the official *Black Rock Gazette*, published Issue 19, 'The Drug Issue', with the outline of the Man drawn in cocaine on a mirror (see Figure 2.4). Inside was an image of an ecstasy pill with the words 'Playa Drug Guide' etched on it. The issue covered the gamut of drugs from acid, absinthe, crystal meth, mushrooms, caffeine, Ecstasy, cocaine, ketamine, alcohol, marijuana, nicotine, nitrous oxide and Valium/Xanax and discussed their properties, ups and downs, and served as a humorous informational guide to 'safe' drug-taking. *Piss Clear* editor Adrian Roberts noticed that the 2,000 copies were gone in an afternoon. He also noticed that a BLM vehicle was parked across from his camp. He didn't want to seem overly paranoid but he was aware of its presence.

Later, when Roberts returned to San Francisco, he learned that the BLM and Pershing County Sheriff's Office had confiscated the boxes of *Piss Clear* and demanded that the BMO remove any copy of the issue from sight. The BMO defended *Piss Clear* by saying that the paper was entitled to freedom of speech like any newspaper in any city and had no affiliation with it. As a response to this action, Roberts created the 'Sex, Drugs & Cops Issue' (see Figure 2.5), in which he exposed the theft and intervention by the authorities in an article 'Please Don't Steal This Issue!'

FIGURE 2.4. 'The Drug Issue'. *Piss Clear* 19 (27 August 2003). Courtesy of Adrian Roberts.

FIGURE 2.5. 'The Sex, Drugs & Cops Issue'. *Piss Clear* 24 (2 September 2004). Courtesy of Adrian Roberts.

Another *Piss Clear* article, 'The Great Blow Job Bust', describes how three men were entangled in a make-out session at the Space Virgins Dome (Anderson 2004). The Pershing County Sheriff's Department reported that the three began to perform fellatio in a variety of positions in a public space. The fun came to a jarring halt when, after the three had put their clothes back on and left the dome, a man in a Metalica T-shirt approached them and informed them they were under arrest for public indecency; he had pictures to prove it. When another undercover deputy walked over and slapped handcuffs on them, the three men realized this was no joke. The men were hauled off to jail in Lovelock, Nevada, two-and-a-half hours away, because they had performed sex acts in public. Finally, no charges were brought against them, but the incident served as a wake-up call to the Burning Man community that the Pershing County Sheriff's Department, which enforces the law at the event, was cracking down on public sex within Black Rock City. According to *Piss Clear*, two of the men believe they were unfairly targeted because they were gay, a notion Sheriff Skinner dismisses: 'It was the luck of the draw' (ibid.). In the arrest report, Reserve Deputy Poffenroth notes, 'There was nobody to monitor the people going in or out of the dome [. . .] whether they were children or adults' (in ibid.).

Another crime that goes mostly unreported in Black Rock City is rape. As in any city, few rapes are reported, as they are usually with someone that the person knows. Being the sexually promiscuous environment that Burning Man is, with people often wearing sexy, little or no clothing, the sexual boundaries are blurred. A blog on Burning Man's *eplaya* listserv posted 16 September 2004 and titled 'Rape Does Occur at Burning Man', begins:

> Someone was overheard on playa this year speaking to a large group saying that there has never been a rape at Burning Man. Sadly, this is not true. It did not happen to me, but to one of my camp mates a few years ago and she has talked to others with similar experiences. None of these women chose to report the rape to authorities, which is their own business, but I think it is important for the community at large to be informed about the risk involved being a female citizen of Black Rock City. My point is that going around saying there has never been a rape creates an inaccurate feeling of safety, which could cause women to behave in an unsafe manner, and end up getting hurt. The last thing I

> would want to do is create bad press about Black Rock City. I love it there. But let's be honest, please. It ain't all playa love out there, and some people do take it too far (Kegynalonglank 2004).

This initial blog posting was met with over a hundred responses on the theme of rape at Burning Man. In several instances, people reported being in a delicate situation where comfort boundaries were crossed or seeing others in those situations. In response to rape and other sexually related violations at Burning Man, an activist group called the 'Bureau of Erotic Discourse' (BED) emerged as a support group to give safe sex-talks in Black Rock City.

Burning Man and the Media

The influx of media attention has forced the BMO to create a strict media policy that requires press representatives to attend the entire event and buy their own ticket (many want to just show up the day before the Burn). The media submit an online application by June stating their purpose. By July, they are notified about whether or not their application has been accepted.[6] Once on-site, they have to register at 'Media Mecca' in Center Camp and receive laminated badges for all cameras and video equipment. Technically, no video camera without a badge is allowed to be used to photograph any part of the event, although many people take pictures anyway as it is impossible to monitor the entire city. They also receive a badge that states, 'This media badge entitles you to absolutely nothing.'

While the BMO is careful about the media invasion, it recognizes that it depends on media coverage for survival. This, along with word of mouth and viral marketing on the Internet, is what keeps Burning Man going. In 2005, independent film crews from Switzerland, photographers from *Smithsonian* magazine, *Rolling Stone* reporters and international TV media from Russia, France, England, Spain, Japan and the Ukraine made their way to Black Rock City. There were 182 approved registrations in all, not including another 50 or so walk-up ones.

When the media first started covering the event, it was described as a pagan festival, full of drugs and nudists; but, as the event has matured, the media coverage has grown more sophisticated and in-depth. Increasingly, documentary filmmakers, news outlets, photographers and scholars are conducting coverage that addresses the more complex aspects of the

Burning Man project. Since 2001, filmmakers, photographers and reporters have gone beyond the general overview of the event by covering topics ranging from political activism at Burning Man (a significant theme in the election years, 2004 and 2008) to individual artists and city planning. The BMO does attempt to regulate the number of crews filming the event so as not to infringe on the participants' experience, and those denied permission to document the event are porn websites seeking photos of nude and topless women, and narrative filmmakers hoping to use Black Rock City as a backdrop for a fictional story.

The media coverage ranges from praise to scathing criticism. The *Rolling Stone* article from 22 September 2005, 'White Madness' by Matt Taibbi, is a harsh, yet candid critique:

> In the twentieth year of Burning Man, a new religion takes shape—or maybe it's just an excuse for stressed-out yuppies to get naked and take a lot of drugs. [. . .] This year, the curtain went up on Burning Man in the wee hours of the morning of August 29th, just as Hurricane Katrina made her landfall on the shores of Louisiana. While the rest of the country sat glued to the TV watching the biggest natural disaster in our history, a steady stream of America's best and brightest descended as pilgrims to a remote spot two hours north of Reno, Nevada, where by the thousands they would disappear behind a sandstorm, not to emerge for a week. Alice-like, I followed them there, expecting magic and wonder [. . .] (2005: 2).

I too was highly aware of this paradox of being in the 'Land of Oz' while the rest of the country was dealing with the devastation of Katrina in Louisiana and Mississippi. Taibbi calls Harvey the 'wizard of Oz' and describes him as a mechanic or refrigerator repairman rather than an artist:

> Then I went into Burning Man and actually experienced the thing [. . .] It came down to a few basic truths: It is a bunch of hairy art snobs running around with no pants on in the middle of the remotest desert, calling themselves agents for transforming social change. It is educated upper-middle-class white people rebelling against nothing they can put their fingers on (ibid.: 2).

There is no doubt some truth to Taibbi's statement. However, it is more complicated then just a shallow festival of excess, although that certainly is how some may see it.

On the flipside, the *San Francisco Chronicle* has been covering the event extensively since 2001 with more favourable stories. In 2005, it did a round-the-clock, week-long story of the event called 'Burning Man at Twenty'. A group of on-site embedded *Chronicle* reporters wrote 30 articles over the week, posted daily blogs and had a webcam tracking the week's activities. Articles focused on Burning Man artists, such as Christian Davies who created the *Dicky Box* and Mark Perez who designed the life-size *Mousetrap*; interviews with Burning Man veterans; and a portrait studio called the 'Faces of Burning Man'. The media obsession with the event offers the BMO valuable publicity. For better or worse, the media is largely responsible for bringing Burning Man into mainstream consciousness. Burning Man is often referenced on TV—on talk shows such as the *Daily Show*, *Jay Leno* and *David Letterman*; as well as in cartoons such as *South Park* and *The Simpsons*, indicating the extent to which this counterculture event is being acknowledged and consumed, if not accepted, by the mainstream.

Where the Wild Things Are: Children and Sex in Black Rock City

Another major concern for the law enforcement is the exposure of minors to the sexually promiscuous environment. In 2004, the presence of children at Burning Man sparked an intra-community debate among the organizers, the authorities and the participants. The Pershing County Sheriff's Department's concerns about children being exposed to 'obscene art', or anything sexually related, caused a ripple throughout the community. The authorities' desire to 'protect' children should not have come as a surprise to Black Rock City residents; it is a strong and recurrent theme in US society.

In *Abnormal* (1999), Foucault noted that, since the eighteenth century, children's 'bodies, actions, attitudes, appearance, facial features, beds, linens, stains and so forth are brought under surveillance' (ibid.: 263). The child's body is 'given an economic and an affective value, a fear is created around this body, and a fear is installed around sexuality as source of the dangers incurred by the child and his body; [. . .] setting out an obligatory, statutory closeness between parents and children' (ibid.: 265). Children must be protected not only from society but also from themselves, their own desires and their own bodies—childhood 'must be protected against every possible danger, and therefore any possible act or attack' (Foucault 1988: 280). The family space must be a space of continual surveillance and it is the parents' responsibility to monitor and observe the 'physical existence of their children', ensuring their safety and survival (1999: 256). Children must be 'watched over when they are washing, going to bed, getting up and while they sleep. Parents must keep a lookout all around the children, over their clothes and bodies. The child's body must be the object of their permanent attention' (ibid.: 245).

The spatial division and segregation of children's bodies from the sexually oriented theme camps and the uninhibited adult bodies parading around the playa and through the streets of Black Rock City is a central concern. The cellular mapping of bodies appears as a form of control and surveillance. In *Discipline and Punish: The Birth of the Prison* (1979), Foucault articulates how power is maintained by 'organizing "cells", "places" and "ranks", the disciplines create complex spaces that are at once architectural, functional and hierarchical' (ibid.: 148).[7] The cellular beehive structure of Black Rock City allows for the regulation and choreography of bodies and practices into precise, geographical locations that can be monitored through networks of surveillance that are 'silent, mysterious, unperceived vigilance. [. . .] It is the eye of the government ceaselessly open and watching without distinction over all citizens' (ibid.: 280). With the well-being of the children in mind, it is necessary to establish the sexual mosaic of Black Rock City in order to find a place for the child to safely exist within that universe.

Driven to the desert to practice temporary freedoms, thousands of citizens enact some of their wildest fantasies through visual art, performances, costumes, sexual activity and radical self-expression. Focusing on the sexual, in a carnivalesque and playful fashion, Black Rock City is infused with displays of pleasure, desire and promiscuity, both gay and straight. Of the 479 theme camps at Burning Man 2004—'Vault of Heaven'—over 50 had a sexual theme. Of the 26 villages, on one extreme was 'Kidsville', formed in 1997 for participants with children, and on the other, 'Penetration Village: JiffyLube', advertised as 'a gathering of gay and bisexual camps who collectively encourage a sex-positive atmosphere and playground on the playa' (BMO 2004c). Among other camps in 2004 with sexually related themes were the 'Safer Sex Camp', 'Best Genitals

Camp', 'Camp Fuck', 'The Genital Portrait Studio', 'The Green Penis', 'Opulent Temple' and 'Smoochdome'. In 2005, in order to enter the tantric sex camp 'Opulent Temple', you needed to be invited by a friend of the camp and fill out a questionnaire about what activities you were or were not comfortable with along with your sexual history. A volunteer guarded the door all night to prevent uninvited people from strolling in, which not only protected the participants inside but also prevented wanderers from entering an environment unsuitable for them. Only 30 people were allowed into the dome per evening and by invitation only. These perimeters were set up to ensure a 'safe sex' environment with all consenting adults.

These sex-themed camps, laced throughout the City, are just one arena for the pervasive sexual promiscuity. Besides the camps, hundreds of free workshops are offered daily throughout the City, on everything from yoga to body-painting, costume-making and theme parades. In 2004, 25 per cent of these workshops were related to sexually oriented activities including: Spiritual Sexuality Forum, Sensual Play 101, Sacred Sexual Massage for Women, Next Top Stripper Contest, Fetish Attire-making Workshop, Catholic School Girl Nite, Free Uranus: A Cosmic Cocktail Party for Intergalactic Gay Guys and Gals, and The Female Orgasm: A Class for Men (ibid.). To give a sense of the variety and texture of these offerings I have selected a few examples from the programme 'What? When? Where?'; some humorous, some ironic, some serious—all exceptionally imaginative:

> **JiffyLube**: Man2Man4Play. All Day. Fast grinding action all nite. Get in. Get off. Get out.
>
> **Beginner/Advanced Rope Bondage**: We provide rope, direct instruction and a comfortable dome. You may wish to bring pillows, water or your own favorite rope.
>
> **Carpet Munching Workshop**: This is a hands on interactive event. Bring your own carpet, hardwood floor is welcome. Single carpets will be accommodated. Please properly shampoo the rug or mop the floor before coming. This is not a spectator event, bring no cameras!
>
> **Fetish Night:** Come out to play at the Second Freak Show. All fetishes welcome and celebrated (ibid.: 1, 18, 23, 26).

The programme also designates a tongue-in-cheek sexual objective for each day of the week: 'Make-out Monday', 'Oral Sex Tuesday', 'Hump Day Wednesday' and 'Three-some Thursday' (BMO 2004c). The interplay

FIGURE 2.6. 'Save the Children Issue'. *Piss Clear* 23 (1 September 2004). Courtesy of Adrian Roberts.

of these activities creates a playground of flesh, and a sexual mosaic where nearly every pleasure, fantasy and desire can be performed and experienced. Not surprisingly, the Pershing County Sheriff's Department worries about the children in this environment.

As if anticipating the response of authorities, the official *Burning Man Journal* (Summer–Fall 2004) featured an article entitled 'Kids!' that celebrated the role of children within the Burning Man community (see Harvey 2004b). The article addresses two audiences: the authorities and the parents. The authors of the article demonstrate to the authorities that adults with children at Burning Man are responsible parents; then, they address the parents, warning them of the rules and responsibilities of bringing children into this 'adult' environment—and the consequences if these rules are not obeyed. The article begins, 'Kids have always been a part of Burning Man. When Jerry James and Larry Harvey first burned a Man in 1986, they included their sons, Tristan and Robin. Tristan was six and Robin was seven years old. [. . .] Burning Man has become a gigantic playground for children as well as adults' (BMO 2004e). Then the tone shifts to address the spatial segregation of children from sexually explicit behaviour. The article describes the effort to separate sex-related camps from family-oriented camps, stationing the latter in a 'family quarter' called 'Kidsville'. They also encouraged the adult theme camps to take responsibility and provide doorkeepers to prevent minors from entering these environments. To prevent parents from losing track of their children, they recommended identity bracelets with the child's playa address.

In response to the article, *Piss Clear* (Issue 23) featured an article by Adrian Roberts titled 'Save the Children! Kids at Burning Man' (see Figure 2.6):

> Geez, if it's that big of a deal, why don't they just quarantine Kidsville? I mean, let's face it, Black Rock City is already a totalitarian dictatorship—let's just take it all the way! We can build a wall down 5:00 and 6:00—it'll be just like Berlin in the 1960s! Of course, I'm kidding. But still—anything so we don't have to constantly hear about how we need to 'protect the children'. It's the parents' responsibility, not ours. They brought them out here (2004a: 4).

The rhetoric of protection, duty, responsibility and moral judgement infused the debate. In 'Confessions of an Eleven-Year-Old Burner' in the same issue of *Piss Clear*, young Kalea Holden voices her opinion:

> This year it seems that everyone is all hypersensitive about kids. I've been here longer than a lot of adults, so I don't see why I should be treated like some little kid! I hate ageism [. . .]. I'm the only one who knows if I'm uncomfortable with something. I mean, really, I am NOT going to get drunk (beer stinks) or high (so does weed) and sex is stupid and gross. So for once, will the world have just a little faith in us kids? (2004: 4).

These perspectives highlight the central concerns of the debate over 'protecting' the children from illicit sexual behaviour for fear of corrupting them, the need to constantly monitor and keep children under strict surveillance and the responsibility of parents towards their children and their obligation to guarantee their safety, both physical and 'moral'. Pressure from outside critics forced the community to examine and impose a discipline upon itself that otherwise might not have existed or even been necessary. In reality, there is no way to protect children from the nudity, sexuality and promiscuity that runs rampant throughout the City. Parents run the risk of exposing their children to explicit sexual behaviour; at the same time, they are exposing them to a beautiful, utopian world where adults are not afraid to express themselves and their desires. While embedded in the matrix of surveillance, Burning Man, as a point of resistance, challenges normative models of sexual expression and parenting, offering an alternative model for both in a city that is far more liberal than in any other American city. In *Love the Sin: Sexual Regulation and the Limits of Religious Tolerance*, Janet R. Jakobsen and Ann Pellegrini call for radically reoriented understanding of 'our practices of freedom, including sexual freedom. Sex is not a luxury, but a good: a vital resource for remaking the social and saving our lives' (2003: 151). They ask, 'is it really possible to practice freedom in the American context?' (ibid.: 103). Perhaps Burning Man doesn't pose a serious risk to children but, rather, offers a great liberation from the repressive mechanisms of everyday life. Maybe it doesn't damage them, but instead offers children a new vision of how the world could be and what freedom might look like.

Under the Veil of Utopia: Civic Volunteerism in Black Rock City

A fundamental aspect of all utopian experiments is the balance between work and play. What is the relationship between work and leisure within the Burning Man community? Why do people spend their precious vacation days volunteering at Burning Man? Why would people choose to take time off from their 'real' work to participate in 'play' work? What can Burning Man tell us about the relationship between work and leisure, capitalism and ideal communism? As Rosabeth Moss Kanter suggests, utopias are held together by commitment and cooperation that is self-created and self-chosen, not imposed by the repressive apparatus of the state (1972: 1).[8] Work is performed by choice, not coerced, which is the key to the success of volunteerism at Burning Man. While only a handful of people receive a salary, more than 95 per cent of the workforce at Burning Man consists of volunteers. Burning Man creates a temporary utopian alternative that participants actively *work* towards. The dependence on volunteers is articulated in the BMO's mission statement, which emphasizes the need for members and event attendees to actively participate in the creation of Burning Man. Each year, several thousand volunteers dedicate time, energy and money to building the civic structure of Black Rock City: the Black Rock Rangers, the DPW, the Café, the Lamplighters, the Fire Conclave, the commissary, the post office and the DMV, in addition to the theme camps, performances and art installations.

In 1994, the volunteer coordinator Harley K. Dubois had every gate and Café shift filled. However, she learned her lesson early about volunteerism—only one person showed up. She realized that volunteers should not gain free entry to the event but be reimbursed after, once work has been completed. She found it to be the only way of guaranteeing a commitment from them. In 2007, Dubois established a mentoring system to assist volunteers. When she sees a problem, she analyses the breakdown in communication to find out why individuals are not getting the information they need, whether it is in the training, coaching or mentoring. If volunteers do not fit their assigned job, she tries to find something more appropriate for them (Dubois 2008).

In her essay on volunteerism at Burning Man, Katherine Chen tries to understand people's motives for dedicating so much time and effort to this project (2005). Reasons for volunteering are diverse; some people do it for fun, for a sense of community or for public recognition. Volunteers enjoy their work because they have the freedom to select their tasks, coworkers and leaders (ibid.: 117). In other words, even volunteering at Burning Man is utopian. Volunteering also may lead to permanent change, inspiring some to leave their day jobs back home to find more fulfilling work (ibid.: 118). Chen found that many volunteers felt the work at Burning Man was more creative and fulfilling than their regular jobs.

When I interviewed a volunteer at REMSA, Burning Man's medical camp, who worked in Reno as an ambulance driver, she told me that she spent her one-week vacation a year at the desert event. When I asked her why, she responded that people at Burning Man say 'thank you' and that made everything she did the rest of the year worth it—she finally felt appreciated. I asked two Black Rock Rangers why they spend eight hours a day patrolling the City for no pay. They both responded that it was a great way to meet people you would otherwise never get to know. The job gave them the opportunity to go to all parts of the City and talk to all sorts of people. It also gave them a sense of purpose and community, a feeling that they were doing their bit. They also appreciate the respect and praise for the work they do, which makes them return year after year to patrol the dusty desert streets. Both have been Rangers for three years and buy full-price tickets to the event.

Nevertheless, the system has its drawbacks. Many volunteers are too casual and often do not show up for their scheduled assignments. Because people are not paid, the organizers have less leverage to demand timeliness and accountability (ibid.: 111). In his typically cynical tone, Chicken John shares his thoughts about volunteerism at Burning Man, 'I would say that 80 per cent of the volunteers do nothing; 20 per cent of the volunteers do *all* the work. They claim to need all these volunteers but they actually don't. Volunteerism has become part of their marketing. Get involved. They don't need any of these people' (Rinaldi 2006). To guarantee that they are not understaffed, the BMO inflates the number of volunteers. But while some experience their jobs as part of a carefree holiday, many take their roles seriously and work so hard that they suffer 'burn out' (ibid.: 119). Because there is no limit on the number of hours a volunteer can work, some people simply work themselves to the point of exhaustion.

The Ambivalence of the 'Gift Economy'

Even more difficult to quantify than the elaborate network of volunteers, is the Burning Man 'gift economy' prescribed by Harvey: no vending, advertising, buying or selling of anything is permitted. The idea of a gift economy in the context of Burning Man is filled with contradictions. In a lecture titled 'La Vie Boheme' at the Walker Art Center in Minneapolis in 2000, Harvey proudly asked, 'Have you ever been in a city of thousands of people where you couldn't buy or sell anything?' (2000a). Harvey draws his philosophy of the gift economy from Lewis Hyde's *The Gift: Imagination and the Erotic Life of Property* (1983). The cardinal difference between gift and commodity exchange, according to Hyde, is that a gift establishes a permanent bond between two people, while the sale of a commodity does not necessarily leave a connection (ibid.: 56). The exchange of gifts creates a series of interconnected relationships, which builds community and serves as a vehicle for culture-making. A gift, when given without the promise of anything in return, creates a different kind of expectation that builds a bond within a community. For the gift economy to function, the exchange should contain a minimum of three people rather than the usual one-to-one reciprocal giving. In order to sustain this communal bond, gifts need to keep moving from hand to hand in a circular pattern, which Hyde likens to a river (ibid.: 4). Should the flow of the gift halt, the chain of the gift economy is broken. As Hyde notes, 'when the gift moves in a circle its motion is beyond the control of the personal ego, and so each bearer must be a part of the group and each donation is an act of social faith' (ibid.: 16). The gift is to be used up, consumed, or even destroyed as in the practice of the Native American potlatch in order for it to be efficacious (ibid.: 8).

Harvey believes that burning the Man has always been a gift and that gifting is the tissue that holds the community together (Van Rhey 2002). When I asked Harvey how the concept of the gift economy emerged, he said:

> It evolved organically, with no plan or theory attached. At first, there were sporadic attempts to sell things but those failed because no one bought anything; everyone came over prepared with food, water and other necessities. Originally, of course, it would have been gauche, and in the worst possible form—like going to a family picnic or a picnic of friends and trying to sell someone your stuffed olives. It would disrespect the relationships—the implied social contracts (Harvey 2004a).

As the event grew, further attempts at commerce were made, but they too failed. In 1997, the Black Rock City LLC realized that this failure was in fact a blessing and then incorporated a 'no-vending' policy into its by-laws. The no-vending policy went hand-in-hand with the adoption of the gift-economy philosophy. The simple decision to ban vending has had a central impact on the formation and development of the Burning Man culture and ethos:

> If you are living in a gift economy, it means you give without expectation of return. It is an unconditional relationship. When those kinds of interactions happen on a sufficient scale within any society it leads to a kind of general sense of cohesiveness—of belonging together. [. . .] Our clean up is done 90 percent by people on their own free will when they leave. When was the last time you had a wild party at your house and before they left your guests said, 'We're going to vacuum your floor now.' That is what they do here but on a civic scale (ibid.).

Harvey noted in 'Viva Las Xmas', his Cooper Union speech in New York City on 25 April 2002, that sociologist Robert Putnam found that bonding 'social capital' is rapidly eroding in the US today (see Harvey 2002). Drawing on Putnam's research, Harvey notes that the average US household owns 2.4 television sets; each family member sits in a separate room with a separate TV set, watching a different programme with different commercials. This lifestyle is isolating and alienating, creating a world in which no one interacts any more. Harvey believes that a gift economy can create 'social capital' and the exchange of gifts can serve as the glue that holds the community together in the form of binding social contracts.

Harvey is also concerned about the rapid disappearance of public spaces and the erosion of grassroots culture. Living in San Francisco, a city known for its thriving bohemian culture, he has noticed the ever-shrinking locally-owned coffee houses where you used to be able to place flyers to advertise a local event. Now, many have been replaced by the franchises that are taking over the United States. For Harvey, Burning Man is 'a life lesson in civics for an entire generation that has grown up thinking that the world is made of malls and that society is one big vending machine. Some people learn citizenship in Black Rock City for the first time' (2004a).

Harvey emphasizes the distinction between bartering and gift-giving: bartering is a market transaction, an exchange of items or services of equal value, while a gift requires no exchange. Unfortunately, some participants confuse the two and there is an expectation of equal reciprocation. Harvey believes the gift economy is misunderstood by some Burners:

> People actually demand goods. 'Wadda ya got?' they'll say, then paw through someone's cache of goods in search of something rare and valuable. They must think we're Mardi Gras. I've even heard of bartenders demanding that people humiliate themselves in exchange for a drink. It isn't playful, and it's not a gift. A gift comes from the heart, and more than anything, it's not about exchange. [. . .] Gifts are things we give away without an expectation of return. If we do expect something back in exchange, even if it's counting on an expression of gratitude, we ruin the gift. [. . .] The true value of a gift is unconditional (Van Rhey 2002).

French sociologist, Marcel Mauss, author of *The Gift: Forms and Functions of Exchange in Archaic Societies* (1967) would strongly disagree, arguing that there is no such thing as a 'free gift', that the exchange of a gift is actually an archaic form of contract that leaves the recipient in debt to the gift-giver. By accepting a gift, one is committing oneself to a binding contract with a burden attached (ibid.: 41). While Harvey holds that the gift is 'unconditional', there is among Burners an unspoken contract that your participation in the community is an obligation to give and receive gifts. Theme camps, art installations, workshops, free food and drink—all could be considered forms of gifts. In exchange for roaming the City all day and benefiting from acts of unconditional gift-giving, it is expected that you will give something in exchange, more like in a barter system.[9] Originally, gift-giving was an organic exchange of items of some value to the giver; but, increasingly, gifts are store-bought trinkets without value or meaning ordered in mass quantities to be distributed ad hoc, many of which end up as Matter Out of Place (MOOP): Harvey states, 'That's because people don't really care about them. [. . .] Simply do someone a kindness or contribute to the life of our city instead of passing out so many tangible souvenirs' (Van Rhey 2002).

In many ways, Burning Man functions like the Native American potlatch and many parallels can be drawn between the two. Mauss translated 'potlatch' in terms of nourishment, however, more commonly the word is taken to mean 'gift' or 'giving'. A potlatch is a form of gift economy—a total system of giving and exchange—practised traditionally by Northwest Coast Native Americans. It assumes a social contract in which one tribe gives gifts of blankets, whale oil and other valuable and symbolic items with the expectation that these gifts will be returned the following year two-fold, what Philip Drucker and Robert Fleming Heizer call a 'double return', as they have noted in their study of the Southern Kwakiutl potlatch (1967: 53). Oftentimes, the gifts were destroyed and burned as a symbolic gesture of status, wealth and power.[10] This form of contract is both symbolic and functional, serving to bind the community. Yet many societies were ruined by the practice of potlatch. Burning Man participants sometimes go too far, overextending themselves financially and in the process ruining their lives.

At Burning Man, items of value take months to fabricate and construct, only to be destroyed on a vast scale. But unlike in the potlatch system, at Burning Man the giver and the destroyer are one and the same. The display of one theme camp's assets is a form of gift to the others in attendance and creates a binding network of exchange. This reciprocal relationship carries over from year to year and builds in momentum and scale. The idea of 'double return' can be seen in the community's commitment to double the ambition and scale of the year before, and the theme camps, art installations and costumes continue to grow exponentially more elaborate and complex each year.[11] Consequently, each year the level of destruction increases two-fold, as the community outdoes itself, competing with levels of generosity followed by competitive destruction. The wholesale destruction, often through fire, of art, the temple (see Chapter 5) and the Man are symbolic acts that demonstrate the ability to let go of material possessions.

The essential difference between a potlatch and what goes on at Burning Man is that in most cases participants return to their lives in the same economic bracket as when they arrived. However, some Burning Man participants are ruined financially, having poured their life's savings into an installation or artwork that is eventually burned. What is at stake in the potlatch and at Burning Man is honour and prestige.

Burning Man as an Experience Economy

Harvey describes his experience of going to Las Vegas for the first time and experiencing firsthand a Retail Entertainment District (RED). REDs are the fastest growing trend in retail; they come in all shapes and sizes: Disneyland, Times Square and Las Vegas are prime examples. According to B. Joseph Pine II and James H. Gilmore in their book *The Experience Economy: Work Is Theatre and Every Business Is a Stage* (1999), these are examples of an 'experience economy', in which interactivity and immersive environments are key: 'experiences represent an existing but previously unarticulated genre of economic output. [. . .] Only when companies constitute it in the form of information services—or informational goods and informing experiences—do they create economic value' (ibid.: x). Las Vegas and Disneyland, the experience capitals of the US, are designed to create a complete experience for the consumer:

> Virtually *everything* about Vegas is a designated experience, from the slot machines at the airport to the gambling casinos that line the Strip; from the themed hotels and restaurants to the singing, circus and magic shows; and from the Forum Shops mall that recreates ancient Rome to the amusement parks, thrill rides, video arcades, and carnival-style games that attract the twentysomethings and give older parents a reason to bring their kids in tow (ibid.: xi).

These highly artificial environments stage experience by engaging customers in a personal and memorable way. The experience is designed to be individualized so that each participant has a different emotional, physical, intellectual, even spiritual, response—a custom-designed experience that targets the individual (ibid.: 12). These immersive, integrated systems of escalators, bridges, elevators, tramways and a variety of other mechanical devices are designed to choreograph the shopper's movements from one retail venue to the next. When Harvey walked onto the strip in Las Vegas, he found the similarities remarkable:

> This is just like Burning Man! We, too, create a scene, a fantasy environment. [. . .] We are a themed environment! What is more, we fill it with interaction and ambient entertainment. [. . .] The theme camps are magnet attractions. [. . .] It's an immersive environment. The only difference is that you must struggle to survive. The only difference is that you are seldom more than 10 feet away from opportunities to interact with art and other human beings. The only difference is that you must give of yourself. The only difference, finally, is that it is *real*. [. . .] The great difference between us and the consumer marketplace, however, is that we have inverted the essential nature of the capitalist system. We may be like Disneyland, but we are like Disneyland turned inside out (Harvey 2002).

In contrast to Disneyland and Las Vegas' artificially streamlined experience economies, Burning Man has emerged as an organic interactive environment that has evolved into an experience economy over time. In a speech given to the Burning Man community in 1998, Harvey defended

Burning Man against the accusation that it was getting too commercial and selling out: 'We charge to get in. And I'll tell you that's commerce, but we've never been against commerce. I mean commerce is civilization—commerce was the silk route. [. . .] Nothing wrong with commerce. We're against commodification. That's what we don't do here' (1998a).

However, in a 2005 interview with *The Economist*, Harvey remarked on the brilliance of capitalism while advocating the gift economy as a model for the 'ideal' economy (in McMahon and Morris 2005). The line between his use of the terms 'commerce' and 'commodification' is deliberately blurred and he uses them in different ways depending on the context, thus highlighting the central contradiction that plagues the event. On the one hand, Burning Man is a for-profit enterprise that participates in 'commerce' and operates on a 14-million-dollar annual budget (in 2008) driven by ticket sales; on the other, it advocates a commerce-free decommodified world within Black Rock City. Burning Man is a business, one that sells a nicely packaged participatory experience of an allegedly commerce-free world, a utopian product that many want to buy. Any event you charge money for is a commercial event and Burning Man is no different.

Ultimately, Burning Man is like any other business, the only difference is that the product is affective and ephemeral—'experience', 'participation' and 'community' rather than a tangible commodity. It is the commerce of 'experience' and 'creativity', one that has value for many of the participants. As Harvey demonstrated in his 'Viva Las Xmas' (2002) speech at Cooper Union in New York City, community, participation and creativity are lacking in people's everyday lives and Burning Man has filled a niche market. While the event began as countercultural and marginal, as it has gained mainstream popularity it has had to adapt and evolve with the pressures of supply and demand for this type of 'experience economy'. As Roger confirmed, 'We're no different than any other business' (2005).

Outside Black Rock City, the BMO has reached an economic status that gives them political leverage and power. It makes a concerted effort to invite congressional representatives and public Nevada officials to attend the event as guests; they often arrive at the Black Rock City airport via helicopter or plane to do a brief tour of the City on an art bus. Board member Goodell has noticed that 'usually as they leave they say, "What can we do for you?"' (2004).

This generosity on the part of public officials is most certainly linked to their realization that Burning Man is an economically profitable event, not only for the organizers but for the surrounding towns, governmental organizations and the state of Nevada. It is in everyone's financial interest to ensure that the event continues, a position the BMO was not in 10 years ago. This is not to say that the relationship between the authorities and the BMO is stable or can be taken for granted, but it endows Burning Man with political leverage.

Imagining A Commerce-Free World

Robert V. Kozinets, a professor at the Kellogg School of Management, and John F. Sherry, an anthropology professor in the Mendoza College, University of Notre Dame, who together conducted a study of temporary communities such as Burning Man, speculated on the existence of life outside the marketplace (see Kozinets and Sherry 2005: 87). They thought Burning Man would be a perfect place to study life outside the market, but when they first arrived in Black Rock City they observed:

> How amazingly ironic it was, then, to walk through Burning Man for the first time, to walk through the vast neon-tubed, electroluminescent-wired, über-strip mall of the place, the signs competing for attention, the touristic cameras, the elevated RVs on prime real estate, the lowly K-Mart tent shanty-towns. [. . .] We found a sign that mocked capitalism while also celebrating it—the familiar sign of the Hard Rock Café, that read, 'Welcome to the Black Rock Café.' [. . .] We had gone a long way to penetrate the anti-marketing zone, only to be once again confronted by popular brands and commodities for sale (ibid.: 88).

Kozinets and Sherry read Burning Man as a demonstration of the powerful lengths to which consumers feel they must go in order to decommodify products, services, even their own identities (ibid.: 101). Products are 'purified' through the acts of decommodification, which include customizing, masking or transforming brand names; burning branded objects and turning products into gifts (ibid.: 20). Still, brand names are ubiquitous. Upon entering Black Rock City, one sees a vista of Budget and U-Haul rental trucks, RVs and cars,[12] creatively transformed to become a temporary shelter for a week, some disguised but many still boldly displaying the corporate logos. The irony behind covering a logo, on a Pepsi can for example, is that you are still drinking a Pepsi and you still bought the product at the supermarket before you entered the desert.

As Kozinets and Sherry's research demonstrates, this anti-brand event also uses the language of brands to parody and invert images from the market. On the back of *Piss Clear* (Issue 23), a series of fake ads humorously inverts popular mainstream ads, with the Man holding an iPod (see Figure 2.7); an ad that reads, 'Whatever it is you're burning for, do it eBay' (Roberts 2004b) (see Figure 2.8); an Expedia.com ad of a lawnchair in front of the Burn; and a Mastercard ad of someone in the Thunderdome that reads: 'Geodesic dome: $10,000; Bungie Cables: $200; Ticket to Burning Man: $165; Cool Black Costume: $70; Blow to Ego: $ underestimated' (ibid.). Another instance of culture jamming, these fake ads distort and invert commercial symbols, transforming them into humour and satire. As with all parody, there is the question of whether the ads, even though they are fake and entertaining, are also reinforcing brands and products of the market.

Kozinets and Sherry's guiding question—whether consumers can actually get outside the grips of the market—has led to the realization that one cannot. They found that Burning Man is what A. Fuat Firat and Nikhilesh Dholakia would call a 'theatre of consumption' (1998),[13] a temporary enclave that represents a lively, expressive and creative model for consumption. Theatres of consumption, as theorized by Firat and Dholakia, emerge as alternative models of commerce within the dominant market economy. As Kozinets and Sherry point out, Burning Man, in its festive celebration of abundance and excess, holds much in common with the mood and tenor of ancient marketplaces (2005: 101). What they call 'indulgent consumption' is demonstrated by the amount each individual spends before arriving in Black Rock City. Their research indicates the average amount spent per person was between $500 and $750, with a considerable percentage spending thousands of dollars (ibid.: 99).

In an interview I conducted in 2005, one participant said he had spent $150,000 on a brand new circus tent. In 2006, the installation *Uchronia* (also known as the Belgian Waffle), designed by Belgian architects Jan Kriekels and Arne Quinze, was one of the most ambitious installations

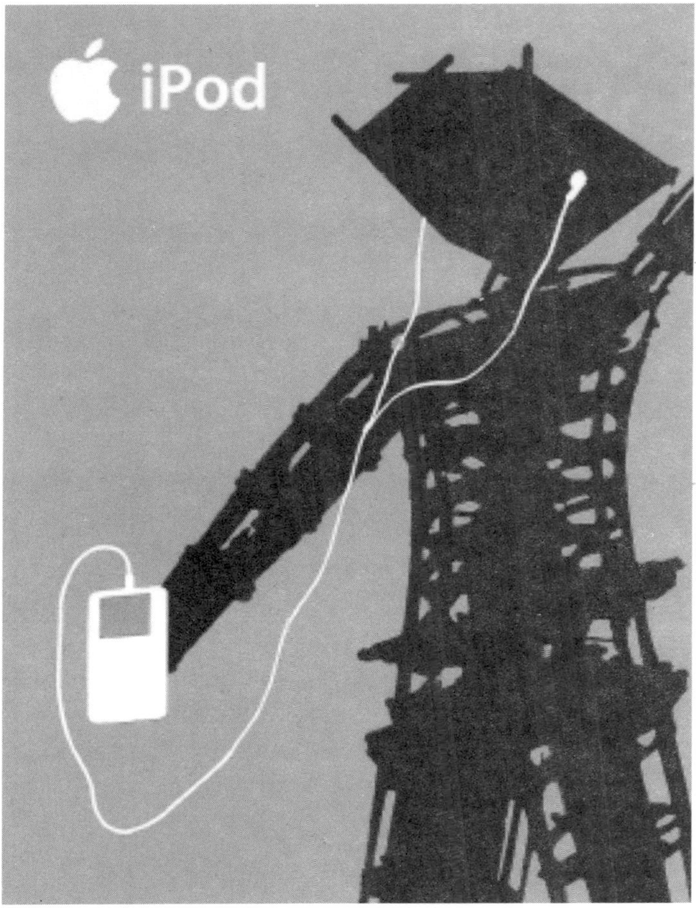

FIGURE 2.7. Ipod fake ad, *Piss Clear* 23 (1 September 2004). Courtesy of Adrian Roberts

FIGURE 2.8. eBay fake ad, *Piss Clear* 23 (1 September 2004). Courtesy of Adrian Roberts

at Burning Man to date. It was 50 feet tall, 200 feet long and 100 feet wide. It was built by a team of 90 volunteers, cost $250,000 and was finally burnt. Another group spent $14,000 on their elaborate tent structure, not to mention sound systems, RV rentals, food, costumes, shade structures and art cars. If you added the untold amount spent by each individual and theme camp, the figure would be astronomical. One participant that Kozinets and Sherry interviewed remarked that she had never seen so many people consuming so much in her entire life (2005: 99).

Bombarded by the scopic regime of the mainstream, Burning Man attempts to escape into a world without logos and corporate sponsorship, yet the inherent contradiction of attempting to erase a product's surface demonstrates the impossibility of this enterprise. As Louis-Ferdinand Celine accurately remarks, 'There is no escaping American business' (in Hardt and Negri 2000: 370). Burning Man functions as an attempt to escape the commodity and the reigns of the global empire of exchange, yet inevitably fails. One participant interviewed by Sherry and Kozinets remarked, 'I'm walking around with no cash. I love that! It's great! It would certainly be idealistic if everything worked on a barter system—that would be beautiful. Of course, the real world doesn't operate like that but then again this isn't the real world. This is like an experiment, creating some semblance of utopia' (in Kozinets 2002: 6). But consider the amount of cash spent before the interviewee-with-no-cash crossed the threshold into Black Rock's utopian universe. In my own experience, the preparation to enter 'utopia' cost over $1,000 for two people for airfares, entrance tickets, car rental, food, water and camping gear. It costs money to create the temporary illusion of a commerce-free world; utopia is an expensive endeavour.

William Morris, in *News from Nowhere: Or, an Epoch of Rest, Being Some Chapters from a Utopian Romance* (1890), argues that utopian concepts are bound to be failures because of their 'lack of perception' about economic reality; and, according to Thorsten Bagschik, every utopian system struggles with the fundamental economic problem of how to provide and sustain the community with necessary supplies (1996: 10, 179). In the case of Burning Man, the gift economy is inherently ambiguous as it contradicts the realities of running a for-profit LLC. While Burning Man offers a rehearsal of utopia, like all other utopias, it is impossible to achieve.

Participants pay over $250 to enter into the ephemeral playground to play at survival. While the harsh desert conditions are real, it is self-imposed and could be seen as a form of play. Without an agricultural foundation or access to natural resources such as water to maintain and feed the community, ultimately Burning Man could never be a self-sustaining community in the desert. No matter how much it tries to escape, it is intimately bound to the economic reality of capitalism. According to historical paradigms, the inability of a utopian community to sustain itself would be a sure sign of failure but I would argue that, in fact, Burning Man could be seen as an incubator—a social laboratory of how utopian ideals can rehearse alternatives within the realm of globalization.

It is beyond the seven days in the desert that the seeds of an alternative creative way of living are planted. Burning Man doesn't pretend to be self-sustaining; in fact, it celebrates its ephemerality and disappearance as a radical, political act. Perhaps it is its inherent ephemerality that makes this experiment such a success. In *Utopian Lights: The Evolution of the Idea of Social Progress* (1989), Bronislaw Baczko writes, 'When utopian dreams light up the horizon, a horizon of expectations and collective or individual hopes, they shed new light on the social landscape. [. . .] Caught in the light of utopia, glances are turned toward visions of an alternative society, contrasting with the existing society' (ibid.: i). Burning Man rehearses and stages an alternative model of how the world 'should' be within the limitations of the actual world. Quintessentially hopeful but not necessarily utopian, full of contradictions and ambiguities, Burning Man is perched on the edge of utopia, a timely intervention that creates an alternative vision for being in the world.

Notes

1 Since the fifteenth century, when Garcia Ordonez de Montalvo coined a new word, 'California', for 'an imaginary island rich in pearls and gold, the name has called up visions of utopia. Centuries afterward, applied to Baja California and gradually to the vast, unexplored regions northward, the term for the land of fertile coastal valleys and rugged mountains continued to carry the hint of an earthly paradise' (Hine 1966: ix).

2 Jill Dolan expands upon J. L. Austin's performative utterance, the speech

act, in which words become action such as 'I do' in a wedding ceremony, which performs the act of marriage.

3 Michel Foucault coined the term 'heterotopia' in 1967:

> [Heterotopias as] found within the culture, are simultaneously represented, contested, and inverted. Places of this kind are outside of all places, even though it may be possible to indicate their location in reality. [. . .] Museums, libraries, zoos, and cemeteries are heterotopic spaces. [. . .] Fairgrounds, these marvelous empty sites on the outskirts of cities that teem once or twice a year with stands, displays, heteroclite objects, wrestlers, snakewomen, fortune-tellers, and so forth. [. . .] The heterotopia of the festival (1986: 24).

4 Foucault states that to get into a heterotopia, 'one must have a certain permission and make certain gestures. Moreover, there are even heterotopias that are entirely consecrated to these activities of purification—purification that is partly religious and partly hygienic, such as the hammin of the Moslems, or else purification that appears to be purely hygienic, as in Scandinavian saunas' (in ibid.).

5 The sundial/clockface has been a popular civic shape used by Burning Man for: 'The Body' (2000), 'The Seven Ages of Man' (2001), 'Vault of Heaven' (2004), 'Psyche' (2005), 'Hope and Fear' (2006), 'The Green Man' (2007) and 'The American Dream' (2008).

6 This process is also required of researchers and scholars documenting the event. In 2004, 2005 and 2008, I registered as media to be able to photograph and videotape the event.

7 In his discussion of the carceral city, Foucault explains that at its centre 'there is not the center of power, not a network of forces but a multiple network of diverse elements—walls, space, institution, rules, discourse . . . a strategic distribution of elements of different natures and levels' (1979: 307).

8 Most utopian communities abolish private property and require all participants to do work for the public good. Jobs are rotated so that no one gets stuck doing the 'dirty work'. Often the community is money-free, agricultural and self-sustaining (Morgan 1946: 45). Utopian communities are social laboratories defined by their spirit of experimentation, in which members are conscious of themselves as a community—who belongs and who does not—and their role in history (Kanter 1972: 52).

9 Two random acts of gift-giving I benefited from in 2004: a woman on a bicycle gave me an ice-cold ice-cream cone in the middle of the desert and rode on by with no expectation of anything in return; and a guy on

a bicycle, the 'Black Rock Pizza Delivery,' randomly gave out slices of hot pizza to passersby. There were other times when the gift is offered with the phrase, 'What do you have for me?' which is no longer a gift but a barter exchange.

10 As Marcel Mauss argues:

> To refuse to give, to fail to invite, just as to refuse to accept, is tantamount to declaring war; it is to reject the bond of alliance and commonality. [. . .] All the forms of potlatch in the American Northwest know this theme of destruction. [. . .] Material and moral life, and exchange, function within it in a form that is both disinterested and obligatory (1967: 13, 16).

11 According to Helen Codere who conducted a study on the Kwakiutl potlatch, the potlatch is a public giving and destruction of what she calls 'surplus economy' of goods (1950: 63). As Codere notes, the potlatch produces a vast network of 'debtor–creditor' relations based on accumulations that double each time. The potlatch is the distribution as well as destruction of property (ibid.: 77). As John W. Adams observed in the Gitksan potlatch, gifting is a sign of social status and prestige (1973: iii).

12 Many rental companies will not rent to you if they know you are going to Burning Man because the fine playa dust is impossible to remove from any vehicle. Many rental companies have adopted a policy of a 500-dollar deposit if you plan to bring their vehicle to Burning Man.

13 As A. Fuat Firat and Nikhilesh Dholakia further note:

> The emergence and multiplication of such permeable but distinct, porous but bounded, life mode cultures promises the possibility of the new theatres of consumption that can break the hegemony of the market in contemporary human life. As modes of life that do mediate all relationships and interactions through the market are sampled and found to be meaningful, as they become experiences that are sought and preferred, therefore, repeatedly returned to (1998: 158).

PART TWO

REALMS OF PERFORMANCE

Stilters walking around Black Rock City at sunrise in the 'White Procession', 2007. Photograph by Scott London.

CHAPTER 3
SPONTANEOUS ACTS: FROM PERFORMANCES OF EVERYDAY LIFE TO THE CARNIVALESQUE

FIGURE 3.1. Person sitting on sculpture, 2001. Photograph by Rick Egan.

> The American desert is an extraordinary piece of drama. [. . .] It is purely, geologically dramatic, bringing together the sharpest, most ductile shapes with the gentlest, most lascivious underwater forms (Baudrillard 1988: 69).

> Burning Man is an experiment in temporary community. Each year we design a city to serve as a vessel for community and a model of civilization, and place it like a Petri dish in the Black Rock Desert. We study the result, note how culture thrives, survives and replicates itself within our test tube world, then wipe the sterile surface of the playa clean and start again (Harvey 1999).

> At Burning Man you are the fantasy. People do not come to this event to be distracted from themselves; they come here to discover and distill what they uniquely are. Burning Man is based on your immediate experience (Harvey 1997a).

It is the epic scale of the playa that makes movement across it inherently theatrical. The opening image for this chapter (see Figure 3.1), evocative of a still from a Robert Wilson production, is actually a participant sitting on a sculpture and staring into the Black Rock Desert. In *The Presentation of Self in Everyday Life* (1959), Erving Goffman cogently denies Shakespeare's quote from *As You Like It*, arguing that, 'All the world is not, of course, a stage, but the crucial ways in which it isn't are not easy to specify' (ibid.: 72).[1] Goffman's theory is useful for understanding the performances within Black Rock City as a series of staged encounters.

The grassroots evolution of the event has informed the culture of Burning Man and creates an environment in which participants have a stake in the event and are responsible for its existence. They are willing to dedicate time, energy and resources towards building a world in which each person has the responsibility of its creation. This investment in time and energy creates a fertile space for creativity and play—an environment where everyone is involved and each participant is a player. In fact, a cardinal rule governing Black Rock City is the mandate to participate—bold letters on the admission ticket spell out, 'PARTICIPATE!' Burning Man is a temporary republic, where art and creativity govern the community and its citizens are obligated to leave behind the pressures of everyday American life. Black Rock City is an opportunity for artists and activists to create an ideal world, one where art and creativity hold central importance.

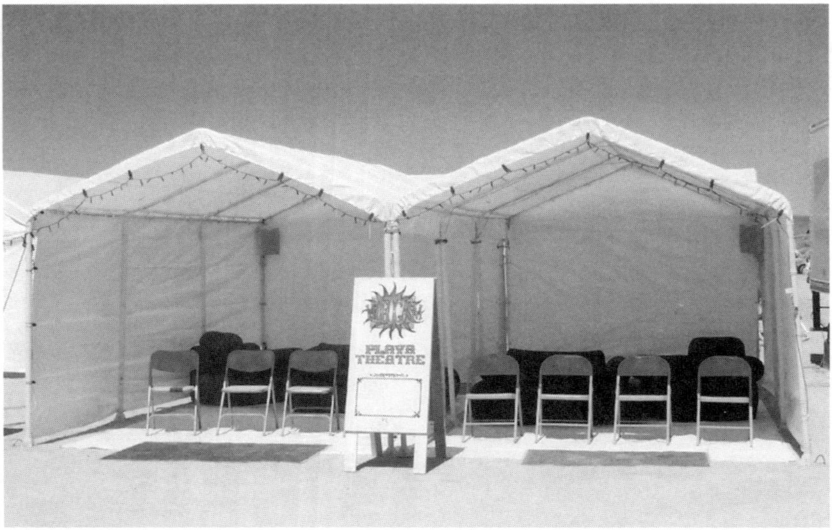

FIGURE 3.2. Playa Theatre, 2005.
Photograph by John Tzelepis.

The 'Playa Theatre' is a commentary on the role of spectatorship in Black Rock City. It is an empty tent facing the Esplanade where you can sit and watch the performance of Black Rock City pass by in front of you (see Figure 3.2). The tent is always empty; no one wants to play the role of spectator. Anyone who enters within the boundary of the City is in essence a performer, and any action, movement or gesture within this arena becomes a performance. The role of spectatorship becomes increasingly complicated as participants adopt the dual roles of performer and spectator. As Stuart Mangrum states in the *Burning Man Summer Newsletter* (1998):

> Unlike a rave or a concert, Burning Man is not a spectacle/commodity that can be experienced passively. That's the real meaning behind the 'No Spectators' tag: not to draw lines of exclusion, but to remind us of our mutual agreement to entertain each other. There is no official bandstand, just the vast empty stage of the desert, with no proscenium to separate the audience from the players. You are the show (ibid.).

Travelling through Black Rock City, one notices the conspicuous absence of a 'main stage'—something that is the main focus of any other festival. The only exception is on the night of the Burn, when all attention is on the one staging area around the Man. There was, at one point in Burning Man history, a main stage-type of event put on by the Burning Man Opera but the organizers felt that its presence created a division between audience and performers; that the Opera was in competition with everything else that was happening in Black Rock City, thus going against the fundamental Burning Man mandate of participation.

The Burning Man Opera, which existed from 1996 to 2000, was a spectacular annual pageant involving hundreds of elaborately costumed performers enacting epic narratives conceived by Pepe Ozan, a sculptor, filmmaker and theatre practitioner from Argentina (see Chapter 4). The Opera involved the entire community, yet maintained the distinction between 'performer' and 'spectator'. As Chicken John remembers the spectacle, the entire city shut down to watch the opera: 'In the middle of the performance there were a 100 people just freaking out, dancing like they were never going to dance again' (Rinaldi 2006). Shutting down the city for several hours for one event created the 'main stage' effect that the organizers wanted to avoid.

One hazard of mandating participation is that participants feel pressured to comply, to in fact conform to this nonconformity. Harvey recounts an example of how the 'participate' mantra has been misunderstood: a man had spent hundreds of hours building a theme camp but himself dressed conventionally, as Harvey himself does. When he walked down the street in Black Rock City, he was harassed for not 'participating'. As Harvey noted, 'Apparently they thought he should be wearing a costume. [. . .] Sometimes I wish we'd never promoted the phrase "no spectators". Who are these people to say that these individuals aren't participating?' (Harvey 2000b: n.p.). Perhaps ironically, or by clever intention, Harvey is the most understated dresser on the playa—his signature style consists of the famous pearl grey hat that seldom leaves his head, along with dark aviator glasses and a cigarette dangling from his lips.

Burning Man as Environmental Theatre and Modern-Day Happening

In Black Rock City, new relationships that blur boundaries between participant, performer and spectator open up possibilities for interaction, participation and transformation. Bracketing the ordinary and making the everyday strange—as in Marcel Duchamp's *Fountain* (1917), in which he transformed an everyday item (a urinal) into an artwork, or Andy Warhol's *Brillo Box* (1964), a painting of a household object—offers opportunities for experiencing life as a work of art (Kaprow 2003: 102).[2] This notion of blurring the boundaries between art and life can be traced back to the early Dadaists, but was further developed in the 1950s and 1960s by Allan Kaprow and other Happenings and proto-performance artists. Blurring the distinction between art and everyday life is a basic tenet of Burning Man: 'At Burning Man the distinction blurs between real life and performance. We are all performers, on stage or off. On stage you just tend to attract more of an audience. But of necessity we are all spectators too' (Harvey 2000b).

In a 1959 essay on Jackson Pollock, Kaprow coined the term 'Happenings' based on the leap that Pollock sensed but never took (Kelley 2003: xx). Pollock's paintings are records of movement; their enormous scale resulted in environments that confronted viewers and drew them into the canvas (ibid.: 6). Kaprow and others explain the origins of 'environments' as 'the pieces of the paper that curled up off the canvas and spilled into the gallery' (Kaprow et al. 1966: 165). It is in these constructed environments that Kaprow developed the concept of Happenings, which flourished in New York City in the 1960s and that can be traced to other locations in the US, Europe and Asia. Influenced by philosopher John Dewey, author of *Art as Experience* (1958), Kaprow embraced the idea that experiences could have shapes, beginnings, endings, plots, moods, patterns and meanings. According to Kaprow, Happenings were an experiment in a sensory and perceptual awakening that re-engaged the environment, the performers and the spectators (2003).

In the late 1950s and 1960s, the traditional modes of theatre and artistic practice began to break down, blurring the boundaries between theatre and politics, art and life, performance event and social event, stage and auditorium. Breaking out of the proscenium, the action of Happenings moved beyond the art gallery and into the streets, lofts, forests, swimming pools, boxing rings and a myriad of found alternative spaces for audiences frequently numbering less than 100 people (Kirby 1994: 4). Implicating the audience influences the rhythm and outcome of the performance, unravelling orthodox theatrical structures, throwing the

FIGURE 3.3. Costumed participants with pink wings dancing on the playa, 2001. Photograph by Rick Egan.

exchange into radical uncertainty (Schechner 1973: 45). In Kaprow's first Happening, *18 Happenings in 6 Parts*, presented at the Reuben Gallery in 1959, spectators were expected to move through a three-room environment to witness seemingly random activities performed by actors, accompanied by projections and a soundtrack (Kirby 1994: 34). According to Kaprow, themes, materials and inspiration should come from life, not other artworks, and there should be no audience; everyone should be a participant in the event (2003: 62).

Performance studies scholar Michael Kirby defined Happenings as a new category of performance that was a 'purposefully composed form of theatre in which diverse alogical elements, including nonmatrixed performing, are organized in a compartmented structure' (1994: 11). He defined nonmatrixed performance as a departure from the traditional use of time, place and character by eliminating imaginary locations and plots, and often rehearsals (Kaprow 2003: 173).[3] Largely nonverbal, Happenings abandoned story structure and were typically arranged in a series of scored, sequential and/or simultaneous actions determined in advance, sometimes through chance techniques.

Kaprow's definition of Happenings as 'unrehearsed and performed by nonprofessionals, once only' (ibid.: 63) offers a way to understand the chance encounters of Black Rock City as a kind of Happening. Many of the performances on the playa eliminate actors, plots and rehearsals, yet maintain a basic structure and score. Concept and costumes are often constructed and planned in advance but the element of chance plays an enormous role in the actual performance, and the chance encounters of participants on the playa keep the work alive and surprising. While many of the performances on the playa are not as structured or scored as the Happenings of the 1960s, they evoke a similar quality of an encounter, with the juxtaposition of chance elements and the blurring of participant and spectator relationships.

As in many of the performances at Burning Man, Happenings involved nonprofessionals who performed functionary roles and carried out mundane tasks, leaving to the audience the job of putting together their own associations (Kirby 1994: 7). As Jeff Kelley notes:

> Participation is whole. It engages both our minds and bodies in actions that transform art into experience and aesthetics into meaning. Our

> experience as participants is one of meaningful transformation. [. . .] Participation invites [the] spectator to become a participant and make a choice of some kind. To participate in something is to cross the psychological boundaries between the self and other and to feel the defining social tensions of those boundaries. The experience of participating transforms the participant as well as the game (2003: xxii).

While performance at Burning Man does not conform to the model of traditional theatre, it does fit Schechner's definition of 'environmental theatre'—that which 'surrounds, sustains, envelops, contains, and nests' a performance, a theory Schechner developed by drawing on Kaprow's use of the term 'environment' (1973: x). Environmental theatre also synthesizes many of the ideas of Dada and Happenings with more conventional theatre. All of the spaces within Black Rock City constitute a single, charged performance environment where 'anything' can happen.

Taken as a time-space unit, Burning Man, with its myriad of installations and performances, camps and venues, creates what Kirby called a 'total' experience; no spectator-participant can see all of the performances at once (in Kirby and Dine 1965). Burning Man's environmental theatrical landscape comes alive, charged with possibility and potential. Not only does Burning Man transform the desert into a city and a performance space, it is also constantly negotiating the harsh conditions of the desert from drastic temperature changes and strong winds to dust storms and heat waves. The artificial environment of Black Rock City is connected to the unpredictable nature of the Black Rock Desert, and this in turn affects the citizens and performances within those boundaries.

The layers of Burning Man's environmental theatrical landscape come *alive*, charged with possibility and potential by engaging in a complex system of transformation where entirely new relationships are possible. The flexible environment surrounds, envelops and nests the participant/citizen/spectator in a multisensory experience. Sensation and a tactile relationship to the space are part of the overall experience. As the week in the desert progresses, citizens not only move through the bounded space but also wear the desert on their skin. The thin, opaque white dust of the playa clings to every pore, every piece of clothing and every object, so that, by the end of the week, the participants, the desert and the environment have synthesized and merged into one. Part of the game and the challenge is surviving the harsh desert conditions. Burning Man optimizes Schechner's ideal for an environmental theatre, where all the elements of space, body, environment and participation collide.

Two installations that particularly illustrate this participatory ethos are Spencer Tunick's performative sculpture installation *Krystl* (1997), part of his *Reaction Zone Series* (2000), and *The Dicky Box* (2005) created by San Francisco artists Christian Davies and Logan Mitro. New York-based installation artist Tunick is known for creating installations of masses of nudes in urban landscapes such as the Brooklyn Bridge, Times Square or Grand Central Station, as well as other locations throughout the US and elsewhere in the world. In 1997, Tunick staged a similar installation on the playa, using the citizens of Black Rock City (BMO 1997a). Advertising the event in the *Black Rock Gazette*, Tunick asked participants to appear at 8.30 a.m. and to be prepared to get naked for a few minutes. In an elegant swirl, bodies became paint on the canvas of the playa, fusing flesh with desert. After momentary cohesion, the group dispersed. A performative moment occurred, was captured as a photographic image, then vanished like a mirage.

In a similar vein, Burning Man's 2005 theme, 'Psyche', inspired Mirto and Davies to create *The Dicky Box*. *The Dicky Box* plays with the notion of an isolated psyche as part of a community consciousness. For the duration of Burning Man, Christian Davies, or 'Dicky', was locked into a 10' x 10' plexiglass room on the open playa, where his perceptions of isolation were tested, celebrated and delivered as a gift to the community. Evocative of Marina Abramovic's *The House with an Ocean View*, performed at the Sean Kelly Gallery in New York City for 12 days in November 2002, *The Dicky Box* tested Davies's endurance in full public view.[4] The central difference is that Abramovic fasted and took a vow of silence, while Davies was given enough food and water to survive the event and a medical staff was on hand to ensure his safety. He performed all his daily functions in full public view, including eating and sleeping; he went to the bathroom in full view in a chemical toilet. He was not able to leave the box nor was anyone able to join him, and his only interaction with the outside world was through a standard-size parcel slot and a screened 6" x 6" portal. Everything he received was at the discretion of Black Rock City's citizens, literally acting out Harvey's gift economy. Day and night, people gathered around *The Dicky Box* offering food, gifts and conversation. Sometimes, Dicky would entertain a small crowd by telling jokes or answering questions, often bringing roars of laughter from his audience. Dicky's portal was filled with candy, necklaces, Doritos, condoms, fruit, pictures and various other items throughout the event. The generosity of the community was on full display.

The Daily Rhythms of Black Rock City

To begin to understand the complex cultural landscape of the Burning Man community, it is necessary to walk through Black Rock City, a feast for the senses. Mike Pearson and Michael Shanks's notion of 'desire mapping' (2001) and Michel de Certeau's concept of 'walking the city' (1984) offer ways of navigating and mapping Black Rock City. By becoming a 'flaneur',[5] a term introduced by Charles Baudelaire and expanded upon by Walter Benjamin to describe a person who walks through the city in order to experience it, a product of modern life, by tracing more or less random movements carefully on a map and moving by impulse and inspiration—one can gain a deeper understanding of the micro-shifts in the urban desert society. Pearson and Shanks speak of 'deep maps' and 'desire maps'. 'Deep maps' start with traces, fragments and artefacts in an attempt to reconstruct the past. 'Desire maps' on the other hand are constructed when one knows the object of interest and proceeds without a fixed itinerary or without a map. It requires a sense of curiosity and discovery, of being open to the unexpected (2001: 140–7). Weaving deep mapping with desire mapping, the Burner can discover, encounter and experience the rhythms and energies of Black Rock City. The wanderer thinks of the City as a series of free-flowing excursions, 'moving between sites of leisure, consumption, exchange, and display' (ibid.: 149). The overall design of Black Rock City organizes bodies socially and spatially, creating a complex choreography of bodies in space and encouraging the random flow of movement.

De Certeau distinguishes between the 'voyeur' and the 'walker', each having its own spatial vantage point. The voyeur is the Man, elevated high above the City, capable of overseeing the urban desert sea below like an omniscient god. De Certeau's walker/wanderer embodies the thick and thin of an urban landscape without being able to read it. Networks of bodies moving through space compose a complex story in which each participant plays a single role in the epic narrative. The city becomes a readable text only when one experiences it on the ground, with footsteps as well as a tactile and kinesthetic awareness (De Certeau 1984: 92). According to de Certeau, pedestrian movements form a system of flows that makes up the city, and the operation of walking or wandering locates points that draw a concrete and reversible line on a map (ibid.: 97). The act of passing by is marked by a series of encounters in which pedestrians discover stories that accumulate, creating within the city a 'metaphorical' city. In practice, the movements of bodies in space weave spatial narratives that transform space into place (ibid.: 117).

The organic ebb and flow of bodies through the desert landscape forms the elementary experience of the pedestrian city. The physical contact with the desert floor and the paths through space transform the blank canvas into a written, multivalent narrative. If we understand this movement as a text, we can read it as a universe that is constantly exploding with the possibility of encounter. For his part, Harvey's metaphor for Black Rock City is the ocean, seemingly the opposite of its desert reality:

> I don't know if you have ever hung around a beach, with the sound and the pulse of the tide; it instils an almost trancelike feeling, and you have this huge natural occurrence and that's our notion of infinity. It certainly feels like a great magnitude. [. . .] This [the playa] is just like the ocean except that it doesn't move. But it is as volatile as the ocean. So, those two factors—just the eminence and immediacy of the cosmic—of unmediated nature is still very much a core factor that defines this (2004a).

Harvey's ocean is an apt metaphor for Black Rock City—a city that never stands still; a city that never sleeps. The energy of the City is also a series of hot and cold pulses: a pulse of energy occurs, there is an encounter, a crowd forms, experiences something, then dissipates 'coolly' until the next encounter. These rhizomatic pulses occur simultaneously throughout the urban landscape like waves in the ocean or the shifting sands of a desert.

The rhythm of these pulses, though, changes over the course of each day and throughout the week. Monday begins with a slow pulse, which gradually builds momentum as the week progresses, reaching a new height on Friday night and climaxing on Saturday night with the burning of the Man. While each day has its own unique rhythm and flow, people's individual and daily rhythms vary drastically: some party all night and sleep all day, others wake up early, enjoy the day and go to sleep early.

Mornings in the City are generally peaceful; people linger at their campsites in sleeping gear that is as creative and funky as the outfits seen throughout the day: eccentric and colourful bathrobes or lingerie, combat boots and dust goggles, sarongs, flip-flops and long johns. The crisp, cool desert morning light streaks down the avenues and boulevards as colourfully decorated bicycles weave in and out through groups of pedestrians. Everything moves at a calm, languid pace. Some people are just waking up, others just going to bed. Some are sprawled out in their geodesic domes, others are preparing breakfast: some camps dedicate their gift-giving to morning coffee and pancakes. There is usually a line at the porta-potties and people socialize while waiting. Other people stroll into Center Camp Café to get their morning coffee or chai or listen to mellow sitar music wafting through the camp. Morning is also the best time to get ice from Camp Arctica—the lines are short and the day is still cool. By 2 p.m., over a hundred people are in line under the hot sun, standing for a half hour or more for ice. By midday, Center Camp is bustling, and the energy picks up as people emerge in new and ever more exciting costumes. The pace becomes increasingly frantic as bicycles and art cars dodge pedestrians en route to a myriad of destinations—everyone is going somewhere, meeting up with friends, attending workshops and exploring the art. Others retreat from the heat to the calm of shade structures.

Around twilight, another shift occurs: the energy dissipates as people return to their camps to change into warm clothing for the chilly desert evenings when the temperature can drop down to the 40s. Camps eat dinner, often communally, and prepare for the evening. As night falls, the city begins to twinkle with electroluminescent lights and fires. Night is when the City is most energized—the Esplanade is bustling with activity and pedestrians making their way from one event to another. People's costumes, theme camps and art cars transform into black light spectacles for the nightly festivities. Sculptures are set on fire and fire performers of all types emerge. The majority of the large-scale spectacular performances occur at night, avoiding the daytime heat.

Rave/techno camps, such as Lush Camp, Xara or House of Lotus, placed at the edges of the city at 2 and 10, remain quiet during the day but now burst into action, drawing huge crowds. The pulse is strongest at night, when, for example, a huge fire installation spouts 50-foot flames, and hundreds of people converge from all directions to watch the performance. After the show, the crowd is drawn to the next fiery spectacle. This rhythmic pattern of gathering and dispersing gains momentum through the night, often lasting until sunrise, when the cycle begins all over again. This cycle builds in intensity until the Burn on Saturday night (see Chapter 6).

Front Stage of Black Rock City

Goffman divides quotidian space into public space, the 'front' or the 'stage', and private space, the 'backstage' or 'back region' (1959: 107–12), two areas that generate two very different types of performances. The distinctions that Goffman makes are paralleled by Roberto da Matta in his analysis of the Rio de Janeiro Carnival (1991). Da Matta discerns two carnival 'planes': the house (private) and the street (public). Both these sets of distinctions are evident in Black Rock City's various public and private spaces that function as venues for different forms of behaviours and performances. In Black Rock City, the street is the stage, the public space for displaying the unpredictable, ludic world of the Burning Man carnival. The 'base camp' is home—the backstage where participants prepare meals, sleep, shower and unwind. Theme camps are liminal spaces positioned in-between front- and backstage, between interior and exterior worlds of the City.

The two most popular 'frontstage' public spaces of Black Rock City are the Esplanade and the Center Camp Café. The nucleus and social hub of Black Rock City is the Café with its 38,000 square feet of shade. Open to the public 24 hours a day and always bustling with activity,[6] the Café is a structure held up by two concentric wooden rings and secured by high-tension cable capable of withstanding 120 mph winds and drastic weather changes. Designed by Rod Garrett, Black Rock City's urban designer, the Café was first conceived as a huge circular hub that tapered out to the desert floor like a Bedouin tent, causing the wind to push down on the structure rather than to lift it. The central apex is left open as an exit for internal forces such as wind and dust storms. While the event is a 'no commerce zone', two venues are permitted to sell: Center Camp Café and Camp Arctica.[7] In 2004, 80,000 cups of coffee were brewed by more than 300 volunteers working over 1,000 shifts (BMO 2004b).[8] The Café operates on four-hour shifts, 24 hours a day, starting at 7 a.m. on Monday until

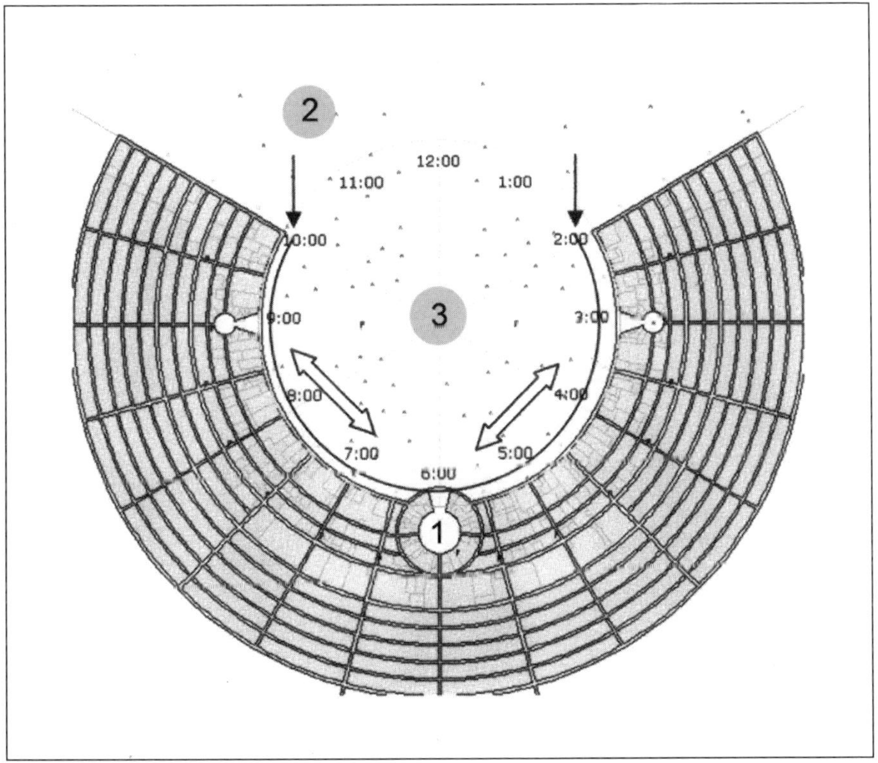

Map of Esplanade and Center Camp (2004)

1. Center Camp is at 6:00
2. Black line is the Esplanade (Black Rock City's main thoroughfare) from 10:00 to 2:00
3. The Man

FIGURE 3.4. Map of Esplanade and Center Camp. Created by the author.

3 p.m. the following Monday. Volunteers serve as preparers, cashiers and support staff.

The Center Camp Café is Black Rock City's biggest theme camp and offers a relaxed chill-out area and central meeting point. It features a shaded art gallery with dozens of couches, three small stages and a circular performing space that functions as a theatre-in-the-round. The music stage has scheduled acts all day from 8 a.m. to 3 a.m., leaving time in the afternoons for walk-in performers. The spoken-word stage schedules slots from 9 a.m. to 5 p.m., offering a range of performance activities, including poetry, theatre, comedy and spoken word. In the theatre-in-the-round, one can see aerial performances, large participatory performance groups such as the monkey chant, hula hoopers, dancers and jugglers at various times during the day.

Performing at Center Camp is a high-profile way for participants to share their talents with the community. Several stage managers and a team of volunteers help coordinate the performances and ensure events run smoothly, from the arrival of the performers, setting up and running the technical equipment, to the transition to the next performance. There is a dedicated crew of 500 volunteers who help run Center Camp Café, from pre-playa decor planning and prop-making to on-site construction and the coffee-shop operation. To be guaranteed a spot on the Center Camp stage, performers must submit an application and a sample CD of their music or spoken word on the Burning Man website by 1 August. Even though the Center Camp stage managers maintain a programme of scheduled events, these are not actually listed in any comprehensive manner for the public. Some are listed in the 'What? When? Where?' event bulletin but not always, giving the impression that the performances are spontaneous.

The Esplanade is Black Rock City's main thoroughfare, located on the inner circle of the City, and functions much like the midways of the world's fairs.[9] To be featured on the Esplanade, a theme camp has to have a fully articulated concept or visual theme. The Esplanade draws a colourful kaleidoscope of activity, with performances and theme camps competing for attention. Some of the performances are listed in the 'What? When? Where?' programme; most are spontaneous. The Esplanade is reserved for pedestrians and bicyclists, so no vehicles disrupt the flow of activity and performances. As one moves up and down the Esplanade, the sonic landscape is never completely silent: there might be German Oktoberfest music from the Black Rock Biergarten, hardcore techno from a rave camp, and the berimbau as a group plays capoeira. One day in 2005, as I strolled the Esplanade, I heard 1970s disco, rap, Frank Sinatra, psychedelic trance, gongs, chimes, a didgeridoo, thrash punk metal, hardcore grunge, 1950s lounge music, mash-up, jazz, a sitar and Bollywood remixed with techno.

Backstage at Black Rock City

Asylum Village, where I camped in 2004 and 2005, exemplifies how these front and backstage worlds function. Located at 7 o'clock and Esplanade, Asylum Village was one of Burning Man's New York City camps comprising several smaller theme camps: Kostume Kult, Whirligig, Whiskey and Whores, New Day's Eve, Super Lucky, Camp Power Exchange and Smooch Dome.

The dark grey space in Figure 3.5 indicates the public space open to all Black Rock citizens. The light grey areas are private or backstage at Asylum Village—areas where only Asylum residents or guests invited by a resident are welcome. This behind-the-scene space accommodates cars, RVs, tents and communal shade structures to be enjoyed by Asylum residents. There is a communal kitchen tent designated for food preparation, with two folding tables and several folding chairs, and two Coleman stove burners. At Asylum, cooking was not communal, although some meals were shared (but not preplanned). Bins of food, labelled by each group were stored under the tables. People drifted in and out of the kitchen tent all day long, with most of the activity around mealtimes. But breakfast, lunch and dinner timings varied from person to person. The kitchen was the social nucleus of the camp as people chatted informally while preparing add-water-and-stir meals, such as canned soup, noodles, oatmeal or burritos. Others attempted more appetizing gourmet meals that involved elaborate preparation.

As Goffman notes, backstage areas allow people to drop their social masks and public fronts; it serves as a space where people relax and recharge before reentering the 'stage' (1959: 112). At Asylum, the kitchen was a casual, safe space for people to let down their guard. They often entered the kitchen in pajamas or states of undress, sometimes removing

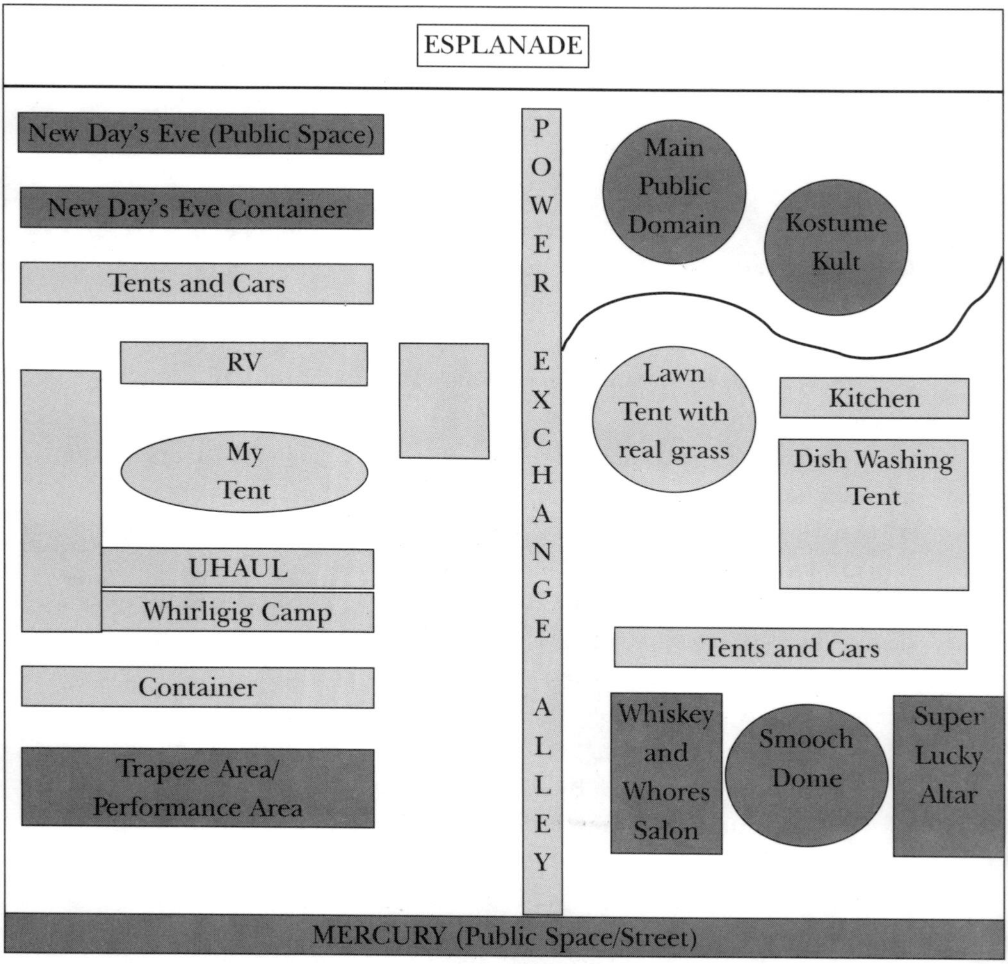

FIGURE 3.5. Diagram of Asylum Village, 2004.
Created by author.

costumes, hats and goggles once inside. It was also the 'preparation' area: people helped one another into their often-elaborate costumes and did each other's makeup, asking all those present for their opinion on the final result. Typically, before leaving the tent, there would be some form of final preparation, such as putting on goggles or dust masks, in the case of a dust storm, or replacing costumes pieces. Next to the kitchen was a smaller dishwashing tent where, with the help of a hand pump and plastic sink, people rinsed dishes before reuse. 'Grey' water was collected in buckets and left in the sun to evaporate. This was a functionary space, not a social one—people washed their dishes and left.

The communal shade areas and a lawn tent made of real sod and maintained by sprinklers, served as a chill-out space protected from the midday heat and sun. With cushions, couches and pillows, these spaces served as sites for rejuvenation and restoration. People sprawled about, napping or engaging in quiet conversation, reading or writing. These spaces were used both for relaxation and preparation—a type of greenroom or backstage area typical of many theme camps. Increasingly, laminated badges are used by camps to distinguish campers, who have paid their dues (often ranging from $100 to $300 for the week) from the general population.

In Asylum Village, in 2004 and 2005, New Day's Eve camp hosted a party each night at midnight which was open to the general public. About half an hour before midnight, a huge crowd gathered around the camp in festive New Year's Eve outfits: ball gowns, tuxedos, sequined dresses and fancy hats to celebrate the new day New York Times Square-style.[10] A large freight container was the base for a cardboard cut out of the New York skyline, with the Twin Towers decorated like the US flag. Below it was a stage for the DJ booth and disco ball emulating the Times Square ball. A huge digital clock counted down the hours and minutes to the new day as a DJ played Frank Sinatra and other oldies. New Day's Eve camp members handed out streamers, party favours, noisemakers and other paraphernalia associated with New Year's celebrations. On the small stage, two MCs announced the dawning of a new day: 'Welcome to Times Square, Nevada. Times Square Playa. Shout to the Man, let him hear you!' Everyone screamed, and champagne glasses were handed out as 1970s disco funk played in the background. As midnight approached, the Esplanade crowd grew larger, to about 250 people. Then the countdown began: 10, 9, 8 and so on. The ball dropped, fireworks were launched, everyone cheered, hugged, kissed and extended 'happy new day' greetings. The tuxedoed announcer proclaimed, 'This is a new day, anything is possible out here—forget yesterday, make today matter—this is a new day!' Everyone sang along with Sinatra's 'New York, New York' as fireworks continued to explode. Just one of countless public performances occurring simultaneously all over the playa.

Burning Man as a Modern-Day Saturnalia

While Black Rock City is full of performances of the everyday, planned and unplanned Happenings and elaborate spectacles, it has also evolved into a society based on play. The chief organizing tool of this society is art—but it is art that is meant to be played with. Like the formalized play of carnival, it is a break from everyday life, what Alessandro Falassi calls 'time out of time' (1987).[11] Crossing the threshold into Black Rock City, the metaphoric line drawn in the sand, one enters a modern-day incarnation of Rabelais's world of sixteenth-century carnival as theorized by Mikhail Bakhtin—a multidimensional world that temporarily transforms and inverts the normative social world, suspending business, commerce and motorized traffic, opening the streets to pedestrians (1984). In the case of Burning Man, a full year of preparation and planning transforms a barren desert into bustling city streets, plazas and performance spaces for seven days. It is a festive time during which Burners enter a temporary utopian realm of community, freedom, equality and abundance (ibid.: 11); for the duration of carnival, there is no other life outside it. The two-world condition of carnival serves as a social pressure valve, allowing participants to negotiate and redefine their freedoms and to act upon their wildest fantasies by reinventing themselves and designing new personas (ibid.: 255). The oceanic experience of total participation and belonging to the second world results in what Turner would call *spontaneous communitas*, or anti-structure (1969). Merging action with awareness, a sense of loss of ego and the complete fusion with the individual, the community and the surroundings, participants experience what Mihaly Csikszentmihalyi calls *flow*, a necessary condition for *communitas* (1975: 42).[12] Black Rock City provides the backdrop for a variety of transcendental activities that allow both the experience of flow and a sense of *communitas* to flourish.

Bakhtin traces the roots of Renaissance carnival to the Roman Saturnalia, an escape from officialdom, where participants create a second world in which official rules and conduct are turned inside out. As Photeine P. Bourboule argues in *Ancient Festivals of the 'Saturnalia' Type* (1964), the Saturnalia goes back to age immemorial in the history of human culture and can be traced back to the lithic age (ibid.: 37). A seven-day festival in honour of Saturn, the god of seed, it was a time when all customary restraints of law and morality, all restrictions on social inversion, feasting, masking and effigy-burning were lifted. Common in ancient Italy, Greece and Mesopotamia, the great festival of the Roman year was celebrated shortly before the winter solstice in the Augustan age (ibid.: 9), and human effigies were offered to Saturn as substitutes for human sacrifices (ibid.: 12). The Roman Saturnalia was marked with gift-giving, the wearing of disguises, excessive consumption of food and promiscuous sexual behaviour, signifying the end of an old life and the beginning of a new one. The Greek Saturnalia festivals in early spring were connected to the worship of Dionysus, the god of wine, and were celebrated with delirious enthusiasm, orgy, frenzy and ecstasy (ibid.: 51).

As play theorist Roger Caillois points out in *Man and the Sacred* (1959), excess is key in such events: 'the amount of food and wealth ostentatiously consumed or spent, and even destroyed and wasted, for destruction and waste, as forms of excess, are at the heart of the festival' (ibid.: 98). The carnivalesque body—with exaggerated and celebrated protrusions and orifices such as genital organs, phallus, nose, anus, mouth, belly and buttocks (Bakhtin 1984: 26)—is an example of excess on display throughout Burning Man. The exaggeration of scale that captures the essence of grotesque folk-festival forms is vividly on display in the enormous expanse of the playa that allows for large-scale art installations.

The cosmic topography of Rabelais's carnivalesque body is governed by duality and ambiguity In the cosmological universe of carnival, upwards points to heaven and downwards to earth, privileging themes of fertility, copulation, pregnancy, birth, growth, old age and death, which are intimately linked to natural life-cycles (ibid.: 25). One example of the grotesque body is *Cradle* (2001), a six-foot vagina sculpture created by Deirdre de Franceaux and Jann Nunn, which allowed participants to enact their own symbolic rebirth, another prevalent carnival theme. The giant eyeball bicycles built by John Krieger in 2005 are both surrealistic and carnivalesque; the illuminated pair meanders at night through the streets of Black Rock City. The exaggeration of scale celebrates both the carnivalesque grotesque body and the artist's sense of humour.

Playa As Playground

Black Rock City is an enormous playground—a hermetically sealed universe bound by rules determined in advance, rules that define a temporary world of play. Burning Man is a finite game with a definitive beginning, middle and end—with finite spatial and temporal boundaries—while Burning Man culture is an infinite game that is recreated each year, opening up possibilities of endless variations within the very finite world of Black Rock City.[13] At this level, Burning Man is a paradox: an infinite game contained within a finite one; Burning Man happens inside Black Rock City and yet extends—conceptually and in terms of the play world created—beyond its limits. Even more paradoxically, the infinitude of Burning Man is possible only when the limits of Black Rock City are accepted by all players, including those not actually part of Burning Man: the BLM, the local Nevada authorities and so on.

Once the rules and boundaries of Black Rock City are accepted, there is room for infinite artistic freedom and experiences; if these rules are transgressed, the whole play-world collapses. As play theorist Johan Huizinga notes, 'the play-community generally tends to become permanent, continuing even after the game is over' (1970: 12). Distinguishing between work and play helps to clarify why so many people spend their vacation days from 'real work' engaging in the 'play work' of building Black Rock City. As a volunteer, the 'work' is fulfilling and enjoyable because it is self-selected and intrinsically motivated, therefore fitting into the category of play.

Huizinga characterizes two types of human activity: *homo faber* (Man the Maker, the 'serious') and *homo luden* (Man the Player, the 'ephemeral'). Both types are instrumental in the Burning Man community, weaving together the serious work ethic needed to build the City with the more serendipitous play that creates the art and breathes life into it. It is out of this combination of a dedicated work ethic with playfulness and creativity that the alternative community emerges. Combining and synthesizing various forms of play, as they are defined by Brian Sutton-Smith (1997)—

play with identity, play of the self, play of the imagination and frivolous play—Burning Man is a complex, multitiered game that is in a constant state of flux and transformation.[14] Participants engage in games of imagination and fantasy, solitary play, playful behaviours, informal social play and risky or deep play.

Some of the most playful, imaginative creations that come out of Black Rock City are the art cars—the 'mutant vehicles'. A mutant vehicle is a vehicle that has been significantly and permanently 'mutated'—altered—so that the original appearance is no longer evident. Before bringing a mutant vehicle to Black Rock City, it must be registered online at the DMV and obtain a license plate. The DMV has two types of licenses: day and night. To pass inspection, the vehicle must be fully mutated and decorated beyond recognition. To receive a night license, the vehicle must be fully illuminated. Art cars are required to observe a 5-mph speed limit and are not allowed onto the Esplanade. These cars are arguably the most eccentric art at Burning Man and are largely responsible for the surrealist aesthetic that pervades Black Rock City.

Alongside the national venues for showcasing art cars, such as Houston's annual Art Car Weekend, the northern California ArtCar Fest (since 1997) and ArtCar West Fest in San Francisco organized by Harrod Blank and Philo Northrup, Burning Man has become one of the largest destinations for art cars in America. Art cars come in all shapes and sizes, including vehicles disguised as cupcakes, bunny slippers, large mammoth skeletons, pirate ships, jellyfish, eyeballs, dragons, whales and larger-than-life tricycles, to name a few of the most successful. *La Contessa*, one of Black Rock City's most ambitious art cars, first appeared in 2002 for the theme 'Floating World' and returns year after year to the playa. The ship was built around a yellow school bus and the inside was decorated like the gallows of an old pirate ship (see Figure 3.6). *La Contessa* moved at 5 mph across the desert surface and appeared to be floating in a dust storm. Unfortunately, in 2006, *La Contessa* was the victim of an arson fire at the ranch where she was being stored—the magnificent structure was reduced to ashes.

The art cars are one example of the kind of play Caillois characterizes as *ludus*. Caillois determined two principles of play: *paidia*, play that is free and spontaneous, the epitome of anti-structure manifesting a kind of uncontrolled fantasy; and *ludus*, play that is calculated, regulated, hier-

FIGURE 3.6. *La Contessa*, created by Simon Cheffins and the Extra Action Marching Band, 2005. Photograph by John Tzelepis.

archical and rule-bound (1961: 28). Most of the playing experienced at Burning Man appears to be *paidia*. However, even a little digging reveals that a lot of what is going on is *ludus*. Behind every moment of seemingly free play is both a lot of planning by the players and close oversight by the organizers and the authorities.

In *Man, Play, and Games* (1961), Caillois divides play into four types: *alea*, mimicry, *agon* and *ilinx*. *Alea* is Latin for the game of dice and covers all games of chance. The state lottery, Russian roulette, slot machines, and raffles all fall into this category. Agonistic games include all competitive sports and board games. *Ilinx*, associated with vertigo, applies to a wide range of activities from rollercoasters to illicit sexual relationships: anything that undulates and disorients (ibid.: 23–8). One can find all of these modes of play in Black Rock City but *alea* serves as Burning Man's connective tissue. Chance encounters and spontaneous activities make any journey through Black Rock City an unpredictable, exciting and surprising experience. One never knows what will be waiting around the corner, what spectacle or activity might cross your path at any given time. The City is charged with the electric energy of the unknown. Chance as a technique of artistic creation was used in the twentieth century by the Dadaists. And more than 80 years later, concepts of chance and indeterminacy are one of the chief governing forces of Black Rock City. Surrealists Tristan Tzara and André Breton would be in seventh heaven if they could wander through the City and see their ideas and theories so effectively realized.

One example of this kind of spontaneous chance collision occurred in 2004 when the annual Pink Parade crossed paths with the Black Rock City Animal Patrol (BRCAP). The BRCAP is another spoof of a civic organization whose job is to capture and detain all the furry beasts—people costumed as animals—wandering on the playa. The patrollers wear red jumpsuits and carry large nets with which to catch the 'creatures'. As the Pink Parade approached with pink furry creatures of all kinds and two bunny-slipper art cars, the BRCAP patrollers began chasing the pink bunnies with large nets in hand. A crowd instantly formed to witness the absurdity; then a third party coalesced, shouting protests and carrying picket signs that read, 'Free the Animals!' This melee continued for about 15 minutes until each entity went on their way. This spontaneous encounter is just one example of the hundreds of collisions occurring daily throughout Black Rock City.

Caillois's category *ilinx* is derived from the Greek word for dizziness (*ilingos*). *Ilinx* temporarily destabilizes perception and creates a sense of vertigo. Stilt- and tightrope-walking, hula-hooping, trapeze, acrobatics, fire performance and skydiving, all popular Black Rock City activities, induce this off-kilter sensation. Some installations are designed to induce a sense of *ilinx*, as seen in Peter Hudson's *Deeper* (2004)—a rapidly revolving diorama lit by a strobe light that at night produced the optical illusion of a single figure repeatedly diving into the playa. Other forms of *ilinx* play are rave dancing and the use of psychedelic drugs.[15] Rave dancing to various forms of techno music is common throughout Black Rock City, but by no means pervasive. One popular mode of *ilinx* is hula-hooping, where the performer undulates and twirls inside a spinning hoop. As the hoop glides effortlessly from the hips to the neck to the hand, the body is in constant motion, gyrating elegantly to keep the hoop spiralling up and down the body. Of course, hula-hoops were very popular in the late 1950s and 1960s. After being out of style for more than a decade, they gained new popularity in the early 1990s. Hooping ('hula' has been dropped from the name) is a craze at Burning Man. Today's hoopers construct their own hoops out of irrigation tubing wrapped with speciality holographic or phosphorescent tape. These hoops are much heavier and bigger than the 1950s version. Some are made with fire wicks for fire hooping. Hooping works as a solo act or as part of an ensemble. A Burning Man regular is Groove Hoops, a six-person group from New York City. Founded in 2002 by Jessie Kile and Stefan Pildes, Groove Hoops is the only co-ed hooping ensemble at Burning Man. Kile's goal is to legitimize and professionalize hoop dancing, and she choreographs tight and elaborate routines for her company. Of course, at Burning Man, Groove Hoops performs gratis.

Caillois's category of *agon* refers to conflict and competition engendered through matching skills, speed, endurance, strength or memory. Competitive play can be found in dance forms such as capoeira, and in contests such as the Miss Black Rock City Beauty Pageant and the Death Guild Thunderdome. The Death Guild Thunderdome comes straight out of the *Mad Max* movie in which opponents suspended from a geodesic dome by cables charge at each other with foam staffs (see Figure 3.7). Each

FIGURE 3.7. Death Guild Thunderdrome, 2000.
Photograph by Gregory Zabilski.

night, the entire dome is packed with spectators, screaming and shouting down at the contestants, the screaming itself in competition with the blaring thrashing punk metal. The dome is run by a team of hard-core punks adorned in chains, leather, piercings and tattoos; contestants sign up to fight in advance. The atmosphere is aggressive and violent and someone could easily be injured. A sign outside the dome reads, 'Days since last injury: 0; (1) We are always right; (2) Find your own opponent; (3) Sign up to fight; (4) Start and stop when told; (5) Fight as long as we say; (6) Don't Bitch'. When active, cheers and shouts can be heard across the playa; the violent energy escalates as the opponents beat each other playfully yet aggressively.

Of course, competition—both overt and covert—drives much of what goes on in Black Rock City. People ostensibly collaborate but actually compete in costuming, creating theme camps and putting up art installations. Each is more elaborate and complex than the next, growing larger and more ambitious from year to year.

At Burning Man, people shed their conventional selves and try out different personae. The fourth Caillois category of play is mimicry—disguise, wearing masks, playing parts, dressing up and travesty. In the streets of Black Rock City you may encounter someone dressed like a tropical fish, a rooster, a leopard or a stilt-walker with large green wings. Mimicry, whether in conventional theatre or in role-playing outside a bounded performance, produces a sensation of freedom, a suspension of ordinary reality in favour of a separate play reality. These disguises, as Turner points out in *The Ritual Process: Structure and Anti-Structure* (1969), are closely linked to the reversals and inversions of social roles. During carnival, a factory worker can become a king for the day; a child dressed up for Halloween can become a superhero. Every day, at Burning Man, people dress up in spectacular, elaborate costumes rivalling what can be seen in New Orleans Mardi Gras and Rio de Janeiro Carnival.

Sometimes the mimicry is enacted by a group, creating a single group persona. In 1995, a huge thunderstorm hit the playa, transforming the ancient lakebed into mud. Hundreds of participants stripped down and covered themselves with mud as they celebrated under a full double rainbow. Early pictures of Burning Man often show throngs of people covered in mud running around the playa in Dionysian frenzy. Known as the 'mud people', this look quickly became a playa fashion, evolving from mud into colourful full-body painting. The San Francisco performance troupe BodyCartography did a seven-day performance in 1999, each day fully painting themselves a different colour representing one of the chakras.

All four types of play are present at Burning Man, but mimicry, *alea* and *ilinx* dominate, at least on the surface and in the official literature. Even as citizens of Black Rock City disguise themselves and become whoever and whatever they want to be for seven days, they also compete with each other and conform to the rules of the authorities and the organization.

Personal Transformations: Reinventing the Self

All of this playing often results in personal transformations. People come to the playa to play; they try out new selves by means of mimicry and other modes of play. Sometimes, these new selves and names stick. The playful world of Black Rock City provides an inviting place to be whoever you want to be. In a way, Burning Man realizes an ideal American freedom: self-invention. Burners enjoy their annual opportunity to recreate themselves, adopt new identities and take on 'playa names' which are either given or self-selected and which often stick upon re-entry into the 'default' world. The self as self-consciously constructed is manipulated and influenced by our surroundings. As Goffman argues, we are all social actors continuously 'performing the self':

> Everyone is always and everywhere, more or less consciously, playing a role. [. . .] It is in these roles that we know each other; it is in these roles that we know ourselves. [. . .] The role we are striving to live up to—this mask is our truer self, the self we would like to be. In the end, our conception of our role becomes second nature and an integral part of our personality (1959: 20)

A new identity usually requires a new look, a total costume that masks the old self of the 'default' world. As John Emigh notes, the mask as a physical instrument of transformation creates a potential space for playing with the self in relation to others (1996: 14). A mask hides the identity of the person wearing it, yet at the same time exposes a hidden persona (Falassi 1987: 211). Burning Man board member Michael Mikel marvels at how the idea of costuming from the Cacophony Society was taken to extremes at Burning Man:

> Burning Man gives you the opportunity to 'recreate your identity'. We first have to take people out of their comfort zone. The world around us is largely a construction but people don't realize this. Society and rules have been built up. In order to get to the core of yourself, to think new and fresh, you have to take all of this away. Burning Man strips away who you thought you were. And this is the rebirth that happens at Burning Man. People come to Burning Man with their baggage and it becomes a heavy weight and the world gets stripped away from them. When people say they have these life-changing experiences, it is due to these factors. We do not have rites of passage in our society anymore. That is what we are sadly lacking. There is no coming-of-age ritual and I think it causes us to be spiritually inferior (2008).

Costuming plays an important role in the transformation of self and the creation of a new persona. The cover of the 3 September 2004 *Piss Clear* instructs participants on how to dress like a Burner, replete with platform boots, furry leg warmers, hot pants, goggles, water bottle, sun block, accessories and body paint (see Figure 3.8). This article both celebrates and mocks 'playa fashion'. Once radical and original, various costume styles quickly became trends such as hot pants, platform shoes and furry boots.

From 2003 to 2006, landscape architect Bill Tonnesen and photographer John Romero teamed up to create a photography installation titled *The Box Project* (see Figure 3.9). Positioned near Center Camp, they would select participants from throughout the playa, each of whom was dressed in unique costumes. After filling out a consent form, the participants sat in the box for a photo shoot. The elegant framing of the box captured the complexity and originality of each person who participated. No two costumes were alike. The photographs have subsequently been shown at galleries around the country as documentation of the performative event.

In the unlikely circumstance that a Burner doesn't bring an exotic costume along, there are several outlets that provide costumes for free, such as the Black Rock Boutique[16] and Kostume Kult,[17] which gives away free donated costumes all week long. Kostume Kult offers the positive aspects of the consumer experience without the monetary transaction. Founder Jim Glaser (aka Kostume Jim) explains:

> It is, 'Hi. How are you? How can I help you?' Helping people come out of their shell a little. Giving them something that makes them very

> happy and potentially changing their week. If they have an outfit, that becomes their outfit all week and they come away with a new identity. It is empowering. It is ritual. It is consumer experience. It is the ritual that is most common in America and we do it in a positive way (2006).

Born and raised in the New York metropolitan area, Glaser attended Burning Man for the first time in 2001. After a successful career at a top-level accounting firm, he began a business venture called Costume Network Inc. in 1999 to target what he calls a 'niche entertainment portal'. He feels that one of the reasons why people don't wear costumes is because they don't have ideas, so he created a website to post photographs of costume ideas. The annual New York City Halloween parade and the Coney Island Mermaid Parade is where Glaser realized he loved the whole costume-performance genre because of the way a costume empowers its wearer. He came to believe that costuming has a great potential for transformation when he noticed that, on the nights he wore costumes, he met more people and was able to express himself more creatively:

> If you have exceptional costumes and unique stuff, it brings out the child in you. And then you are compelled to outdo yourself every year. It is addictive in a way. [. . .] Absurdity brings out the child and keeps you young and at the end it is feeling young; feeling vibrant is the drug that is fueling this whole thing. Feeling alive. [. . .] It isn't about getting your Nike Swoosh. It is about figuring out what your own swoosh is going to be (ibid.).

For Glaser, Burning Man was a transformational experience that brought together costuming and community. He calls himself a 'serial subculturalist': 'I was a deadhead. I was a metal head. I was a sci-fi head—all of the above—in search of community I guess. And Burning Man brought so many different elements together. It is not judgemental' (ibid.). When he returned home to New York City after his first experience at Burning Man, he become involved in the New York Burning Man scene and began to devote his time developing the Costume Cultural Society and Kostume Kult.

Since 2001, Glaser has returned every year to Burning Man and Kostume Kult has continued to evolve from seven people in 2002 to several hundred in 2008. While the idea of the Costume Cultural Society began before Burning Man, Kostume Kult has grown and gained in popularity because of Burning Man. The Kostume Kult listserv has 350 subscribers as

piss clear

friday
3 september 2004
issue 25

Black Rock City's favorite alternative newspaper

devil horns ... yes, even attached to a hat

for some reason, the classic cowboy hat just never goes out of style

bad-ass goggles, dust storm optional

Black Rock City is in Nevada, not India – but that doesn't seem to stop anyone from wearing a bindi

jack that hair up in pigtails ... it gets fucking hot out here!

but not so hot that you can't wear a furry vest!

the more chains and necklaces you have on, the better

or a matching furry bra, for that matter

open vest, no shirt, no reason

striped arm sleeves ... just because, okay?

a backpack full of stupid playa gifts that people gave you, because you didn't want to seem rude

show everyone how fucking cool you are – you've got a Burning Man laminate!

obligatory body paint – this is the bare minimum permissable

hot pants ... if you're a Burner chick, these are practically mandatory

the more bracelets and jewelry you have on, the better

SPF 30 sunblock – anything less and you're just asking for skin cancer

your most important accessory: your water bottle! Shown here conveniently latched onto utility belt

furry leg warmers ... the epitomy of pointless playa fashion. Who started this and why? Brilliant in a form-over-function kinda way

nothing says 'Burner dude' like a Utilikilt – especially if it's stuffed full of tools, sunblock, flashlight, gifts, drugs, etc.

platform boots with a filled-in chunky heel – keeps you a few inches above the playa dust

if your boots are this clean, then you're *not* in Black Rock City

How to dress like a Burner

and more style tips in our second annual Fashion Issue

FIGURE 3.8. 'How to Dress Like a Burner'. *Piss Clear* 25 (3 September 2004). Courtesy of Adrian Roberts.

FIGURE 3.9. *The Box Project* by Bill Tonnesen and John Romero, 2003–06. Photographs by Bill Tonnesen and John Romero.

of 2008 as well as a discussion board of over 100 members. New Yorkers make up 60 per cent of the subscribers and the rest are from around the country as well as internationally. There is a board of directors with nine members and a core leadership group called 'KKabal' of 30 people.

The 'k' in Kostume Kult, as Glaser explains, is an element of culture jamming—turning the world upside down and infusing it with new meaning. Like the Cacophony Society, Kostume Kult is an open social network, not an exclusive club. Kostume Kult plans all year for their trip to the playa hosting at least four fundraisers in New York City throughout the year.[18] In 2005, the Costume Cultural Society began to get press coverage from the National Public Radio, the *New York Post*, the *Village Voice* and the *New York Times*, highlighting the growing trend in 'costume culture', also known as 'participatory culture'. I would argue that Burning Man is largely responsible for this national trend.

While costuming is an important aspect of carnival, so are parades and processions, which thrive in Black Rock City. Every day, there is at least one parade, often more, hosted by various camps, such as the Pink Parade hosted by the Pink Pleasure Palace, the French Maid Brigade Parade, the Burning Marching Band and the Orange Parade. Traditionally, Friday is the day for the annual Critical Dicks and Critical Tits Bike ride—segregated gender-specific events, that sometimes have over a thousand participants biking naked through the streets. The parades of Black Rock City are open to anyone and for the most part are a source of laughter and merriment both for those participating and for those spectating. The parades give the various camps a chance to display themselves to the rest of the community, participating in what Schechner would call 'direct theatre' (1993: 83).[19] For the most part, the parades are not protest marches directed against the authorities; they are not rebellious but celebratory.

Carnival Laughter and Political Performance

As Bakhtin points out, laughter during sixteenth-century carnivals were deeply ambivalent, mocking and satirical (1984: 12). Black Rock City voices a similar penchant for the language of the grotesque—curses, profanities, excessive praises and abuses. The best example of carnivalesque satire and parody can be found in *Piss Clear*, Burning Man's alternative newspaper, which provides a more humorous, often biting commentary than the *Black Rock Gazette*, now the *Black Rock Beacon*.[20] *Piss Clear* gets its title from the survival axiom, 'Drink so much water that you piss clear'. Editor-in-chief Adrian Roberts contributes a daily column, 'Adrian's Rant' and *Piss Clear* staff writer Steve Courtney (aka Malderor) writes 'Malderor's Rant' in which they freely speak their minds in a sarcastic, frank manner. In the 31 August 2004 issue, Malderor began his rant, entitled 'Raise Your Own Damn Money!' with: 'Welcome to the Crankiest Column on the Playa! If you live in San Francisco like ME, you probably received the same deluge of annoying invitations to fundraisers to help get various theme camps out to Burning Man. What the HELL ever happened to SELF-SUFFICIENCY? [. . .] Why should I PAY for Trance-Box to get to the playa?' In another rant mocking the gift economy, titled 'I Don't Want Your Stupid Gifts!', Malderor complained, 'Okay, goddamitt, please stop giving me your trinkets' For god's sake, I don't WANT your necklaces, your friendship bracelets, your homemade water pipes, or frickin' WHATEVER!' (2005).

These satirical articles humorously play with the concept of the 'gift economy' but at the same time point out a hidden truth about the economics of getting to Burning Man. Each year, San Francisco is flooded with fundraisers planned by various groups to get their theme camps to Burning Man, and Malderor makes a valid point: Why should he or anyone else underwrite those expenses? He also comments on the 'trinkets' that many people distribute as 'gifts'. As the event has grown, the values of a 'gift economy' have been distorted to the point that Burners have taken to buying mass quantities of valueless souvenirs that no one cares about.

Parody, another feature of carnival, is also popular at Burning Man. In 1997, 2003, 2005 and 2007, the BMO invited performer Bill Talen, known for his portrayal of the character Reverend Billy. While Reverend Billy and the Church of Stop Shopping did not originate in conjunction with Burning Man, Talen's clever, witty and satirical work parallels the culture jamming that is the essence of the event. The organization partially funded Reverend Billy and gave him permission to perform at the base of the Man, an honour not many people are afforded. Reverend Billy and his 30-member Church of Stop Shopping choir perform a parody of evangelical preaching aimed against American consumerism and right-wing politics. The message is clear and, even as the audience roared with laughter, it got the point. Ironically, Reverend Billy preached the word of 'stop shopping' and 'anti-consumerism' to a crowd who had just purchased untold amounts of supplies to construct Black Rock City and survive a full week without commerce.

In 2004, with the presidential elections at hand, political satire and parody were the order of the day. While the BMO claims political neutrality, it was clear that most of those on the playa were against the Iraq War and anti-Bush. One memorable installation consisted of the image of George Bush's face projected on two white geodesic domes. Bush's voice was electronically manipulated and loudly amplified for those on the Esplanade. His familiar sayings were carefully edited so that the President was heard proclaiming: 'Lies, lies, lies', 'Fear and terror', 'Your enemy is leading your country', 'VP Cheney will be killed', 'I am addicted to oil. I am addicted to power', 'Innocent people will be killed', 'If you're against me, be afraid', 'Americans will be killed', 'Many Iraqis will be killed', 'I am addicted to God', 'God will kill many Americans', 'If you search for Cheney, you will be killed.' As the recorded voice of Bush continued to speak, passersby paused to listen and laugh.

One camp called 'Baghdad' was covered with Chinese, Cuban, Iraqi and Palestinian flags, pictures of Che, and a target practice with Bush's face that read 'war monger' (see Figure 3.10). Many of the porta-potties had signs on them reading 'Republican Voting Booth' (see Figure 3.11). Anti-Iraq War signs appeared throughout the City. Center Camp had a voting station adorned with the US map and a sign that asked you to place a red or blue pin where you would be on 2 November 2004. New York, San Francisco, Los Angeles and Phoenix were covered with the most pins and all but four pins were blue. Not that this is a surprise, but it clearly indicates the political orientation of Black Rock citizens. Especially during the 2004 presidential elections and after the 2005 Hurricane Katrina disaster in New Orleans and the Gulf Coast, which occurred during Burning Man, events in the 'real world' inevitably impacted the community and informed its ideology.

FIGURE 3.10 (FACING PAGE). Target practice poster from 'Baghdad' camp, 2004. Photograph by John Tzelepis.

TARGET
BUSH
WAR
MONGER
BOMB TOSS PRACTICE

FIGURE 3.11. A sign over the public urinal transformed it into a 'Republican Voting Booth', 2004.
Photograph by John Tzelepis.

In fact, since the start of the Iraq War in 2003, politically oriented art has become more common. Three installations from 2005 are direct commentaries on the war in Iraq and the atrocities at Abu Ghraib. *Peace Boots* by Sheilah Morgan is a pathway of army boots representing all the US soldiers killed in the war in Iraq. In *Hellfire Weenie Roast*, five headless figures, which at night spewed fire, prayed in front of a lectern. Behind them, a yellow warning sign of a soldier decapitating a kneeling figure evoked media graphics of the war in Iraq—in this case the US soldiers captured and beheaded.

In 2005 and 2006, two installations of white crosses haunted the playa surface, echoing the endless sea of crosses at Omaha Beach in Normandy, France, a mass grave in honour of those killed on D-Day during World War II. The installation *In Memoriam* (2005; see Figure 3.12) placed crosses sporadically around the playa with the date of a soldier's death and a replica of his/her dog tag. *What Remains* by Chris Meyers (2006; see Figure 3.13) expanded on this image: 2,600 crosses represented the US soldiers killed in Iraq to date, each including a photo, name, age, hometown and cause of death inscribed on the cross. Walking through a seemingly infinite sea of crosses spatialized and amplified the magnitude of loss and the human tragedy of war. The severity of the installation within the festive atmosphere of Black Rock City was a constant reminder of real-world politics. Clearly, despite a general feeling of the carnivalesque and the adamant intention to get away from the everyday world, concerns and problems from the other 51 weeks of the year cannot be fully shut out or ignored. In fact, Black Rock City becomes a fertile landscape for political action and performance—an opportunity for political critique and activism for an audience of 49,000 spectators.

As was true for the Saturnalia and the sixteenth-century folk carnival as analysed by Bakhtin in *Rabelais and His World*, inversion is a common theme at Burning Man. One major difference is that Burning Man does not inspire the same inversion of social hierarchy as is found in carnival: Larry Harvey, his organization, and state and local authorities are still in power throughout the event. While there is evidence of *spontaneous communitas* on one level, *normative communitas* (the expected) ultimately prevails. What is expected at Burning Man is that people will dress in carnivalesque attire and become participants rather than observers; it is

FIGURE 3.12. *In Memoriam* (artist unknown), 2005. Photograph by Tom Pendergast.

FIGURE 3.13. *What Remains* by Chris Meyers, 2006.
Photograph by Rick Egan.

an orderly Saturnalia—a special moment for excess, bounded by regulation. While there is little chance of the extraordinary behaviour spinning out of control, it is always a possibility—but then the event would be shut down by the authorities. Black Rock City is a multitiered game in which modes of everyday performance and the carnivalesque play out in a myriad of ways. I take seriously Turner's assertion that the way a culture plays their games, rituals and festivals is more revealing than the way they work (in Falassi 1987: 76). Both the very serious and the seemingly frivolous play of Burning Man are a testament to Bakhtin's pronouncement: 'All the acts of the drama of world history were performed before a chorus of laughing people. Without hearing this chorus we cannot understand the drama as a whole' (1984: 474).

Notes

1 The theme in 2001, 'The Seven Ages of Man', was inspired by Shakespeare's lines from *As You Like It*. The playa served as an enormous theatre where players moved through all the various stages of life from birth to death.

2 The Dada notion of blurring art and life was further developed by John Cage and the original Happenings artist, Allan Kaprow.

3 This nonmatrixed performing, compartmented structure, and the methodological use of chance methods can be traced back to the Futurists and Dadaists. Each participant becomes a necessary part of a nonmatrixed performance (Kirby 1994: 17).

4 Marina Abramovic lived in a loft-like platform that was divided into three rooms, each accessible by a ladder built with butcher knives as rungs. She remained there, in the Sean Kelly Gallery in New York, without eating or speaking for 12 days. Spectators could watch from the gallery floor below and view her up close through a high-powered telescope (Abramovic et al. 2004).

5 According to Mike Pearson and Michael Shanks, with the advent of the modern city, 'the concept of the *flaneur* has come to stand as a metaphor for the contemporary urban dweller, moving through the flux of the city, as a mode of being in the world, in relation to the dazzling consumer spectacles; in a modern shopping center we are all flaneurs: gazing, grazing, consuming' (2001: 149).

6 P. Segal started the Center Camp Café in 1995 and ran it as her own business until 2001. As the population grew, the job became too much for one person, so the Café is now managed by the BMO and all profits go back into the organization (BMO 2001).

7 At Camp Arctica, in 2004, they sold thousands of bags of ice to the community at two dollars a bag, with 19 semi trucks loaded with ice entering Black Rock City during the week. All the proceeds went to charities in Reno, Gerlach, Empire and San Francisco (BMO 2004b).

8 The Center Camp Café sells hot or iced chai ($3), coffee ($2), cappuccino ($3), tea ($2), espresso ($2), lattes ($3), mochas ($3), hot chocolate ($2), lemonade ($3) and electrolyte powder ($3) (prices from 2004 and 2005). Water is not sold because all participants are required to bring their own (BMO 2004b).

9 According to Robert W. Rydell in *All the World's a Fair: Visions of Empire at American International Expositions, 1876–1916* (1984), the midway 'Possessed the features of the circus, the menagerie, the museum and the vaudeville, with an odd collection of strange nationalities forming a unique anthropological exhibit' (ibid.: 94)

10 This performance was reminiscent of the first 'zone trip' to the playa in 1990, when participants wore ball gowns and tuxedos to burn the Man.

11 The etymology of 'carnival' traces the word from the Latin *caro*, 'flesh', and *levare*, 'put away'. Carnival is also connected to the mediaeval Latin phrase, *carne vale* [meat, farewell!] marking the four-day period of revelry just before Lent culminating on Mardi Gras or Fat Tuesday. Rooted in the pre-Christian pagan past, carnival has affinities with the Roman Saturnalia and the mediaeval Feast of Fools (Falassi 1987: 14).

12 Csikszentmihalyi offers chess, rock-climbing, painting, yoga, dancing and surgery as examples of flow activities (1975: 11) and distinguishes between three types of flow: (1) Deep flow—total engagement with activity; (2) Micro flow—events such as watching TV, stretching or taking a coffee break; and (3) Flow deprivation—the anxiety and boredom caused by lack of flow activities. Csikszentmihalyi argues that we need flow in order to be productive and healthy. Play and leisure time increases our productivity, concentration and motivation while at work (ibid.: 12).

13 Finite games are the games of life that have a definite beginning, middle and end—where there are winners and losers—such as in politics, religion, war and social structures (Carse 1986: 45). Infinite games eliminate boundaries and have no distinct beginning, middle or end; they are ongoing, opening up the players to a new relationship with time (ibid.: 8).

14 In the *Ambiguity of Play* (1997), Brian Sutton-Smith examines the complexity of play, finding that almost anything can be understood through the lens of play: tourism as play, television as play, daydreaming as play, sexual intimacy as play, travel as play, politics as play and so on (ibid.: 3–5).

15 The use of hallucinogenic drugs often intensifies the *ilinx* factor when combined with dancing and can induce trance and other forms of ecstatic experience. However, drugs are not a part of everyone's experience at Burning Man, although they are present and a major concern for the authorities.

16 The Black Rock Boutique sews their label into everything they distribute—their wares are more about fashion than costuming. You are supposed to bring the costume back but 80 per cent don't. The Boutique has been around longer than Kostume Kult but is less popular.

17 Kostume Kult was mentioned four times in the 2005 novel *The Man Burns Tonight: A Black Rock City Mystery*, a murder mystery set at Burning Man by Donn Cortez. The adventure takes place in Black Rock City and revolves around a big 'killer' bunny who keeps coming back to Kostume Kult to change his disguise.

18 Their themed New York City fundraiser costume parties in 2005 and 2006 included 'Horned Ball', 'Black and Light Ball', 'Carousel' and the 'Alternative Oscars' (Glaser 2006).

19 As Susan G. Davis notes in *Parades and Power: Street Theatre in Nineteenth Century Philadelphia* (1986), parades and public ceremonies can serve as an opportunity for a group to display itself to the community (ibid.: 5).

20 *Piss Clear* is fully funded by Adrian Roberts and does not receive any grant money from the BMO. *Black Rock Gazette* was supported by the BMO as the official newspaper. However, in 2005, the BMO decided to stop its financial support; it was concerned that the *Gazette* portrayed a negative image of Burning Man that might be taken by local and state authorities as the official representation of the BMO's views and values. In protest, the writers and editors of the *Black Rock Gazette* formed their own newspaper, *Black Rock Beacon*, supported by the editors and writers themselves.

CHAPTER 4
DARK CARNIVAL: THE NEW AMERICAN ALTERNATIVE CIRCUS

> Whether escaping the boundaries of gravity, playing with fire or balancing a swirling hoop, dancers and choreographers are adopting elements from the fantastic, magical realm of circus, nightclub and even children's playthings into sophisticated choreographic works, adding their own artistic stamp in the process. The cross-pollination is inspiring new ways of moving, expanding the audience as well as the definition of a dancer and developing entirely new performance venues. [. . .] The latest trends in 'extreme dance' are propelling the art form into the future (Sims 2005: 47–53).

> The score is like a glass inside which a candle is burning. The glass is solid; it contains and guides the flame. But it is not the flame. The flame is what illuminates the score, what the spectators see through the score. The flame is alive. Just as the flame in the glass moves, flutters, rises and falls, almost goes out, suddenly glows brightly, responds to each breath of wind [. . .] (Ryczard Cieslak, in Schechner 1973: 295).

The above quote, about the 'candle in the glass', uttered by Ryczard Cieslak, Jerzy Grotowski's lead actor, captures the essence of this chapter. While performances of everyday life and spontaneous outbursts of artistic collaboration infuse the playa with playfulness and the carnivalesque, at the other end of the spectrum are the many rehearsed performances by amateur and professional groups. Black Rock City is a magnet for performance troupes of all kinds. My aim here is not to give an encyclopaedic overview of, or even list, every group that has performed at Burning Man, but to focus on five performance groups that represent the variety of performance on the playa: Burning Man Opera, AWD, Xeno, El Circo and Cirque Berzerk. These troupes are part of the 'new American alternative circus' movement (also known as the Indie Circus) that emerged around 1990.

The Birth of the New American Alternative Circus

John Bill Ricketts brought the first circus to the United States in 1793, and, in 1871 at the Brooklyn World's Fair, P. T. Barnum introduced the world's first three-ring circus (Babinski and Manchester 2004: 20).[1] For decades, the American circus remained a staple and stable entertainment. Then, in the 1950s, alternative circuses began to emerge. This 'new American circus', as it was called, was a radical rethinking of the genre—and, as we shall see, there are direct connections between this trend and Burning Man. The first generation of the new American circuses included Peter Schumann's Bread and Puppet 'Our Domestic Resurrection Circus' (1962), Larry Pisoni and Peggy Snider's Pickle Family Circus (1975), Paul Binder's Big Apple Circus (1977) and Montreal's Cirque du Soleil, founded in 1984 by Guy Laliberte and Guy Caron. The performance arena shrank from three rings to one and animals were no longer a central attraction. The people involved in the new American circus wanted their work to be regarded as an art form and to elevate the circus from its reputation as a low art form created by outsiders, vagabonds and gypsies (Eckley 1984: 8). Unlike the traditional circuses, none of these founders came from circus families. In San Francisco, New York City, Vermont and Montreal, these new circuses attracted a different audience: more affluent, more receptive to new ideas, and consisted of more adults than children (ibid.: 11).

Another flurry of activity in the new American circus movement began in 1990, one in which Burning Man plays a significant role. While it is not clear when the term 'new American alternative circus' was first used, J. Dee Hill's *Freaks and Fire: The Underground Reinvention of Circus* (2004) is a thorough portrait of this movement and defines its parameters. Her research covers groups such as Flam Chen, Bantu Mystic Family Circus,[2] Yard Dogs Road Show and Bindlestiff Family Cirkus, among others. All are a part of this new genre and have performed at Burning Man over the years.[3]

The Bindlestiff Family Cirkus, founded in New York City in 1995 by Stephanie Monseu (aka Philomena) and Keith Nelson (aka Mr Pennygaffe), performed at Burning Man in 1997. An adult-oriented circus, it features whip crackers, knife-throwers, stilt-walkers, aerialists, contortionists, clowning, vaudeville and burlesque. The Yard Dogs Road Show—founded by Eddy Joe Cotton, Five Livered Larry and Voodoo Freddy—embraces the hobo spirit and the aesthetic of the local junkyard, weaving together a mélange inspired by 1880s burlesque, jug bands and vaudeville (ibid.: 121). Founded in 1994 by Nadia Hagen in Tucson, Arizona, as a finale for the local All Soul's Day Procession,[4] Flam Chen is an aerial fire circus troupe known for its signature otherworldly style in which the characters are costumed as warriors and animal spirits. A significant quality of these groups is what Hill calls their 'tribal aspect': tattooing, scarification, fire performance, drumming and ritual (ibid.: xii). These circuses have grown up contemporaneously with other countercultural events such as the Rainbow Family gatherings held annually in US national forests, the Oregon Country Fair and Burning Man; the influence among all of these postmodern cultural outpourings has been reciprocal.

Alternative circuses performing at festivals, underground raves and nightclubs project a darker vision of the world than their more easygoing counterparts, such as the Pickle Family Circus or Big Apple Circus. In the alternative circuses, many of the performers have had no formal training in circus techniques or acrobatics; however, many have gone on to seek out training to improve their skills, and to study the history of the genre to deepen their knowledge of the form (ibid.: xii). The ritual and neo-tribal nature of the alternative circus is central. As Hill notes, 'The phenomenon of alternative circus performance can be seen as the theatrical dimension to one generation's wholesale rediscovery of the concept of the tribe. A return to tribalism is taking place but reinvented from their perspective' (ibid.: xii). Hill points out that an anti-consumer ethic is perva-

FIGURE 4.1. Apsara at opening night premiere party for Cirque du Soleil's *Corteo* in San Francisco, 2005. Photograph by Spencer Hansen.

sive throughout the movement, along with performance styles that bring audience members onstage or even break down the performer–spectator barrier altogether (ibid.: xv). And these same elements of the alternative circus movement can be felt throughout all of Burning Man, and Burning Man, in turn, has a significant influence on the shaping of this circus aesthetic.

In one sense, Burning Man could be seen as one enormous alternative circus. At any time, day or night, one might encounter a group of stilt-walkers, fire performers or hoopers creating a circus-like atmosphere throughout the City. However, some groups take it to the next level, rehearsing and mounting fully realized performances. Although these groups are not strictly circuses, they borrow and adapt the circus aesthetic in their own unique, homemade ways.

The Burning Man Opera

One of the most elaborate of these circus-like spectacles is the Burning Man Opera, which was performed from 1996 to 2000. These Operas were spectacular pageants involving hundreds of performers, epic mythological narratives, flaming *lingam* towers and ritualistic initiations masterminded by San Francisco-based Argentinean visual artist, filmmaker and sculptor, Pepe Ozan. According to Burning Man Opera performer and organizer Paradox Pollack (also a core member of the Mystic Family Circus), who has participated every year, the history of performance at Burning Man, including the Opera, can be traced to an event called *Desert Site Works*, organized by photographer William Binzen. It was at *Desert Site Works* that Pollack first met Ozan.

Desert Site Works, performed each year from 1993 to 1995, occurred simultaneously with Burning Man. Also in the Black Rock Desert but just a few miles away, *Desert Site Works* took place each year in a different location—Black Rock Hot Springs, the Trego Hot Springs and the Bordello Hot Springs. Binzen organized a group of approximately 30 artists to perform a 24-hour, continuous performance ritual of the life cycle from conception to death. He assembled four directors, each responsible for a different stage of development. As one of the four, Pollack took people on an interactive journey through the various rites of passage. The only rule was that there always had to be a witness—and Pepe Ozan sculpted a ‘wit-

FIGURE 4.2. Set for the 1998 Burning Man Opera.
Courtesy of the Burning Man Opera.

ness chair' for that purpose. Pollack vividly remembers that the Trego Hot Springs served as the birth canal, where one person would be a 'child' for three hours and two 'parents' would be caregivers. Pollack was familiar with the immersive paratheatrical work of Jerzy Grotowski and Peter Brook's 'holy theatre' from the *Empty Space* but only retrospectively does he recognize their influence on these interactive experiences.

The following year, the same group created an equally epic immersive performance based on the mysticism of the Kabbalah in a different location in the Black Rock Desert, the Bordello Hot Springs. The tree of life became an interactive performance where each of the major arcana of the Tarot was represented. Ozan designed and constructed his first 30-foot tower or, *lingam*, using trees, metal stucco mesh, plaster and the natural clay from the hot springs. Once the clay dried, it cracked creating an ornate texture, which Ozan had not expected. Like all of his *lingams*, the tower was burned at the end of the event. *Desert Site Works* rehearsed for three months, developing interactive themes and game structures so that someone could enter at any stage of life At each station a character played one of the archetypes of the major arcana around the tree of life, such as the Devil or the High Priestess. You could interact with one person, such as the Devil, who had cigarettes, booze and bones. He would watch you closely and command that you go see the High Priestess. Pollack recalls:

> It was about readings. Every person that came in was being read, challenged and passed onto the next archetype. It was very powerful work. That year I buried myself on the death tarot and I dug my grave. They buried me, put a dead raven on my chest, and went to Burning Man. They came back 12 hours later. I was still in the hole (2008).

The group began to call themselves the Ape Theatre, later to become Dream Circus.

In 1995, one of Burning Man's founders, John Law, invited Pepe Ozan to build a tower for Burning Man. The Dream Circus from *Desert Site Works* went over to Burning Man that year and performed around the 40-foot tower while it burned. Pollack recalls his first experience at Burning Man as being very spontaneous: 'The crew we had been working with for three months became primal beasts. We were just going for it! Going completely mad! Images of primal looks on our faces. Throwing dirt into the fire, saying prayers, and casting spells. It was very deep. Ozan said that was the inspiration for the operas, watching the Dream Circus around his *lingam*' (ibid.). The following year, Ozan created the first Burning Man Opera and he discusses his inspiration:

> What inspires me mostly is religion, although I don't profess religious ideas. I'm closer to being an agnostic, an atheist, than anything else. Although I think religion is impregnated with incredible possibilities of beauty. Let me tell you a story: I was in the Shiva temple in Chidambaram, many years ago, and I saw this ceremony, this procession. They were bringing fire on their shoulders, and there were elephants, horns, drums . . . I had goose bumps, and I was absolutely taken by this 'spectacle'! And so I realized that a good spectacle, because it really hits you, doesn't need an anecdote, doesn't need a story to be told. And that was the basis of the idea of the Opera. So I owe my inspiration of using rituals for art here to India (in Kamakshi 2007).

The 'Tower Project' or 'Fire Lingam' set the stage for what became known as the 'Burning Man Opera'. Ozan realized he wanted to create a ritualistic ceremony around the burning of the *lingam* where the audience would not need to understand or share a mythology as long as the ritual resonated on a spiritual and aesthetic level. At a certain point, he realized his ideas for an epic ritual could be turned into an opera, a Wagnerian *Gesamtkunstwerk* fusing dance, music, song, theatre and spectacle.

Each year, the Opera appropriated a different mythology and culture and these infused the entire week leading up to the actual performance. Ozan took this to the extreme by conducting in-depth research for each opera. In an interview with the *Black Rock Gazette*, Ozan describes the opera as a tableau: 'There is no plot in the literal sense, and no specific symbolic meaning: the performance is simply meant to be experienced immediately and directly. [. . .] The opera tends to be an experience rather than a story' (BMO 1999b).

For the first opera, inspired by the Byzantine Empire in Constantinople, Ozan travelled to Turkey to learn Byzantine history and mythology. The BMO provided Ozan with two sound systems and paid for all Opera-related expenses. When he first started, he admits, he had no idea what he was doing. His goal was to give all the performers total freedom to do whatever they chose within the performative mythological structure he had created, from designing their own costumes to their actions, which inspired tremendous creativity (Hawthorne and Mikel 2003).

FIGURE 4.3. Set for the 1996 Burning Man Opera. Courtesy of the Burning Man Opera.

The 1996 theme was 'Inferno', inspired by Dante's *Divine Comedy*, and the first opera, *The Arrival of Empress Zoe*, followed the soul's journey from birth to death. The Burning Man Opera was the first interactive performance of this magnitude and complexity on the playa. For the first two Operas, Ozan had to do most of the labour from concept to costuming, posters, set design and choreography; but soon he gathered a group of artists, composers, singers, musicians and performers to handle the various responsibilities. At first there were 35 volunteers; by 2000, over 200 people were working to organize and perform the Opera, which also became a haven for performers of all kinds. According to Ozan, 'If you are a performer and you go to Burning Man, what do you do? The opera was the place for singers, dancers and performers. [. . .] The opera had choreography, music, a sound system, you name it' (ibid.). For several years, Ozan invited composers, musicians and performers from CalArts to help coordinate and create the operas. The crew typically arrived three weeks early to begin setting up and constructing the *lingams*.

Louis M. Brill announced the first opera performance in the *Black Rock Gazette* (1996), which was scheduled to take place on Saturday night around midnight, 'It's opera folks! Wear your best finery!' Consisting of about 50 people, including performers, musicians, sculptors, special effects technicians and costume designers, the centrepiece of the opera was a series of *lingam* towers—hollow, phallic tubes constructed out of rebar, mesh and mud, which went up in flames for the finale. One theme of carnival as described by Bakhtin is the underworld and the representation of hell—the vertical conception of the world, with heaven on top and hell below (1984: 401). According to him, the set that depicted hell was solemnly burned at the peak of the festivities; it was represented in the form of a globe ejecting flames and was known as the 'jaws of hell' (ibid.: 91). The Burning Man Opera, like carnival, embodied this spirit of creative destruction. The mythology surrounding the first Opera was as follows:

> It is the year of 1158 AD in the Byzantine Empire in Constantinople. The hermaphrodite condition of Empress Zoë has been revealed by Cardinal Petroccelly, one of her passive homosexual lovers. Condemned by the Holy See to be drowned in the Bosphorous, the Empress managed to take to the waters the Light of the Casiksi Diamond, which assured her the favor of the Demons. Steffanos, the High Priest of Hell, possessed by desire at the sight of the Empress, incites the jealousy of the Graces who

> assist him in the Infinite Recreation of Fire. Pretending to help in the production of the Dust of Darkness to spray the Empress out of existence, the Graces plot the destruction of their rival, the hideous Lil-llik to ascend in the Hierarchy of the Nine Circles. Satan, embodied in a goat to please His wife, is amused by the events that threaten the very balance of the universe. As chaos erupted, the Mantra singing of 50 devotees and 1000 participating audience helped to save the universe (Burning Man Opera 2008).

The music for the piece was composed and played by Chris Cunningham and sung by Lili Oldfield, Pat Bregant, Sean Steward and Todd Nelson. This legendary story was performed by Justin Miller as Empress Zoë, Steffanos X as the High Priest of Hell, Sussy as the Devil, and Paradox Pollack as the master of ceremonies and choreographer. The Graces of Hell were represented by CC, Shari Greenfield, Martha Thomson and Susanne Couture. The opera did receive some criticism for being exclusive, too spectacular and not participatory enough, thus going against Burning Man's principles. As longtime Burner Chicken John remembers:

> They built a giant thing and then it was going to burn for 45 minutes but it burned for four hours. In the middle of the performance they had a hundred people, just freaking out, dancing like they were never going to dance again. There was a chant for four hours. If you've never seen hundreds of people, naked, dressed in glitter dancing—it was an amazing spectacle! When the opera was first being organized anyone could do whatever one wanted. [. . .] Watching it was really cool, but you could never do that again. You can never ask everybody to shut down for your event. That's not fair (Rinaldi 2006).

In 1997, the opera the *Daughters of Istar*, which took place on the Hualapai Playa on Saturday, 30 August, reenacted a 6,000-year-old Sumerian death-and-resurrection ritual. Still inspired by his visit to Turkey, Ozan wanted to produce an opera rich with design, mosaics and gold, so he based the Opera around the ancient mythological goddess of love, Ishtar. In an interview, Ozan tells the story of death and resurrection:

> Ishtar kills her lover Tamuz every year in winter—that's why we have the desolate landscape of winter—and then she starts remembering and desiring his company by the springtime. So then Ishtar goes to the underworld, rescues Tamuz and brings him back to life. The whole myth of Ishtar and Tamuz is a vision of the process of death and resurrection

> in Nature. Verses that were sung in the Opera were taken from the original that were written on stone 5,000 years ago, like the phrases of Ishtar in the role of desire, when Tamuz is in the underworld, she sings 'Who will plough my vulva?' for instance. Those are original old verses that we used. It was beautiful to be working with that material (in Kamakshi 2007).

The performance culminated in the immolation of the towering *lingam*. Once again, the theme of death, rebirth and the triumph of life through the mystery of reproduction infused the narrative.[5]

The 1998 *Temple of Rudra* was developed after Ozan's three-month trip to India, where he studied Hindu mythology and lived in temples. The Opera consisted of four different sects based on the humours. Documentarian Dean Mermell produced *Eye of Rudra* (2000), about the creation of the *Temple of Rudra* Opera. In an interview with Joyce Slaton in *Wired*, Mermell states that he believes the Burning Man Opera is a window into what he calls 'chaos culture'. He feels Burning Man is so overloaded with random imagery that those trying to document it often fail to capture the human side of the experience (in Slaton 2000). Rather than focus on the spectacle, Mermell investigated why performers, set builders, choreographers and costume-makers spent almost a year planning and rehearsing for a single performance in which the sets were set on fire and destroyed. After gathering 50 hours of footage, Mermell captured all that went into the staging of *Temple of Rudra*. Slaton reviewed the film:

> In a tribal ritual, hundreds of costumed performers, giant pyres, and stage sets formed of steel mesh and desert mud create 30-foot towers and human-insect figures. We get a glimpse of the people who made it happen as they discuss their roles, create their costumes and prepare for what seems more like a religious ritual than a theatrical performance. [. . .] People need a connection with something deeper than day-to-day life. We've lost touch with that need in modern times and that's the nerve that a ritual like Burning Man and the Opera has touched (ibid.).

According to Mermell, the Opera may appear to be a haphazard melee of performance and fire but to the participants it is a sacred experience and one that has been carefully thought out. For *Temple of Rudra*, a core group of leaders and organizers met for months in San Francisco to plan and coordinate the performance. During the week on the playa, the 'Opera Camp' recruited and initiated several hundred new performers by offering workshops that served as rudimentary rehearsals for the final performance.

In 1998, the Burning Man Opera Camp divided the participants into four groups, corresponding to the four humours: Cholerics, Phlegmatics, Melancholics and Sanguines, each with specific roles. The Cholerics' sacred tasks were to bear torches and light fires as they embodied such mythical characters as Kali, Loki, Legba and Medea. Their costumes—yellow body paint with elaborate tribal geometric patterns—accentuated their fiery, frantic, athletic movements. At the other end of the spectrum, the Phlegmatics' temperament was 'indifference' and they embodied the mythic figures and icons of Aphrodite, Isis, Atlantis and mermaids. Adorned with aqua body paint evoking their element water, their sacred duties were to sprinkle holy water and do Tai Chi. The Melancholics, represented by the element air, were adorned in black to represent angst, desire and melancholia. Their sacred duty—purifying the space with incense—was suitably gloomy yet somewhat elegant. Adorned with white body paint and black clothing, they were the keepers of the funeral pyre, ancestral skulls and the oracle. They represented mythic characters such as Orpheus, Osiris and vampires. And finally, the Sanguines, adorned in red, earthy body paint, represented fertility. Their movements were animal-like and their temperament was cheerful and lusty, capturing the essence of mythic icons such as Pan, Dionysus, wood nymphs and Ceres.

As people started arriving on the playa for the 1998 *Temple of Rudra*, each sect created its own initiation ceremony for neophytes. Pollack, who was a hierophant, remembers undergoing an initiation conducted by the Melancholics. Naked and blindfolded, he was led by four gothic women through a half-hour private ceremony, which he describes as a ritual of surrender that included drops and suspensions. It left him transformed. As he fondly recalls:

> The high point of Burning Man was being able to design and immerse people into these initiations. [. . .] When you actually bring intention there, and get people to focus on a specific energy, huge things happen and huge transformations happen. Aesthetically, the operas have this 'oh this is a bunch of naked fire dancers and fire spinning.' Visually, it is nothing. The fire, the spectacle, it is there. And the fact that a huge number of people are moving in space is awesome. But the ritual aspect was very powerful. I got to be a part of bringing people through (2008).

FIGURE 4.4 (ABOVE). Procession of the Melancholics, 1998. Courtesy of the Burning Man Opera.

FIGURE 4.5 (BELOW). Rehearsal, *Temple of Rudra*, 1998. Courtesy of the Burning Man Opera.

According to Pollack, the desert allowed for a complete commitment from each sect, and participants adopted the qualities of their group to such a degree that all were completely transformed into their roles.

In 1999, the Opera was the final act in a large-scale pageant, with the theme 'Wheel of Time' capturing the anxiety on the brink of the millennium. The layout of the performance area on the playa was designed as a giant clock face with 6 o'clock to 9 o'clock representing the immediate past of the twentieth century, from 6 o'clock to 3 o'clock signifying the future, and the open playa between 3 o'clock to 9 o'clock called the 'primordium' or the ancestral past. At the 3 o'clock position the *Le Mystere de Papa Loko* Voodoo Opera was performed.

This Opera was the result of year-round preparation, developing roles based on dramaturgical research inspired by Haitian culture. In order to fully grasp the nature of voodoo rituals, Ozan, Opera co-producer Twan Huljez, and Burning Man Opera director Christopher Fuelling spent several weeks in Haiti conducting intensive research; by the time they returned home, they were fully initiated voodoo priests. Based on their research, they fabricated a new religion symbolized by five different sects, each centred around a different *Lwa* (a voodoo spirit of which there are hundreds): the veiled white divas of Ezili, the fiery red warriors of Ogoun, the zombies of Guede, the temple builders of Couzin Azaka and the rainbow serpents Dambala and Aida. Each of the sects had a rich spiritual and organizational community that developed rites of initiation unique to itself. Participants were encouraged to join the sect that spoke to them personally.

One Opera sect, the Ounsi, led the entire Opera village in nightly singing, dancing and drumming ceremonies. Each Opera participant was required to undergo a personal initiation that had three successive phases. There were two sacred spaces: Tower Lakou and the Temenos around an open-air voodoo temple. At the centre of the Temenos, where the Opera was performed, stood the Portal of Life and Death, two 40-foot-tall totems covered with three-dimensional images depicting allegoric scenes of the cycle of life and death, supporting a large vertical pentagon between them. The ground was painted with a pentagon, and in each corner was a large pyre that was lit during the Opera. Haitian, African and Native American drumming and singing by the Ounsi created the sonic landscape for the performance.

The five *Lwas* acted out the three-part drama. Act 1, 'Calling the Heavens', portrayed the violence enacted by colonialism throughout history as well as how traditional African belief systems were forced to assimilate Western imagery and beliefs. The first phase of Act 1, 'Invocation of Alewa', was marked by the silent entrance of Alewa, the supreme ancient African deity and controller of the spirit realm—identifiable by his gruesome mask and giant erect phallus. In phase two, 'Calling of the *Lwas*', the performers sang five short Haitian songs while participants who represented deities performed a cleansing ritual. At this point, the five sects or *Lwas* entered with their altars, led by a choreographed flag dance and large puppets representing spirits. By the end of this phase, each sect had reached its pyre.

Act 2, 'Rites of Transformation', was set in current times and used three stages. Through the three phases of Act 2—'Requiem for Time', 'The Breach' and 'The Ordeal'—devotees or neophytes removed and burned all their clothing, as a form of ritual cleansing and a means of shedding their previous identities. Through performance, they were ritually reborn as the Children of Ogoun.

The third and final act, 'Ecstasy', was composed of three phases, beginning with the 'Shamanic Descent'. A haunting female aria broke the silence as all the naked and painted deities dropped to the ground. After the aria, the deities rose from the ground as slowly as Butoh dancers. As they descended from the stage, they set it on fire and initiated a call-and-response Afro-Haitian song. The Children of Ogoun ended the ritual with the swirling of torches as they set the Portal of Life and Death on fire, inviting participants to follow them symbolically into the new millennium.

The final full-scale Opera was performed on 1 September 2000, inspired by the mythology of the submerged city of Atlantis that fused history with fantasy. The Opera village boasted a three-story white pyramid with upper floors reserved for initiation rituals and Tarot readings; the building's surface served as a projection screen at night. In order to perform in the Opera, participants had to undergo an initiation ceremony into the Atlantean mysteries. In my interview with fire dancer Cassandra Marshall, she described Ozan's Opera as a rite of passage:

> We went through the whole rite-of-passage. [. . .] Literally, you are initiated at the Opera. They made us stay up all night. They took all our

FIGURE 4.6. Rehearsal, *Le Mystere de Papa Loko*, 1998.
Courtesy of the Burning Man Opera.

> clothes and made us stand naked for hours. The Opera was always Friday night and people would get dressed up. That was the first time that you would change out of your everyday clothes. [. . .] And you would get dressed up and go to the cocktail party and then to the Opera. And that was a big deal. Everyone would go to this. So, the rite-of-passage got you naked. You would go to the initiation of the Opera, which was usually two days before the actual Opera and you just never put your clothes back on. When you talk about rite-of-passage, it is really a big part of stripping your identity away and giving you a new one. They give you a new name. That is where a lot of people get their playa names whether they stick or not (2004).

According to Marshall's account, the initiation literally and metaphorically stripped the neophytes of their past lives, forced them to shed their clothes and their given names and adopt a new identity.

Of all the operas, *Atlantis*, also known as *The Great Rite of Cosmic Union*, was the most 'new age' in terms of material and content. The primary characters were the Atlantean hermaphrodites: the masculine moon-bull in blue body paint and the feminine sun snakes in radiant gold, each representing the two halves of a whole. Other characters included 16 flag bearers and 22 Tarot characters. The aim of the ritual reconstruction of Atlantean society was to evoke the spirit of 'pure love' and revisit an ancient understanding of sexuality and gender. This Opera was perhaps the most elaborate: performers even went so far as to invent their own language and alphabet, which then became the material for the Opera. The group created 'Sacred Collective Utterance for the Birthing of Atlantis', also known as SCUBA, to generate a collection of 'radiant' words before the group arrived at Burning Man. Each person then took a piece of paper with a word on it and repeated it over and over again—like a mantra—along with other chanters to create harmonic glossolalia or sacred nonsense. The chants and songs for the Opera were developed from these incantations.

Each night of the 2000 Burning Man, a 'vortex dance' served as a rehearsal for a dance that was ultimately performed as part of the Opera. The dance was influenced by Gabrielle Roth's 5 Rhythm Wave™, a simple meditation exercise that includes five types of movement qualities: 'flowing' (fluid and continuous motions), 'staccato' (percussive, sharp, angular motions), 'chaos' (dancing that is unplanned and spontaneous), 'lyrical' (the rhythm of trance and lightness) and 'stillness' (dancing slowly or being completely still) (Roth 2008).[6] The set design consisted of a 40-foot phallic *lingam* on one side of an oval space and at the other, about 200 feet away, an 18-foot *yoni* (or vagina) representing the male–female aspect of the universe. Midway between the organs stood the *kundalingam*, the meeting point of the two forces. With an overture, five acts—Entrance, Seduction, Chaos, Joy and Cosmic Union—and an epilogue, the Opera was an epic staging of the lunar bulls and solar snakes ceremonially dragging the flaming *lingam* to meet the *yoni* in ritualistic heterosexual intercourse. This corresponded with the 2000 Burning Man theme, 'The Body'.

After 2000, Ozan decided to take a break from the Opera to pursue other artistic ventures such as documentary filmmaking in India. The Opera crew maintained contact and, in 2001, created the Opera Diaspora Camp. Ozan returned in 2002 and created, on a much smaller scale, the *Ark of the Nereids* for that year's theme, 'Floating World'. He still creates large-scale sculptures for Burning Man each year and remains actively involved with the community. In an interview when he was asked how his 15-year involvement with the Burning Man Festival had affected his experience as an artist and individual, he responded:

> It changed my life. It was a big jump in my career. Burning Man is an art event of radical expression, participation and community. [. . .] When we have an idea, we talk to Larry Harvey, who is the number one guy there, 'Hey, Larry, we have this idea, what do you think?' 'Oh yeah, how much money do you need?' 'Ah, this much. Okay, it's yours.' [. . .] That's like a dream for an artist, and most of the Operas were just like that (in Kamakshi 2007).

Twan, a long-time Burning Man Opera collaborator, sees it as:

> A forum for self-expression, a place for willing people to lend their creative skills, in some cases skills they didn't even know they possessed. It is about ritual celebration, which is sorely lacking in modern society. [. . .] Somewhere along the road of time, we have lost this necessary activity. The opera is about having the time of your life (BMO 1999b).

A blog on the Burning Man Opera website posted audience responses, including these: 'I would definitely say that the Opera was my peak experience of the Burning Man Festival this year. What a beautiful and spirit moving performance!' 'I was totally mesmerized by the whole thing!' 'The Opera changed our lives!' (Burning Man Opera 2008). While the epic spectacles of the early operas no longer exist, other groups quickly took up the torch. The Burning Man Opera paved the way for both professional and amateur groups to create structured, rehearsed performances on the playa, although none would ever attain the magnitude and complexity of the Burning Man Operas.[7]

AWD and Xeno

Another group that brought spectacle to the playa, although not on as large a scale as the Burning Man Opera, is AWD. Founded by Raquel Reyna in 1996, AWD was dedicated to combining mixed media with dance, theatre, acrobatics and esoteric shamanic dream work. The original members of AWD included Raquel Reyna (dancer, fire dancer, acrobat, aerialist, writer and spoken-word performer), Richard 'Spark' Szpigiel (dancer, actor, writer, acrobat, aerialist, fire dancer, spoken-word performer, bass player and production designer), Robert 'Ra' Miller (dancer, writer, spoken word performer and visual artist), Scott Sterling (drummer/percussionist, composer, visual artist, graphic designer and writer), Lisa Reutter (singer, composer, lyricist, visual artist and accountant), Tiffany Parish (dancer, fire dancer, writer, scenic construction, executive producer and dance instructor) and Kimberly 'Dragonfly' Hampton (singer, guitarist, composer and lyricist) (Szpigiel 2006).[8]

Many AWD members came from the Stephanie Gilliland Dance Company. Gilliland, a dancer and choreographer with great athleticism and invention, was never bound by any of the constricting mores and aesthetic fads of her comrades, including Wim Vandekeybus, Mehmet Sander and Elizabeth Streb in the late 1980s and early 1990s. Gilliland's work:

> Sped flesh and bone toward chairs, tables and floors; bodies bouncing off the walls, over and through an open wooden cube, and even warped time by breaking the aggressive pacing with Gilliland's glacially slow, lyrical solos. There was also a lot of conscious gender neutralization through costuming and counterintuitive partnering (men in skirts, smaller women hefting and throwing the larger men (ibid.).

With the foundations of the Gilliland Company work, the group moved into the San Francisco performance scene. Reyna remembers:

> I started AWD in the living room of my house. I gathered together some amazing artists and we began to create. We did it for the joy, beauty and fun of creation. I had a big dream and vision for the group. Primarily, I wanted to create a group of artists who had the freedom to fully express themselves and delve deep into the psyche because there was the safety, the freedom and the encouragement to do so (2008a).

As a spiritual seeker, Reyna considers dance, music and all creative forms to be divine paths to spiritual awakening. She recalls, 'I saw AWD as a spiritual as well as creative journey' (2008b).

Upon their arrival in San Francisco, AWD heard of the recent demise of Contraband, a group of talented San Francisco performers who had created many site-specific pieces in a stylistic and thematic vein that the new group wanted to explore. AWD sought to occupy the niche Contraband had left open and take it to the next level. At first, they were accused of plagiarism even though they had never seen Contraband's work. As Szpigiel recalls, they were also charged publicly with being 'derivative', 'insouciant', 'irresponsibly loud', 'obscurely mystical', 'overly deep' and 'frivolous' (2008). However, they took this criticism with a pinch of salt and kept working to forge their own unique aesthetic.

The name 'AWD' looks like an acronym but does not stand for anything. They took the sound of the word 'odd' and the word 'awed' and combined the two to create 'AWD'. They made up five or six names that the acronym supposedly stood for so that the conflicting stories would generate an urban legend about the group: All Wheel Drive, Acrobatic Warrior Dancers, and so on (Szpigiel 2006).

At first, AWD received little support from San Francisco's dance and theatre community. However, they presented their first piece in January 1996 as part of an evening called *Local 7* at Footworks/Dancer's Group, which received a positive response. The untitled 10-minute piece was rehearsed for musical, choreographic and acrobatic precision but left open enough for improvisation (ibid.). Szpigiel describes it thus: 'The goal was to astound with thematic breadth, theatrical surprise, tonal contrast, emotional vulnerability, physical risk, startling proximity, jovial familiarity, non-linear fantasy and large-scale group ecstasy' (ibid.).

A year later, in 1997, under the fiscal umbrella of Dance Brigade, AWD produced their first full-evening show at Krissy Keefer's studio on 60 Brady Street. The response was favourable: 'After the first groundbreak-

FIGURE 4.7 (FACING PAGE). Aerialist Tiffany Parish at Art on Fire, San Francisco, 2006.
FIGURE 4.8 (ABOVE). Performers Tiffany Parish and Richard 'Spark' Szpigiel at the Vau de Vire Society Twisted Cabaret Tent at the Vegoose Festival, 2006.

Photographs by Sharlene Stephens.

ing show at the Brady Street Dance Center, we had a standing ovation at every show and realized, people really loved the excitement, the energy, and the power we were creating' (Reyna 2008a). The AWD shows finally drew the attention of Anon Salon's Joegh Bullock and Marcia Crosby, who host the Burning Man Decompression parties in San Francisco. Climate Theatre, a not-for-profit production company founded by Bullock and Crosby, produced AWD's show for a six-week run at San Francisco's Eureka Theatre in 1999, giving the group the momentum to continue their work. In the programme, AWD set forth their manifesto:

> The AWD Performance Band began forming in San Francisco in January of 1996 with the specific intention of changing the way artists work together to affect the world. This ever-evolving process empowers the individual by shedding the limiting factors of hierarchy, censorship, ego and separation, so that s/he may create from a place of truth, community, higher vibration, and magic. [. . .] Dare we change the world? (Schwartz and Szpigiel 1999).

Connections between the tech community and the fringe arts scene in San Francisco were solidifying, and with the tech boom came funds for the development and promotion of art and performance. Early on in their existence, AWD gained the attention of Craig Newmark, founder of Craigslist. He started his web juggernaut in 1995 out of his apartment in Cole Valley, next door to Tassajara Bakery where Szpigiel worked. Szpigiel served Newmark coffee and danish pastries in the mornings and they would discuss both of their projects. Newmark helped to advertise AWD shows to Craigslist users, which, during that first year, grew in number from about 1,200 to 2,500. On the cusp of the now-infamous Dotcom Boom (later to become the Dotcom Bust), the group benefited from the windfall and received lots of attention—at the same time, their rent jumped so high that they could no longer keep the warehouse where they had settled in to create their work. Literally overnight, their rent at The Vortex warehouse in the South of Market district (SoMa) went from $2,500 per month to $10,000.

Around the same time, members of the Burning Man community began supporting the group, including Larry Harvey and Crimson Rose who learned about them in 1998 (Szpigiel 2006). That year, the BMO offered them free performer tickets to bring their act to Center Camp. Reyna fondly recounts their first year at Burning Man:

> I think that one of our most powerful shows was actually the first year we performed at Burning Man. We were a modern dance company performing in theaters. I had never seen anything like Burning Man at all. What a shock! This was when Burning Man still had a main stage. They invited us to perform and paid for all of our tickets. They do not do this anymore, so I feel lucky we had this opportunity. They built a huge stage with scaffolding and professional lighting. It was amazing! We climbed all over that stage and at one point we flew from the top and leapt into the audience. We had a huge screaming crowd with dust flying everywhere. It was definitely a turning point in our careers. We developed a huge following and broke free from traditional modern dance venues and began to perform everywhere (2008a).

Performing in harsh desert conditions places extreme limitations on physical acts. The heat, the thin air and the alkaline playa dust take their toll. Szpigiel recalls their full-length show on the Thursday before the 1999 Burn:

> There were extremely high winds and it was very cold, dust blowing everywhere and people waited around for two hours. The playa dust was making the stage slippery. Trying to do intensely acrobatic physical performance in these conditions is challenging. The first year we went, in 1998, we performed on Friday at Center Camp. We also performed Thursday at Cataclysmic Megashear Ranch. A lot of the choreography involves falling flat on the ground. One of our performers breathed in the dust and got sick, ran off, and vomited and then returned to the performance. You think you are just in dust and sand, but the alkali, the crushed skeletons of the ancient sea animals can make you sick, and we had to deal with that every year. But you have an obligation to perform, especially when the Organization gave us free tickets, and if you don't come through, you jeopardize the relationship. But they are watching. If they are not satisfied with what was agreed upon, then they aren't going to give you free artist tickets (2006).

Performing these physical feats under the hazardous playa conditions forces the performers to engage with their bodies on a visceral, elemental level. Often, performers are covered with playa dust—wearing the playa on their skin. AWD's last year at Burning Man was 1999.

AWD had no central artistic director; each member had an equal say in the collaborative process. Originally, the troupe was modelled after a music band rather than a theatre company:

> When you auditioned into AWD, you made a commitment to be in a band, in the classic sense of the word. As in a band of brothers and sisters. It was called a performance band and everyone was a player. The guitarist doesn't tell the drummer what to play. Everyone creates together in harmony; there is nobody dictating, there is no single author. There is an overall communal vision. The individual elements are authored by each contributor. Ultimately, it all just fits together, like a collage. When there is no power struggle, the system works. But with the strong personalities required for an electrifying performance, there is often a duel of wills (ibid.).

They were interested in creating new kinds of virtuosity; the ability to sustain a full evening of nonstop multi-genre, multi-sensory, risk-filled, high-intensity entertainment, without the benefit of a formulized script and performed by a small cast of people who were the sole creators of their own individual contributions (ibid.). To generate original imagery and ideas, AWD would conduct 'dream labs' based on lucid dreaming (when the dreamer knows she is dreaming), a Yaqui Native American shamanic technique Reyna learned from her association with Don Miguel Ruiz, author of *The Four Agreements: A Practical Guide to Personal Freedom* (1997) and *Mastery of Love: A Practical Guide to the Art of Relationship* (1999). Reyna had met Ruiz before he was famous and he taught her the power of dreams and how to explore them through ceremony.

Once a month, AWD members would gather early in the evening to eat dinner and then to do all-night lucid dreaming workshops. Every hour, two people would get up and remain awake; then, after an hour, they would ring a chime softly. The idea was to cultivate a shallow sleep and prevent people from fully submerging into REM sleep. Lucid dreaming occurs during sub-REM sleep. Scott Sterling would drum for six to eight hours while people were sleeping—a sonic environment that would generate dreams—creating a conduit between the dream space and the physical realm. The dream labs were held over the course of a year at their Vortex warehouse space (Szpigiel 2006).

The dream labs culminated in free-association writing sessions and were mined for their imagery. AWD would discuss for 10 minutes, then write for 20, then discuss for 10 minutes, then write for another 20 and so on. A lot of the unedited material was incorporated directly into their performances, much like the Surrealist automatic-poetry techniques developed by Tristan Tzara. A lot of AWD's work was self-reflexive, combining the group's experience as dancers and performers with lucid dreaming techniques. AWD created an esoteric, dreamlike world, asking such reflexive questions as, 'What does it mean to be doing this kind of work?'

> Upon starting our journey together, we felt that, while these ideas signalled the dawn of our own artistic renaissance, they had probably been already embraced on some level by many artists in the world and that we would be taken as arrogant and dilettantish if we put them forward as any kind of creed (even though, amongst ourselves, we were convinced we were now going to shake the foundations of art and, Samson-like, bring down the rigid establishment of aesthetics) (ibid.).

AWD was sometimes criticized for being too introspective. In 1997, AWD wanted to expand and held auditions. The group, which began with seven people, had by 1998 grown to 15 members before settling at 11 members in 1999. With the addition of new members, the group took a new direction, shifting away from its original intentions. In fact, those who later formed Xeno became less and less interested in the structured dream labs.

The newcomers, while talented and visionary in their own ways, brought an electrifying (yet friction-inducing) rock-star attitude to the already ethereal mix and dissension formed in the group about artistic process (ibid.). By 1999, AWD was at the height of its popularity and idealism. What had begun with esoteric aspirations was threatening to become a bitter power struggle. Creative, personal and political tensions had left the seven original members with a bad taste in their mouths and ultimately each would bow out of active creation with AWD, beginning with the withdrawal of Reyna. Realizing she needed to discover her own spiritual path alone, Reyna left the performance world altogether and sought deeper aspects of her own path through the study of spiritual psychology. Szpigiel articulates the dilemma:

> As the parents and protectors of this vision, we feared destroying it with our possessiveness. [. . .] If we grappled over this gift, it would be torn asunder, leaving nothing but sad wreckage. It was, after all, a living, breathing thing. Painful as it was to say it to ourselves, who were we to claim ownership of it? [. . .] We had dreamed it into existence, watched it grow and attract new talent, and now, observed with what we hoped was equanimity as it moved inexorably toward entropy and disintegration (ibid.).

The idea arose to transform AWD into 'AWD Presents', a production company, and divide into two new groups: Genetyx and Ignus (later changed to Xeno, the Greek word for 'strange' or 'foreign'). Genetyx was all the people who had started AWD—Reyna, Reutter, Sterling and Szpigiel; Xeno consisted of Austin Lewis (composer, singer, lyricist, dancer, clown, production design and company manager), Tiffany Parish (choreographer, fire dancer, aerialist, Pilates instructor, company manager and accountant), Danielle Hooper (choreographer, aerialist, graphic artist, fire dancer, executive producer and accountant), Billy Conti (choreographer, acrobat, aerialist, fire dancer, writer, costume design and construction), Cooper Hazen (singer, fire performer, composer, writer, lyricist, actor and production design), Janine Fondiller (aerialist, fire dancer and Pilates instructor), Steve Pagan (new media producer, audio engineer, DJ and percussion) and Tom Byrne (video artist and performer) who would benefit from the production services of AWD Presents. Many performers, designers and musicians moved in and out of the group including Tommy Cappell, Aimee Flora, Joanna Fasl, Scott Sterling, Richard 'Spark' Szpigiel, Maria Kramer, Juri Koll, Reggie Ballard, Doug Rhodes, Shawn O'Docharty and Sharlene Stephens. From 2000 to 2006, Xeno performed at Burning Man at Center Camp Café and at Lush Camp, a popular San Francisco rave camp with a 10-year history.

Xeno's goal was to connect visual artists and performers within the community. In 2001, it acquired a warehouse space in the Mission district of San Francisco, which the group called the Xenodrome; it became a locus for circus, performance and dance parties and the venue for collaborations between Xeno, Mystic Family Circus and other dance, theatre and circus companies. In 2008, Xeno lost its space due to rising rents and, in October, officially disbanded as a company—with members at a crossroads, choosing to pursue their own artistic paths.[9] According to Reyna, Richard 'Spark' Szpigiel followed AWD from the beginning and all the way through Xeno, the most dedicated member of the group. 'He really saw it all' (2008b). As Szpigiel fondly remembers, 'It was the longest and most complicated relationship any of us have ever had' (2008).

El Circo

The performance troupe El Circo locks like a cross between Clan of the Cave Bear and Madmax. Weaving the ritualistic use of fire with fashion, burlesque and stilting, El Circo creates a desert chic that seems both ancient and futuristic. Adorned in feathered headdresses, beads, horns and ornate makeup, performers fuse animal and human spirits. As a contrast to the rapid spinning of poi and other recreational uses of fire on the playa, El Circo tames the flames and uses them like paint on a canvas to create visual tableaux.

Originally from Ashland, Oregon, El Circo is an umbrella organization that is part production company and part multimedia performance troupe. These various components exist throughout the year, but it is out on the playa at Burning Man that all these energies come together in one place (Dowlen 2005). Formed in 1999 by Matty Dowlen, Tiffa Novoa, Diego Novoa, Opie Snow Heyerman, Random Rab, Darrah Danielle, Karen Sachitano and Rueben Davis, El Circo started as a local performance fashion show.[10] Loosely inspired by Cirque du Soleil with a darker, underground edge, their aim was to create a visually compelling interactive spectacle. For its first performance, the stage was designed like a cake top with musicians above and the fashion show circling below (ibid.). El Circo attended Burning Man for the first time in 1999—not yet under the name El Circo—and presented its fashion show performance in a 44-foot dome built by the group. Its camp was very small and it gathered a group of people off the playa to be in the fashion show and model the innovative designs created by Tiffa Novoa. After the fashion show, the group performed a fire show outside the dome. The show was rehearsed in Oregon but the invited participants added an element of spontaneity.

The event was such a success that El Circo decided to bring their act back to the playa in 2000. This time they built a stage and a 60-foot dome. Unfortunately, there was a 70-mph dust storm and the dome was crushed. Learning from experience, Dowlen recalls they built a much stronger frame for their dome the next year. El Circo began to accumulate the various elements needed to create their show: a sound system, a stage, the costumes and the performers. Bringing over 150,000 dollars-worth of sound and lighting equipment out to the playa has its hazards: once the week in the desert is over, it takes months to clean the fine dust out of the system, but El Circo has a couple of investors who underwrite the cost of the equipment and its maintenance.

Reflecting on the state of the group in 2005, Dowlen said there were still a lot of the original members, although they were not as tight as they used to be. The group is now spread out over Oregon, San Francisco, Los Angeles, New York and Bali, Indonesia. Membership in El Circo is very fluid; members can come and go as they please. There are typically 10 core members, although hundreds may be involved in any given performance: Dowlen notes, 'I'd say it could range up to a hundred people who have been a part of it at some point, who put forth a lot of energy and are still a part of it sometimes. Some shows there are just five of us performers' (ibid.).

For Shawna Hofmann—performer, DJ and fashion designer—El Circo is a collective process, but she credits Tiffa Novoa as the visionary dreamer:

> Much of Tiffa's inspiration came from her dream world. The storyline would unfold through bouncing back her vision with the troupe members often by phone calls and emails; being that members resided in different places. Tiffa could tap into an individual's creature archetype. She would weave that archetype character into the story line with her passion in the unfolding of this vision. Tiffa's enthusiasm was compelling and infectious, inspiring the members to fully embody that creature character. Sometimes she would just dream up a character and manifest it into the form of a costume, then find the person to enter that costume (2008).

Novoa did all the sewing for the shows and paid for the costumes out of her own pocket. She recouped the money by selling them at her fashion shows off the playa. She researched art history, fashion, mythology and spirituality across cultures to construct her elaborate, otherworldly designs. As El Circo performer Malakai remembers, 'Tiffa took everyone's ideas to the fullest level of the vision and was able to articulate and manifest it' (2008). Like El Circo, the fire performance troupe Apsara draws inspiration from tribal culture and spirituality. Aspara has become a major group under the El Circo umbrella and often performs with them. Malakai, originally an Apsara member, believes the two groups gravitated towards each other because they were 'sisters in vision and style' and describes their collective aesthetic as 'tribal edgy magical high art' (ibid.). Both groups heavily influenced each other, fusing two similar aesthetics into one—each bringing their strengths to the table. Both Hofmann and Malakai concur that Apsara and El Circo were trendsetters in the Bay Area for fashion, design and performance, largely due to Novoa's unique aesthetic and the collective vision of the group.

Up until 2000, the Burning Man Opera was presented on Friday night with El Circo performing on Wednesday. But after the last Opera in 2000, the organizers let El Circo take the Friday night slot. In 2001, El Circo created *Iris*, bringing together performance troupes such as Apsara, Phoenix Rising and Infinite Chaos. For *Iris*, the biggest challenge, as Hofmann remembers, 'was getting everyone together at the same time for rehearsals on the playa when nobody is wearing a watch' (2008). Despite the challenges of having rehearsals on the playa, *Iris* was a huge success and showed the group their own potential to produce full-length large-scale events: 'It wasn't just a fire show; it wasn't just a fashion show; it was a huge theatrical spectacle' (Dowlen 2005).

El Circo performs year-round in Oregon and San Francisco at many underground events and clubs, as well as some corporate events. But these shows are not the size of the Burning Man spectacle. Dowlen feels that Burning Man is where he can really have fun because the landscape is so vast and full of potential: 'You have the unlimited input of 35,000 people who are open. [. . .] One of the things I wanted to bring to Burning Man that I felt was lacking was an organic tribal ambiance of fire and ritual' (ibid.). For Dowlen, the neon glow of the club atmosphere does not match the beautiful but treacherous landscape of the playa. He wanted to create something darker—as he puts it, 'a cross between Madmax and space galactic cowboys' (ibid.). In preparing for the show in 2005, Dowlen geared up for a change, a stripping away of layers, both metaphorically and physically:

> This show is going to be a lot different this year; it isn't going to be a fashion show. It's going to be more of a sun dance ritual. It is going to be a pulling away of the layers. This year's theme is 'Psyche'—bringing us down to our inner core. And after this big number, everything else is a celebration after that. It is definitely not going to be what we did last year (ibid.).

At about 10 p.m. on Friday night in 2005, I crossed the playa to the El Circo dome located at 10 o'clock and Esplanade. When I arrived, a few

FIGURE 4.9. Apsara and El Circo performer Malakai wearing Tiffa Novoa's headdress. Photograph by Austin Young.

FIGURE 4.10. Joshuadavid Reno sitting on a bed of nails.
Photograph by Sequoia Emmanuelle.

El Circo performers and tech people were doing last-minute preparations and there was a sense of excitement and anticipation. By that time the dedicated El Circo followers had filled up the first few rows; I was lucky to get a seat in the front row. At the back of the geodesic dome was a rental truck being used as the dressing room and I could see one or two women being adorned with elaborate headdresses of feathers, beads and shells as they were transformed into otherworldly animal spirits.

The crowd continued to build and the excitement became palpable, amplified by the loud pre-show music. By 10.30 p.m. the entire floor of the dome was filled. The audience garb was as ornate as El Circo's, with their desert chic feathers and beaded headdresses, elaborate makeup, decorated handmade costumes and the mandatory goggles. The luminous white playa powder of the desert gave dreadlocks, braids and tattoos a weathered, earthy complexion. It was an audience like no other—each member sporting their uniquely constructed alternative identity, their manifestation of a fantastical self. By 10.45 p.m., there was standing room only inside the dome and a crowd of art cars gathered around the outside forming a balcony of seats.

El Circo started pretty much on time as advertised in the 'What? When? Where?' event guide, a rare occurrence on the playa. The pre-show music was provided by a solo female singer, Lily Rose Love, wearing black high heels, a black skirt and white shirt, with her own live backup band. The stage was a six-pointed star elevated about two feet above the playa floor. A large drum was suspended from the ceiling of the dome. An MC ringleader, Leighton Kelly of the Yard Dogs Road Show, introduced the show. In a deep, sarcastic and cynical voice he announced, 'Welcome to El Circo Dome!' He sang several songs to set a dark carnival mood and was then lifted on a large metal ring, where he sang a throaty, melancholy number. Then the lights went out; a spotlight circled the dome as music blasted from the speakers. Auberon Schull entered in a long, multicoloured skirt and feathered mask, her arms outstretched. In the dark, two people ran in and attached her to a cable. The strobe lights flashed to create a frenzy of light as the music grew louder and faster.

The dancer in the feathered headdress rose like a phoenix, undulating and moving both sensually and violently like a trapped bird. Performers with fire fingers and other flaming fire tools slithered around the frenzied bird. Shanti entered topless with elegant flaming fire wings and perched like an eagle on a stool. Then Simone Thayer, Shawna Hofmann, Jonny Cota, Chris Sia and Auberon Schull entered in elaborate feathered headdresses and costumes flirting seductively with the audience. The stage was a frenzy of flesh and fire. One by one, the performers left. Dowlen entered and did an elegant dance with a flaming staff, throwing the staff into the air and catching it as it spun. Then Simone Thayer followed him on stilts with huge fire fingers that were ignited by a fire dancer (see Cover image). The mood shifted when Chenoa, a Liza Minnelli-esque performer in stilettos, fishnets, hot pants and corset, did the famous Ann Corio flaming parasol burlesque act. At one point, the feather in her hat caught fire but it was quickly extinguished by the fire-safety person and she continued her act unscathed.

After the flaming parasol dance, four girls (Phoebe Minona aka Gypsy Joblinsky, Shay Askins aka Shenandoa Sassafras, Victoria Hawkins aka Tuesday Blue and Zoe Jakes) from the Yard Dogs Road Show, dressed in jailhouse costumes and using chairs as props, did a burlesque striptease, slowly ripping off their uniforms to reveal sexy lingerie. Next, a deep-voiced burlesque singer, Shay Askins (aka Shenandoa Sassafras), entered in a white dress, with the same four dancers, wearing white panties and pasties and deftly manipulating traditional Sally Rand burlesque white feather fans. They danced the fine line between stripping and the art of burlesque, flirting with the audience with winks and sexy gestures—moves that conform to the 'revealing less is more' dictum of traditional burlesque. For the finale, the entire cast reappeared onstage as the crowd roared with appreciation and gave a thunderous ovation. The performance lasted for 45 minutes; afterward, the audience was invited onstage to dance with the cast. A huge dance party erupted; gradually, the cast separated and, one by one, left the stage—a seamless transition from the stage performance to a dance party that lasted well into the night.

While El Circo calls themselves a circus, like many of the troupes in the new American alternative circus movement, the group borrows circus-like techniques, such as fire performance and stilting, and infuses them with cabaret and burlesque, creating a hybrid form. The level of training and expertise within the group ranges from amateur to professional; among them are gymnasts, modern dancers, belly dancers and fire dancers. Some started with El Circo as novice performers and found a new character that they developed over the years. The group rehearses the show primarily in San Francisco and Ashland. Parts of the 2005 circus had been performed for six months, but the whole show didn't come together until the group got to the playa. Storing all their props, costumes and equipment in a 20,000-square-foot warehouse space in San Francisco (donated to them by Obscure Digital) gives El Circo a lot of resources to pull from. They rent the truck that transports the equipment to the playa, but they own all the RVs that form the circle around their camp's central shade structure. They usually get to Black Rock City a few days early to set up the dome and camp, and to rehearse. The group does not get funding from Burning Man except indirectly: in 2005, it received 10 free tickets and 30 discounted tickets at $145 each. To raise the $25,000 needed to bring their act out to the desert, El Circo holds fundraising parties year round.

While no one working in the El Circo dome gets paid, various performance-related expenses are covered. As Dowlen explains: 'Everything is being donated—everyone is giving time, talent and energy. It is really the giving part of it. And that's what makes it fun' (ibid.). When I asked Dowlen if he felt that Burning Man had shaped their aesthetic, he replied:

> We saw what we liked, we admired it, we adored it and we became it. And then we added on our own touch. I like to think that we have our own aesthetic that has kind of evolved out here. One of the hardest parts is that people feel it is hard to enter into what we've created sometimes. It gets so passionate that it is a pretty scary thing to walk into (ibid.).

In Malakai's opinion, the 2007 show *Eye of the Storm* was the most successful and ambitious performance to date. Based around themes of war and destruction, the performance began with a political war video, followed by an old opera song about two warring countries. At that point, Shawna Hofmann entered wearing a cheetah headdress and danced with fire fingers while Rigzin Tromge sang a Tibetan chant. As Malakai recalls, 'It felt ancient and modern at the same time' (2008). Then Malakai entered in a huge Native American headdress doing a dance about the power of human struggle. Like all of their shows, technology is mixed with ancient spirituality and pagan elements that are nature- and spirit-based. For Malakai, the work evokes the 'ancient future', fusing images of the past with dreams of the unknown future. The show had special significance for the group because Tiffa Novoa, their visionary leader and collaborator, died in an unfortunate accident in Bali, Indonesia, 16 October 2007, only two months after the show. Novoa was living and working in Bali with her daughter and partner Evan Sugerman on their fashion line 'Ernte' when the accident occurred.

In retrospect, Malakai sees their magnum opus on the playa as a rite of passage, a culmination of Novoa's creative life. The *Eye of the Storm* deeply affected people both as a ritual and as a performance. At one point during the performance, Joshuadavid Reno (aka Faux Pas), was suspended with hooks in his back as a ritual sacrifice. Retrospectively, Malakai sees each moment in the show as a premonition and rite of separation, although of course unaware of the significance at the time (ibid.). The group held a public memorial service for Novoa at the Tropical Chime in San Francisco, followed by a private ceremony at Rigzin Tromge's property in Northern California, where they spread Novoa's ashes. In 2008, El Circo did not return to Burning Man as a group, finding it too difficult without Novoa. The future of the group and the direction it will take is uncertain—only time will tell. For now, it is a time of collective healing and renewal.

Cirque Berzerk

Directly across the playa from El Circo, a very different type of circus was set up at the 2 o'clock location. Cirque Berzerk, of all the troupes that perform at Burning Man, comes closest to evoking a traditional circus while maintaining the rough, homemade quality of the first troupes in the new American alternative circus movement. Cirque Berzerk is the co-creation of Kevin Bourque (a drummer in the successful Burning Man performance group The Mutaytor) and Suzanne Bernel. Like most other groups, Cirque Berzerk holds fundraisers to underwrite the trip to the desert. It held a dinner theatre fundraiser in 2005 with a six-course meal and circus performances to be able to purchase its $15,000 circus tent, which it brought along for the first time to the playa in 2005.

In 2005, I entered the large, brand-new tent through the only entrance—a single tent flap. I listened as the tent creaked and heaved, assaulted by the howling wind outside. The tent was a refuge from the harsh desert conditions. I introduced myself to Neal Everett, an aerial artist from Los Angeles who started out as a dancer. He became involved with Cirque Berzerk when Bernel, his friend and aerial student, asked him to join. He had been planning to attend Burning Man for several years and the circus gave him the opportunity.

Also in the tent was Eric Newton, an aerial artist who used to perform with Cirque du Soleil.[11] Newton was doing yoga stretches in the corner, apparently oblivious to the commotion around him. I sat quietly as Newton effortlessly lifted himself up the silk onto the trapeze, then gracefully shifted his stout muscular body from formation to formation. Newton danced 20 feet in the air without a safety net, moving with precision, grace and confidence; two spotters stood below in case of an accident. The people inside the tent froze in silence to focus on Newton's practice session. After five minutes of continuous movement on the static trapeze, Newton lowered himself to the ground, barely breaking into a sweat. Everyone clapped and cheered.

The next day, Everett had just finished rehearsing when I arrived. I watched Bernel practice—one of Newton's students, her movements were graceful but her sweaty and reddened face indicated the incredible effort she put into performing her routines on the suspended silks. In the middle of the day, the desert conditions clearly took their toll on performers.

During my interview with Newton, Bernel called a meeting for all the performers to review the sequence for that evening's performance. About 18 people assembled around the stage as she read over the order of events. In contrast to El Circo, Cirque Berzerk was a group of independent artists who were pulled together for this performance and 2005 was their first year on the playa marking the birth of Cirque Berzerk. As Bernel read the script to the company, there was tension and anxiety among the performers. Their performance had been delayed by two days because severe winds had stalled the tent installation.

Later that night, I returned to the Cirque Berzerk tent to see the dress rehearsal. The energy was chaotic and frenetic as they finished preparations for their first performance on the playa. A few techies ran around doing last-minute sound and lighting checks; performers milled about, stretching and socializing. Bernel tried to get everyone together for a dress rehearsal—their only one. Show time was at 11 p.m., the same time as El Circo's show. Cirque Berzerk and El Circo would be vying for the same audience from opposite ends of Black Rock City.

FIGURE 4.11. Cirque Berzerk, 2007.
Photograph by Suzanne Bernel.

Newton, always serious, warmed up with total concentration. He changed the silks, climbing to the top of the tent on the sweaty, dirty rehearsal silk to attach the fresh, clean performance silk, dangling effortlessly upside down from the 25-foot rig. In one corner, a juggler was practising with three pins. A woman practised her hoops in another. The tent heaved and moaned with the desert winds of a dust storm swirling around outside, and the tent flap fluttered as dust was driven through the small cracks. Where the lighting was being focused, large dramatic shadows of the rig loomed across the white canvas tent. About 25 performers gathered around Bernel, talking through the show sequence for the second time.

To one side of the tent was an installation of five jars set upon red velvet, filled with what looked like animal organs. A recorded voice muttered indecipherably, creating a creepy freak show feeling. The floor of the tent was covered with long plastic sheets and duct tape to keep the desert dust out, but, over the course of the week, the playa had filtered in, forming a thin layer of white dust. Techno blared from the rave camp next door, but inside Cirque Berzerk's tent the level of concentration and anticipation was palpable.

Cirque Berzerk borrowed some traditional circus techniques to define the performance space, including the 42-foot Astley ring. The scenario featured Kevin Bourque as the ringmaster/MC. He evoked a turn-of-the-twentieth-century seedy freak-show announcer, promising a dark and terrifying show full of oddities and marvels. The opening act was Everett on a flying strap, a daring performance to Marilyn Manson's *Sweet Dreams*, a dark rendition of Annie Lennox's original. Everett was whisked into the air, flying in spirals around the perimeter of the ring below. In describing his piece, Everett said that he chose the music to capture the dark carnival atmosphere of Cirque Berzerk, which emulates a 1920s burlesque style and lives up to their motto: 'circus of assault' (2005).

Unlike El Circo, which has one person design the entire show including all the costumes, Cirque Berzerk performers create their own costumes and do their own makeup. Everett decided to wear something black and blue with feathers coming out of his hair and elaborately painted eye makeup, appropriating Cirque du Soleil's dramatic aesthetic. Everett's act was followed by eight others that included juggling, hooping, clowning, music and aerial acts. The final number was Newton on a static trapeze. After the circus, Bourque's band, *Skin*, played in the Cirque Berzerk tent while Everett and Bernel continued to perform aerial acts.

Since buying its own tent, Cirque Berzerk has received offers to perform elsewhere, offering Everett hope for the future of the organization: 'Now it looks as if the circus is going to continue. It is being born. It is the very beginning of the creation process for us' (ibid.). It also gives the performers encouragement and holds out the possibility that they will be able to continue with their work. Both Newton and Everett started their aerial work late in life, but both found they had a natural ability and learned the ropes quickly. Everett has performed with Newton's Eye of Newt Circus and Dream Circus and hopes to find a circus home some day. His dream circus would tour in a circus tent, travelling from place to place and staying in each location for a month—just like the Ringling Bros and Barnum & Bailey. When I interviewed him, Everett was transitioning from working on a series of random jobs to working full-time as an aerialist. In 2008, Everett was invited to a one-month workshop as an aerialist for Julie Taymor's *Spiderman* on Broadway. Now, he is torn between the seduction of lucrative commercial work and the opportunity to shape and create his ideal circus with Cirque Berzerk (ibid.).

Newton is a freelance aerialist, an actor and a clown. He performed a five-person rope act with Cirque du Soleil in the 2002 North American tour of Quidam. He has also worked with Cirque L'Eloize and Make-A-Circus, and now owns his own company in Los Angeles, Eye of Newt Circus (Newton 2005). In 2002, teaching at a circus school in Hollywood, Newton met Bernel who was a student in one of his aerial silk (also known as Tissu) classes. Bernel is a professional photographer, who started being an aerialist as a hobby—one that she is extremely dedicated to and passionate about. She would like to transition to becoming a full-time aerialist. In 2004, Newton and Bernel went to Burning Man, bringing two freestanding rigs with them. Newton had been hearing about Burning Man for a long time, but corporate gigs scheduled at the end of August prevented him from attending.

Between performances Everett and Newton rehearse their routines on the static trapeze or silks, stretch, do yoga and condition their muscles. For an aerialist, the training never stops. Going to the gym is not typical for aerialists, but Everett goes to build strength in his arms. 'We are always training,' he says. 'Get in the air, work on more choreography. Stretching, conditioning. Working on toning. You build a lot of strength being up there' (2005).

On the playa, there is a broad spectrum of talent and commitment, from novices to professionals like Newton and Everett. What does Burning Man offer these professionals, what attracts them to perform for free? Newton responds:

> I love the underground scene of it. The most meaningful thing is the art for art's sake, the people being kind for no reason. [. . .] It is a total disconnect from the commercial world. As much of what I do is about the joy of performing, the giving and receiving from an audience, it is all really based on commercialism. At Cirque du Soleil, tickets are very expensive and all circuses have to sell tickets to survive. And in Los Angeles everything is at the mercy of the industry. If you are trying to do theatre there, you have to put money and creative energy into it; unless someone is signing a big check, which is rare. You break your back trying to get your work out there. As far as a collection of artists, these people do amazing things in their 'real' lives that allow them to do this. Gabe is a rocket scientist and an amazing DJ. Sue is an amazing photographer. Evan is an editor. And there are others that are professional aerialists, circus performers and dancers. This is all about their passions. We wanted to make something unique and special (2005).

Newton has strong opinions about the influence of Cirque du Soleil on the new American alternative circus and on how budding amateur troupes pose a threat to professional performers such as himself and Everett. Cirque du Soleil has given the public an awareness of a different kind of circus aesthetic, unlike that of Ringling Brothers and other more traditional circuses. The growing popularity and acceptance of circus arts is flooding the market with performers at many different skill levels. Unfortunately, amateur performers, who often will perform for free, jeopardize the income of professionals. But, ultimately it is passion that drives these performers, both amateur and professional, to spend months preparing and planning acts

FIGURE 4.12 (FACING PAGE). Neal Everett and Tari Schultz on a flying strap, 2008. Photograph by Pixie Vision Productions.

for the desert. They want to share with a community of likeminded people who give and receive with no financial gain.

In 2008, Cirque Berzerk developed *Beneath*, its first full-length circus, loosely based on the story of Orpheus. It erected its big top in the State Historic Park in Los Angeles for four sold-out performances from 24 to 27 July.[12] It added two more performances, which also sold out. Cirque Berzerk has now incorporated to become a limited liability company (LLC) to professionalize the group and its performances. During the year it performs individual acts at corporate and private events and parties, with the goal of supporting the entire company year round. Bernel's aim is to tighten the company to become as professional as possible by skill-sharing and continuous training (Bernel 2008). The company has received financial backing to remount *Beneath* in Los Angeles in 2009 for a two-month run in a tent three times the size of their first one (Everett 2008).

Cirque Berzerk returned to Burning Man with its circus and tent in 2006, 2007 and 2008. In 2006, Cirque Berzerk joined forces with several other performance groups—Gooferman, Vau de Vire Society and The Mutaytor—to form a large circus camp called the 'Red Nose District'. In 2008, the camp of 150 members featured the big top tent, a stilt bar and a private backstage area called 'The Nome'—a shaded industrial tent structure that had a full kitchen, three shower stalls, a massage room, a chill-out lounge and a dining room. In order to enter 'The Nome', you needed to have a laminated badge that said 'staff', which all 150 camp members were given. Each member paid $120 to camp in the 'Red Nose District', which gave them access to private porta-potties, the kitchen, the showers and the chill-out area. Centrally located at 5 o'clock and the Esplanade, the camp had a steady stream of pedestrian traffic. During the day, the big top tent served as a cool shaded chill-out space and at night, as the nexus of circus performance in Black Rock City.

Each night, the 'Red Nose District' hosted a happy hour at the stilt bar followed by a series of performances by Gooferman, The Mutaytor and Vau de Vire Society. Thursday night, Cirque Berzerk presented segments from its circus show *Beneath*, which included cabaret dancing, fire performances, a five-person aerial act, balancing acts, solo silk and static trapeze acts and sword swallowing. Over 1,000 people crammed into the big top, spilling out onto the playa in every direction. In less than four years, Cirque Berzerk has emerged as one of the most successful performance groups to come out of Burning Man, its success continuing year round beyond the borders of Black Rock City.

Counter-Study: Cockroach Theatre

In contrast to groups like AWD, Xeno, El Circo and Cirque Berzerk, the Cockroach Theatre from Las Vegas presented a scripted play, Richard Foreman's *Brain Damage*, the only one on the playa in 2005. It performed every night at 10 p.m. and midnight. One night, around midnight, I got a place on a couch in the front row of the small audience. The gathering filled the two rows of couches and chairs, with two rows of standing room. The set was an enclosed plexiglass room with a red carpet, bordered on all four sides by a 2-foot-deep playing area. There were two actors outside of the room and one actor inside. The performance began with the actor inside the plexiglass room reciting Foreman's text as the other actors silently moved around the exterior. Two masked figures entered the interior space and began to manipulate the man inside the plexiglass as if he were a puppet. The narrator on the outside talked about how the man inside the box did not know what was happening to him, that he was being manipulated. Many audience members fell asleep, lulled by the monotonous dialogue. By the end of the performance, about 10 people were left and passersby on the Esplanade strolled by without a second glance. The movement and acting were amateurish, not engaging in any way.

Brain Damage failed because the actors spoke the text disconnectedly, with no physical or emotional engagement. The play's lack of spectacle was no competition for the bright fiery orbs of the poi dancer next door or the exploding sculpture across the Esplanade. As a counter-study, the Cockroach Theatre demonstrates the challenges of producing predominantly text-based theatre on the playa, even when the text is by someone of the calibre of Richard Foreman. In order to hold the attention of an audience in a place with so many distractions, the work needs to be spectacular, awe-inspiring, visual, visceral and physically demanding. Text—especially one as complex as Foreman's—requires the audience to actively listen and participate intellectually. At Burning Man, if a performance is not visually engaging, people lose interest and move on to the next thing.

One of the reasons circus and fire performances thrive in this environment is that their visual allure and daredevil quality keep audiences gripped and engaged. Words will not hold a Burning Man audience unless they are delivered through a megaphone or surrounded by carnivalesque spectacle.

The kaleidoscopic flurry of activity on the playa forces performers to be bigger and more spectacular in order to seize and keep the crowd's attention. While each show does not compete for financial box-office gain, they do compete for attention, what Mikel calls an 'attention economy' (2008). This popularity contest has inspired a rigour and aesthetic that often follows artists and audiences off the playa and back into the 'default' world, creating a fluid cross-pollination. When I asked Szpigiel (AWD/Xeno) what the hallmarks of performance at Burning Man were, he replied:

> Part of it is an unfettered sexuality. An aggressive, almost fetishistic sensuality and for someone who has never explored that, it starts to pervade their work. It's wearing less and tighter things than you've ever worn before while still doing serious dance. So the idea is that the aesthetic of the performance style creates an end-of-the-world feeling. It's very post-apocalyptic. [. . .] All this is already there in San Francisco and has been going on since the 1960s. It's the logical conclusion, taking these ideas to the desert. [. . .] Burning Man came from San Francisco. More than anything else, what Burning Man has done is create a community in San Francisco. [. . .] Your whole life becomes that. Everyone becomes connected in that way in the city. It's a motivational trigger more than anything else (2006).

Performance groups have changed their names and/or membership, recycled alumni, broken up and started over again; some are quite well known and some have been resigned to oblivion—but they all have found a voice and a home in Black Rock City. AWD frequently used dream labs to generate original material, while performers in Cirque Berzerk have spent years training to perform on the trapeze and aerial silks. El Circo spends months conceptualizing and rehearsing their shows. Once on the desert, the performers need to adjust to the fierce winds and dust. They warm-up accordingly, preparing for physically rigorous work in unfamiliar conditions. All the preparation, workshops and training pays off when the crowds show their appreciation for the performances by saluting the performers with whistles and cheers.

While no money is exchanged, most performers feel that the gratitude and praise they receive far exceeds any monetary value. It is this bond, this feeling of acceptance by the Burning Man community, that draws these groups and performers back year after year. The performances have a lasting impact, as the performers return to their local communities often much more famous than before playing at Burning Man. Many individuals cohere into groups at Black Rock City and continue at home what they started on the playa. Groups such as the Burning Man Opera, AWD, El Circo and Cirque Berzerk bring to Burning Man all the spectacle of Cirque du Soleil but with a much darker, sinister and apocalyptic aesthetic, pushing fire performance, trapeze, stilt-walking, hooping, aerial silks and burlesque to new and risky frontiers. At Burning Man, the new American alternative circus rises to new heights.

Notes

1 The modern circus was born in 1770 when Philip Astley of Great Britain opened his 'Riding House' in London, featuring a circus ring that was 42 feet in diameter, the size still predominantly used in circuses. Astley gradually added variety acts to his horse show, including a pyramid of acrobats, tightrope walkers, jugglers, mimes, dancing dogs and clowns derived from the Commedia Dell'Arte (Fenner and Fenner 1970: 15).

2 Founded in 1999 by Carmenchu Caballero, Tekeba Bantu and Moondoggy, the Bantu Mystic Family Circus is a nomadic, healing arts circus collective, weaving together myth, circus and healing arts. It performed at Burning Man in 2000, 2001 and 2002 and has, over time, evolved into an umbrella organization with over 300 members, acting more like a talent agency than a circus (Pollack 2008). In an interview with J. Dee Hill, Moondoogy remarked, 'We're the most permeable membrane in show business. [. . .] Anyone who thinks they're a part of Mystic Family Circus probably is' (in Hill 2004: 94). This inclusivity echoes the Cacophony spirit of 'You might already be a member.'Mystic was spawned by an event called the Yoga Tai Chi Collective, comprising a Tai Chi class taught by a man named Patrick Luther King, followed by yoga and then a dance party. Today, Mystic Family Circus brings together jugglers, dancers, capoeira dancers, DJ sound poets, Tai Chi practitioners, stilt-walkers and aerialists, drawing their inspiration from myths and stories from around the world to create a unique theatrical experi-

ence. Mystic has been compared to Cirque du Soleil, not in terms of skill but in its flamboyance and the emotional content of its performances. Mystic Family combines storytelling with a contemporary social awareness, mixing and matching epics from a variety of sources and cultures. Its process usually begins with a story about raising eco-consciousness and from there incorporates circus acts. Its mission is to educate audiences about bio-diesel and other ecologically-minded projects such as the water car, using transcultural circus performance techniques and incorporating storytelling from Africa and the West.

3 At Burning Man, Flam Chen, Apsara, the Mutaytor, Groove Hoops, Firefly Aerial Dance, Clan Destino, BodyCartography, Circus Redickuless, the Bindlestiff Family Cirkus, Gooferman, Vau de Vire Society and Capacitor are among the myriad of groups that have performed on the playa and are part of the 'new American alternative circus' movement.

4 The All Soul's Day Procession in Tucson, Arizona, inspired by Mexico's Dia de Los Muertos, was founded in 1990 by Susan Johnson and organized by Many Mouths One Stomach, a non-profit arts collective. Johnson ran it for seven years before it was taken over by Nadia Hagen, founder of Flam Chen. Over 20,000 participants walk the 2-mile procession route, ending in a ritual burning of an urn filled with hopes, offerings and wishes that are placed there by participants in the procession (Many Mouths One Stomach 2008).

5 The principle Opera organizers and performers were Pepe Ozan, Leon Rosen, Steffanos X, Adawna De Vine, Glenda Soler, Shari Greenfield, Kara Blanc, Rina Hedly Wells, Kim Leary, Brynne Cortez, Morgan Raimond, Al Honig, Sean Stewart, Christine Heath and Leo Nash.

6 Gabrielle Roth developed the 5 Rhythms Movement Practice: a 'simple, powerful moving meditation that anyone—of any age, size, or physical ability—can practice. There are no steps to follow, no choreography to learn, no way to do it wrong. [. . .] Just like light, sound or ocean waves, a dancing body when moving freely passes through 5 distinct rhythmic patterns. These patterns continuously repeat themselves in a wave of motion' (2008).

7 Founded by Ronnie Nelson, the Rock Opera attempts to recreate the epic scale of the Burning Man Opera. The performance in 2008 was disappointing to say the least. It consisted of a series of fire performers scaling a pyramid structure. It lacked any kind of narrative or the complexity of Ozan's operas. The performance culminated in the immolation of the pyramid. It was not well received.

8 Other members included Austin Forbord, Aimee Flora, David Schwartz, Austin Lewis, Sophia Mallie-Ferrera, Billy Conti, Cooper Hazen, Shelley Trott-Forbord, Cheryl Graham, Janine Fondiller, Leighton Kelly, Danielle Hooper, Tom Byrne, Joegan Bullock, Helen Sebastian Chang, Doug Rhodes, Reggie Ballard, Eenor, DJ Steve Pagan, Tobias Roberson, Eliot Bates, DJ Goldilox, Piki Chappell, DJ 80 Bug, Channel 23, Marcia Crosby and Scott Paul Cannon (Szpigiel 2008).

9 As of 2008, Austin Lewis, Tiffany Parish and Cooper Hazen are currently part of The Bohemian Carnival with Vau de Vire Society. Billy Conti is now part of New York's bustling fashion industry as a designer and pattern-maker. Danielle Hooper continues to be a successful accountant in San Francisco. Tiffany Parish and Janine Fondiller work as Pilates instructors in San Francisco. Parish is also a member of Vau de Vire Society & The Nekiya (with Scott Sterling), a belly dance group in Oakland, CA. Richard 'Spark' Szpigiel left Xeno in 2006 and is currently a performer, rigger and stagehand in New York City. Tom Byrne and Juri Koll are both in film production in Los Angeles and San Francisco. Steve Pagan is a DJ, new-media producer and web optimization specialist in New York City. David Schwartz is a Broadway producer and entertainment lawyer in New York City. Kimberly Dragonfly is a musician/composer/producer in North Carolina. Lisa Reutter is an accountant in Oakland, CA. Raquel Reyna received her Master's degree in Spiritual Psychology. She is a life coach in Los Angeles. Austin and Shelley Trott-Forbord are filmmakers in San Francisco, CA. Tommy Cappell is a drummer/composer/producer in Oakland, CA. Aimee Flora is a trapeze artist in Berkeley, CA. Scott Sterling is composer and bandleader for The Nekiya, belly dance company in Oakland, CA. Leighton Kelly is a primary performer in the Yard Dogs Road Show (Szpigiel 2008).

10 As of 2008, El Circo members include Shawna Hofmann, Malakai, Opie Snow Heyerman, Joshua Brott, Rab Clinton, Darrah Danielle, Joshuadavid Reno (aka Faux Pas), Karen Sachitano, Jason Bernard, Eli (Budge), Benny Cochran, Denise Guillot, Rylan Heyerman, Jochen Ziems, Rueben Davis, Chris Houchin, Giselle Pereira, Gaston Albanel, Siouzen Kang, Rigzin Tromge, Sage, David Altmire, Ooah Mayer, Laura Howett, Lorin Ashton (aka Bassnectar), Chris Sia, Simone Thayer, Tom Sepe, Shmichael Norris, Auberon Shull, Jonny Cota, Cassidy Haley, Evan Sugerman, Ashley Knight, Jan Hilmer, Indeara St Claire, Neptune Merrick, Carolyn Craft, Tzaddi Heatherstone, Tyone Raymond, Andrew Jones, Ana Sia, Alesha Rognes, Lycee LaChance and Rainen Janes among others (Dowlen 2008).

11 Eric Newton left the Cirque du Soleil North American tour of Quidam in 2002 for personal reasons and rejoined them in 2008 (Everett 2008).

12 Performers in *Beneath* (2008) included Suzanne Bernel, Kevin Bourque, Neal Everett, Kystal Bell, Jen Shields, Roo Ruane, Tami Beers, Briana Hamilton, Mark Wildman, Eric Gradman, Chantel Durelli, Gabrielle Scott and Happe Roberts, among others.

PART THREE

REALMS OF RITUAL

The Lamplighter procession with large puppet, 2002.
Photograph by Gregory Zabilski.

CHAPTER 5
REINVENTING RITUAL IN BLACK ROCK CITY

FIGURE 5.1. Ken Hamazaki performing a Japanese tea ceremony on the playa, 2003. Photograph by Gabe Kirchheimer.

> Underlying all rituals is an ultimate danger, lurking beneath the smallest and largest of them, the more banal and the most ambitious—the possibility that we will encounter ourselves making up our conceptions of the world, society, our very selves. We may slip in that fatal perspective of recognizing culture as our construct, arbitrary, conventional, invented by mortals (Moore and Myerhoff 1977: 18).

> The core ritual around the Man was the raising and the burning. Essentially, we didn't have to assign any meaning to it. We did it because it was fun. What we have done, as time goes on, is evolve rituals. There are two methods we have come to employ in formulating ritual: work and play (Harvey 2001).

Black Rock City is a rich environment where new and hybrid rituals that draw on traditional practices abound. Borrowing, reworking and refashioning ritual practices, Black Rock citizens create a patchwork that forges the unique, heterogeneous identities of the participants into a temporarily harmonious community. The spectrum of reinvented ritual in Black Rock City runs from the parodic—tongue-in-cheek, comic rituals—to the efficacious—serious ritual practice that is meaningful to the participants. Many engage in both forms throughout the week at Burning Man.

Each year, the week begins with the Opening Fire Ceremony at sunset on Monday at the Center Camp cauldron, led by Crimson Rose, one of the six Black Rock City LLC board members. In 2004, at around 6 p.m. as the sun was sinking below the horizon, Bay Area's Gamelan X,[1] a group of over 100 Gamelan players and dancers, dressed in black-and-white checkered sarongs with silver and gold sashes, entered Center Camp. The procession slowly moved towards a steel cauldron in front of the Café, drawing a crowd of several hundred. Drummers followed in droves, forming a circle around the cauldron, and the Gamelan music soon transitioned into drumming.

Once the performers were assembled, Rose entered the centre area. A striking woman, she wore her long silver hair in a braid that snaked down her naked back; her black sarong was embellished with yellow and orange flames. She held a long piece of rolled paper like a wand as she circled the playing area, moving and dancing in front of the crowd, to the beat of the drum. In a strong and authoritative voice, she commanded the crowd to pay attention—the initiation ceremony was about to begin. The crowd continued to grow. Then Rose gestured to the drummers to pick up the pace. She philosophized about the meaning of the flame, the fire and the Man, commanding the crowd to keep the fire alive all week long, for this would be the fire that would release the Man on Saturday night. Rose addressed the circle: 'You are the Man—the Man is within each of you. [. . .] The fire is in each of you. [. . .] Fire comes from within. [. . .] Each one of us will be released' (2004b). Everyone clapped to the beat of the drum as she began to dance around the cauldron. A man walked into the circle with a large silver disc and pointed it at the sun as Rose held the baton of paper in the magnified light. The baton instantly burst into flames and the crowd roared with cheers and whistles. Rose then lit the cauldron filled with wood, and the circle of spectators erupted into spontaneous dancing around the cauldron.

The flame is kept alive all week until it is transferred from the cauldron to the Luminferous (a transportable metal urn) and carried from its position at Center Camp towards the Man in a procession by the Fire Conclave, a group of over 650 fire performers. Once it reaches the Man, the Luminferous is carried clockwise around the circle used to ignite the Fire Conclave. Up until 2000, the same flame was used to ignite the Man on Saturday night. However, due to safety concerns, he is now lit by a professional pyrotechnic team. The ritual of creating fire captured by the sun, invented by Rose in the mid-1990s as a personal ritual dedication to the Man, now marks the official start of Burning Man.

The Eclectic Rituals of Burning Man

The opening fire ritual described above is one example of the many invented rituals in Black Rock City. At Burning Man, one can see how the sacred infuses the secular, how ordinary life is turned into ritual, blurring the boundaries between the sacred and profane and forging a complex relationship between performance, visual arts, ritual practices and spirituality. Burning Man is a peculiarly American event, a conglomeration of New Age religious beliefs and practices, pop art, high art and hedonism. The secular, invented rituals of Burning Man structure the community's social reality and embody its ethos, offering participants a way to create meaning and a sense of place and belonging.[2]

In the 2005 annual census conducted by the BMO, surveying 20 per cent of the population, data indicated that over 75 per cent of those responding to the survey reported that Burning Man was a spiritual experience for them. In 2006, 55 per cent had a spiritual experience and 23 per cent had a 'somewhat' spiritual experience. The census in 2003 and 2004 did not collect data on spirituality; however, the themes 'Beyond Belief' (2003) and 'Vault of Heaven' (2004) played right into the spiritual impulses of many who attended. These impulses are not necessarily inclined towards the practices and beliefs of Christianity, Judaism, Islam, Buddhism or Hinduism. The reach instead is towards activities and beliefs that are more 'New Age': combined elements from many different religions, from the 'great religions' to Wicca (witchcraft) and Animism. Burning Man from its inception incorporated much that was 'spiritual' in the New Age sense. But, in 2003 and 2004, there was a superabundance of spiritual eclecticism. Of the 466 theme camps, at least 23 and over 100 workshops were dedicated to ritual or spiritual content. This inundation of spiritual information lays the groundwork for what Denny Sargent calls the 'eclectic ritualist' (1993: 165). Sargent argues that this phenomenon is predominantly American, and that the eclectic ritualist flips through various religious practices and sacred rituals like channels on the TV, weaving together a new system of beliefs according to spiritual wishes and needs. Throughout the week, a Burner could wander through Black Rock City and sample a variety of rituals, becoming an eclectic ritualist.

From the Temple of Reverie, the Temple of Venus and the 24-Hour Confessional to the 7 Sins Lounge, Camp Israel, Kabala Kabana, Sanctuary Village and The God Box, each camp offered a site for spiritual experimentation and sampling. These venues were not the ordinary church, mosque or synagogue, but spirituality refracted through the lens of Burning Man: erotic, playful and New Age. One could join sunrise and sunset meditations, full moon and new moon rituals, and even a sunrise sacrifice in which a stuffed animal was sacrificed and offered to the sun. Oracles are another popular activity, with numerous groups hosting Tarot readings, rune stone-making workshops, vision quests, sunrise pow-wows, guided shamanistic journeys and talking circles.

FIGURE 5.2. The 'Talk to God' telephone booth, 2004.
Photograph by John Tzelepis.

Humorous Ritual Practice from the 2004 and 2005 'What? When? Where?' event guides

Spiritual Accounting Office **hosted by Hippocampus**

Our crack team of spiritual accountants and refund specialists are here to assist and serve. Our records indicate that YOU are due! Please come file your return and help us bring the universal accounts back into balance.

AAA 24-Hour Confessional

Father Nick makes his triumphant return to the playa with a whole rectory full of playa-bound priests ready to hear your very best confessions, grant you eternal absolution, and assuming your confession is good enough, get you good and drunk. Be pure, get absolved, and meet some really cool priests—remember, we've got god on our side!

7 Sins Lounge

Come embrace the heat at the 7 Sins Lounge! Why take a chance on Eternal Damnation when our Church-sanctioned Get Out of Hell Free cards can save the day!

Camp Israel

Love Israel? Love the Dead Sea? Love the spirituality and the mystics? Love Jewish stories? Love to dance? Love life? Love learning? Love family? Love community? Love food? Camp Israel has something for everyone!

Kabala Kabana

Under the Vault of Heaven there are many maps to help you find your way—the Kabala, Runes, the Medicine Wheel, Tarot, Twister. Kabana offers a participatory experience with metaphysical and just plain physical fun. Rune and Tarot readings will be available throughout the week, or come and make your own set of runes

Sanctuary Village

Sanctuary is a village of long-time Burners who offer spiritual exploration and physical celebration in a hospitable and inviting environment. Visit us daily for yoga, meditation, full body adornment, clothing gifts, discussions on shamanism and journeys of the mind, tea service, and nightly audio/visual presentations—and enjoy our sacred refuge from the outside environment.

The Temple of Venus

The Temple of Venus will be a full-service salon for the goddesses of the playa, serving their bodily, spiritual, psychic, emotional, and sensual

> needs. Temple priests and priestesses will attend to the needs and desires of each goddess individually.
>
> **The Messiah Complex**
>
> Discover the savior within you! The Messiah Complex will help you build a new religion that features YOU as the founding prophet. Through our mystical methods of divine contact, you will learn the deepest secrets of the universe, which you will spread to the infidels. If you can gather the largest flock, you can brand everyone else heretics! The Messiah Complex features a holy symbol and vestment workshop. Paint, sew, or mold your very own sacred artifact, pendant, or banner. Stitch up a genuine prophet's robe, kimono, or other priestly garb (BMO 2004c and 2005b).

The creation of altars is a common practice and they often serve as sites for the blurring of the sacred and the profane—some serious, some ludicrous. At Super Lucky Camp, in the centre of the altar was a large ceramic Maneki Neko (the 'beckoning cat' thought to bring good luck) surrounded by three smaller versions, Chinese Hell money, fans and fake candles. By the end of the week, the altar was covered with offerings which included Kit-Kat chocolate bars, candy and Hello Kitty toys, thus serving as a powerful symbol of consumer worship. The altar, like many others scattered throughout Black Rock City, highlights the inherent contradictions that run throughout the City—between the 'commerce-free' world and the realities of the event's economics, between the sacred and the profane.

Both New Age practices and the 'great religions' were represented on the playa. The ritual sampler could take a course in Judaism, participate in a Shabbat dinner, attend a Quaker meeting and share in a moment of Unitarian Universalist worship. In 2004, the Zenplicity camp created a Zen rock garden where you could meditate in the shade or design a personalized card for Tsunami survivors, to be delivered to the affected regions on the first anniversary of the tragedy in South East Asia.

Three Jewish camps—Kosher Camp, Camp Israel and the Black Rock JCC—offered a variety of activities in 2004, including a potluck Shabbat dinner, question-and-answer sessions about the Jewish faith and Kabbalah workshops in Jewish mysticism. The Black Rock JCC held two events that were open to all, regardless of affiliation or knowledge of Judaism. In

2005, it gave a midnight workshop called the 'Jewish Shamanic Journey and Meditation', which fused elements of Jewish shamanic and mystical practice. Camp Israel also offered a Kabbalah workshop on Friday afternoon, or you could just stop by to be painted the blue of the Jewish star on the Israeli flag—fusing the humorous and political with the religious.

Not only did the 2003 and 2004 themes inspire a flurry of spiritual activities and rituals, they also were the impetus for a number of art installations dedicated to spiritual or sacred iconography. In 2004, these included the *Heavens on Earth* by Frank John Piwarski and Aldebran Dawn Larson, *Universal Awe* by Jerelyn Hanrahan, *Cosmic Dance* by Daniel Dunkle, *Cosmos* by Royce Carlson, *Celestial Stone Circle* by Jeremy Bryant, *Celestial Body* by Michael Christian, *Cosmic Cocoon* by Ellen Henrici, *Heaven's Gate* by Todd Reed, *Wheel of the Sacred Earth Year* by Kasia Wojnarski and *Heaven's Point* by Kern Atma. Both Daniel Dunkle's *Cosmic Dance* (also known as *Foucault's Pendulum*) and Ellen Henrici's *Cosmic Cocoon* created interactive spaces where participants could engage with metaphysical questions while moving through or inside the work. According to Dunkle:

> All that we are and perceive, including the fundamental foundation of the earth itself, is truly in motion through the larger Cosmos. In the stillness of the vast desert, Black Rock City rotates through endless spirals, mostly outside of our awareness. *Cosmic Dance* brings this perpetual motion into the realm of our ordinary senses, using a centuries-old yet still relevant technology, the Foucault Pendulum. The continual spinning of Planet Earth, and the passage of what we call time, can be remarked as the pendulum swings, pegs are toppled at regular intervals, and audible tones are emitted by the resonant harmonics of Celestial Motion (2004).

Henrici's *Cosmic Cocoon* was a walk-in canvas womb; its inside was painted with a depiction of the birth of the universe and the formation of the stars, with an ambient soundscape. Through installations such as these scattered around the playa, Black Rock City becomes a sensorium in which participants see, hear, feel, smell and taste a selection of ritual elements from around the world.

Rites of Passage

Rites of passage, both playful and serious, are rehearsed and performed throughout Black Rock City. Crossing the threshold into the City is itself a rite of passage in Arnold van Gennep's sense of the term. Participants separate from the profane world of everyday life and move towards the margins of society. The gates of the City are the threshold or limen into a new world, where entrants become in essence neophytes or initiates (van Gennep 1960: 3). In Turner's elaboration of van Gennep's basic idea, novices undergoing a rite of passage are stripped of their secular clothing and identities as they pass through a symbolic gateway. They are 'levelled', their former names and selves discarded (1969: 108). In Black Rock City new playa names are taken, quotidian clothing is shed and highly imaginative costumes—or nakedness, a costume of a different kind—are donned. Sometimes these new identities stick and are carried back into the 'default' world of everyday life after Burning Man is over.

In ritual, clock time is transformed into 'event' time. During the week in Black Rock City, the neophyte exists in a liminal state of event time and endures tests of survival, engages in ritualistic activity and forms new bonds of community. Afterward, the former neophyte, now changed, reintegrates into his/her community (ibid.: 94). Some are permanently transformed while others only temporarily transported, a distinction put forth by Turner, Schechner and others. While this may seem like a romanticized scenario, many participants do in fact experience such a transformation when attending Burning Man for the first time. Even a few of the veteran Burners still undergo changes during their week on the playa. While some enjoy Burning Man as one big party, many others find the experience to be deeply personal, affecting real-life changes. For most, however, the week in Black Rock City is both fun and meaningful.

A wedding is a rite of passage that, in many cultures, is both enjoyable and serious. Each year on the playa, dozens of marriages, real and pretend, take place. At the Black Rock Wedding Chapel, furnished with a seven-foot Elvis head and a spin-a-vow wheel, both faux and real weddings are staged, Las Vegas-style. Others choose more intimate settings within their camps, inviting friends as well as strangers to partake in their playa nuptials. In 2004, two participants, Squeeze and Mistress Ann, planned their interactive wedding at the El Circo Dome. Invitations were distributed randomly on the playa, which specified a dress code of burnt oranges, yellows, reds and ice blue. Guests were provided with food and drinks, and a dance party followed the ceremony.

The death rituals in Black Rock City play with fire in the figurative sense; some of the death enactments come closer to the real thing than one might at first imagine. The advertisement for the Black Rock Cemetery reads:

> Die in style and reserve your plot in the Black Rock Cemetery of the Deceased and Deranged. We'll kill you, judge you, accept confessions, send you to Heaven or Hell, punish or reward you, entertain or bore you, accuse or pardon you, photograph you, mist you, relax you, and costume you for the inevitable afterlife (not exactly in that order) (BMO 2004c).

At Camp Hex in 2005, a person could stage his/her own death and funeral by lying in a real coffin donated by a San Francisco funeral home. One woman invited her friends to perform her funeral while she lay in the coffin. Dressed in all black, they brought poems they had written, left her flowers and delivered eulogies. After the ceremony, the woman's friends helped her out of the coffin and went on their way.

The Lamplighters of Black Rock City

One of the most enduring rituals in Black Rock City is the civic ritual of the Lamplighters. Every evening, as soon as the sun slips behind the Black Rock mountain range, several hundred Lamplighters emerge from the Lamplighter Chapel. Their white gowns edged with orange and yellow flames suggest membership of some mediaeval guild and evoke a solemn atmosphere. Each Lamplighter carries a wooden bar behind his/her neck and across the shoulders from which five kerosene lanterns hang on either side.

As the sound of gongs and cowbells fill the air, a tall man, sporting a kilt, a leather whip and leather suspenders, addresses the crowd. His billowing voice slices through the desert air as his incantation, which I recorded in 2004, introduces the Lamplighters to the community:

> We are the Lamplighters lighting our city. The Lamplighters give us light. [. . .] As a gift to you, within each one of these lamps burns a flame, a flame of hope and a flame of creativity. A flame that enlightens each and every one of us to the endless possibilities that our friendships and

FIGURE 5.3. The Lamplighter procession, 2001.
Photograph by Stewart Harvey.

> experiences here can provide. Now in honour of the playa and the boundlessness of our dreams and visions we will hang our lanterns high. Now, hurry, the night is upon us and the festivities are about to begin. Lamplighters, light our city!!! Citizens, make way for the Lamplighters! (Lamplighters 2004)

The crowd cheers and screams, 'Lamplighters, we love you!' The sea of people parts out of respect as the Lamplighters go forth to light the City.

The ritual of the Lamplighters was invented and designed by Larry Harvey, once a Lamplighter himself. In 1993, Steve Mobia and Harvey placed 24 lanterns on the ground leading up to the Man, creating a ceremonial pathway of light. Several of the lanterns were stolen; hence, the following year, Mobia painted them with the Burning Man logo. This time they were all stolen. As a preventive measure, and an aesthetic choice, 12 foot-tall spires were erected to put the lanterns out of reach. Mobia, who retired from the Lamplighters in 1997, noted: 'These lampposts give the sense of an urban space to what might otherwise be a haphazard camp. The lamps are controlled flames as opposed to the passionate flames of the Man: a balance of fires' (BMO 1997b).

These 24 lanterns doubled every year; by 2007, over 800 illuminated the streets of Black Rock City. Burning Man is the largest user of kerosene lamps in the United States, with Disneyland a distant second; both are supplied by W. T. Kirkman of Ramona, California—the largest importer and distributor of kerosene lamps in the country (BMO 2003a). Over the course of the seven days of Burning Man, the 800 lanterns consume seven 55-gallon drums of kerosene, lighting over three miles of the city each evening.

The Lamplighter Village has become the hub where some Lamplighters live and where they all gather each evening. By 2004, the Lamplighter Village lounge was a 4,000-square-foot shaded communal area covered in AstroTurf and featuring a small waterfall. The 750-square-foot kitchen—with four sinks, a water tank, a fridge and a two-burner stove acquired through donations—fed almost 150 Lamplighters every night.

The central Lamplighter workspace, where the lanterns are prepared each evening, is known as the Chapel. Every day, 150 volunteers clean, fuel, light, carry and lift the lanterns into place. The Lamplighters make their own robes from donated bedsheets. Mikel recalls how Louise Jarmilowicz (aka Edwina Pythagoras), a former Suicide Club and Cacophony Society member, designed—gold lamé with red flames sewn on the bottom edge—and sewed the first Lamplighter robes in 1995. (Mikel has the only one out of the first six ever made.) Jarmilowicz's design was adapted and simplified so that the robes could be easily reproduced.

Around 5 p.m. each evening, the Lamplighter Chapel is bustling with activity. A freight container is filled with the robes of the Lamplighters. All the sooty lantern globes are washed and cleaned, the lamps filled with kerosene and the lanterns are arranged, loaded onto the poles and made ready for carrying. Everything is done in a precise, methodical manner, mostly in silence.

In 2004, people who wanted to volunteer or were trying to find their group of Lamplighters surrounded a white eraser board outside the Chapel. The City had been divided into six regions with routes drawn and designated: (1) Center Camp to the Man, (2) from 6 and 10, (3) from 6 to 2, (4) from 3 to 9 including both plazas, (5) from the Man to the Temple and (6) the Temple complex. Each region was assigned six to eight Lamplighter volunteers which were divided into three groups: lifters, carriers and support. These routes change only slightly from year to year. Another crew of four to eight people works in the kitchen, preparing the meal that is shared once the city has been lit; each villager is required to provide one ingredient for one of the meals. The next day, a few early risers set out after dawn in the Lamplighter staff vehicle—dubbed 'Lucifer' (aka 'Lucy')—to take down the lanterns before the City wakes up.

A huge dust storm broke out during 2004, as I observed the Lamplighters' preparations. Regardless, about 100 people, wearing dust masks and goggles, continued their diligent efforts to get the lamps out and up. Was this work or play? Clearly, the experience was not 'fun'—they were struggling to see and breathe in the dust—but they worked with dedication and commitment despite the harsh conditions. Volunteerism had turned into sacred duty: they would not let the City down; the City would be lit no matter what the conditions. And, perhaps at some level, the comradeship and dedication made the task 'fun'.

If a person camps in the Lamplighter Village, it is expected that s/he will lamplight almost every night, although the requirement is somewhat flexible. Despite all their work, the Lamplighters are required to buy full-priced tickets. The Lamplighter Council is composed of three veteran and three new members who work year-round on the project—organizing the camp, coordinating the set-up crew for the village, ordering the kerosene and planning the meals. To join the Lamplighters, you have to fill out an online questionnaire on the Burning Man website participation section. Once the questionnaire has been completed, the volunteer gets a password to access the Lamplighter listserv. In his second year on the playa in 1999, Terry Schoop[3] (aka Retro) joined the Lamplighters and held several roles from Volunteer Coordinator to Council Member to Project Manager in 2004. As Schoop notes, 'We have this core group of labour in the village and then people walk in at 5 o'clock and help us. We are all over the city, we open it up to everybody, you don't have to live in the village to be a Lamplighter' (2004). While the Lamplighters are an inclusive group, the core members who return year after year run and maintain the Lamplighter Village. The Lamplighters actively recruit in Black Rock City by hosting cocktail parties serving sangria and Bloody Marys to entice new volunteers on a night-to-night basis.

When I asked Schoop if he felt the Lamplighters represented any particular religious affiliation or symbolized something specific, he replied, 'It's hanging lanterns. We are kind of like the Pacific Gas and Electric of Black Rock. I have to respect that some people do see it that way [as religious]. I appreciate and respect their beliefs. One thing we do is we signal the difference of the changing between the afternoons, the heat of the day and the cool nights. The transition from day to night' (ibid.). For Schoop, being a Lamplighter connected him to a large network of like-minded individuals in the San Francisco artistic community and beyond.[4] While the Lamplighters serve a civic ritual function, it is the temples by David Best that serve as Black Rock City's sacred centre.

The *Temple of Tears*: Rites of Separation

> For the Egyptians and the Babylonians, as for us, the temple represents the principle of ordering the universe. It is the *omphalos* 'navel' around which the earth is organized. The temple is a scale model of the universe,

> [. . .] a very important feature of every town in our contemporary civilization, as in the ancient world. [. . .] The temple as the center of the universe may be a myth, but it is the most powerful myth that ever possessed the human race (Nibley and Norton 1992: 15, 170).

One of Burning Man's most magnificent artistic efforts, merging visual art and ritual on a grand scale, are the ephemeral temples designed and constructed by San Francisco-based artist David Best. Prior to Best, there had been other temple-like structures, such as Pepe Ozan's *Temple of Rudra* (1998), but it is Best who managed to fill the spiritual void for processing grief and loss—his temples serve as sites for the expression of beliefs within the Burning Man community. Since 2000, Best's temples have become sanctuaries—a quiet space of prayer, meditation and reflection—where the community performs rituals of mourning, memory and loss. Each temple, which is built to be destroyed, is burned on Sunday night, after the Man burns on Saturday night.

Before coming to Burning Man for the first time in 1997, David Best, a striking man in his 60s with a white beard and piercing blue eyes, made his living in San Francisco working primarily with painting, prints and sculpture. The temples mark a tremendous evolution in his work as an artist. In 1997, he was invited by a neighbour to attend Burning Man, and he took along a bunch of junk to make things with. Over the first two years, he created an art car that he calls his 'rocket car'—a converted Cadillac convertible shaped like a rocket.

On his way to Burning Man in 2000, Michael Heflen, one of the young people working with Best, was killed in a motorcycle accident. This tragedy gave rise to the first temple of Black Rock City, *Temple of the Mind*, constructed out of recycled scraps from a dinosaur jigsaw puzzle factory in Petaluma, California. Best reminisces, 'So we were going to build something but we had no idea what. There was no meaning to it. We were collecting material and a week before we were coming up one of the kids that was working with us was killed on a motorcycle. We built this structure and it became a tribute to Michael' (2005). As he constructed the first impromptu temple, about 10 participants wandered up and offered to help build the structure, a wave of generosity that Best had not expected. He ended up with a crew of about 80 volunteers. Over the years, this initial group of volunteers became known as the 'Temple Crew', a group dedicated to helping Best construct his temple structures.

The structure of the temple synthesized various styles and quickly became a site of mourning and meditation. By the end of the week, every surface was inscribed with dedications to the dead, makeshift altars were erected and rituals invented within the space. Working with his Temple Crew of volunteers, Best designed and built more elaborate structures with every passing year.

Best designs the temple ahead of time in Petaluma, California, but his design is only a rough sketch, leaving his crew the freedom to embellish and improvise, to add their own personal touches. At first, Best simply took leftover scraps from the jigsaw factory dumpsters but, as his pieces grew larger and more ambitious, he began to buy the scraps to ensure he had enough material. Sorting and colour-coding the recycled material begins in May each year in a warehouse in Petaluma (not always the same one). Each year, a 45-foot flatbed trailer loaded with the sorted and coded Russian birch plywood puzzle pieces arrives at the Nevada Burning Man Ranch and Black Rock City. The first step is to build the temple's frame. Then the crew spends several weeks on the construction and ornamentation of the interior.

While the Temple Crew is all volunteers, some get free tickets to Burning Man though most pay full price for their tickets. One crew member, William Dire Wolfe, a computer programmer turned musician, usually bought his ticket but was given one in 2005. As Wolfe explained, 'Not all of them get in free, some of them pay for tickets. It all depends on your financial situation. I didn't have any money because I was out of a job and the Temple Crew took care of me' (2005).

Wolfe's first year at Burning Man was 1996 but he didn't join the Temple Crew until 2001, the year of the *Temple of Tears*. Initially, Wolfe thought his role in the Temple Crew was limited to that of a musician but, slowly, his responsibilities grew. Now he does almost everything from construction and painting to picking up trash. One of his jobs is to drive to all the recycling centres in San Francisco collecting scrap wood. For Wolfe, the most important thing that Burning Man and the Temple Crew have given him is the feeling that he is a part of something. The crew has become his life inside and outside of Burning Man. Stories like Wolfe's abound at Burning Man. Best described his crew's devotion to the temple:

> We are so committed to one another. If I said, 'Let's make this thing out of aluminum foil or push-pins,' they would do it. [. . .] The beauty comes from Dire working on it, from Maureen working on it, from Tim working on it, and it comes from all these different people with different aesthetics. If you just have good aesthetics, if you just had a perfect thing, it wouldn't work, as far as I am concerned. The thing that makes the temple for me is when it is imperfect. It is when someone has built this beautiful altar and then someone comes up with the nail gun and goes 'gunk gunk gunk'. You don't say, 'You've screwed it up!' You say, 'Great, can you just come over here for a minute and help me with something. I need to get a sandwich. [. . .] Will you come over and sit with me for a minute?' You graciously pull the person away from what they've just done. Then I go over to Dire and I say, 'Dire, could you do me a favour. Could you go over and put another layer over that?' And then the other person doesn't feel as if they were disrespected. And they weren't disrespected. It is just layering. So then Dire puts 10 pieces over it—what you have is four people's labour melded into one (2005).

Considering the building process, Best tells an anecdote that he believes epitomizes the temple experience and explains its success. The night before I interviewed him, Best was standing quietly, visiting the construction of *The Machine*, an installation by the Seattle Regional Crew. Best recalls what happened:

> Last night I just happened to be out there talking to someone. I told them they were doing a fantastic job. He was out there at 12 o'clock at night still working with a smile on his face, like our crew has done. Someone else came up and said, 'Who is the boss?' and here is the key to our success right there. [. . .] The guy said, 'No one is the boss in this. We don't have a boss.' Maybe one or two people's vision but we are all working together, and we all have different skill levels, and everyone is contributing what they can. Someone who studies office management and corporate management—our method would certainly not fit into any corporate situations (ibid.).

Inside each temple, participants can practise any chosen belief. Best considers his temples to be the ultimate temple—where all religions and belief systems are welcomed and celebrated, challenging French sociologist Emile Durkheim's assumption that churches and temples house only one ideology and belief system (1996: 143).

Due to the popularity of the *Temple of the Mind* in 2000, the BMO asked Best to build his 2001 temple to fit in with their theme, 'Seven Ages of Man'. Designed by Best and Jack Haye, the *Temple of Tears* was constructed as the final stage of a symbolic journey from life to death through seven rites of passage.[5] The *Temple of Tears* was reminiscent of South East Asian temples as it shared several of their architectural features; yet it maintained a uniquely original shape and form (see Figure 5.4). The inner sanctuary was dark and shady, with rays of light streaking through the recycled wood lattice and forming patterns on the playa floor. The dark space provided a break from the glare of the desert sun outside, and the intricate latticework created a 'sky door' effect, allowing the sun and sky to flicker into the sanctuary. A sky door, according to architect Anthony Lawlor, connects a building to the cosmos, drawing attention towards the sky and the sun. This draws the spirit upwards, igniting human inspiration and imagination (1994: 57). For this reason, many temples and churches have windows and openings near the ceiling. The *cella* or inner room of the Greek temple faces the entrance and is a sanctuary for reflection and meditation (Fox 1988: 33). Wolfe recalls: 'Sometimes, it would be these big biker guys or something, dressed in leather and chains, just lying on the ground crying their eyes out. And then beautiful women around them, holding them and crying too. People from all different walks of life, all different sizes, suddenly joined together to comfort each other' (2005).

I asked Best why he built his temples:

> If I am building a temple, what is this about? Is it a Buddhist temple? Is it a Baptist Church? Is it a synagogue? I thought about all of those religions and there is a stigma about not being able to be buried with the rest of the dead if you have taken your own life. You put all your life into a religion and then all of a sudden because for some reason if one of your wires isn't right they won't bury you? This temple is dedicated to suicide (2005).

Best estimated that in 2001 he talked with at least 100 people who had lost someone to suicide, be it their mothers, fathers, brothers, sons, daughters, spouses or friends. One of his most memorable moments at the burning of the 2001 Temple was when a man in an Eddie Bauer outfit, who looked like a lawyer or doctor, came up to him and said, 'My son committed suicide and you set him free' (ibid.). Best feels a tremendous sense of honour and responsibility to be able to build something that evokes that kind of emotional, personal response. The temple has become Black Rock City's sacred centre, or *omphalos*, a powerful destination for those members of the community who are grieving or processing a loss.

FIGURE 5.4. The *Temple of Tears*, 2001.
Photograph by Gabe Kirchheimer.

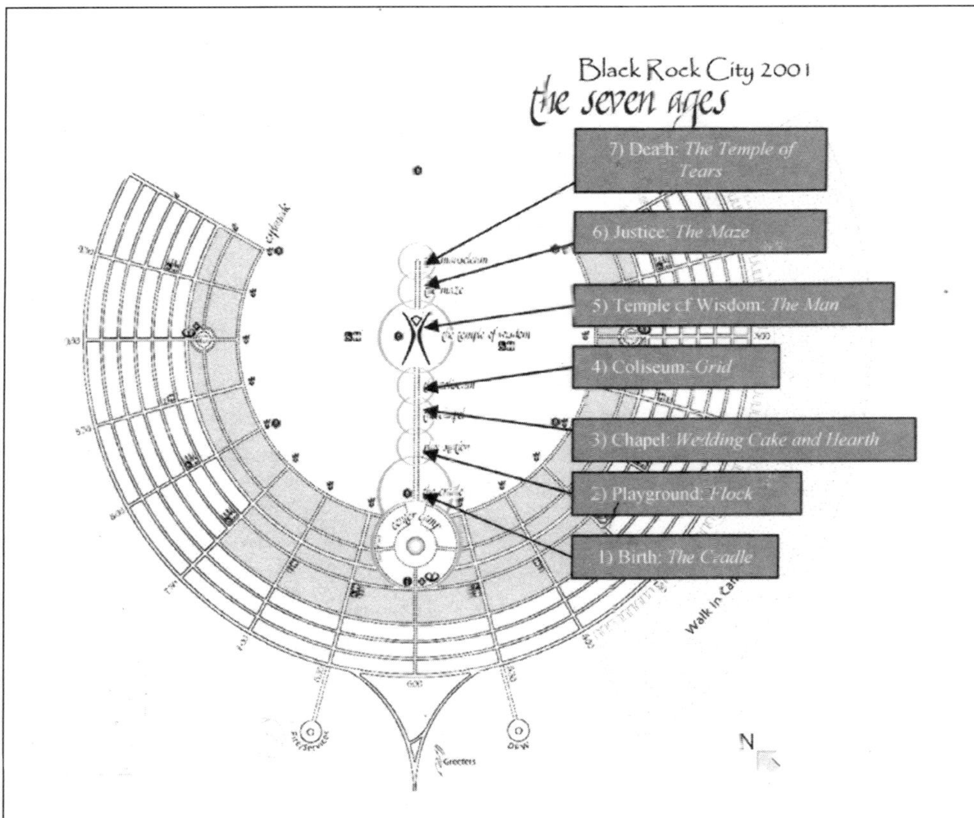

FIGURE 5.5. Map of the seven stages of life in Black Rock City, 2001. Created by the author.

Best was so overwhelmed by the emotion evoked by the *Temple of Tears* that he told Larry Harvey he would create the *Temple of Joy* for the summer of 2002. By changing the name, he hoped it would still wield the same power yet allow people to tell jokes about their father in hospital undergoing chemotherapy or recall their mother's favourite joke. They may still cry but there would be a sense of joy and the possibility of laughter (ibid.).

Then 9/11 happened. The *Temple of Joy* was dedicated to all those who died at the World Trade Center and Pentagon attacks; its altars expressed grief and sorrow while offering a place for reflection. An American flag was placed at the entrance, and a chest containing the names of those killed in the attack was set atop of the main altar (Pike 2005: 208). A firefighter from New York City was invited to set alight the temple at the end of the week. Lee Gilmore remembers that, at the burning of the temple in 2002, the silence gave way to a spontaneous performance of 'New York, New York' (2005a: 50).[6]

Best realized he had filled a necessary void in the community. But he also wondered how he was going to rid himself of the responsibility of having to build the temple each year. He was 60 years old and didn't want to assume the sole burden of building the temple:

> How I am going to be able to make the temple evolve so that someone else can do it? I've got an idea, I'll do it out of paper. I thought by using a different material, it would open the door to someone else who could help me. So, I made the *Temple of Honor* [2003] out of paper. That was probably the world's dumbest thing to do, to come to the desert with wallpaper and paste in a desert storm and try to glue stuff to the temple at 70 feet in the air! (2005)

Best dedicated the *Temple of Honor* to forgiveness (see Figure 5.7). Towering above the playa, the paper temple looked to some like a mosque, but Best said the structure had 'nothing to do with the war in the Middle East, Bush, or patriotism' (ibid.)—it was a place where people could come to be forgiven or grant forgiveness. He said, 'I get the opportunity to make a place where someone is going to walk in and forgive themselves or their mother' (Shipwreck 2003). While rewarding for Best and visually intriguing, this temple seemed to him to lack the emotional potency of its predecessors.

FIGURE 5.6. Sketch for David Best's *Temple of Honor*, 2003, created by David Best.

FIGURE 5.7. The *Temple of Honor*, 2003, created by David Best. Photograph by Rick Egan.

A year later, in 2004, Best challenged himself and his crew to build their largest and most elaborate temple yet, the *Temple of Stars*. Unfortunately, there was a moment of panic when one of the trucks bearing the main building materials was late—the crew feared that the driver may have cheated them, leaving them without the essential materials to complete the temple. But Best remained calm; he had absolute faith in his crew's commitment and knew that, no matter what, the temple would be built with whatever materials were available, even if they had to drive to Reno for plastic bottles from the recycling centre (Best 2005). The materials did finally arrive and the temple was completed late, opening to the Burning Man community on the Friday of the festival. It was up for only two days in its finished form before being burned on Sunday night.

Around dusk on Wednesday, before the temple was completed and opened to the citizens of the city, I walked over to the *Temple of Stars* Camp at Esplanade and 2 o'clock to find Best. The camp was the headquarters for the Temple Crew and its intricately designed eating area with lattice walls was made from the same dinosaur jigsaw puzzle remnants used to construct the temple. A man at the entrance asked, 'Can I help you?' and I said I was looking for Best. He told me he was at the temple that was still under construction; they were behind schedule—it was Wednesday and the temple was still not complete. The man was Leo Nash, co-author with Daniel Pinchbeck of *Burning Man: Art in the Desert* (2007) and the temple's lighting designer. Nash told me he was about to light up the temple and asked if I would like a ride to it in Best's art car, a 30-foot Cadillac. I couldn't refuse.

After a 5-mph trek to the outer limit of the City, we arrived at twilight to see the silhouette of the intricate temple latticework against the azure blue sky. Since the temple was not officially open, it was empty and entirely silent. I watched Nash use a crane to climb high into the temple vault. He asked me to hold a spotlight on him as he muddled about for a bit. Then, suddenly, the entire temple lit up like a thousand stars.

Once it was officially opened on Friday, 3 September 2004, I returned around 11 a.m. Located on the furthest margins of the city, directly behind the Man, one must embark on a pilgrimage to get there. From the centre of Black Rock City, the temple was a small dot in the distance. As you walked away from the City and towards the temple, the blinding white surface of the playa met the horizon ringed by majestic mountains. The thumping sounds of the City faded to near silence, and all you heard was your own breathing, the beating of your heart and the crunching of the playa beneath your feet. During the day, the sun's blinding glare made the walk an arduous journey. Some flew by on bicycles or in art cars but the real experience lay in making the journey on foot. Gradually, the vision of the sprawling two-storey temple complex appeared, extending a quarter of a mile along the horizon. Two long ramps led up on either side to the second level, marked by two small, spired stations. A central altar dominated the interior and rose up into the steeple.[7]

Several hundred people were milling around inside, on the ramps, up in the rest stations and in the main temple. Inside, the atmosphere was sombre, hushed; people were crying, meditating, praying, consoling and writing messages to loved ones. Someone began to play a guitar; someone else on the upper level hit a Tibetan gong that resonated throughout the temple and vibrated out into the desert. From the highest point, Black Rock City was a distant cloud of dust just barely visible. While it was a magnificent structure, Best noted one major flaw: he did not like that people on the second level could look down on those grieving on the first.

The central altar was covered with mementos, photographs, paintings, portraits, flags, candles, burning incense and sage, books and beads. There was a pile of circular disks of wood left by the Temple Crew onto which people could inscribe their feelings and thoughts. Mementos to the dead, wishes and blessings covered all surfaces on the way up to the second level of the 2004 *Temple of Stars*:

> 'I love you dad'; 'Hi Grandpa'; 'May this burn release me from my cocaine addiction'; 'Sorrow and pain, I thank you for your lessons'; 'This is Erika and John letting go'; 'Hari, what is it like over there?'; 'My empty womb'; 'Here today gone tomorrow'; 'Burn my dishonesty'; 'Miss you mom'; 'To all I have hurt, I'm sorry'; 'Praying for a cure, a release from needle bondage'.

In *The Gift: Imagination and the Erotic Life of Property* Lewis Hyde speaks of 'threshold gifts' or 'gifts of passage' that aid in rites of separation (1983: 41) and that serve as actual agents of individual transformation and change. Leaving a memento, a poem, a photograph or drawing at a site of mourning, such as the temple, acts as a symbolic gesture to the deceased: 'Passing the gift along is the act of gratitude that finishes the labour. The transformation is not accomplished until we have the power to give the gift on our own terms. [. . .] Art acts as an agent of transformation that we may correctly speak of it as a gift. A lively culture will have transformative gifts as a general feature' (ibid.: 47). The temples become portals through which Black Rock citizens can pay their respects to those they have lost through gifts of art, inscriptions and performative gestures. As in Chinese funerary rites, the burning of effigies and symbolic paper objects such as cars, houses, money and other material possessions releases them into the afterlife. The burning of the temple, and with it the inscriptions and gifts, performs a similar symbolic function of release and transfer. According to John M. Lundquist, the temple is 'associated with the realm of the dead, the underworld, the afterlife, the grave. The temple is the link between this world and the next. It has been called "an antechamber between two worlds"' (1993: 104). Temples are liminal spaces for divine human encounter, for illumination, transformation and passage. Best's temples are conduits for performing what van Gennep would call 'rites of separation' or funerary rites. Participants become ritual agents transforming their grief and sorrow into release (1996: 532).

When the temple was finally completed, Best had the opportunity to walk through it one last time before its incineration:

> When I got up to the temple itself, and looked at it, I was blown away like anyone else would have been blown away. I realized that this was the last time I was going to walk from it and I couldn't turn around to look at it. I really wanted to turn and look because this was the last time I was going to see it. And yet, I also knew that it wouldn't be fair to look back. I had to keep walking. And then this young girl started to jump off the ramp, and I said, 'Hey, you can't do that, you have to walk *all* the way to the end.' Suicide is where people jump off. There are a lot of places where people bail midway through life. You can look back at your life and say, 'Wow, that was incredible, I had such a great life and now it is so shitty. It's shitty but it's life.' You have to walk all the way through life. You can't just stop walking because it is not as free as it used to be. And by looking back you look longingly for the past instead of living in the present. I didn't realize any of that when I made it. It was only when I was walking on it that I realized what it meant (2005).

Best believes that if he hadn't built the temples, someone else would have; he is just fortunate enough to be the one who had that opportunity. He has become a celebrity of sorts within the Burning Man community, receiving praise and respect for his powerful work.

Changing Hands: The *Temple of Dreams*, 2005

While Best is still an active member of the Burning Man community and a board member of the BRAF, in 2005 he handed the responsibility of designing and building the *Temple of Dreams* to artist and builder Mark Grieve. Best decided to take the year off to pursue other art installation projects. Grieve earned his degree from the San Francisco Art Institute and, inspired by Best's temples, in 2003 created a small, intricate pagoda complex out of sticks. In 2004, Best invited Grieve to create an installation of sticks in front of his own main temple before handing over full responsibility in 2005. Grieve's temple was a light salmon pink, with a main temple and several smaller temple huts evocative of a Shinto shrine—beautiful but smaller in scale and less complex than Best's temples. The *Temple of Dreams* was dedicated to the memory of Stevie,[8] a young woman who was a beloved member of the Burning Man community and was killed leaving Black Rock City in 2004 when her RV flipped over on the highway.

Constructing the *Temple of Dreams* turned out to be very difficult for the crew, who were used to working with Best:

> A new person came on [Mark Grieve] and it was *really* hard to inherit 60 people that every night I give a kiss goodnight to. And he [Grieve] is not a person who does that. Six months working with these people, he doesn't know how to give a kiss good night. I've known every one of them for five years now. [. . .] The long and the short, for the Temple Crew, even though this has been a hard year for them, I am hoping we can bring the crew together again (Best 2005).

In 2005, Burning Man took place the same week as Hurricane Katrina hit New Orleans and the Gulf Coast. With limited access to the Internet or the media, news was slow to reach the playa. Media Mecca was turned into the New Orleans Disaster Relief Center, where free satellite phones and a laptop were made available for those who needed to reach their families in the devastated areas. During the event, over $35,000 in cash donations were collected and thousands of pounds of food and water were delivered to the Salvation Army for hurricane survivors displaced to Reno. In an article featured in *Wired*, 'Burning Man Mourns the Big Easy', Daniel Terdiman writes:

> On Sunday afternoon, hundreds took part in a New Orleans-style memorial for the flooded city at Mark Grieve's *Temple of Dreams*. The service organized by the anti-consumerist Reverend Billy of the Church of Stop Shopping, mixed angry political rhetoric with heartfelt sadness. Singer Joan Baez led the audience in a sing-along of 'Swing Low, Sweet Chariot' and 'Amazing Grace' (2005).

Once again, the temple had become a site for processing national trauma, just as the *Temple of Joy* was for mourning the victims of September 11.

For the 2006 Burning Man, Grieve and the Temple Crew designed and built the *Temple of Hope*. Constructed out of wood and white fabric, a series of conical towers formed a courtyard, evoking a futuristic science fiction landscape. As was the case with the *Temple of Dreams*, participants could wander through the labyrinth of pillars and inscribe messages to the dead on their surfaces. The same year, the Seattle Temple Crew built the *Temple of Light* as a memorial to the victims of the Capitol Hill shooting on 25 March 2006, when six young members of their community were killed. Their aim was to provide a quiet space for reflection, grieving and to leave messages.

When I asked Best in 2005 if he would build another temple, he replied: 'Not for a couple of years. But I will do other things with the Temple Crew. I am 60 years old; I think for the next 10 years I would like to work with Dire, Tim, Maureen, and all of the crew; we are so much stronger as a team than as individuals' (2005). However in 2007, Best returned to team up with Tim Dawson to design and build the *Temple of Forgiveness*, a simple yet elegant structure that captured the intimacy of his earlier temples (see Figure 5.8). Four grand entrances converged on a central altar and an interior *cella*. An open tower above the altar provided a sky-door effect, with long curved beams reflecting the arc of the horizon. Using his trademark lattice of jigsaw puzzle scraps, Best added subtle details within the frame to create undulations of light and shadow. Once again, Best managed to create an intimate yet complex space, unmatched in uniqueness and emotional potency.

In 2008, responsibility for the design and building of the temple changed hands yet again. Pasadena artists Shrine and Tuktuk built *Basura Sagrada*, a temple inspired by Antoni Gaudi's *Sagrada Familia* (*basura* is Spanish for garbage). Shrine and Tuktuk first created the Basura Sagrada

FIGURE 5.8. The *Temple of Forgiveness*, 2007, designed by David Best and Tim Dawson. Photograph by Scott London.

Collaboratory to collect materials for the temple. They established a website to post designs and sent a call out to the Burning Man community for recyclable materials such as windows, doors, plywood, lumber, cardboard, sheet metal, driftwood, branches and frames. The surfaces of the two-storey temple structure was ornately painted in a swirling pattern and the central spire housed a large wind chime made of recycled aluminum that filled the interior of the temple with a percussive symphony of sound. As in the temples by Best, shrines, altars and messages of farewell, regret and hope filled every surface until their release into flames on Sunday night. Best's desire to transfer the responsibility for designing and building the temple was complete. With or without him, the temple has marked its place within Black Rock City as an enduring and necessary part of Burning Man's ever-changing culture and identity.

A Temple Like No Other

What distinguishes Best's from ordinary temples in the 'default' world? Firstly, Best's are artworks made to disappear, built to be destroyed. Secondly, by the end of the week, every surface of the temple is inscribed with dedications to the dead, impromptu altars are erected inside the temple and rituals are invented and performed in the space. The temples are meant to be places of mourning, of remembering the dead, especially those lost to suicide, and Best forbids anything other than memorials. He wants to create a space free of slogans or propaganda or anything that is not a remembrance of the dead:

> If a Republican's son had just gotten killed, I wouldn't want them to feel that they couldn't walk into the temple. [. . .] It is not my place to make a political statement. I can make a lot of political statements, but the temple is not a place to make those statements It is a place to grieve and be forgiven, a place to say goodbye (2005).

Thirdly, Best considers his temples to be nondenominational, where all religions and belief systems are welcomed and celebrated. Inside the temple, participants can practise whatever beliefs they choose. And finally, Best's temples are perhaps the only temples in the world you can enter naked, wearing a G-string, a corset, or lingerie with knee-high platform boots. No priest, mullah, rabbi or bishop governs this temple and it is home to no single doctrine or belief. In her essay, 'Fires of the Heart:

Ritual, Pilgrimage, and Transformation at Burning Man', Gilmore poignantly argues that Burning Man offers an 'experience of ritual without dogma' (2005a: 45). Best's temples are an example of this, non-denominational spaces where people process and release grief. Best believes that the temple was an inevitable and necessary part of Black Rock City: 'I see the temple as an integral part of the community here now. You couldn't have Burning Man without the porta-potties; you couldn't have Burning Man without the Café, and you couldn't have Burning Man without the temple' (2005).

While Best had not previously studied other temple structures, he believes his inspiration was drawn from the innate need to construct and decorate. The recycled lattice wood does dictate the design to some degree. He believes that if you put 100 people in a field with a sack of seeds within a matter of minutes, they would be casting seeds in a rhythm and within 10 minutes would be singing a song (ibid.). Given a pile of sticks, the same people would start to build a structure. 'You get a bunch of people out here with a cup of water, and a little bit of that water spilled, the rest is divided up to drink, someone would get that little bit of mud and put it on their face. We have decoration within us' (ibid.).

Best may be a utopian dreamer but many are keen to follow him and his dreams. Formerly a solo artist, Best found a community at Burning Man and discovered that working collaboratively can be deeply fulfilling, both for the individual and the community. Although he no longer takes sole responsibility for the temples, he remains actively involved in Burning Man and serves on the board of directors of the BRAF. However, his long-term goals extend far beyond the Black Rock Desert—he plans to build his ephemeral temples across the US.

Before the 2005 Burning Man, Best and his crew worked on two temple projects outside of Black Rock City: the *Chapel of the Day Laborer* (2005) and the *Temple at Hayes Green* (2005), both in San Francisco. *Chapel of the Day Laborer* was planned as a temporary art installation in San Rafael, a small city in Marin County, just north of San Francisco. The Chapel, some 30-feet tall, was designed for a green space beside the main entrance to a market in the Canal District of San Rafael, a neighbourhood that is home to many Hispanic day-labourers. Writing in the 2005 *Burning Man Summer newsletter*, Kristin Hale reported:

> It [the Chapel] was conceived as a tribute to the courage and an acknowledgment of the hardship inherent in leaving one's home country with the uncertain hope of finding work in the United States. The project was also meant to honor those whose lives take place invisibly around us, neatly tucked behind the scenes of our affluent society (in Hale and Pritchcett 2005).

Best obtained permission to build the *Chapel* from representatives of the City of San Rafael as well as the storeowner who occupied the site. However, the landowner had not been informed and ordered him to tear it down. With that, the building department of San Rafael cordoned off the site with yellow tape and laid a red tag to stop construction next to the accumulated offerings left by the people of the neighbourhood. Best had to comply: 'I wanted to break into a poor community, to build a central location where the laborers could reflect. This is where people come to buy groceries and make phone calls. It's a hub, and a place where someone can go and sit and cry about not being with family' (in ibid.).

Best and crew disassembled the *Chapel* but, when members of the San Francisco Arts Commission saw a front-page article in the *San Francisco Chronicle* detailing the rise and fall of San Rafael's *Chapel of the Day Laborer*, the Director of Public Art telephoned Best asking the BRAF to help undertake a similar project on public property in San Francisco, on a new green space at the intersection of Hayes and Octavia scheduled to open in June. Best agreed. The temple was on display from June to November of 2005. Once the Hayes Green Temple was complete, it was quickly inscribed with messages. While it was meaningful to the community, the temple, set as it was amidst the crowded urban landscape, did not have the same visual impact achieved on the stark playa.

The Burning of the Temple

The temples, like every other structure at Burning Man, are built to be destroyed. On Sunday night at the end of the week-long event, the temple is set afire—significantly, the day after the Man is set alight. The effect of the two spectacles is very different. For some, the burning of the Man is like a wild party while the burning of the temple is a spiritual experience. I asked Best about the potential competition between the temple and the Man:

FIGURE 5.9. The burning of the *Temple of Forgiveness*, 2007. Photograph by Gabe Kirchheimer.

> Looking at the Man and looking at where the temple is at, they [the BMO] could have fought the temple. They tried a bit last year and the year before to call the Man the temple. No matter what they did, the temple still is the temple. There might be a year that they make a hundred temples, but there will only be one temple, and that's the temple where people go to put their son's ashes, their dog's ashes, their dad's ashes, or their mother's. There is only one. And I think they've seen that. They are my friends, not adversaries, but I think they have seen that the temple is a separate thing. They are not trying to compete with it and I am not trying to compete with the Man (2005).

Wolfe adds his perspective on the significance of the temple within the Burning Man community:

> Last night, when I went out to the temple there were people doing shamanistic rituals, and there were musicians playing sitars on the steps. I feel like the temple has become an entity of its own. Even without David and the crew, it is possible that the temple could go on at Burning Man. People come out here to participate. You come out here and people have been working all year on some of this—they expect it and they need it. So, someone could build the temple in theory and new people would come and do their thing We don't need to make it happen anymore, necessarily (2005).

Wolfe isn't sure he wants to continue building temples at Burning Man, but he is committed to working with Best on future projects. Wolfe appreciates the distinction between the temple and the rest of Burning Man: the burning of the temple is a quiet event, whereas the burning of the Man is more primal. When the temple burns, people are crying and mourning; they are silent and sombre. I asked Wolfe about the relationship between the Man and the temple:

> The Man is like a party and the temple is like a spiritual experience. The central atmosphere at the burning of the temple is one of quiet, whereas the Burning Man is more about 'let's all release and scream'. The circle around the temple, people are crying, people are still mourning. They put their stuff in the temple, and they are going to watch it burn. They are going to release something. There are people partying too, but sometimes it is totally silent and sombre. David s temples have all had perfect acoustics, not by design, just by chance. I played my guitar out there, and I thought the sound was just going to be dead but it just rings inside of it. I would bring my guitar to the *Temple of Tears* and just play, and people would come in and start crying (2005).

In her essay 'No Novenas for the Dead: Ritual Action and Communal Memory at the Temple of Tears', Sarah M. Pike shares her experience of the Temple Burn in 2001: 'Thousands of people gathered around the perimeter of the circle about a hundred yards across. An opera singer began the ritual with a rendition of "Amazing Grace". Then fireworks exploded and the temple was lit. Spirals of flame, ash and dust flew from the temple, releasing wishes, promises, grief, and joy' (2005: 211).

Like the laborious ritual of Tibetan butter sculptures or the intricate patterns and colours of Navaho sand paintings, David Best's temples are carefully constructed over many months with dedication and artistic mastery. Then, like Black Rock City itself, the temple vanishes. Prayers, pleas and pronouncements are burned and released from the temple in the rising smoke.[9] From the mundane to the sublime, a broad spectrum of invented ritual practices are celebrated in a kaleidoscopic flurry throughout Black Rock City. Whether humorous or serious, Burning Man offers a fertile space for experimentation with belief, allowing each participant to create his/her own life rituals. The efficacy of these rituals is evident in the process alone, in the dedication of time, resources and energy spent in building Black Rock City and its annual community of participants, infusing the playa with life, culture, meaning and belief.

Notes

1 Gamelan X is a Bay Area-based music ensemble that weaves Indonesian, Balkan, African, Indian and American rhythms and melodies to create a unique fusion of sound. It has performed extensively throughout California and the United Stated as well as internationally in Bali and Jogjakarta, Indonesia (Gamelan X 2008).

2 In *Secular Ritual* (1977), Sally F. Moore and Barbara G. Myerhoff argue that the sacred is a wider category than religion, rejecting Emile Durkheim's binary of the profane and the sacred. Secular rituals can be found in all contexts, including court trials, graduations and other formal gatherings that make up the fabric of social life (ibid.: 4).

3 In 2004, Terry Schoop resigned as head of the Lamplighters to accept a new senior staff position within the BMO, overseeing the management of all Black Rock City Community Service Departments: airport, ice distribution at Camp Arctica, the Burning Man radio station, Center Camp

Café, Earth Guardians, Greeters, Lamplighters, placement of camps, Playa Info, Recycle Camp, the shuttle bus and the Volunteer Resource Team (BMO 2008b).

4 During the year, the lanterns and supplies are stored in three railroad containers at the Burning Man Ranch: one container for the kitchen equipment, one for the lounge and one for their workspace, the Chapel (BMO 2004b).

5 The first stage, or birth, was named the 'Infant'. It was situated along the promenade directly in front of Center Camp and was represented by *Cradle*, an art installation by Deirdre de Franceaux and Jann Nunn consisting of three six-foot-high sculptures of vaginal openings. *Cradle* was designed for participants to re-experience the wonder and excitement of being born, the sensory overload associated with experiencing the world for the first time. Next, one passed through childhood, 'The Playground', represented by Michael Christian's *Flock*, a 42-foot-high headless creature with four legs, constructed out of gnarled metal wire. The third stage, adulthood was called 'The Chapel', symbolizing rites of passage such as marriage and made manifest by William Lai's *Wedding Cake* and Charlie Smith and Syd Klinge's large metallic, flaming heart *Hearth*. The fourth stage, life's struggles at 'The Coliseum' was depicted by *Grid* created by Russell Wilcox. *Grid* was a lattice of laser beams creating an energy field one foot off the ground. If participants blocked the laser, the field would disappear; and it became a challenging game of jumping over and under the beams to keep them active. The fifth stage was enlightenment, which could be found at the *Temple of Wisdom* constructed as the base of the Man. The sixth stage was 'Justice' represented by *The Maze* designed by Todd Dworman and Charles Trapolin, a labyrinth of rooms that participants had to navigate through. Finally one arrived at the final stage—death—experienced through Best and Haye's *Temple of Tears*, also known as 'the Mausoleum'.

6 According to Sarah Pike, the Delaware Burning Man contingent, Playa del Fuego, planned their annual Beach Burn on a stretch of Delaware coastline a month after 11 September 2001 (2005: 208). Pike notes, 'Several hundred gathered there, many of them from New York City, and built their own mausoleum out of remnants brought home from the *Temple of Tears*' (ibid.: 208).

7 In the *Temple in the House*, Lawlor points out that the steeple embodies 'principles of the masculine, [. . .] found in three archetypal forms: axial pillars, sky doors, and world mountains, whereas sanctuaries offer shelter, nurturing, stability, and loving embrace' (1994: 52). It is the energies

of both the steeple and the sanctuary that evoke feelings of the sacred (ibid.: 51). According to Lawlor, 'the altar balances and integrates the energies of the steeple and is the focal point of the sanctuary, signaling a place of arrival and rebirth: the world navel' (ibid.: 64–72).

8 Stevie's last name is deliberately left out to protect her identity.

9 The temple releases personal messages to the afterlife. In Chinese funerals, hell money and paper effigies are burnt as a symbolic offering, transferring these goods to the afterlife:

> Paper products in all shapes and sizes are produced in China to be burned as offerings to dead relatives, either at the annual Ching Ming Festival or on the anniversary of a relative's death. These objects are copies of a vast array of products, mainly luxury goods or items indicating wealth and affluence: gold bars, gold credit cards, cash from Hell's Bank, mobile phones, laptop computers and digital cameras. [. . .] According to traditional Chinese beliefs, it is up to the living to make sure that their departed relatives are looked after financially and materially, as the dead cannot take anything with them to the next life. The act of burning the paper products 'sends' it to the underworld. If the departed live well on the other side, it is believed they will bestow blessings on the living (Oliver 2001).

CHAPTER 6
DANCING WITH FIRE: THE ULTIMATE EFFIGY

Shiva dances and destroys the world with his mate Kali, the all devouring. [. . .] The current age is considered the Kali Yuga (Age of Kali), another apt symbol of the current situation in mythic terms. We are demolishing the inner myths and old structures, to make way for the new (Sargent 1993: 169).

Every man regards himself as the center of the universe around him. There is a real center, but it is also relative There is also each person's awareness that other people have their centers too, unless you're a solipsist or something similar. Since there are other people, there must be other centers. For the purposes of getting together, can we agree on one center—a fictitious center, a model of some sort, and act as if that were the center? (Nibley and Norton 1992: 140).

When there is a communion between people, when you are facing the flame, you are no longer afraid of anything—it is as if you have been released from a bondage, as if everything was joyful, as if the whole of the circulation of life in us is joyful, as if we ourselves were the circulation of life. If we are facing the flame, that flame is also in us (Grotowski in Croyden 1993: x).

In 20 years, as Burning Man has evolved from a personal solstice celebration to an ephemeral city of 49,000 participants, themes have changed, people have come and gone, but the one constant element has been fire—the essence of Burning Man. The final act of this seven-day performance is the immolation of the Man. Fire fuses the community through performance, ritual, carnival and spectacle. In an interview with Nash, Harvey remarks, 'Fire is the primal attractant. This shared experience, symbolized by our species' attraction to fire, forms a central and necessary basis for our community. People are fascinated by fire, and when you combine fire with the human form, I think it has a significance that certainly transcended our intent' (in Nash 1995).

The use of fire in ritual can be mapped historically, and it is the primal element that draws the Burning Man community together in the present as well as connects it to the past. There are fire sculptures, fire performances and the Fire Conclave, one of the largest gatherings of fire performers in the United States. The grand fire finale of the festival is the burning of the effigy, of the Man. What does the Man mean to the community? What do they experience as they form complex rings of spectatorship around the Man on the night of the Burn?

The Alchemy and Art of Fire

From the very beginning of human culture, there has been an intimate relationship between fire and ritual. The use of fire can be traced back to the earliest Palaeolithic rituals, part of a system of hunting: following food sources according to a seasonal schedule, meeting other hunting bands and performing ritualistic celebrations around cooking fires. Why does fire continue to fascinate and compel humans? Part of our fascination with fire is its variability and unpredictability. As Hazel Rossotti notes in *Fire* (1993), the element has many attributes: 'with its power to warm, to light, to comfort, and to destroy utterly, it is little wonder that fire was worshipped as well as used, and that even today, fire has many religious and social, as well as utilitarian applications' (ibid.: 3). Fire, Rossotti points out, is often represented in the arts because of its inherent symbolism and power to evoke passion and desire, to inspire vitality and curiosity, to provoke destruction, to represent purity and to give comfort—all at the same time.

FIGURE 6.1. *Fire in the Belly* by Susan Glover and John Wilson, with Zachary Coffin's *Rock* at its centre, 2001. Photograph by Richard Jones.

Fire played an important role in the development of religion, and many cultures evolved deities associated with fire. To name only a few: the Egyptian goddess Sekhet, who represented destructive heat; the Japanese fire goddess who lived in a volcano, worshipped by the Ainu; the Icelandic Surtr, a god of volcanic fire; the Hindu goddess Devi, who dwells in natural fires; the Greek goddess Hestia and her Roman counterpart Vesta, who presided over the hearth and home; and the Yoruba Shango, the god of thunder (ibid.: 241).

Agni, the Vedic god of fire, is often depicted with two faces, one good and one evil. His three limbs represent the sun, promoting growth and fertility; lightning, promoting vengeance; and earthly fire, promoting humanity and warmth (ibid.). The Zoroastrians of Iran also worship fire. Zoroaster, the founding prophet of the religion, engaged in spiritual contemplation on a mountaintop and escaped unscathed when the entire mountain was destroyed by fire (Heesterman 1993: 71). For his followers, fire symbolized both sacred purification and communication of their prayer to their god.

Fire is also essential to carnival. As Bakhtin points out, the Roman Carnival ended with the fire festival of Moccoli ('candle stumps'), a grand pageant along the Corso in Rome with each participant carrying a paper lantern illuminated by a burning candle (1984: 248). The entire Corso is flooded with the glow of lighted candles and torches, and the objective of Moccoli is for participants to blow out each other's candles and yell, '*Sia ammazzato*'—'You're murdered!' (Goethe in Falassi 1987: 32). Symbolic death is a recurrent theme of 'carnival' as it is at Burning Man.

Throughout the world, people assemble and celebrate around bonfires and burn effigies: the British celebrate Guy Fawkes Night on 5 November;[1] the Gaelic celebrate Beltane on 1 May;[2] Germans burn a straw effigy of Judas on Easter's Eve; the Yaqui burn piles of Judas masks (*chapayekam*) at the climax of their Easter celebrations (Schechner 1993: 113); and the demon Ravana is burned in the many Ramlilas[3] of north India. In many places, walking on or through fire, or leaping over it, is both a magical feat and a means of spiritual purification.

In the US Southwest, the burning of the Zozobra effigy in the Fiesta of Santa Fe, New Mexico, is a relatively recent fire rite. Although the Fiesta dates back to 1712, Santa Fe artist Will Shuster was inspired by the Yaqui and, at the fiesta he held in his home, added the burning of the Zozobra effigy in 1924. The name 'Zozobra' derives from the Spanish word for 'the gloomy one' and is the epitome of anguish and anxiety. Burning the Zozobra—a 50-foot marionette that moans, groans and rolls his head until he goes up in a blaze of fireworks—dispels the hardships and trials of the past year (see Goodwin 1998). Zozobra, drawing a crowd of more than 30,000, is burned over the Labour Day weekend, the same time as Burning Man.[4] Whether or not Harvey had any direct knowledge of these predecessors, his Man too is a figure of purification, celebration, destruction and rebirth.

What is fire besides a chemical reaction? Gaston Bachelard, in *The Psychoanalysis of Fire* (1964), approaches fire as an entity possessing multiple personalities. Inherently ambiguous, it is intimate, passionate and loving—the hearth, the candle and the stove—yet also angry, dangerous and deadly: 'It is a pleasure for the good child sitting by the hearth; yet it punishes any disobedience when the child wishes to play too close to its flames' (ibid.: 7). Indeed, the first thing we teach a child about fire is to stay away from it. But flames captivate us; they are calming and relaxing, and allow us to enter into a deep state of reflection. Bachelard calls this intoxication the 'Empedocles Complex':

> Fire suggests the desire to change, to speed up the passage of time, to bring all of life to its conclusion, to its hereafter. In these circumstances the reverie becomes truly fascinating and dramatic; it magnifies human destiny; it links the small to the great, the hearth to the volcano, the life of a log to the life of a world. For him destruction is more than a change, it is a renewal (ibid.: 16).

Bachelard further argues that humans harbour a secret desire for 'an apotheosis through fire; [. . .] the call of the all-consuming funeral pyre, of the inner funeral pyre' (ibid.: 97).

Another aspect of fire considered by Bachelard is the 'Prometheus complex', which 'impels us to know as much as our fathers, more than our fathers, as much as our teachers, more than our teachers' (ibid.). The 'Prometheus complex' is the Oedipus complex of the life of the intellect (ibid.: 12). Then there is the 'Novalis complex' driving people to understand the origins of fire through legends and mythologies. Fire is also often associated with sex—heat generated by friction, by rubbing one substance against another. All of these feelings and ideas radiate through the Burning Man community, where fire is regarded with the utmost respect, almost worshipped.

The Myth of the Phoenix

The question remains: why do so many people make the pilgrimage to the Black Rock Desert and go through the trouble of building an elaborate city and erecting installations, temples, theme camps, and art cars, then watch as the centrepiece of their efforts goes up in flames and the entire city vanishes even more quickly than it arose? What is it about the effigy of a man burning that casts such potent spell over the community? Could Black Rock City exist without the Man as its *axis mundi*? Could the community exist without fire?

In analysing the motives of the Burning Man community, it is impossible to pinpoint any single answer. Motivations vary from person to person and are often deeply personal: some are drawn to the party in the desert, others come in search of community, still others look to be inspired by, or create, art and performance. Many are there to find a deeper meaning to life or to find the sacred. When I asked participants, 'What does Burning Man mean to you?' I received a wide range of responses, but it soon became clear that everyone who finds his/her way to the City is in some way a 'seeker' of experience and personal transformation.

The Man symbolizes different things to different people. The theme of the phoenix rising out of its own ashes occurred in many responses as people spoke of burning the old and allowing the new to be reborn; of the cycle of death and rebirth; of an opportunity to reinvent oneself anew each year. The phoenix is, according to myth and legend, a bird reborn from its ashes. Thought to be the size of an eagle, a peacock or heron, its tears have healing properties and only one phoenix exists at a time with a lifespan of between 500 and 1,400 years. When the phoenix senses that death is near, it builds a pyre of aromatic wood (some myths say cinnamon bark), then it sets the pyre on fire and is consumed by its own flames. Out of the ashes is born a new bird. This myth is told and pictured in many cultures, including the Chinese (Feng-Huang), Japanese (Ho-oo), Russian (Firebird), Egyptian (Benu) and Native American (Yel), for example (Eason 2008: 60). In each version, the bird is identified with the sun.

Some depict it engulfed in flames, while others think of it as a bird of shining colours. The Egyptians depicted it as a bird of brilliant shades of red, making it look as though it was enveloped in flames.

Newton from Cirque Berzerk described his experience: 'It is kind of a rebirth. It is the celebration of our lives and our collective spirit. And then starting all over again from the ashes. Like waking up again, it is like a new year. But it is something that means more than just January 1st' (2005). Everett, also from Cirque Berzerk added, 'I guess the Man is everyone's idea of what kind of person they want to be, what they are looking for here. Almost everyone is looking for something here, a creative outlet, something spiritual, something life-altering and changing. Maybe that is what he is the symbol for. Definitely for me' (2005). For Glaser (aka Kostume Jim) from Kostume Kult, the burning of the Man is like a New Year's Eve celebration, the ball dropping in Times Square:

> It's release. For all of us that create something that is so breathtaking and just turn it into a pile of ashes at the end, it is very poignant. I think he is a really cool icon, I am not going to wax philosophic on whether it is wicker man or anything else. It is a brand. It is a logo. It is a lot of things. (2006).

When I asked Wolfe of the Temple Crew what the Man represented to him, he replied:

> I've never put much thought into paganism throughout my life, but once I got lost in a dust storm and I came out by that Burning Man guy and I looked up, and I could just feel the power coming off him. So now, all these people come out here, and they put all their energy up there into the Man and he broadcasts it back out to the city. That is very powerful (2005).

Chris Sia of El Circo credits Burning Man with changing his life. As an artist, an activist and a pilgrim, he finds Burning Man to be the ultimate platform for self-expression: 'This is my temple. It is definitely life changing. [. . .] It is my Hajj. The whole thing feels like a ritual. Collectively, it seems like everyone comes out here to celebrate things that we value—freedom, happiness, the evolution of consciousness. I think people are coming out here to step outside of themselves' (2005).

For Sia, the Man represents a process of surrendering and letting go, 'like a serpent shedding skins'. His least favourite aspect of Burning Man is that it ends too soon. He tries to carry what he has learned in the desert back into his everyday life, and admits, 'In some ways, I am always continuously preparing for the next one' (ibid.).

Daniel Pinchbeck, author of *Breaking Open the Head: A Psychedelic Journey into the Heart of Contemporary Shamanism* (2002), describes Burning Man as:

> Dionysian revel, mother goddess worship, new age psycho-spiritual detritus, coming together to create something. It feels like a laboratory experiment. It also feels incredibly necessary because mainstream culture is so flatly materialistic and one tone/one note. This is a little crucible for an experiment in what could be the proper opposition to that cultural note. It is a cult in that there is a central symbol and people wear symbols, vibe with it and identify with it (in Pinchbeck 2004).

For Dowlen of El Circo, the Man is a focal point and a place for him to release 'a primal rage that is in all of us that needs to escape. [. . .] It is really about releasing something that allows you to throw away what you don't need and take in what you do need to grow' (2005).

Szpigiel from AWD/Xeno, has yet another perspective, and believes that Harvey's personal ritual became the transpersonal. Many people are affected emotionally and psychologically by the very basic concept of burning the old to make way for the new. The desire to recreate oneself is a huge draw: 'Everybody wants to burn him/herself down and start over again. Everybody wants to be reborn. [. . .] By giving yourself to this transformative process, by taking control and putting yourself in this environment, you are actually relinquishing control. That is the paradox' (Szpigiel 2006).

Another Burner, Rebecca Rosenthal (aka Darlinda), a burlesque dancer from Manhattan, tells how Burning Man changed her: 'Burning Man has totally changed my life. I've changed with an internal recognition of who I am. It has changed what performance means to me, what creativity means to me. There are all these creative people that just give off this juice. That's what flames Burning Man' (2004).

Alan,[5] a 59-year-old participant from Marina Del Ray, is an ex-hippie from the 1960s and a civil servant. He told me that 2004 was his first year at Burning Man, and that it brought out his inner child. For Alan, Burning Man is a combination of a Fellini, Spielberg and Lucas movie. He feels that the connective tissue of the event is 'uncommonness' and that each individual's difference is respected and celebrated:

> The people here are so in-sync that it looks almost like chaos. The vibe here is perfect. All these things you dream about when you are a kid. [. . .] I went on a full-size rocking horse today. It's like a giant playground. Last night, I went on a huge Ferris wheel. I'm planning on doing this every year. I can see how something like this could keep you young in spirit (2004).

Harvey has his own relationship with the Man:

> We never said what the Man represents very deliberately. He doesn't represent anything. The Man is a fixed point so that everything else around can be free to be spontaneous and chaotic. It certainly has to do with change. And if you want to go back to the story about the break-up, it meant change, it meant letting go, it meant life. Those are the immediate things. Fire is huge, it always has been. We started with essentially the two first human technologies: fire and the lever. The elemental—well, it is just primal. Gathering around a fire has a potent psychological effect on people and I think it always will (2004a).

Burning Man board member Will Roger's relationship with the Man has evolved over the years. Roger moved from Rochester, New York, to Oakland, California, about 15 years ago, after teaching fine art and photography as well as a course called 'In Search of the Mystical Image' at the Rochester Institute of Technology. He chuckled when he told me:

> Now I found it. It's ironic. I think I was going through the mythical midlife crisis. I had just gotten divorced, my dad had just died, and I was having trouble with the curriculum there and teaching the same courses. I took a sabbatical and never returned. I just took six months off and realized that I was dying. And I needed a change (2005).

He attended the event for the first time in 1994 with his girlfriend, board member Crimson Rose, and in 1996 became the head of Burning Man's Nevada operations and its business manager.

For the first time in 2005, he was the project manager for the construction of the Man: 'I'm going to be out there when it burns, looking into the eyes of those who built it. [. . .] There is a beautiful fire and you are affected by it. It goes into your memory. And then you start the cycle over again' (ibid.). When I asked Roger if he would ever get tired of burning the Man, he replied he would not: each year is unique offering a symbolic rebirth, each year the phoenix rises anew from the ashes. After every Burn, according to Roger, the board members go through cycles of emotion, debriefings and decompressions, and they have retreats where each department of the organization draws up elaborate self-reflexive *Afterburn Reports*.

I asked Rose what the Man means to her: 'He belongs to me, but he also belongs to everybody.' When I asked her what connects the entire community, she laughed and replied, 'We're all black sheep!' (2004a). Back in 1992, her first performance was to climb and dance on the Man wearing large white wings (see Figure 1.14 in Chapter 1). She feels like his guardian and wants to ensure he is immolated correctly each year. As much as they control the Burn, there is always an element of chance, of not knowing what is going to happen: 'Once the flame goes you really don't know what is going to happen. [. . .] I've seen him over the years where he would just crumble into nothingness, which has a whole other feeling as opposed to just falling over. So it is always my hope that he just crumbles into nothing' (ibid.). Rose feels intrinsically connected to the Black Rock Desert and being there feels like Brigadoon: 'I feel the other reality is like sleeping. [. . .] When people say "welcome home", it is like coming home. Being on the edge where you have to deal with nature, where you have to deal with your camp blowing away. It is so real. It is always a test' (ibid.). Burning Man, according to Rose, shows people different possibilities and perspectives of how the world can be, and that they have the ability to enact change in their lives. The desert forces people to come face to face with their own limitations and presents a different challenge to each person. Her philosophy: 'There is something about going to the desert that just opens everything up. To me, I see it as the reflection of one's self. That there is always something else that is possible. That you don't have to stay with what you have done before' (2008). These transformational stories are not uncommon and often cause a permanent shift in people's lives.

While the Burning Man experience was transformative and life-altering for the majority of the participants I interviewed, not everyone feels this way. In an article in the *Burning Man Summer Newsletter* in 2000, Julie Hollar argues that no one really knows what the Man stands for.

While some people have constructed elaborate theories or myths, others don't really care and they are just there to party:

> No one can really say what it all means, because it means something different to almost everyone. To some it means escaping the constraints of modern society and being free to walk around in purple body paint or, on a grander scale, to live free of money, full of art. To others it's just a great party, deep meaning be damned (2000: 2).

In the *Rolling Stone* article 'White Madness', Taibbi offers his opinion on why people attend the event:

> Burning Man looks like God's own playground. In fact, it is impossible to imagine a more perfect synthesis of an adult's subtle artistic sensibility and a child's raw passion for indulgent fun. [. . .] It's the perfect religion for the corporate age: all drugs and the hot music and the sexual permissiveness of Woodstock, with none of the idealist ardor or threatening dogma. And for all the talk about community, the only shared value of Burning Man is a collective dedication to self-indulgence. [. . .] For many, Burning Man is a place where people can go to blow off their anti-corporate steam for a week, then return to the system, fully charged (2005: 2).

In a posting from September 2006 on the 'My Name Is Timmy' blog, titled 'Achtung Hippie! Reflection on the Burning Man Scam', Patrick Mulroy wrote, 'The idea of holding a massive event in one of the hottest, nastiest, driest places on the planet seems stupid on the face of it. Why would almost 40,000 people pay over $200 for a ticket and probably $1,000–1,500 total to suffer in this godforsaken place for a week or more?' He claims his common sense kept him away, just as it prompted him to avoid 'backpacking in Afghanistan, running an ultra-marathon in Death Valley or eating bacon wrapped hot dogs from the vendor carts in Tijuana' (ibid.). He had heard glowing reports of 'magic', 'transformation' and 'Burning Man changed my life!' from his friends and therefore felt conned into wasting a week of his life and $1500. According to Mulroy, it is our desperate desire to stop smoking, lose weight and fall in love that the Burning Man organizers capitalize on—the desire for change and transformation. He read numerous accounts of how dull people now lead exciting lives thanks to what he calls 'the Burning Man cure'. He claims it was these stories that seduced him and others: 'I wanted to drink the spiked Kool-aid and search for magic in the nothingness of the Black Rock Desert. Nothing could have prepared me for the stupidity of this event, except perhaps an honest account of how truly awful it was' (ibid.). After his 'wasted week', Mulroy searched for similar accounts but couldn't find any. So he posted his warning to:

> Save potential burn victims a week of vacation and at least a grand in misspent cash. [. . .] Whatever Burning Man supporters claim, know this, the event is a 24/7 bacchanal of booze, drugs, nudity, S&M, public sex and bad art, all done in a scorching flat dry oasis of misery that reminded me of the surface of Mars (ibid.).

Mulroy's blog got over 199 responses, both in support of the article as well as in defense of Burning Man.

Burning Man is not for everyone and involves a significant amount of time, money and energy. And while a large majority of participants have a transformational 'phoenix-like' experience, the heat, the dust and the chaos are all part of the Burning Man 'package' that comes with the $250 ticket. You buy a ticket to participate in the 'experience economy' and the organization's strong selling point is 'personal transformation', a commodity like any other. Some people like what they buy; others do not.

Flaming Objects

Burning Man, a community founded on the love of fire, is one of the largest venues for fire arts in the world. At Burning Man and elsewhere, fire installations, fire breathing, fire dancing and fire eating have emerged from the sideshow to become a trendy performance medium worldwide, but with a concentration on the West Coast of the United States. Burning Man has become the principal destination for fire artists, an incubator for artists experimenting with larger-than-life, risky work not viable in a more conventional setting. Night in Black Rock City is a carnival of fiery delight with many fire installations, as well as planned and spontaneous fire performances.

Art at Burning Man should be experienced and interacted with, walked through and pushed against. The open expanse of the desert allows artists to create mammoth, interactive installations, many of which include fire. Burning Man is changing how artists conceptualize and construct their work, inviting them to make work that will be burned and destroyed—a potlatch of art, so to speak. Cynthia Kiki Pettit, Dan Das

Mann, Syd Klinge, Charlie Smith and the Flaming Lotus Girls, among others, are all known at Burning Man for their ambitious work as fire artists. In 1998, veteran Burning Man artist Dan Das Mann created the *One Tree* sculpture out of recycled copper pipe. *One Tree* was a social watering hole and gathering place during the day, spouting water out of its leaves; at night, it spouted fire. For the 'Body' themed Burning Man, Syd Klinge and Charlie Smith designed *Hearth* (2000), an enormous heart made of steel that was filled with wood and kept burning throughout the week, serving both as a meeting point and a place to get warm during the chilly desert evenings. In 2001, Cynthia Kiki Pettit created a work entitled *FireFall*, a sculpture of metal, ceramic, water and fire.

The Flaming Lotus Girls[6] have been among the 30–40 annual recipients of the BMO's theme-based artists' grants, which range from $3,000 to $15,000. Founded in 1999, the Flaming Lotus Girls, a collective of metal sculptors from San Francisco, is dedicated to pushing the boundaries of fire art. The Flaming Lotus Girls begins planning its installations based on the annual Burning Man theme, and the group spends months in San Francisco fabricating the sculptures in a large warehouse studio. In 2003, the group constructed *Flaming Flower Garden* where participants could wander through the installation and press buttons to shoot out flames from metal lotus flowers. Its *Seven Sisters* (2004) consisted of seven large fire-breathing metal installations. The central sculpture, *Electra*, was a flame-thrower using nitrogen, kerosene and propane to propel a stream of flames a hundred feet in the air, according to Flaming Lotus Girls artist, Colinne Hemrich (2004). The installation cost $13,500; $8,500 came from the BMO and the artists raised $5,000 on their own. Each performance used between 400 and 500 gallons of propane, costing about $5,000 in total for the week. The propane, a dangerous substance in such quantities, was delivered to the playa by licensed vendors and stored in a locked depot at a safe distance from the city. Artists using fire are required to comply with strict guidelines and safety codes imposed by the BMO.

During the performance, 15 people were needed to operate the controls; there were two control boxes with one person at each tank in case of an emergency. As Hemrich noted, 'Once the kerosene gets shot, the nitrogen is the propellant that shoots the kerosene through and the propane is the igniter. Once that goes flying in the air, if we have a misfire you have probably 10 gallons of kerosene just flying through the air like hairspray and it is pretty dangerous for the crowd' (ibid.).

In 2005, it created *Angel of the Apocalypse*, two 20-foot pyres that formed the flaming wings of a phoenix on fire. The tremendous heat and the light reflecting off of everyone's skin forced participation on a visceral level—one example among many at Burning Man of art designed to be experienced rather than merely viewed. In 2007, the group was commissioned to create *Serpent Mother*, a larger-than-life flaming serpent; and in 2008, *Mutopia*, 13 seed pods that adapted and mutated in an evolutionary series to create a giant spiralling formation. All their work pushes the limits of audience interactivity as spectators wander through, under and around the flaming metal structures.

Playing with Fire: The Fire Conclave

According to Crimson Rose (aka the Naked Fire Goddess), one of six LLC board members and fire performance director of Burning Man's Fire Conclave, when she first attended Burning Man in 1991 she was one of the only people playing with fire. Today, the playa is full of poi, staff, flaming hula hoops, stilt-walkers with fire wings, fire jump ropes, fire fingers, fire bowls, fire costumes, fire hoop skirts, fire breathing, fire swords, fire fans, fire double staff, crossed staff, flaming geometric shapes, fire chains and fire eating to name a few.

Rose began dancing with fire when a friend told her to stick her fingers in a bowl of alcohol and touch a candle. This playing with fire directly on the skin is called 'fire contact':

> I handle it. I put it on my body. I'll have a bowl of fire that has rubbing alcohol in it; I'll get my fingers wet, so I can literally pull off a flame from the fire. I'll torch my torso and neck. It's a very empowering feeling, which is what drew me to it. I almost feel like the fire is manipulating me (in Moses 2001: 1).

Playing with fire, according to Rose, plays with our primal fears—it is seductive, dangerous and unpredictable. Performers come in contact with fire and emerge apparently unscathed.

Rose says she loves fire because of its theatrical quality, and she incorporates it into both her personal rituals and her public performances. In

FIGURE 6.2. Performer with fire fingers, 2007.
Photograph by Scott London.

1991, Rose had the honour of lighting the Man and continued to do so for many years until neon and fireworks were added to the Man in 1999 and required a professional pyrotechnic team. Long on the Burning Man board of directors, Rose took charge of anything dealing with fire to ensure the safety of all fire artists and their audiences. Over the years, the number of fire performers has increased exponentially and experimentation has produced new fire props. As Rose notes, fire performers are continuously devising new tools to play with, 'People are expanding all the time. People attaching things to their bodies, fans, head ornaments. The imagination is very fertile' (2004a).

The most popular fire performance tool at Burning Man is known as poi, a fire prop derived from the Maori of New Zealand. 'Poi' is Maori for 'ball' and, originally, it was a flax bag used to carry small objects such as eggs. The Maori also use poi as a bag to crush food in, and it was even adapted as a tool for warriors—to help develop strength, flexibility and coordination. Later, it was adapted for performance. The traditional performance poi (a light ball made of *raupo*—a swamp plant—attached to a long or short flax rope) can be found in Maori action songs and dances, where it is swung around rhythmically to produce a percussive sound (Starzecka 1996: 46). Lighting poi on fire is not a traditional part of Maori culture and is a practice that developed outside of New Zealand. Fire poi are made of Kevlar wicks attached to ropes or chains. The wicks are soaked in fuel, usually paraffin or white gas (Coleman fuel), and twirled around by the poi performer.

Poi caught on so fast that Seattle's Pyro Boy, Wally Glenn, dubbed it 'the yo-yo of the new millennium' (in Moses 2001: 1). Everyone learns a set of basic moves, then adds their own twist. A group of fire spinners may use similar equipment but end up with wildly varying styles. The choreography of poi includes moves called weaves, crossovers, windmills and the butterfly, among others. Dancing with poi requires manual dexterity, coordination and concentration. Two poi are usually spun in parallel planes, and in the same direction (weaves) or in the opposite (butterflies). Moves such as stalls and wraps can change the direction of one or both poi. The 'basic weave' is considered by many poi swingers to be one of the staple moves; the basic three-beat weave is often one of the first tricks learned. The butterfly is a simple trick: the hands are held close together in front of the spinner and the poi spin in opposite directions to create the appearance of butterfly wings flapping, a dynamic visual flurry of fire. Beginners often start with practice poi made of two heavy plastic balls about the size of a billiard ball, with a two-and-a-half foot chain and a leather strap with two finger holds. Fire performer Cassandra Marshall explained the 'butterfly grip' as sticking your middle and ring fingers into the leather finger holds and wrapping the strap around your thumb to create a solid grip. Only when you have coordinated the moves and have solid technique is it safe to light up the poi.

Fire performance involves Caillois's four types of play: *agon* (competition)—each group competes to create complex choreography and invent new tools; *alea* (chance)—playing with fire is inherently risky; *mimicry*—each group develops personas and costuming; and *ilinx* (disorientation)—primarily for the spectators, as a fire performer must be in control at all times (1961: 17). Dancing with fire requires speed, endurance, strength, memory, skill and ingenuity. In their own way, skilled fire artists are ideal performers, according to Russian avant-garde director Vsevolod Meyerhold's definition. His ideal was for the performer's body to become a finely tuned musical instrument; for an acute awareness of the body in space, arrived at through rigorous training: 'The body is a machine, and it must discover the center of gravity, equilibrium, stability, coordination of bodily movements, orientation in space, and gesture as the result of the motion of the entire body. [Performing] becomes colored by the agility of sportsmen' (in Rudnitsky 1981: 296). It is this focus, balance, stability and coordination, along with a heightened awareness of the body in space, that is required of fire performers. While playing with fire, the performer is in what Csikszentmihalyi would call 'flow' (1975), the total fusion of action and awareness; a break in this flow (or concentration) could be extremely dangerous, resulting in severe burns.

The Risks of Playing with Fire

Obviously, fire performing is very dangerous, and, at Burning Man, not all fire performers are sufficiently aware of the risk. In *Fire Eating: A Manual of Instruction*, Benjamin Mack warns that the sport is so dangerous that his advice is to, 'Try sword swallowing. The swords taste better and you don't have to worry about the wind' (in Moses 2001: 1). A San

Francisco fire performer said that she practised for a year before lighting up her fire props: 'A lot of these fire dancers don't realize they can't go out there solo, they have to have a fire extinguisher, a blanket; you really do need someone to train you. I've heard some really gruesome stories about people lighting their faces on fire. You are playing with fire' (in ibid.).

Poi can also cause burns because the metal chains become very hot and transfer heat very efficiently. Costumes worn during fire spinning should be made of natural materials, such as cotton and leather. Any time someone spins fire, a fire-safety person needs to be on standby with a damp towel or fire extinguisher. At the Fire Conclave finale in 2001, Tedward[7] of the Los Angeles Fire Conclave seriously burned his hand when he was trying out a new set of fire tools with three wicks on a stick. He did not realize that fuel had saturated the stick and half of his hand; when he ignited the instrument, both the stick and his entire hand caught on fire. He was burned down to the bone. Even more dangerous than poi are fire breathing and fire eating. Tedward told me that a Fire Conclave performer he knows set his whole face on fire. These catastrophes rarely happen; however, performers often receive minor burns. In the LA Fire Conclave, someone gets burned at least once a month.

Regulating Fire Performance

Because it is so risky, it is very difficult for performers to find places to rehearse outside Black Rock City. On 20 February 2003, in Providence, Rhode Island, a pyrotechnic performance during the *Great White* show at the Station nightclub got out of control and more than 90 people were burned to death or suffocated (Romano 2003). After the Rhode Island tragedy, fire performances were banned in many parts of the country. Tedward took the lead in educating performers and fire departments alike so that safe fire performing could be practised. Joined by other dedicated fire performers, Tedward set up the North American Fire Arts Association (NAFAA) to not only inform authorities about fire arts but also to establish a national fire performance safety code to allow fire performers to practise and perform safely. He has had only limited success. Tedward attends quarterly fire marshal meetings in Los Angeles and has a working relationship with the Los Angeles Fire Department. As a result, the LA Fire Conclave has received a permit (costing $100 per year) to do fire performances in one specified area of the city (Tedward 2006).

Working with LA fire marshals, Tedward located a vacant lot where he and his Burn Club are allowed to spin each Wednesday. At the Burn Club, donations are solicited to cover the $25 per day cost of insurance and use of the public space. The Burn Club's arrangement was one of the first legal open-area fire performance venues on the West Coast. Similar arrangements have been made across the country. For example, the NAFAA Fire Safety Code is now the law in Philadelphia. According to Rose, the situation for fire performers outside Burning Man varies widely: different cities have different permits and some are stricter than others, Los Angeles being one of the strictest. The situation for fire performers in San Francisco is improving.

Since 2001, the nonprofit community arts venue The Crucible has hosted the *Fire Arts Festival*, which brings together many Burning Man fire artists such as Dan Das Mann, Karen Cusolito, the Flaming Lotus Girls and Charles Gadeken, as well as performance groups Xeno, Gooferman, Vau de Vire Society[8] and members of the Fire Conclave such as Phoenix Rising, Pyronauts, Nocturnal Sunshine and Controlled Burn. The festival is supported by the city of Oakland, the Oakland Museum of California, and the Oakland fire and police departments (The Crucible 2008). Attracting over 10,000 people annually from all over the country, the main feature in 2007 was *The Fire Odyssey*, a modernized interpretation of Homer's epic poem. Designed and produced by The Crucible's founder and executive director, Michael Shurtz, *The Fire Odyssey* was composed of 11 acts that took the audience on an epic journey using ballet, opera, hip hop, aerial dance and fire performance.

However, it is at Burning Man itself where fire performance reigns supreme. Around 1997, Rose invited a group of fire performers to dance around the Man before he burned. This group evolved into the Fire Conclave. By 2000, the Conclave had approximately 300 members. By 2008, it had grown into one of the largest gatherings of fire performers in the country, if not the world, with over 650 members. Rose maintains a steadily growing listserv, which as of 2008 went out to 1,300 fire performers. It was in 2001 that Rose realized the Conclave was getting too big for a single organization. She went to Seattle, Portland, New York and Los Angeles to find a representative from each region, called a *shin*, which means 'mother fire' in Hebrew, 'hot' or 'fire' in Japanese, also extra spicy—or as Tedward, *shin* of the Los Angeles Fire Conclave, jokingly adds, it can be translated as 'flaming hot mother' (2006). The first year there were only four *shins*; by 2008, there were 34.

The responsibility of the *shin* is to be the group leader and to provide Rose with safety rules that the group follows and a list of the performers' names: 'The *shin* has to have enough responsibility and respect to command that group. [. . .] If someone in the group messes up they have to answer for it' (2004a). In the beginning, Rose allowed anyone who was proficient at spinning fire into the circle; however, over time, her standards have become stricter and entry into the Fire Conclave more competitive. Rose developed what she called 'Show Me Salons' in New York, Reno, Seattle, Portland, Los Angeles, Santa Barbara and San Diego where she holds auditions for the Fire Conclave.

Taking Fire Performance at Burning Man to New Heights

Until 2004, Rose held Conclave rehearsals in San Francisco months before Burning Man. Groups had the freedom to perform whatever they chose as long as they were safe, but Rose was determined to do more. After watching the same moves year after year, Rose wanted to challenge the Conclave to perform a choreographed, synchronized fire spectacle. She met with some resistance, as many performers believed that they should do whatever they wanted at Burning Man. But Rose wanted to harness the chaos and energy into a harmonious fiery spectacle that would affect people in a deep way (2004a).

In May 2004, Rose went to Los Angeles to choreograph a two-and-a-half-minute piece called *The Pulse*, with eight dancers from the LA Fire Conclave. Together, they developed a simple routine that would be easy to learn. The LA Fire Conclave conducted a survey and found poi to be the most popular tool, followed by the staff, so Rose and the group set the choreography using poi. Rose started working with Reed Defever, a musician who created a drum piece for 80 drummers. After three nights of working on the choreography, the sequence was videotaped and placed online for performers all across the country to learn. Each *shin* was also sent a CD of the choreography. Rose's expectations were high: 'If it only goes for the first two counts of eight I will be delighted. [. . .] If they can do the first two and a half minutes, I'll be ecstatic. [. . .] If they can repeat this five times I will feel like *okay*!' (2004a). Her goal was to unify all the different groups from around the country into one cohesive group and to surprise the Burning Man crowd, used to seeing chaos, with a beautifully choreographed performance: 'I want to get them to think it's not just chaos but theatricality. [. . .] On a scale of pageantry, how do you move people through a space and tap into what they are really good at?' (ibid.). Her ultimate challenge was to have all the fire go out at once—something yet to happen.

Rose was criticized by some performers who felt constricted by conforming to set choreography. All the same, in 2004, 650 dancers learned the moves. They were required to audition for Rose on the playa, Friday night before the Burn, and prove that they knew the routine. If not, they would not be allowed in the circle. On Friday night, I headed over to the Fire Conclave Convergence at dusk to watch the audition. A large gathering of several hundred fire performers stood anxiously, waiting for Rose to audition them and decide whether or not they could be a part of the 'Great Circle' around the Man.

Rose stood tall on a platform above the Conclave and spoke into a megaphone. She wore a yellow robe with orange flames and gave a goddess-like nod to welcome everyone. She read off the list of all the different troupes that had pre-registered and groups cheered as she read their names. Then she reeled off the order of events, the importance of safety, and her goal to have everyone synchronize for five sets. Then, she reviewed the choreography, the role of the drummers and the signals from those wielding light batons that would guide the drummers. She warned them, 'If you screw up, your *shins* are the ones who are going to take the heat.' Then the groups broke up into their regional areas. There was a tremendous sense of anticipation and nervousness as they rehearsed their choreography without fire. Finally, a circle formed around Rose as she called the first group to present their routine: eight counts of a combination of seven parts, including the simple clockwise spinning called 'home', stalling, the butterfly, turns, weaves and the Mexican wave.

According to the *2004 Afterburn Report*, each of the 29 groups that auditioned made it into the Great Circle from nine different states plus Canada.[9] The 29 groups were organized around the Man using points of reference based on the orientation of the city—3, 6, 9 and 12—as markers to divide the 'Great Circle' (BMO 2004b). To separate fire performers from the huge amount of pyrotechnic material loaded inside the platform of the Man, a 75-foot perimeter circle was created so that no one could cross the line except for the Pyro Crew. Outside that circle, controlled chaos could happen as long as safety and communication was maintained. Each spot designated for a Fire Conclave group had its own refuelling station, a Radio Head and a Fire Watch—someone to monitor the group's performance and make sure performers were safe. Because the main stage manager cannot be everywhere at once, the position of Radio Head was created several years ago to relay instructions.

Unfortunately, the performance did not go according to plan. Rose reported that the 80 drummers (Helmsmen) could not keep the rhythm, and the dancers lost their way because they couldn't hear the beat. It was an impossible feat to coordinate 650 fire performers from across the country, but it was a valiant attempt. In retrospect, Rose felt the performance was an important exercise in the evolution of the Fire Conclave. In general, she believes the skills of the performers and the quality of the performances are reaching new heights due to experimentation with form, content, choreography, costuming and fire tools. Through elaborate costuming and makeup, groups are each beginning to establish a distinctive look and style. Fire performers as well as fire performance itself are maturing as groups take big risks with the medium. *The Pulse* served as a catalyst for groups to take the Conclave to the next level.

In 2005, rather than attempting another synchronized spectacle, Rose urged the individual groups to devise an original piece of choreography to perform in the Circle. The process became more formal, requiring groups to submit a sample of their choreography via DVD by 1 July of each year. This same application and audition process was repeated in 2006, 2007 and 2008. Each group is required to reapply every year with a new piece of choreography: 'It doesn't make sense if you come back and keep doing the same dance. It becomes stale' (2008). Only a fraction of the groups who audition actually end up in the circle. In 2005, 45 groups totalling over 850 performers produced their routines around the Great Circle.

While some felt that the imposition of choreography restricted their creativity, Rose defended her position:

> My goal is to get people to actually be part of a group and take it seriously. It doesn't take away from their own creativity and style but when you join a group you have to let go of a little bit of your own ego. I find it also challenges them to think more creatively. [. . .] Most of the fire performers are so inventive that they will take an idea and they will go with it. They will start inventing new tools, new movements; that to me is exciting. They are all keeping it very much alive as an art form and moving the medium forward (ibid.).

Rose is the sole curator of the Fire Conclave, wielding her authority and control over the Conclave's aesthetic and artistic direction. In regular contact with each group, Rose encourages fire performers to take inspiration from the outside world and incorporate that into the performance. She often gives specific suggestions to groups about the direction they should take. For example, in 2006, Rose encouraged the LA Conclave to use the film *Memoirs of a Geisha* as inspiration for a new routine, which resulted in a choreographed fan dance.

In 2005, each group was given a specific location and set order to perform around the Great Circle. However, this new configuration caused a different set of problems. As Tedward remembers, the signals on the radio were unclear and his group sat around for a long time waiting to perform. When it finally was their turn, they had less than a minute. In 2005, I observed large gaps of darkness around the Great Circle and it was difficult to see the performances unless they were directly in front of you.

Rose no longer attempts to hold rehearsals on the playa as it takes too much time and energy. Upon arriving in Black Rock City, each fire performer is required to check in at the Fire Conclave Convergence located on the Esplanade. By signing their name and affiliation in a binder, they receive a laminated badge that is distributed the day of the Burn. Performers are not allowed to enter the Great Circle without this badge. Within the Great Circle, each group needs to sustain a high level of energy that can be projected across the vast landscape. Small, intimate movements are lost in the chaotic environment, hence performers need to be larger than life. It is the *shins*' responsibility to drive and push the groups each year to new levels of innovation and experimentation.

Rose soon realized the political nature of her role as Fire Conclave curator. As the Burning Man Regional Network (see Chapter 7) began to expand, she needed to include fire troupes located in each region to help forge ongoing relationships. Each troupe is totally different, with varying degrees of experience, and Rose gives some leeway to groups who do not live in urban settings and have not had much exposure to this type of performance: 'If you are trying to encourage the Regionals to come together and do something—this is another way to encourage them to be a part of something' (ibid.). In the past few years, several international fire ensembles have joined the Conclave, from Finland, Germany, Thailand and Australia, bringing further influences from around the globe into the mix.

In 2005, Rose initiated a new ritual elaborating on her Opening Fire Ceremony that officially begins the event. The flame captured from the sun is kept alive all week and, on the day of the Burn, the flame from the Center Camp Cauldron is transferred to a steel vessel called the Luminferous, forged and fabricated by the Seattle-based collective Iron Gypsy. The vessel is carried by the Lamplighters along with the vocal troupes One Peoples Voice and Gamelan X in a procession surrounded by the Fire Conclave. Once the vessel arrives at the Great Circle at the 6 o'clock position, it moves around the circle clockwise, distributing the flame to each Conclave group.

For Rose, timing is essential and experience has taught her that the threshold of attention around the Man is approximately half an hour—then people begin to get bored. Once all the performers are assembled around the Great Circle, Rose communicates the signal for the Conclave to begin via radio. The Conclave has exactly 25 minutes to perform: 15 minutes of a choreographed routine and 10 minutes of 'zaka', Rose's term for performed chaos. Her challenge remains the same each year: 'How do you keep the energy and timing alive so that people don't get irritated that the man is not on fire?' (Ibid.)

Performing in the Fire Conclave

During the year, the Fire Conclave remains connected via the Internet. Most groups have their own websites and each *shin* maintains a discussion list. In San Francisco, the Fire Conclave meets on the last Sunday of each month to do a fire jam. Many performers are self-taught; others learn from experienced fire performers. A large number of the fire performers that I interviewed learned to spin fire at Burning Man and wanted to continue learning after attending the festival. The website homeofpoi.com has short video clips and instructions on how to dance with poi, and many of the Fire Conclave groups teach fire performance in their home towns.

While many people have been inspired by Burning Man to start fire dancing, many other great performers have quit for one reason or another: burned, burnt out or no longer interested. Szpigiel from AWD/Xeno remembered his experience performing in the 1999 Conclave: 'The first year was pretty chaotic; Rose told the performers, "Okay, whatever your act is, do that"' (2006). But the year after that, rehearsals were mandatory, which turned some performers off. Fire performer Mindbender recalled attending several Conclave rehearsals in San Francisco in 2001 with the agreement that Conclave members would receive a free ticket to Burning Man. She observed a wide variety of skill levels and saw that the choreography they were learning was rudimentary. She went through the entire rehearsal process but, at the last pre-desert rehearsal, Rose announced that they were not going to get free tickets. However, if one attended all the desert rehearsals, one would be given a voucher to get a free ticket the following year. Mindbender was disheartened:

> I got upset with Burning Man because our trust was broken. How can you promise all these people that you are going to give them free tickets and then not come through? We'd made a commitment and Burning Man back-pedalled on their end of the deal. It felt like a big scam. I said, 'Forget it, I am not going to be a part of the Conclave.' That was my first disillusionment with Burning Man (2006).

According to Mindbender, by 2001 a lot of people were disillusioned with Burning Man. But for others, Burning Man and the Fire Conclave has completely changed their lives. Tedward, for example, has been playing with fire since he was a child. Born in Michigan, Tedward discovered his love for fire when his brothers would throw hot campfire coals at him. He learned how to hold the coals and eventually walk on them, quelling his initial fear of fire. Self-trained, Tedward learned to play with other tools such as poi, staffs and fire swords. He moved to Los Angeles in 1995 and held a variety of jobs, mostly in information technology. A friend returned from the 1999 Burning Man raving about the event and Tedward decided to go the following year.

That first year he stayed at what became known as 'Camp Miserable' after the 70-mph winds and three days of 24-hour white-outs, which ended in rain, utterly destroyed his camp. He applied to be in the Fire Conclave, but the Conclave never happened: a short in the neon accidentally triggered the fireworks on the Man two hours early—no one had yet gathered around the Circle. When the Man unexpectedly went off, there was a surge of people from every direction towards the Man, and Tedward was almost crushed. Thrust to the edge of the blazing Man, the heat was so intense that he had to keep rotating to avoid being burned.

Despite the catastrophes of his first year, Tedward started the LA Fire Conclave in 2001 with 25 dancers. By 2006, there were 50. The LA Conclave does not perform at other venues, although small subgroups and individual members do. Once performers become too good, says Tedward, they tend to break off and form their own groups or join other groups that give public performances. He recalls his own first experience performing solo at Burning Man with his handmade fire swords: 'When I first started doing fire, it was about attention. Moontribe was having a party; I snuck in and performed with my fire sword. There was a ton of fire. They treated me like Elvis. It was awesome!' (2005).

At the time, Tedward held a full-time information technology job. He began to get requests for fire tools from other performers and decided to start an online fire tool business, Bearclaw Manufacturing. He quit his technology job and gave himself one year to get the business going. He was successful and now sells fire tools full-time. All the tools are handmade and cost from $30 to several hundred dollars, depending on materials and complexity. Tedward fabricates custom-made poi, torches, fire staves, hoops, swords, whips, fans, wings, fingers, ropes, shoes and clothing. When I asked him how Burning Man affected his life, Tedward responded, 'It completely changed it—I am a full-time Burner now. I am where I am because of Burning Man. I run my own business. I have fans. I am a rock star. I took a completely different direction in my life' (ibid.).

Another fire performer, Cassandra Marshall, saw fire spinning for the first time in the 1997 Burning Man Opera and then in a performance by the group Xeno. She was totally mesmerized. When she moved to New York City, she lived downstairs from a fire performer, Flambeaux, who had never been to Burning Man. Every fire performer she had ever seen previously had *something* to do with Burning Man and she assumed Flambeaux's work would be similar—but she was sorely disappointed. He poured some fuel on the stage, lit it on fire, and then proceeded to eat fire in a mundane manner—nothing like the fire performing in the desert (Marshall 2004). What Marshall noticed was that a unique style of fire performance was developing on the playa—a more visceral and aggressive style than that of the nightclub and circus performers she had seen. The open expanse of the playa allows fire performers the freedom to take risks and push their art to new limits.

These individual stories are representative of the scores of performers who join the Fire Conclave each year. And while they are all rigorously rehearsing and preparing for the night of the Burn, another group is equally busy—the Man Crew. Theirs is the final Burn, the climax of the week-long event.

Axis Mundi and the Construction of the Ultimate Effigy: The Man

Harvey once called Burning Man the 'stagecraft of religion'. Burning Man is full of theatre tricks and it is also very much like a religion—people believe in Burning Man the way some believe in their chosen religion. Like a religion, Burning Man becomes a focus of participants' lives, a community of ideals around which they base their lives and the choices they make. The effigy of the Man stands at the centre of Black Rock City on an altar around which the mythology and belief system of the Burning Man community revolves, similar to other geographic locations designated as the focal point of a people: To'wa Yallanne is the sacred centre of the world to the Zuni; Mt Agung is the 'naval of the earth' for the Balinese; and the Kaaba at Mecca the focal point of Islam. The 2003 theme, 'Beyond Belief' explicitly named the Man as the *axis mundi* on the Black Rock City map. In an interview with his alter-ego, Darryl Van Rhey, Harvey stated that the Man:

> Forms an absolute center; a sort of hub or fixed axis around which everything else is free to revolve. [. . .] He stands at the end of a monumental avenue that is lined with wooden spires. [. . .] It harkens back to an historic moment when science, art, and politics were all one thing, all united in a single sacramental act. All over the world, at the very dawn of

> civilized history, we see evidence of this. Great temples, *axis mundi*—'world navels'—dominated public space. The days before the burning are a kind of Saturnalia (in Van Rhey 1999: 4).

In most religions, idols, physical symbols, effigies, fetishes and the like represent the religion's belief system. Countercultures emerge, according to sociologist Milton Yinger, when a society's myths and symbols lose their meaning (1982: 9). This lack of meaningful symbols in our culture perhaps explains how the icon of the Man emerged as a powerful symbol around which the Burning Man community coalesced. Early on, Harvey noticed that the Man's face formed by an inverted triangle corresponded to the basic pattern of eyes and mouth in a human face. He realized that he had stumbled on a universal primal image that was simple yet significant (Van Rhey 1999: 4). Primary shapes such as circles, triangles and squares are often charged with mythological and symbolic meaning in rituals, and their simplicity and accessibility is the source of their power. For Harvey, the ritual around the Man himself recapitulates a form of primordial experience that transcends culture. Initially, participants gave birth to the Man through a symbolic gesture—by pulling on a rope attached to his navel, like an umbilical cord (Nash 1995: 1). While the participants no longer haul the Man into place, a powerful symbolic connection still exists.

How does this iconic figure get built and who is behind its construction? Initially, Harvey and James constructed a rudimentary Man out of scrap wood—Harvey designed and James built. Very early on, Harvey relinquished control over building the Man. I asked Harvey if the Man was his creation: 'Partially. I drew it in its present form in 1990. Originally, it was Jerry James and I but I let the carpenters take it over. We have kept him essentially the same but everything around him should change' (2004a). James, the primary carpenter, stopped building the Man after 1990 because it became too much of an obligation for him. Soon, other builders got involved—Chris Campbell, Dan Miller, Dale Scott and Ben Stoelting, among others. The construction of the 40-foot wooden Man still follows the original blueprint drawings that Harvey and James made back in 1990, but small embellishments appear each year (Harvey 2005). For example, the base is designed to reflect the annual theme. In the early 1990s, the Man stood on the playa surrounded by bales of hay. On the first day of Burning Man in 1990, the community physically lifted the

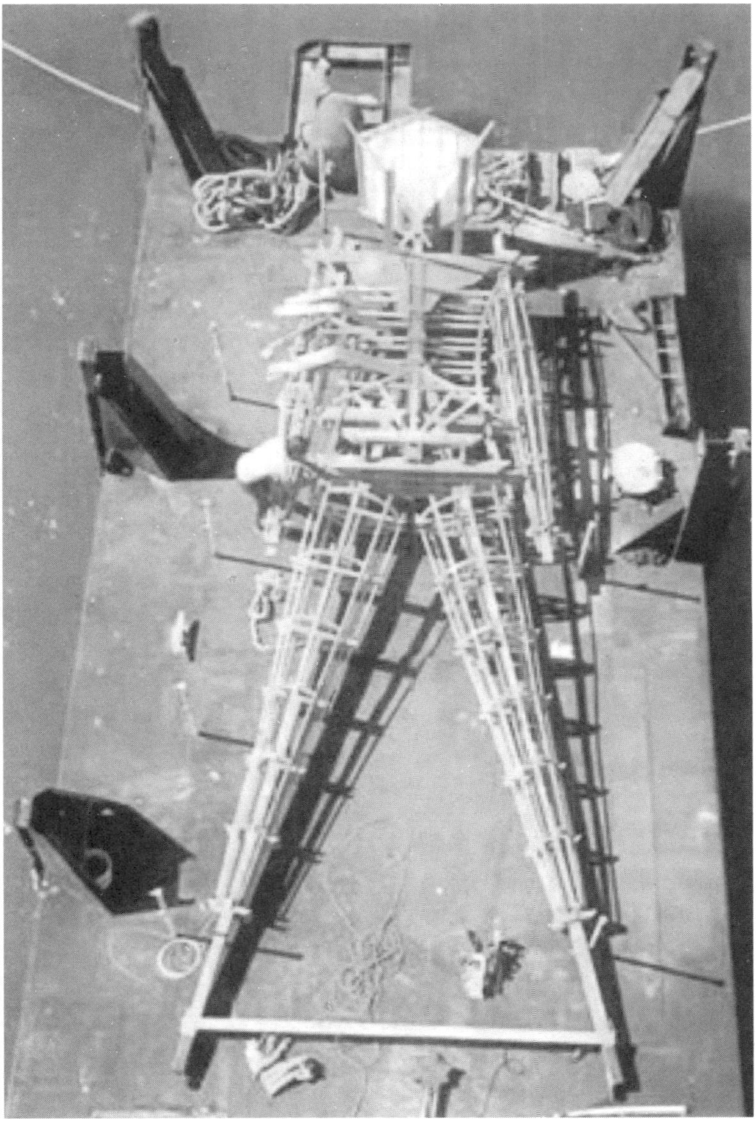

FIGURE 6.3. The Man being constructed on a barge in San Francisco, 1991. Courtesy of the Burning Man Organization.

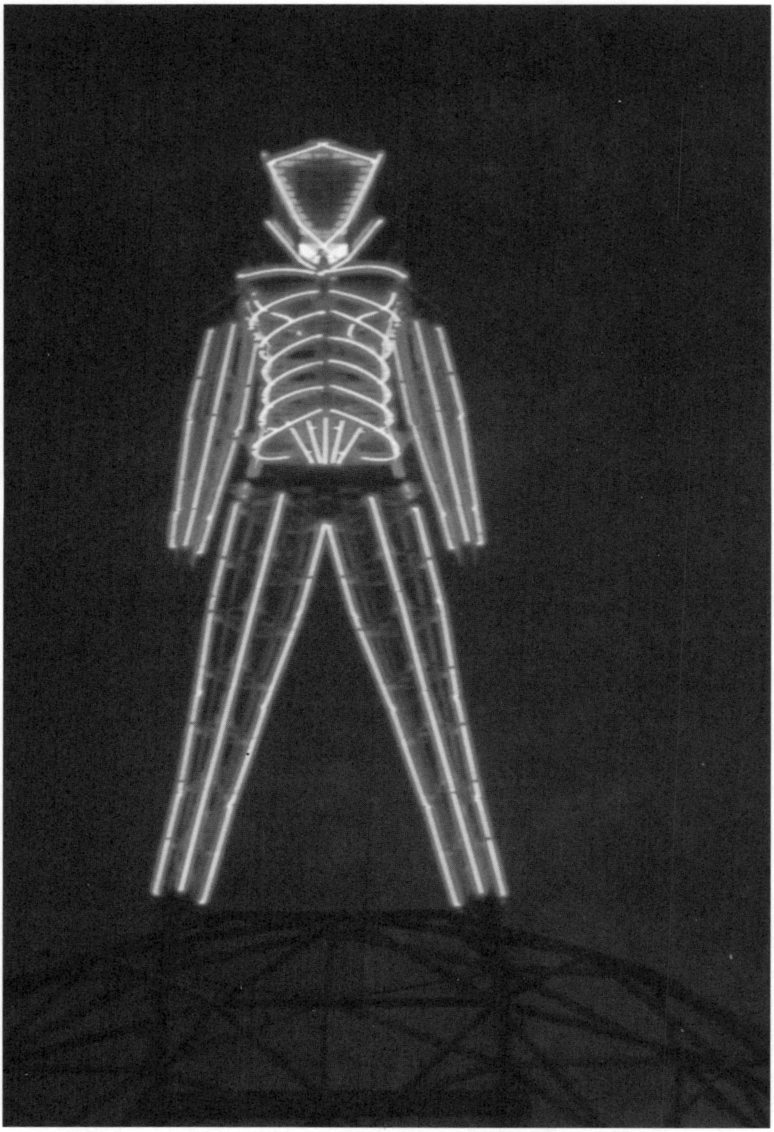

FIGURE 6.4. The Man, 2004.
Photograph by John Tzelepis.

Man into place; for years now, a crane does the job. Constructing the Man requires the coordinated effort of several crews: pedestal, neon, laser, rigging, pyro and the Man himself. A select crew of eight builders called the Man Crew, which is supervised by Rose and Roger, builds the Man.

Man Crew builder Captain Bob, whose default name is Robert Heacock, shed light on the building process. According to him, Harvey does not participate in the building at all. In fact, Harvey never appears at the work ranch during the construction, although he is present when the Man is raised on the playa. Captain Bob, a 56-year-old retiree from the Teamster Union, joined the Man Crew as a volunteer in 2003. He first saw the statue of the Man in 1998 in a vacant lot near the Civic Center in San Francisco and was amazed by its epic scale. In 1998, he went out to Black Rock City for the first time and, during that week, Captain Bob says Burning Man renewed his faith in humanity. He met people who were totally different from the greedy, self-centred, egomaniacs he worked with. He felt a tremendous sense of community that drew him back year after year.

For Captain Bob, Burning Man represents the 'help your neighbour' attitude. In 2003, when Captain Bob retired from the Teamster Union at the age of 56, he wanted to give something back to the Burning Man community. He went to the Burning Man office to donate his time and expertise to the Man Crew and, a few days later, was invited to Nevada on 23 June for a work weekend (Heacock 2006). In 2002, the 25-person crew was too crowded, so today the Man Crew consists of eight core carpenters and a few volunteers. In exchange for their labour, each builder receives two free tickets to Burning Man and meals during workdays. They meet in February to discuss preliminary plans and convene on weekends in June at a work ranch in the Black Rock Desert, north of Black Rock City, to begin the first phase of building the effigy. The BMO owns the 200-acre ranch, which comprises two steel huts, each 200 feet long and 60 feet wide, a woodshop, a metal shop, a shower building, a laundry room, a kitchen and a storage location for the DPW vehicles, oversized art cars, the Lamplighter's street lampposts and 20 broken-down trailers.

During work weekends, all meals are provided by a cook and are paid for by the BMO. Working from 10 rudimentary blueprints, the Man Crew follows a daily schedule that includes breakfast, a morning meeting and then building throughout the day except for a midday meal break. Each person builds the legs, the torso, the arms, or the head. Captain Bob used to hand cut the rings of the legs with a jigsaw, but now the rings are cut by a computer-guided saw to save time and labour. The prepared materials—a total of 350 separate wooden parts—are transported out into the desert where sections of the Man are assembled. Once the sections are together, they are stored in a large container at the ranch until they are brought to Black Rock City in mid-August (ibid.).

Surveying and laying out Black Rock City starts at the beginning of August when the location of 'ground zero'—the Man—is established. The entire city radiates out from this single, metaphysical point in space. At first, an ordinary wooden stake was used to break ground but soon the builders began to ceremonialize the action, using a 'golden' stake to mark the *axis mundi* (Harvey 2008b).

In mid-August, the trash fence—designed to catch any blowing garbage—demarcating the perimeter of the City, goes up, and the Base Crew begins construction. At this point, the Man Crew moves onto the playa for the duration of the building and the event. This crew and others working on the Man are fed in the Commissary,[10] the communal dining hall for all pre-event volunteers. Once the base is complete, the sections of the Man are brought to ground zero and assembled. When the Man is assembled, but before he is lifted onto the base, the Neon Crew moves in to wire the Man. Then highly flammable burlap soaked in wax is wrapped on the inside of the Man's legs, arms and parts of the torso. This is to make sure that once ignited, the fire will swiftly spread and consume the Man. Finally, the Man is lifted into place by a crane.

The Man Crew works hardest the week before the event. In addition to the core of eight, trusted volunteers are selected and placed according to their strengths and skill levels as carpenters, engineers and other specialities. Professional architects and engineers are brought in to inspect all structures and public gathering areas such as the base of the Man and the Center Camp Café to ensure they can withstand the violent wind and other harsh conditions of the desert.

While many crews are crucial to the operation of Black Rock City, Captain Bob feels that the Man Crew receives special attention from the organizers because of the central importance of their job. The Man

Crew is allowed to stand in the inner circle sanctuary around the Man on the night of the Burn, and they have the responsibility of raising the Man's arms via a pulley system. According to Ben Stoelting, the Man Crew chief from 1997 until 2008, 'each year the crew signs the Man's wooden heart, but in 2003 the Man had an electro-flashing heart, so they signed the spine. By tradition, crew who injure themselves drip blood onto the wood' (BMO 2003b: 2).

Captain Bob feels a tremendous connection to the Man; he is 'the focal point, the icon. He is metaphysical. When he is gone, I cry. He feels like a best friend and I have a very intimate relationship with him. [. . .] Being on the Man Crew, everyone praises you constantly, encourages you, and makes you feel good about yourself. There is a tremendous sense of accomplishment' (Heacock 2006). According to Captain Bob, being on the Man Crew elevates you to the status of 'demi-god' within the community: 'You become extremely popular because you are responsible for building the heart of the event, the center of power, the central icon. That is a very powerful thing' (ibid.). For Captain Bob, nothing is more rewarding than being a part of a team that constructs a work of art admired and adored by 49,000 people. Each year he spends hundreds of hours building and each year he watches the Man burn with great emotion.

The Man through Time: 2001–08

In selecting the themes each year, Harvey looks for concepts that are accessible and that will resonate throughout the entire community. Increasingly, he has sought themes that relate to current sociopolitical trends in order to reinforce the idea that Burning Man values and culture resonate in the 'default' world. A central question Harvey asks each year is, 'What is the spirit of this time?' (2008b) and how can that spirit be translated into a central navigating point of departure. In 2001, for 'The Seven Ages of Man', the base was a white monolithic structure that represented the 'Temple of Wisdom' in the game of life. People could walk around the Man but not touch him. The base in 2002 was a lighthouse, reflecting the theme 'Floating World'. A green krypton laser pierced the darkness like a searchlight, with four beams radiating out from the lighthouse. The Man atop his lighthouse was 69 feet tall.

FIGURE 6.5. The Man atop the Great Temple, 2003.
Photograph by Roth Hall.

In 2003, the theme was 'Beyond Belief' and the Man stood on a 40-foot-high altar called the Great Temple (not to be confused with David Best's temples), modelled after the Aztec Templo Major (Great Temple) in Tenochtitlan (today's Mexico City). Deep inside the pyramid, inner sanctuaries housed altars where participants were encouraged to leave cherished items as a sacrificial act. According to Captain Bob, and confirmed in my interview with Best, there was a growing tension between Best and Harvey over their temples. Harvey did not want Best to build his temples higher than the Man. Harvey's Great Temple was 79 feet tall; with the Man standing on top, it was the tallest in the event's history.

Burning Man's 2003 Great Temple base was a pyramid, geometrically reminiscent of bygone structures built according to cosmic alignments. Many ancient structures—from Ur and the Egyptian pyramids to Stonehenge, Chan Chan and the Teotihuacán pyramids—were built according to geographic, astronomic and cosmic orientations linking the structures to the stars and the surrounding landscape. The appropriation of cultural symbols such as the Teotihuacán Pyramids of the Sun and the Moon (AD 200–450) was, according to Harvey, a deliberate choice. His guerrilla strategy is to appropriate symbols and other elements of mass culture that pervade popular consciousness, creating new myths with a postmodern twist. While pop culture and the media transform what he calls 'authentic culture' and grassroots art into commodities, Burning Man reverses this process by turning pop culture back into myth. 'We appropriate the appropriators. It's a survival tactic for the nineties' (Van Rhey 1997).

Harvey believes that in the 'eclectic' age we live in, there is no single unifying idea to rally around, causing us to become 'a nation of dilettantes' and members of disconnected subcultures. For him, every idea or lifestyle is spread out in front of us like an enormous buffet, 'a never-ending post-graduate course', yet we do not know how to take advantage of this freedom (1997a). The appropriation of a Meso-American temple served as a focal point around which disparate mythologies could be reborn. When Glaser (aka Costume Jim), founder of Kostume Kult, learned that there would be portals at the base of the Aztec pyramid where one could stand as a godlike statue, the first iconic symbol that came to his mind was Anubis, the Egyptian god of mummification and the afterlife. Glaser created what he considers his most elaborate costume yet, an

FIGURE 6.6. The Man on the Observatory, 2004.
Photograph by Rick Egan.

electroluminescent Anubis headdress, neckpiece and loincloth. The night before the Man burned, Glaser found himself walking alone at dawn, clad as an Egyptian god. As he approached the pyramid, he could hear the distant mayhem of Black Rock City fading behind him. As he ascended the Great Temple, everyone already gathered there started banging rhythmically on the side of the pyramid. Glaser shared his experience: 'When the first blink of light crested, everybody just sat there. At that moment, you could hear silence. You could hear angels laughing. You could hear devils singing. It was probably one of the most powerful moments of my life. Then after a long time, everybody started clapping. Talk about ritual' (2006). The mythical landscape deliberately created by Harvey and the BMO allows for participants to construct new personal mythologies around the symbols that are provided. These ritual spaces, such as the 79-foot pyramid complex, offer a *tabula rasa* for the invention of ritual practices and the formation of alternative identities.

In 2004, the 2,300-pound Man stood tall upon an enormous geodesic dome called the Observatory. Participants could wander through the dome and gaze up towards the Man and beyond, up into the 'Vault of Heaven'—the theme for that year. Surrounding the Observatory were 10 small stages with various otherworldly landscapes painted on the walls. People were invited to enter the small theatres and create performances. The idea was interesting, in theory, but was not fully realized. Many of the theatres remained empty as participants found better venues to perform in.

For the 2005 theme, 'Psyche', the base of the Man was called the Funhouse, the most playful design for the Man's base to date. From the outside it looked like a circus tent festooned with red neon and adorned with colourful green and pink flags. Entering through one of the four doorways, participants encountered a complicated maze. Moving through tight spaces, narrow doorways and revolving doors, the journey through the Funhouse was an exhilarating, and at times terrifying, experience. After reaching the maze's centre, you could ascend to a platform on the second level for a panoramic view of Black Rock City. The fluorescent green and pink Man weighed 2,200 pounds and rotated on casters and bearings designed for effortless turning when participants pushed a wooden shaft. Roger, who supervised the various crews, said that the base of the Man was a three-storey building built to code with wet-stamped plans from a structural engineer. It was assembled on-site in two and a half days so that everything else could get built. Two designers, Rod Garrett and Todd Dworman, and four project managers were brought in just to build the maze. Roger recalls, 'Before it was completed, one of the carpenters left his hammer in one of the rooms of the maze and he was looking for it for half an hour. He just couldn't find it. That is when we knew the maze was a success' (2005).

For the 2006 theme 'Hope and Fear', the base was an Art Deco palace dubbed 'The Pavilion of the Future', designed by Garrett and Harvey. The Art Deco movement of the 1920s and 1930s, with its streamlined, dynamic forms, espoused a modern, industrial aesthetic and a vision of a utopian future. However, retrospectively, this is a future that never came to pass. With a dystopic twist, Harvey writes, 'Robots do not wait upon us hand and foot, nor do we jet from place to place in private rocket ships. Along the road to a utopia, these science fiction fantasies gave way to traffic jams. The future, it begins to seem, ran out of gas' (2006c). As in 2005, this base was a complicated labyrinth of rooms decorated with visions of a utopian, as well as dystopian, future. The theme was a provocation to define how we create futurity by reflexively examining our deepest hopes and fears. To represent this metaphorical ebb and flow of uncertainty, participants could manipulate levers to make the Man rise and fall. Inside the Pavilion, artists created a variety of voting devices like slot machines where participants could vote for either hope or fear. These results were indicated by light signals—green for hope and red for fear—calculating the community's positive or negative vision of the future at any given moment.

In response to the growing concern about protecting the environment and humanity's relationship with nature, the 2007 theme 'The Green Man', was a concerted effort to 'go green'. The theme was loosely based on an enigmatic figure named the 'Green Man' which was discovered around 1939 etched onto the crevices and walls of mediaeval cathedrals by anonymous craftsmen. As in 2006, the theme posed a question: What do we need to do as a civilization to protect the earth and her resources? The 'Green Theme' Man stood atop a shade structure that resembled a mountain peak. Beneath the cloth, a 30,000-square-foot pavilion provided an exhibition space in the spirit of the World Fairs where participants

FIGURE 6.7. Rendering of the 'Pavilion of the Future', 2006, by Rod Garrett. Courtesy of the Burning Man Organization.

installed interactive artistic and scientific displays about environmental protection. Part of the project was to calculate Burning Man's carbon footprint and to encourage participants to reduce their environmental impact on the desert within their own camps, an ongoing challenge since the first year the event took place in the desert in 1990. To reduce the carbon footprint, the organization used solar panels to charge the Man, which were later donated to a local high school and the Lovelock Medical Center. But the event did not go as planned.

On Tuesday 28 August 2007, at approximately 2.58 a.m., Rose was sitting at First Camp watching the lunar eclipse: 'I just happened to be up and sitting on the deck at First Camp when I started to see emergency vehicles race towards the Man. It took me a while to really realize what was happening' (2008). The Man had been torched by old-time Burner, Paul Addis, a 35-year-old San Francisco playwright, as an act of rebellion against the BMO. In 2000, Addis quit his job as an intellectual property lawyer to pursue a career in the arts. At the time of the incident, Addis was starring in a touring show, *Gonzo, a Brutal Chrysalis*, about journalist Hunter S. Thompson. He climbed up the shade cloth before anybody saw him and set the Man ablaze. Rose, who has known Addis for about 15 years, said, 'He was totally pissed off that we had sold out and it was not like the good old days. Yeah, it is not like the good old days. I think he was trying to draw attention to himself' (ibid.).

Addis was arrested and jailed on felony charges of arson and destruction of property by Pershing County, as well as with a misdemeanour for the possession of fireworks and resisting a police officer. He posted a $25,632 bond and was released. Addis's arraignment on these charges was scheduled for 25 September 2007, at the Pershing County courthouse where he was charged with first-degree arson, destruction of property and the reckless endangerment of human life. He was released on bail and arrested eight weeks after the Burning Man incident for attempted arson at Grace Cathedral in San Francisco. As of October 2008, Addis was being held in a San Francisco jail with a bail of $488,000. He has since been released after serving jail time. There is also a warrant for his arrest in Nevada (BMO 2007b).

Addis defended his action in an interview with *Wired*'s Miyoko Ohtake as a 'badly needed reality check for the desert art festival' (in Ohtake

2007). Later, he claimed full responsibility: 'Burning Man has turned into an "Alterna-Disney", and the act was a protest against the Man's increasing commercialization.' Addis, a member of the anarchist organization, Black Rock Intelligence, claimed, 'This was a Black Rock Intelligence operation. But since the group has been disbanded, they can make no claim to responsibility. [. . .] I am their sole surviving member' (in ibid.). The early Burn was premeditated and planned well in advance. Without arousing suspicion, participants were cleared from the area so that no one would get hurt. Addis felt that Burning Man had lost all spontaneity: 'The Burning Man Organization doesn't have any sense of humor anymore and that streams and trickles down to the participants themselves.' He criticized participants, 'What are they doing when they come back to the cities? Nothing. They go blow their wads for seven days at Burning Man and then go back to their jobs. They don t do anything else for the rest of the year' (in ibid.).

Addis had attended the event in 1996, 1997 and 1998 but didn't go again until 2007 because he felt that Burning Man was 'only advocating social impact and responsibility in the name of its own self-preservation, survival and expansion' (in ibid.) and he was not willing to be a part of that. He showed his rebellious side early on in his history with Burning Man—in 1997, he pulled his first prank on the playa by attaching giant silver balls between the Man's legs—an act he was not charged for. The 2007 early Burn, according to Addis, was his attempt to recapture the original spirit of the event: 'This was not an act of vengeance, it was one of love' (in Garofoli 2007). Addis felt his act of arson was a reminder of why the event started in the first place, an act of radical self-expression, which he believes is no longer possible at the event because it has become too regulated:

> We're being programmed on every level: TV, radio, Internet, advertising. It's everywhere. We believe in the true promise of the American Dream and that should be for everyone no matter what. We're jamming the programme and allowing people the freedom of their minds rather than the programming someone else is trying to sell them. That's the most important thing (in Ohtake 2007).

People had been talking about pulling this prank for years before Addis finally succeeded.

Addis also complained that the 2007 'Green Man' theme was a total sham:

> If you want to know how much of a total lie it is, run a Google satellite photo of Burning Man right now and count the number of RVs there. And they're telling me it's an environmental movement? Bullshit. [. . .] Burning Man is offering no real alternatives to the current environmental crisis. [. . .] 'Green Man' is all about Burning Man getting the most green in their pockets' (in ibid.).

With several fire trucks, the fire was doused within half an hour. Although the Man was severely charred and there was some structural damage, he remained standing. However, for safety reasons, he was removed from his pedestal. 'It was strange to have the event without the central icon of the Man anchoring the city,' Rose recalls (2008). The event continued despite the effacement and displacement of the event's central effigy. Rose admits, 'It was definitely one of the worst nights of my life. We had joked about it for years, and then it happened. It showed me that the Man Crew and the Pavilion Crew were not going to allow somebody to take their energy away' (ibid.). By the time the organizers woke up the next morning, the builders had started rebuilding their Man.

Without any prompting from Harvey or anyone else from the BMO, the Man Crew, the Pavilion Crew and the DPW mobilized to work around the clock to rebuild the Man by Saturday for the scheduled Burn. Goodell laughed, 'In fact, we probably couldn't have stopped it. That is their art, so they rebuilt their art' (2008). The crews utilized the shade structures to rebuild the Man on-site and a cook was sent out to provide meals for the volunteers who worked nonstop. Replacement wood and neon was purchased in Reno. With hundreds of hours of human labour required, the crews who had worked so hard to complete the Man and the Pavilion before the event opened, were right back at it with no break at all. The incident proved to Rose that they could rebuild the Man in record time: 'We triumphed over anybody thinking that they could actually take that away from us' (2008). Usually, the Man itself is built the week leading up to the fourth of July, giving him three months to cure; the rebuilt Man took much longer to burn because it was green wood that had not been cured. Nevertheless, the 2007 Burn was very special, according to Rose, because it let people know that, no matter what, 'we're doing it our way' (ibid.).

FIGURE 6.8. The charred Man after Paul Addis set him on fire., 2007. Photograph by Michael Mikel.

Harvey did not want to have the Man rebuilt. In his opinion, the Man should have been lowered, cut into pieces with a chainsaw, then distributed throughout the entire community. That to him would have been a symbolic and appropriate gesture. In Harvey's opinion, rebuilding the Man confirmed Addis's belief that the event had become too corporate. Harvey wishes he had been the one to make the official announcement to the community but he told me, 'I just didn't have the heart. It made me heartsick' (2008b). The announcement printed in *Black Rock Beacon* read, 'The Man will burn as scheduled.' Harvey feels that this was the wrong language and that it should have been, 'The Man will burn at the appointed time,' which to him represents a very different tone and meaning (ibid.).

The toll exacted by Addis's act was emotional as well as financial. According to LLC board member, Harley K. Dubois, the early Burn broke the spirit of the Black Rock Rangers, the peacekeeping entity of Black Rock City. The group had to be completely restructured in 2008 because the rangers on duty worked overtime to deal with the crisis to ensure the rebuilding of the Man on time (Dubois 2008).

Participants' responses varied. Some supported Addis, shouting, 'Burn the Man!' Others saw the act as disrespectful of the event and the organizers. The early Burn prompted some Burners to rethink their relationship and attachment to the Man, which was one of Addis's goals: 'Why are you really out there? If the burning of the Man means something, if it brings you some sort of cathartic connection, then build your own thing and burn it down. Don't be a passive audience member. Cross the line' (in Ohtake 2007). Reflecting on the incident, Harvey poignantly recalls what he experienced when he learned no one was hurt:

> We started laughing for two hours but I fooled myself, I didn't realize how much it affected me. There has been this tension in the underground against the Man and it goes back to struggles I had with my old partner, John Law, with attempts to deface it and mock it. I wasn't even going to assign any meaning to it but it was mean spirited. It was promoted by jealousy, envy. The community did fine but there was a noxious dialogue on the Internet and he [Addis] became celebrated in the underground as a cultural hero for defacing 'the Man'. [. . .] This teaches us not to reify symbols. Let's not mistake the object for the real thing, which is the community. I handled it well at first, but then I paused to reflect later

> and it was in fact a gut punch. It hurt. They finally succeeded in desecrating this thing (2008b).

The incident was an important moment in the history of the event because it proved that the event could still function with or without the Man. This was a difficult lesson to learn, as Rose realized, 'It kind of woke us up out of being a little bit innocent and naive—that we would allow someone to take advantage of us. However, this is just a little glitch. I think we need to protect things a little better. It just means we need to be more on the ball. I think we will be better prepared for it in the future.' With great concern, she added, 'This is not something I want to repeat' (2008).

In response to the arson in 2007 and in light of the 2008 presidential election, the 2008 theme, 'The American Dream', was about nationality, identity and the nature of patriotism. For Rose, 'The American Dream is Burning Man. Out of nothing came this gathering of people to do this and isn't that part of what the American Dream is, to live your dreams and be a part of something? We are on a journey. It is always a little different every time. We end up having to reinvent something' (ibid.). Guiding questions were designed to provoke participants to consider 'America', what the 'American Dream' actually is and what it means to pursue the 'American Dream'. How can these questions be answered artistically, interactively and performatively?

As a reaction to the attempted arson of the Man by Addis in 2007, the 2008 Man, designed by Garrett and Harvey, was placed far out of reach. Set aloft a tower of flags from around the world, the Man stood as a utopian beacon of international unity and prosperity. Ironically, this phallic effigy of invincibility was erected during a time of economic recession, with a national mortgage crisis and ever-escalating fuel prices, and at the end of the eight-year domination of the Bush Administration and its failed policies in Iraq. The imposing obelisk adorned with flags from around the world reclaims the 'American Dream' and attempts to heal Bush's damaged foreign policy by reuniting the nations into a harmonious whole.

Participants could ascend the tower via a double-helix staircase, like a strand of DNA, to reach the uppermost platform beneath the Man. To prevent another attack on the Man, increased surveillance was required from the Black Rock Rangers and other authorities present on the playa. A ranger was placed at the base of the ascending staircase and only 15 people were allowed up at a time. Another ranger regulated descending participants and a third was placed on the observation deck to monitor participants. The roof of the deck and the base of the Man were ringed with barbed wire to prevent climbing. The Man performatively enacted the unfettered surveillance allowed by the design of Bentham's Panopticon. Once again, the ironic juxtaposition of 'freedom' on one hand and 'surveillance' on the other spiral each other in a continual search for balance. The 2008 design epitomized this quest.

Surrounding the tower of flags were several shade structures and an installation called *Welcome to Ellis Island* that recreated the border crossing into the United States. Participants walked over a wooden bridge to a lectern surrounded by tattered suitcases where they signed their names and wrote down their dreams. Two event posters captured the paradox of the American Dream: one depicted a utopian vision of Lady Liberty looking skyward, crowned with flags from all the nations of the world—a beacon of hope; the other showed a dystopic, apocalyptic version of the American Dream—one ravaged by anarchy and war. Several of the funded art installations captured the irony of the ideals of the 'American Dream' versus today's realities. *Bummer* by Myk Henry was a super-sized Humvee measuring 38 feet long, 18 feet wide and 16 feet tall. Painted a dull, military khaki tan on one end and multicoloured graffiti on the other, it captured the Jekyll-and-Hyde nature of the American Dream and referenced our addiction and dependence on oil. Transforming a military vehicle into a popular civilian luxury car that was quickly absorbed into suburban culture, the Hummer is the epitome of America's consumer mentality and conspicuous consumption.

In classic Warholian fashion, three funded sculptures extended the iconic *Campbell's Soup Can* (1962) series by exploring other infinite multiples: Bruce Bender's *Ketchup*, a 31-foot-tall bottle of Heinz ketchup; Hedy Sirico's *Chasing the American Dream*, a larger-than-life papier-mâché purse covered with catalogues from Pottery Barn, Wal Mart and the like—a comment on the daily bombardment by advertising, marketing and a spend-thrift culture; and Steven Goodman's *Shrine to the Oven Mitt*, a 10-foot-tall oven-mitt windchime fabricated from stainless steel squares—

an ironic take on consumer worship, transforming an everyday utilitarian object into a sacred altar.

Other funded installations addressed political issues, from border crossings and checkpoints to nuclear weapons and the growing tension with Iran. In *Checkpoint DreamYourTopic* by Amsterdam-based Dadara, participants could enact a symbolic border crossing at the 'Department of Dreamland Security', pass a border patrol guard and enter a small interrogation house where a customs officer awaited them. After a series of formal procedures, a passport for the 'Land of Dreams' was issued and stamped with a visa. Once this process was completed, the border barrier opened to allow passage to the destination of your choice. This symbolic game raised questions about illegal immigration: What does the 'land of dreams' and the 'American Dream' mean for illegal immigrants? Who has the right to cross the border and who does not? Who decides? Another piece that echoed the theme of immigration was Defaid Daf a Joe's *Man Gwyn Man Draw*, the Welsh equivalent of 'The grass is always greener on the other side'. The installation consisted of a wheat field and a flock of life-sized sheep that represented the thousands of people who fled Wales in the nineteenth century in the hope of finding their utopia in the United States. Wheat, which can survive even the harshest conditions, is a metaphor for individuals holding their ground when times get tough. The piece explored the conflicts between idealism and reality along with the idea of forging a self-sustaining community in the United States.

In the multimedia installation *Picture of You: Images from Iran* by Yechdosay Chahar, portraits of Iranian citizens are printed on translucent silk while a soundtrack of Iranian civilian life and a light show simulated the passage of time. The work is designed to bring participants face-to-face with the supposed Iranian 'enemy' and to reflect on the humanity and the construction of the dangerous 'other'. Contemplating the 2008 theme, Harvey referred to Americans who live in the:

> Tarnished squalor of a second Gilded Age. By nearly every measure, America has become a more unequal society. A mere one per cent of the population now controls a third of the nation's wealth. [. . .] Forty years of heedless mass-consumption have turned dreams into delusions. America's awash in debt. Embroiled in a wayward war, its citizens are told to shop (2008a).

Set adrift in a delusional state, Americans, according to Harvey, are grasping to find stable ground in uncertain times.

Between 2000 and 2008, the US civic fabric rapidly unravelled, as citizens grew more distrustful of the government; yet deep-seeded values such as 'freedom', 'opportunity' and the 'power to transform oneself' prevailed. At a time of disillusionment, Burning Man has capitalized on these swiftly crumbling core values. At Burning Man, one can performatively reactivate and revitalize the 'American Dream' through a process of discovery and self-reflexive reevaluation. By examining key questions—'Am I living the American Dream?'; 'What do I need to do to change my life so that I can live the American Dream?'; and most importantly, 'What is the American Dream?'—participants have the opportunity to imaginatively reinvent themselves—a quintessentially American trait. The Man becomes a powerful icon for transformation itself. As the image of America has eroded in the eyes of the international community, participants have an opportunity to reclaim their 'American-ness' by forging a new relationship with the world. This returns to the fact that Burning Man itself is an inherently American event. Where else in the world can citizens separate themselves for seven days to construct an imaginary city and sustain themselves with food, water, and every amenity imaginable; to party, create art and performance, forge community and invent rituals?

The Final Act: Rings of Spectatorship

Saturday night the Man burns. All day, Black Rock City is buzzing with anticipation and excitement. Participants often reserve their most elaborate costumes for this special night. The gates are closed and the population of Black Rock City stabilizes—at least in terms of numbers. All theme camps, art installations and performances have been completed by this time. Saturday is officially a day off for everyone except the Black Rock Rangers, the Man Crew and the Fire Conclave—the teams needed for the Burn. During the day, the Man, Base and Pyro Crews are busy loading the Man with fireworks and the Rangers are placed around the base of the Man for safety reasons.

As a salmon-coloured sunset streaks the sky on the night of the 2004 Burn, a troupe of skydivers floats into Black Rock City.[11] As soon as the sun sinks behind the mountain range, participants begin to fill the first ring of the Great Circle. The inside of the first ring of the Circle is lined with an installation called *L2K* made from 2,000 LED lights that send a pulse of red light racing around the circle. On the night of the Burn, this installation serves as a safety barrier between the first row of spectators and the base. By 7 p.m., Rangers are placed outside the Great Circle, between the spectators and the base, to prevent undocumented participants from wandering in. No one can enter without a laminated badge. Those permitted include the Rangers, the Fire Conclave, the Man Crew, the Pyro Crew, the Burning Man LLC, senior staff and fire fighters.

Dressed in carnivalesque Burn attire, I proceed at dusk to the edge of the Circle to claim my front-row seat. Others have already started to sit around the edge, although there is plenty of free space. Inside the circle is a flurry of activity as Rangers, organizers and fire-safety people prepare the Man for the Burn. There is tension and excitement. As night falls, spectators continue to gather.

The first ring, 75 feet immediately around the Man, is reserved for the Pyro Crew and the Burning Man organizers along with a few select guests.[12] Next is the Great Circle, 600 feet in diameter around the Man, guarded by Rangers and within which the Conclave performs. The next ring is the first 15 rows of people seated around the Great Circle on blankets, lawn chairs or directly on the playa. This ring is filled about two hours before the Burn.

Slowly, the rows and circles fill up. Just before 8 p.m., members of the Fire Conclave arrive, showing their badges to the Rangers as they go to their designated spots. Each group in the Conclave has a location assigned by Rose. Large drums are set up about 150 feet apart. As the sun goes down more Rangers arrive. People start passing around glow sticks and glow bracelets. At 8 p.m., when night falls, the Man's neon is turned on by the Neon Crew, and people yell, 'Burn Him!'

Around the seated ring forms the standing-room circle about 40 rows deep. Behind it, a ring of art cars and buses create makeshift balcony seating. Beyond the cars is another ring of parked bicycles and art cars, a sort of parking lot. Surrounding all this is the open expanse of the playa. The best view of the whole event would be from above: 49,000 spectators creating a series of concentric rings around the Man.

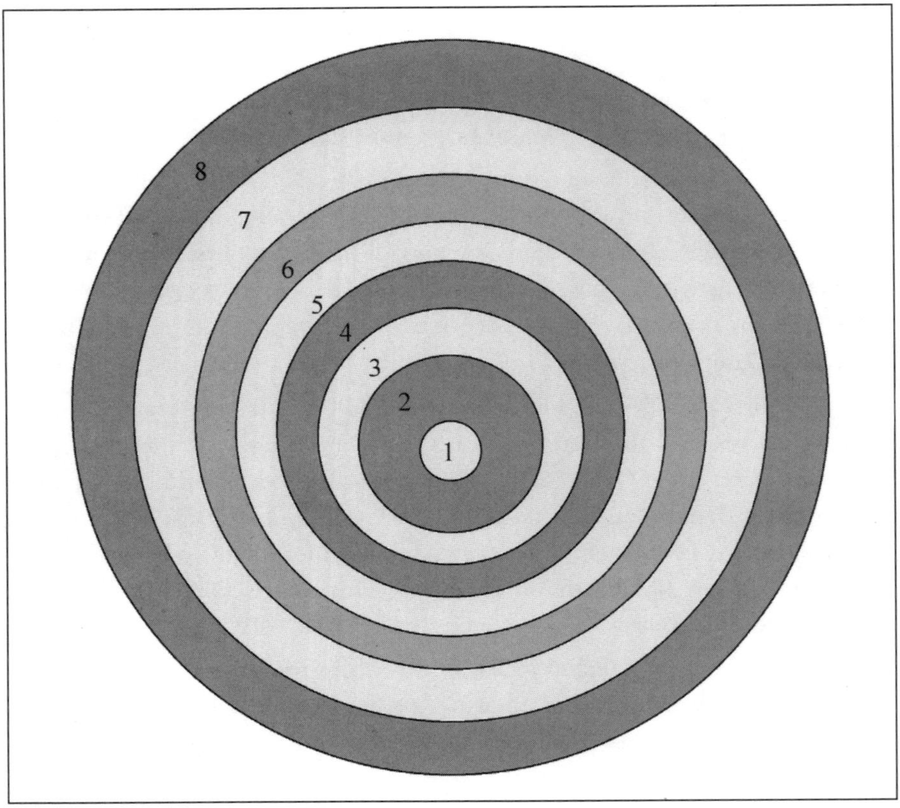

FIGURE 6.9. Rings of spectatorship surrounding the Man on Burn night. 1: The Man, 2: Fire Safety Zone (75 feet around the Man), 3: Fire Conclave: The Great Circle (Barrier of Black Rock Rangers), 4: Early Birds: Seated audience about 15 rows deep, 5: Standing Room: About 40 people deep, 6: Art Cars and Buses: Balcony Seating, 7: Parked Bicycles, 8: Open Playa: Wandering spectators. Created by the author.

The entire City has converged around the Man, waiting for the Burn—and release. Rose is walking around with a walkie-talkie doing last-minute checks and making sure all her groups are in place. The anticipation and excitement are palpable. Two girls from Reno, who have been waiting for hours, say this is their fourth Burn. One woman says, 'Once you've been in the front row, you can't ever go back.' The people sitting behind me are from Mexico and England and this is their first Burn.

At exactly 9 p.m., the Man Crew raises his arms above his head using a pulley system, signalling the beginning of the ceremony. The crowd goes wild, screaming and cheering. The Fire Conclave gets into position—standing in a diamond formation, with a large drum between each group. The drummers begin with a simple rhythm, and each group of 45 spinners follows a Helmsman holding a red light baton. At a signal, the poi are lit simultaneously around the Circle, eliciting an enormous cheer from the crowd. Adhering to the choreography of *The Pulse* (2004) that has been rehearsed for months, the Fire Conclave performs the first synchronized poi spectacle ever of this scale.

The performance must have been spectacular from a bird's-eye view: the simple, beautiful choreography of 650 fire dancers spinning poi, surrounded by thousands and thousands of spectators. On the ground, the Great Circle comes to life with a rhythmic pulse of fire. Sitting in the first row, I hear the Helmsman and the performers counting under their breath to keep the rhythm; the performers seem tense and nervous in their efforts to carry out their tasks and please Rose. When the entire circle is in perfect harmony—and it achieves this synchronicity for only a few seconds at a time—it is mesmerizing to see hundreds of fiery globes swirling simultaneously.

Synchronizing 650 performers is impossible—unless perhaps you are dealing with a military organization. Groups fall out of rhythm with one another; even within the smaller groups, the unity is quickly lost. After five repetitions of *The Pulse* choreography, *zaka*, Rose's term for chaos, the Conclave erupts into a spectacular, energetic frenzy of flame and fury. The entire Circle is a flurry of flames, fire dancing and drumming Poi, fire fingers, fire rope, stilt-walkers with fire wings, fire hula hoops, fire swords and fire staffs dance furiously in the dark, creating a kaleidoscope of light. Orbs of fire glide through the night air forming intricate patterns as the flames lick each dancer's flesh. Silhouettes of skin covered with the luminous white dust of the desert forge a dangerous inferno of delight. The dancers wear the playa on their bodies; traces of the week mark their skin. The dancing and drumming escalate towards a Dionysian frenzy.

After a signal from Rose, one by one, the fires go out. When the last one fades out, there is a roar from the crowd and thunderous applause. Before the applause dies down, fireworks burst out of the Man's head, causing the crowd to go wild and scream even louder—whistles and cheers thunder through the desert air. This was the moment everyone had been waiting for.

Flames begin to lick up the sides of the Observatory as more fireworks explode. The right arm is the first to fall to resounding cheers. Then the left drops, followed by more fireworks. Fire begins to consume the Man, licking up his legs and body and towards his face, devouring the entire bold silhouette. Everyone waits for him to collapse, but he endures, refusing to fall. Suddenly, unexpectedly, he collapses directly into the flames, swallowed whole. Fire whirls spiral off the base of the Man. These whirls are known by the community as 'ancestors', ancient spirits returning to celebrate the ritual Burn. Despite the unpredictable weather of the desert, the Man has never failed to burn. 'This is a funny thing,' Rose observed, 'because of all the years, for some reason it calms down before we go to the Man. I can't explain it. It is almost as if he allows us to burn him and it can storm before and after him but somehow we get to burn him. We have never had to stop the Burn' (2004a).

As soon as the Man falls, people surge towards the fire, like moths to flame. I stand still as a massive wave of screaming bodies rushes past me. Someone runs towards the fire carrying an effigy of a naked George W. Bush as people scream, 'Burn him! Burn him! Burn Bush!' As Bush is thrown into the fire, a huge cheer goes up and the crowd begins to run counterclockwise around the fire. A few people scream, 'Save the Man!' and others holler back, 'The Man is gone!' Chaos and Dionysian frenzy break out, yet no one is trampled or burned. After approximately 15 minutes, many people remain around the roaring fire while others slowly drift back to other parts of the city. What used to be the Man is now a huge bonfire that burns until dawn. Throughout the night, people dance and drum around the pyre.

FIGURE 6.10 (LEFT). Fireworks going off on the Man, 2004. Photograph by John Tzelepis.

FIGURE 6.11 (RIGHT). The Man burning, 2004. Photograph by John Tzelepis.

Cool Down and Aftermath

With the Man gone, it is easy to get disoriented. The City loses its central point of navigation and it is difficult to locate anything or get a sense of distance. Beyond the beehive surrounding what remains of the Man, I watch as the city opens up to a vast sea of people dispersing in every direction. As I move away from the centre and back to camp, the Esplanade is very quiet and dark. All the energy of the city is still swirling around the bonfire remnants of the Man. It is a cold and clear night and the sky above Black Rock City is covered with a blanket of stars. Although the Man is gone and the crowd dispersed, the unifying state of *communitas* and flow persists: the feeling of belonging, ecstasy and total participation stays with each of us as we move back to our camps. After the Burn, the rest of the City slowly comes back to life and after-Burn parties sprout up everywhere. People dance and celebrate until dawn.

As the sun rises over the Black Rock Desert, the sound of the base drum still pulses through the crisp morning desert air and the playa is bathed in a golden light. The centre, where the Man had stood, is at last cool, levelled to ash—only a small wisp of smoke remains. By the time the sun is visible above the horizon, most of Black Rock City is asleep, except for a few still staggering through the streets. The catharsis is complete. After the more sombre temple burns on Sunday night, everyone will go home. The ritual is over—until next year.

As I pull out of Black Rock City, I turn off the playa and onto the tarmac heading towards Gerlach. On the left, the playa is covered in a white, luminous mist—a cloud of dust. I try to get one last glimpse of Black Rock City, but it vanishes like a mirage, leaving only a flicker in my imagination, as if I had merely imagined it. Black Rock City is no longer there.

In 2005, I re-enter the 'default' world to learn that a large portion of New Orleans is underwater. There were rumours during the week that something terrible had happened but we'd had no real news. Those who did know more had begun to collect extra food, clothing and money to send to New Orleans. Gas prices jumped from $2.71 to $3.50 a gallon in seven days, a trend that would continue. It was a startling reality check. Away from the Internet, newspapers, telephones, the everyday modes of communication we take for granted, we were cut off from the rest of the world and the constant stream of information. There had been only the

FIGURE 6.12. The empty playa, 2004.
Photograph by Pixie Vision Productions.

rumour mill and it was hard to distinguish fact from fiction. The devastation of Hurricane Katrina seemed impossible.

Stopping at a diner in Fallon, Nevada, for my first real meal in seven days, I order food at the counter and receive strange looks from the workers, as if I am an alien from another planet. A little boy standing next to me keeps staring at my feet. I look down and see that they and my shoes are caked in white powder even though I had wiped them before I left Black Rock City. Traces of the desert are imprinted on my skin.

I experienced extreme culture shock upon re-entry into 'default' America. Where had I been? What was that place? At Burning Man, I participated in the creation of a community, a temporary, imagined universe that invited artistic experimentation and spiritual growth. But where does this temporary community go after seven days of extremes in the desert? Black Rock City becomes a virtual online community 51 weeks of the year as well as an ever-growing regional network across the United States and the world. Many people leave Burning Man transformed, some only transported. They start new relationships or end old ones, switch careers, decide to move or redesign their lives in other dramatic ways. Few people leave unchanged.

Notes

1 Commemorating the discovery of the Gunpowder Plot on 5 November 1606, Guy Fawkes Night has been celebrated in the United Kingdom ever since. The current celebrations take the form of a series of torch-lit processions through town. Effigies of Guy Fawkes and Pope Paul V, who became head of the Roman Catholic Church in 1605, are featured every year (see Sharpe 2005).

2 Beltane is a specifically Gaelic holiday celebrated on 1 May. Large bonfires herald the arrival of summer in the hope of good harvest, prosperity and well being to all. Need-fires, as they were called, were built to purify cattle of disease and the plague—villages would rush their cattle through the fires to purify the animals as well as themselves. The festival persisted widely until the 1950s and is still celebrated in some places (Adams and Gailey 1977: 5).

3 As Schechner notes, 'Ravana's cremation signals his final surrender to Rama and his release from his demonic self' (1993: 149).

4 Shuster assigned all rights, title and interest in Zozobra in 1964 to the Kiwanis Club of Santa Fe, which owns the trademark and retains the exclusive copyright of the figure (see Goodwin 1998).

5 In my interview with Alan, he preferred not to reveal his surname.

6 As of 2008, members of Flaming Lotus Girls who come and go from the group include: Pouneh Mortazavi, Tamara Li, Charles Gadeken, Lynn Bryant, Rebecca Hotmetal Anders, Tasha Berg, Brent Coons, Lani, Phil Spitler, Steve Monahan, Stella Rubenstein, Brianna Federico, Nicola Ginziler, Ariel and Jon Spear, Liam McNamara, Hazmat Snyder, Mike Prados, Colinne Hemrich, Kezia Z, Cathy Lynch, Mary Newsom, Rich Humphrey, Epona and Phil, Jessica Hobbs, John DeVenezia, Stig, Vanessa Montiel, Aimee Eade, Jacqulynn Schmitz, Karen Cusolito, Dan Das Mann, Jen Clemente, Caroline Miller, Rose Anna Defilippis, Steve Nelson, Wendy Blackburn, Yasmin Mawaz-Khan, Cecilia Camenga, Jeremy Travis, Angela Knowles, Matt Cline, Jordana Joseph, Corey, Olivier Bonin, James Stauffer, Simone Davalos, David Calkins, Jack Shroll, Steven T. Jones, Kiki Petit, Sparky Scott Bartlett, Nick Xanat, Michael Curry, Scott Cotner, Gaspo, Jim Mason and Dave X (Flaming Lotus Girls 2008).

7 'Tedward' is the name he goes by on and off the playa. He chose not to reveal his 'default' name.

8 The Vau de Vire Society calls themselves an 'avant-cabaret community of dancers, actors, aerial and fire artists, acrobats, and beautiful circus freaks' (see Vau de Vire Society 2008). The eclectic ensemble of performers has a carnivalesque aesthetic characteristic of the new American alternative circus.

9 In the past, groups such as Capacitor, Xeno, Nocturnal Sunshine, Thunderdome, Zonerhill and Heebee JeeBee formed the Fire Conclave. Each year, new groups form and old groups fade. The 15 troupes from California in 2004 included Boom Tribe, Burning Otter, Drum Consortium, Fire Arts Collective, Fire Conclave Jugglers, Ganesh, Infinite Kaos, Los Angeles Fire Conclave, Phoenix Projekt, Phoenix Rising, San Francisco Fire Conclave, Santa Cruz Fire Conclave, Santa Barbarians, South Bay Fire Conclave and Temple of Poi. Fire performance troupes from around the country included Third Degree Burn from Missouri, Controlled Burn from Reno, 1337 and Liquid Flame from New York, Northwest Fire Conclave, Pyrosutra and Pyronauts (a conglomerate of solo fire performance artists from around the country) (BMO 2004b).

10 The Commissary operates before, during and after Burning Man to provide food and shade for the DPW, the Black Rock Rangers and the vari-

ous crews that build Black Rock City and the Man. The Commissary used to be a volunteer operation but is now outsourced to caterers. A reported $80,000 is spent to run the Commissary each year (see ibid.).

11 In 2007, there were 151 registered planes at the Black Rock airport, which is managed by 150 volunteers. Hundreds of skydivers float into Black Rock City during the week, especially at sunset (BMO 2007a).

12 Board member Mikel prefers to witness the Burn from the boundary fence.

CHAPTER 7
BURNING MAN DIASPORA: BEYOND BLACK ROCK CITY

> Burning Man is not an event, but a new way of doing and being wherever you are. It is a movement, a force, a river a culture with a thousand tributary streams (Mikel 2001).

> It's like a flower, or more appropriately, like a fire. Maybe it is the impermanence of it that heightens its preciousness (Anisha, in Hollar 2000).

> The return from the play world is like the awakening from a dream: it is always an abrupt fall into the mundane, fraught with the nostalgia of exile (States 1981: 374).

Black Rock City disappears even more abruptly than it appeared. After one week in the desert, its residents disperse and it becomes a virtual online community for the other 51 weeks of the year. The metal sculpture *Passage* (2005) by Dan Das Mann and Karen Cusolito shows a mother and child walking away from the Man and into the world. Trailing behind are 50 flaming footsteps; in front—the vast, open expanse of the playa beckons (see Figure 7.1). At night, fire pours from the mother's hand into the child's, symbolizing transference of knowledge and wisdom. Mother and child have their backs turned to the Man: they are leaving the desert, taking with them the lessons they have learned. *Passage* was selected by the BRAF to be installed on Pier 14 of the San Francisco Embarcadero for the Pier's 16 June 2006 opening, signifying a symbolic transfer of the Burning Man ethos from the desert into the 'default' world.

Radical Vanishing Act: Exodus

The exodus from Black Rock City begins on Sunday and lasts through the week, with the majority of the population leaving on Monday after David Best's Temple Burn on Sunday night—a steady stream of bumper-to-bumper cars inching along towards Route 447. The traffic jam is an active social scene as people run between cars, play music and share leftover food and drinks. After the Black Rock City theme camps and villages are dismantled, all that is left are street signs and survey markers—and the DPW, a group of over 100 individuals. It takes DPW a month to remove every trace of Black Rock City.

On Tuesday begins the major cleanup of large-scale items left behind, including such things as couches, carpets, bicycles and wood. This is followed by a highway cleanup and line sweeps of the desert. For the line sweeps, dozens of volunteer workers walk every inch of Black Rock City, removing any trace of human contact. According to Tony Perez, Black Rock City Superintendent, 'The only way the task can be accomplished is by taking a crew of 30–40 and walking along in lines, going block by block, and bending over constantly to pick up "matter out of place" or MOOP' (BMO 2004b). The line-sweeps of the desert end some time in the first week of October—a full month after Burning Man—before the site inspection date issued by the BLM.

As the DPW gathers the remains of the festival from the desert, what do they do with it? Black Rock City is without trashcans and strictly adheres to the 'leave no trace' motto. So where does all the Black Rock City waste go? Burning Man citizens are discouraged from leaving trash in the nearby towns of Gerlach and Empire, as these small towns cannot handle much garbage. There are two recommended sites for trash disposal: Fernley Sanitation and Lockwood Landfill in Reno, charging

FIGURE 7.1 (FACING PAGE). *Passage* by Dan Das Mann and Karen Cusolito, 2005. Photograph by Gabe Kirchheimer.

between $4 and $6 per cubic yard of trash (ibid.). Many Burners haul their trash back to their points of origin: San Francisco, Los Angeles, Phoenix, Las Vegas and beyond. They store their theme camps, art cars, and other Burning Man paraphernalia in a wide variety of spaces—mostly home garages, warehouse spaces and paid storage units.

The cleanup and disposal of Black Rock City garbage occurs in stages. First, all large-scale debris that can be burned is collected and burned on-site. This takes a few days. 'Ember Reports' are written and submitted by managers from each department, detailing every significant successful attempt to remove waste and every failure. These reports are candid and often critical assessments. This time-consuming effort is then followed by two retreats attended by the six LLC members and senior staff, who use the reports to examine the aftermath of the event in close detail. In 2007, in an effort to reduce waste, the *Afterburn Report* produced a MOOP map that indicated debris left behind. Green indicated minimal debris, yellow was moderate and red was heavy. The heavily populated areas of the Esplanade and the 2 o'clock and 10 o'clock rave camps were the worst offenders.

Each year the Ember Report inventories each item of trash left behind on the site. These items are listed in the annual Burning Man community newsletter in an effort to reduce debris the following year. In 1999, the report indicated the following items were left behind: pistachio shells, peach pits, cantaloupe rinds, gummy bears, lollipop sticks, water-bottle labels, rhinestones, fabric pieces, bobby pins, Q-tips, toilet paper, buttons, feathers, toothpicks, Band-Aids, beads, safety pins, ink pens, shoelaces, ribbons, used condoms, jewellery, nails, screws, nuts, bolts, washers, rings, staples, rivets, cable ties, rope, string, broken glass, melted glass, broken plastic, wire of all kinds, Christmas lights, kitty litter, yarn, earplugs, wood chips, fake leaves and flowers (BMO 2006d). In 2002, pistachio shells, wood chips and cigarette butts were the three biggest offenders (ibid.). The trash fence is the last thing to be removed—in the desert wind, the fence catches up to five hefty bags of trash per day during the event. This takes care of the physical leftovers. But where does the community and Burning Man culture go once the material Black Rock City is cleared away?

Beyond Black Rock City: Burning Man Regionals

The Burning Man community is very active online and participants often record their experiences to share with others, creating what I call the 'affective history' of Burning Man. Many theme camps reconvene through blogs and websites soon after they disperse, to coordinate and organize their camps for the following year. Participants record and document their experiences on personal websites, e-playa (the Burning Man message board; eplaya.burningman.com), or Tribe.net, a widely used site within the community, full of photographs and personal anecdotes. If you googled 'Burning Man' on 1 November 2008, 7,610,000 results would lead you to personal websites and blogs, group websites, media reviews, interviews and more. Burning Man's official website (see BMO 2008a) is a thorough blueprint of the entire community with hundreds of pages, links, photo and event archives, Ember Reports, bios, personnel lists, rules and regulations, questionnaires, Regional Network listings, a chat board, and many other community-related items. Navigating the site is like navigating the playa—full of sensory overload. In addition to the virtual community, live communities continue to spring up and grow.

In his talk 'Viva Las Xmas' at Cooper Union in New York City on 25 April 2002, Harvey reported:

> All over this country, people are starting to organize. They're starting to form networks, and we're organizing to help them. There have now been burns in several states. I want it to feel like a complete model of civilization so that people can go back home with the confidence that they can change the world—that they don't have to be defined by the context that surrounds them—they can define the world by the vision that is inside them (2002).

LLC board members Goodell and Dubois started the Regional Network Programme in 1997 when the BLM and Washoe County officials confiscated all of the admission money collected that year, claiming it as tax. With the BMO in the red and on the verge of collapse, the community reached out to the Organization to ask how it could help save it from financial ruin. The first two regional contacts were Zac Bolan from Calgary, Alberta, and George Paap (aka St Tiki). In 1998, Paap founded Burning Flipside, the first regional art and music festival inspired by Burning Man, held over Memorial Day each year near Austin, Texas. By

FIGURE 7.2. Burning Man Regional Network map, 2008.
Courtesy of the Burning Man Organization.

November 2008, there were 153 registered regional affiliates (with 68 pending) in the United States and 101 international Regionals in 15 different countries from South Africa, China, Japan, Taiwan, Australia, New Zealand, Belgium, France, Germany, Ireland, Italy, the United Kingdom, Spain and Switzerland. There are 34 official regional events around the world (BMO 2008d). Since 1 January 2008, the BMO has interviewed over 60 people and signed on 31 new regional contacts. There have also been 25 official regional Burning Man spin-off events across the country, including Playa Del Fuego (1998) on Delaware's Assateague Island, Burning Toast (2000) in Arizona, Synorgy/Element 11 (1998) in Utah, Interfuse (2003) in Missouri, Firefly (2003) in Vermont, Transformus (2004) in North Carolina, Burning Corn (2005) in Ohio, and Soak (2004) and Critical Massive (2005) in Washington. The Regional Programme is growing faster than the desert event itself (ibid.).

The regional follow-up events bring local Black Rock City citizens together to help each other recover from the culture shock of re-entering the 'default' world. These 'decompression' parties are popular and have taken place in San Francisco, Seattle and New York, cities with large Burning Man populations. Each regional group must receive prior permission from the BMO to use 'decompression' in its event title if admission is charged. Many participants are compelled to make their year-round lives feel more like Black Rock City; this impulse has evolved into a vast global network of Burners.

The New York Regional, started in 1998, was organized and managed in 2008 by Abby Ehmann, Alex Kalmanofsky, David Koren, Cory Mervis and Oscar Yong. Following Burning Man 2001, the 17 November New York decompression *FunKnDeCom* drew over 1,500 Burners to the Lunatarium, a warehouse in Dumbo, Brooklyn. The decompression was hosted by the Madagascar Institute, a Brooklyn-based arts organization spawned by Burners. The 2005 New York decompression, *Psyche's Sideshow*, was held on 19 November at the old Domino Sugar Factory in Williamsburg, Brooklyn. That year, the New York Regional tried to recreate the desert experience on the 40,000-square-foot rooftop with views of Manhattan. The event featured New York-based theme camps such as 'Disorient', 'Kostume Kult' and 'Whiskey and Whores', desert costumes complete with lots of fur, leather and goggles, as well as fire performances, DJs and other Burning Man festivities.

More recently, the BMO began hosting a 'precompression' party in preparation for the desert festival. On Friday, 20 June 2008, the San Francisco precompression party, titled *Dreams and Delusions Flambe*, featured dancing, vaudeville and aerial acts, DJs, a preview of the funded desert installations, and performances by Vau de Vire Society, Gooferman, Fou Fou Ha (Sexy Go Go Buffoons), Kerri Kresinski (acro-vaudeville) and Thrillpeddlers (Grand Guignol Theatre) among other acts.

Harvey argues that although you cannot plan a community, you can create a social niche in which a group will spontaneously coalesce. He attributes the growth of Burning Man culture to its contagious quality. As participants returned to their destinations of origin and attempted to keep the Burning Man spirit and ethos alive by organizing events in a similar vein, they began to return to the main organizers to ask for guidance with building a successful infrastructure to run and manage large events in the spirit of Burning Man. In response, the Burning Man Regional Network was formed.

Harvey said that the BMO's role was clear: it needed to become a leader in the community and assist the regional groups as they tried to find their own identities. As part of this effort, the BMO sought to promote their 10 philosophical principles: radical inclusion, gifting, decommodification, radical self-reliance, radical self-expression, communal effort, civic responsibility, leave no trace, participation and immediacy. It would encourage the Regionals to create radically inclusive interactive environments where social interactions could occur in a decommodified form (Harvey 2004b).

In 2001, in an effort to make contact with regional organizers and draw new crowds to the desert, Burning Man LLC member Mikel ('Danger Ranger') travelled across America to spread the word. On 1 May, he started the Silver Seed Tour of America, a two-month journey departing from the Black Rock Desert and moving east in his 30-year-old RV known as the 'silver seed', a theme camp on wheels. The trip reached 21 states in the southwest, across the Rockies into the Corn Belt, across the Mississippi and into the Midwest, then on to New York. Mikel's mission was to spread the Burning Man ethos and meet local communities face to face (Mikel 2001).

FIGURE 7.3. Precompression: *Dreams and Delusions*, 2008. Courtesy of the Burning Man Organization.

Part of the Regional Network Programme, according to Regional Network coordinator Andie Grace, is to help regional leaders understand their role as community leaders and help them build what she calls 'social architecture' (2005) or what Joseph Beuys would call 'social sculpture'. Beuys's utopian belief in the power of universal human creativity to bring about revolutionary change espoused the idea of society as a Wagnerian *Gesamtkunstwerk*, or total work of art, in which each person becomes an artist and has the power to determine the future social order (see Tisdall 1974). As social agents, regional leaders have the power to affect and instil change within their communities. To become a 'regional contact', an applicant is interviewed over the telephone by Grace to determine whether the individual has leadership abilities and community organizing skills. (The demand to become a regional contact has become increasingly competitive and the wait can be up to a year.) Once selected, the regional contact's job is to bring the local community together at least once a year as well as to distribute information about Burning Man through newsletters, stickers and videos in order to reach new audiences.

Essentially, the regional contact serves as the BMO's marketing arm, although it is not stated in such blunt terms. The rapid growth of Regionals around the country has become a major force in the viral marketing of Burning Man. The Regionals disseminate core Burning Man values and feed the mother organization by promoting ticket sales, which leads to increases in revenue. Since the BMO is dependent solely on ticket sales for revenue, creative strategies for marketing are required. Burning Man uses a combination of word of mouth, the Internet, community newsletters, brochures and postcard mailings to those who purchased tickets in the past. An innovative marketing strategy is 'Film Festival in a Box' (2002), a collection of Burning Man films available to regional groups to show at local events. The proceeds are divided among the regional group, the BMO and the BRAF. Also, promotional materials are sometimes shipped to the contacts to be distributed at local events.

In exchange for marketing the desert event and disseminating Burning Man's cultural values, the regional contact receives one complimentary ticket, a specific email address (yourcity@burningman.com) and a webpage on the main Burning Man website. In an effort to monitor activity across the country as they expanded, the BMO developed a 'regional contract' in 2004, clarifying the relationship between the mother organization and its tributaries. The contract makes it clear that the regional contact is not an employee of Burning Man, and that each assumes independent responsibility for his/her actions. The regional contract, according to Grace, lays out the expectations for both sides and makes the relationship legally binding. It maintains that the 10 principles must be upheld and any profits collected from admission fees are to be reported through transparent bookkeeping. Any funds generated from such events, according to the contract, should 'benefit the local community and the Burning Man community at large, be lawfully constituted, produce real social interaction, avoid commodification and practice some form of open accounting' (Harvey 2004b). Reciprocation can take many forms, from turning local event profits into art installations at the desert event, supporting local theme camps or making financial gifts to the BRAF. While Burning Man does not condone profit-making, if there is any then the organization wants a piece of it.

The regional organizations serve multiple functions: on the one hand, they promote and encourage the Burning Man ethos in their communities; on the other, they serve as local watchdogs for the larger organization and ensure that Burning Man's logo and identity is not being exploited for commercial purposes. In order to prevent the values and culture of the event from being commercially exploited, which has occurred on numerous occasions, the BMO has trademarked words like 'Burning Man', 'Decompression', 'Flambé Lounge' and 'Black Rock City'. Some Regionals try to recreate a simulacra of the desert event even as they are bound by contract not to reproduce Black Rock City exactly. The events can celebrate the 10 principles of Black Rock City and even burn an effigy, but it cannot have the same design as Harvey's and the event cannot be called 'Burning Man'. If money is used for personal gain, the person responsible is removed from his/her position as regional head through a formal complaint procedure involving the affected community, the BMO and the regional leader (BMO 2008d). One major concern held by the BMO is that regional groups will hold Burning Man DJ dance parties that become indistinguishable from commercial entertainment and that the profits will go undocumented, which they have in the past. As Harvey argues in the contract, 'As the national cachet of Burning Man continues to increase, it takes very little imagination to foresee how the core values of our community could eventually be diluted and perverted in the larger world' (Harvey 2004b).

Harvey celebrates the fact that the organization has resisted the temptation of commercial sponsorships, transactions and advertising, and it is ready to protect its culture from such exploitation: 'We resist substituting consumption for participatory experience. [. . .] We have refused commercial sponsorship. We have instituted a ban on vending' (ibid.). Outside the world of the event, the BMO has prevented entrepreneurs from branding their goods with Burning Man's name, image and logo and several lawsuits have been filed to protect the copyright.

While some members of the community liken the Regional Network to a profit-based franchise system modelled on McDonald's or Kentucky Fried Chicken, the contract carefully states (to avoid this impression) that the BMO does not require a percentage of the profits but there are strings attached in the form of 'donations'. Harvey plainly states that the BMO has 'no designs on proceeds gained from such events. We've trademarked "Burning Man" in order to protect the integrity of our culture, not discourage its dissemination. We will, however, encourage donations to the Regional Program and the Black Rock Arts Foundation' (ibid.). He goes on to say that revenue from the desert event is funding all the efforts to establish the Regional Network and, as the programme grows, the BMO will be unable to support a double mission without these valuable donations (ibid.). The bottom line is that the Regionals need to give back and Harvey uses the ethos of the 'gift economy' as a binding contract in which the subtext reads, 'If you are really a member of the community and you believe in the concept of the gift economy, you will share your profits with us in the form of a gift.' Thus, according to Mauss (1967), the gift becomes an obligation and a binding moral contract.

The flipside, as Harvey points out, is that being a regional contact has its financial perks. Since full-time Burning Man organizers receive a salary, he believes that regional organizers can receive financial rewards for their efforts if profits allow. In return for the Regionals' 'gift' to the BMO, from time to time it gifts back to the Regionals money in the form of competitive grants. For example, Harvey boasted that, in 2003, the BRAF received a donation of more than $6,200 from the Seattle decompression (ibid.). In 2005, the Seattle Regional created an $84,000 installation at Burning Man called *The Machine*. Burning Man art curator Christine Kristen (aka Lady Bee) reported that the Seattle group received a $40,000 art grant from the BMO to partially fund their project.

Each year at First Camp in Black Rock City, the BMO hosts a by-invitation-only Regional Network cocktail party for the contacts to meet with the organization leaders. The organizers in turn often travel out to the regional groups to train volunteers and local leadership, because they believe the Regional Programme is the future of the event and serves as a conduit for Burning Man values. Harvey believes that the greatest growth of the community and culture lies beyond the desert event. The pilgrimage to the Black Rock Desert is really an initiation and a catalyst for the formation of a community (2005). Burning Man began as a 'Petri dish', a test tube world that was incubated out in the desert, and has matured and come to fruition:

> It is clear that Burning Man is no longer confined to the Black Rock Desert. Dozens of satellites orbit the Mother Ship; each and every one possesses a unique flavor and character. Burning Man as a cultural movement is still in its youth. The seeds have fallen to the ground, taken root and sprouted. How we nurture this new growth will define the future evolution of the Burning Man movement (Harvey 2004b).

Burners Without Borders

Another seed that has taken root beyond Black Rock City is 'Burners Without Borders', which can be traced to a 2005 effort. After Burning Man in 2005, a group from the Temple Crew went down to Biloxi, Mississippi, to rebuild a Vietnamese Buddhist temple that had been levelled by Hurricane Katrina. Tom Price (aka Thumper), Matt Lindsay (who has worked as a heavy equipment wrangler for David Best's Temple Crew since 2000), and some other crew members and Burners headed directly to Biloxi, along with several tonnes of heavy equipment and nine generators. Lindsay and other crew members moved in and started repairing the temple, using bulldozers and cranes still covered with playa dust. They cleared an adjacent three-acre parking lot of debris, which then became a temporary headquarters for groups like FEMA, OXFAM and the Red Cross, using a 44-foot dome donated by Pacific Domes (well known by Burners). In order to fund the project, they sold T-shirts online and set up a listserv for ongoing donations of materials, food and clothing. A 'Report from the Field' blog was created to document their progress and experience, often threaded with requests for more help and volunteers. They offered a frequent-flyer exchange programme where people could donate miles so that a volunteer could receive a free flight to the devastated areas (BMO 2008e).

'Burners Without Borders' was formed as a result of this outreach. Applying the 10 Burning Man principles, members volunteered their time, labour and resources to the damaged areas, extending the Burning Man project into the everyday in a significant, socially responsible way. 'Burners Without Borders' was the only nongovernmental, or noncharitable organization to assist in the clean-up efforts. The crew worked steadily for four months, with various volunteers rotating in and out of the project. Once the temple was complete, they continued to clear debris and help rebuild devastated areas, primarily helping those uninsured or underinsured. Their mission is to continue to extend volunteer efforts to equally critical projects.

Limits To Black Rock City

In 2005, when I asked Will Roger whether there was a limit to how many people could enter Black Rock City, a point when the event would become too big to manage, he replied, 'I don't have a limit. Maybe 100,000?'. Responding to the same question, Harley K. Dubois candidly replied:

> There is no cap. Only a certain kind of person is going to come out here. It isn't growing that rapidly anymore, only a few thousand [more] each year. [. . .] The questions we continually ask ourselves are: How much space do we have? How many more people can you fit onto this playa? How can you get people into the city safely and how can you get them out? Those are the limiting factors (2005).

According to Crimson Rose, the government still remains the biggest threat because it has the power to shut down the event at any time. She jokes, 'They wish we would go away but they like the money we bring in' (2008). The main factors limiting population growth are the traffic jams on the one lane Highway 447 and Highway 34 as participants enter and leave Black Rock City, the management of the porta-potties and the number of medical, fire and police personnel required to operate the event. However, the population jumped from 30,586 in 2003 to 49,599 in 2008, an increase of 19,013 in five years, the largest growth in the event's history. In 2008, the BLM, for the first time in the event's history, set a population cap of 50,000 and granted the BMO a five-year event permit for rental of the public land. To control the population, 2008 was also the first year that tickets were not sold on the playa.

After 20 years, the BMO has become proficient at managing the event and its attention is shifting to the bigger picture. Harvey considers the for-profit Black Rock City LLC that manages the desert event, the not-for-profit BRAF that funds art projects outside of Burning Man and the Regional Network all as part of the infrastructure of Burning Man culture. Looking out over Black Rock City from First Camp, I asked Roger whether he could have ever imagined that the simple ritual of burning a wooden man on the beach would evolve into this: 'I don't think Larry envisioned anything like this. Now, as we've grown and we've developed a community, we've wanted the community to grow and so we expect it to. But to say that someone had a vision that this was going to happen, no, I don't think so. And we've grown with it' (2005). Each year, Roger is surprised by the scale and ambition of the artwork, as well as the sense of community. His favourite times are before and after the event during the setup and cleanup when there is such an *esprit de corps*: 'That is a force, something tangible that you can feel. The heroes that come together to build this city in such a short period of time, and they work so hard to do it—that's very heartening. It makes you feel good about humanity' (ibid.).

Burning Man continues to grow and evolve organically as a social phenomenon and cultural movement, having had a profound impact—sometimes positive, sometimes not—on hundreds of thousands of lives over 20 years. When one situates it within discourses on secular pilgrimage and utopias, Burning Man enacts the 'not-yet-here', a new paradigm for living in a new and different world, one that is continuously infused with creativity and community. On the downside, there is the ambivalent relationship between commodification and the 'gift economy'. Burning Man does not escape from the commodification it officially rejects; it demonstrates the contradictions of such an attempt to reject the 'default' world. As a utopian political performance, it rehearses the possibility of a 'commerce-free' world, yet at the same time makes evident the fact that one can never fully escape capitalism. It offers participants the illusion of 'total freedom' yet they remain under the constant surveillance of a twenty-first-century panopticon.

Fire at the Heart

Within the ambivalent second world known as Black Rock City, Burning Man serves a carnivalesque function, where participants turn their everyday lives upside down as they experiment with self, identity and community. Black Rock City is a rich space for play on all levels. At Burning Man every participant is expected to be, and most are, a public performer. Performances range from the Burning Man Opera and professional groups such as El Circo, Cirque Berzerk, AWD and Xeno, whose work is informed and transformed by the Burning Man experience and who have collectively created a new genre of performance, the new American alternative circus; to ordinary people dressing up (or down), trying on alternative identities and experimenting in all kinds of ways. What happens in Black Rock City for a week before Labour Day pushes individuals and groups towards their limits of play, ritual and transformational behaviour.

Black Rock City is full of invented rituals, ranging from the solemn to the hilarious to the grotesque. The Lamplighters and the temples of David Best show just how dedicated many of the participants are. These practices and others like them developed out of a sense of play and experimentation, and have become sites for the formation of actual beliefs and ritual transformation. Harvey offers an example of a spontaneously invented ritual: the 'stake' is the humblest but most essential tool to demarcate public space in Black Rock City. This simple object holds a particular symbolic resonance for this community. At the senior staff retreat held at a California-based Tibetan monastery in 2008, Harvey recalls how everyone placed gifts of a symbolic nature on an altar and one staff member brought a bunch of wooden stakes, one of which he began to decorate with art and messages. Other staff members followed suit. At the end of the retreat, the personalized stakes were burned as a symbolic offering to the community. As Harvey proudly pointed out, this ritual was not a prescribed part of the plan, it was spontaneous: 'Everything we do has a communal origin' (2008b).

On 'story night' of the 2008 retreat, as staff members sat around a fire recounting memories, Harvey noticed that through storytelling, the staff rehearsed the history and identity of the event, moving gradually forward in time. The whole story was played out over the evening, starting with the 'elders' moving towards the 'neophytes'. He saw that the concept of 'bosses' dissolved to be replaced by the term 'elders', those who had more experience and wisdom. The ritual retelling of stories is the foundation of myth-making as well as the location for the transmission of knowledge, here creating meaning within the Burning Man culture. It is through these rehearsals of identity and spontaneous rituals that the group's sense of belonging is sustained. A sense of history and connection is established through the repetition of symbolic, expressive gestures from year to year, such as stake-burning and storytelling. 'The lesson of ritual,' said Harvey, 'is that everything is the same but different. Nothing ever stays the same' (ibid.).

At the heart of Burning Man is, of course, fire. The defining ritual of Black Rock City belongs to the Fire Conclave and the burning of the Man. A close look at the formation of the Fire Conclave and the building of the effigy reveals the community's intimate relationship with fire as a transformative catalyst. The reoccurring theme of the phoenix captures the desire to be transformed—to burn your old self and be reborn as someone else. Ultimately, the pilgrimage into the desert is about a need for personal transformation aligned with a need to build community, one that is meaningful and self-selected.

The seven days in the desert are a utopian time of possibility and transformation, a glimpse into how the world could be. But this is not without ambivalence, sacrifice and struggle. The harsh desert conditions create a difficult, uncompromising environment that tests will power and personal strength. While Black Rock City is a simulated environment, the conditions are real, forcing people to interact in immediate and visceral ways. Combining survival with play, Burning Man offers new paradigms for community formation, modes of performance and the invention of rituals that seep back into the mainstream. Like all other countercultural attempts to subvert mainstream values, Burning Man is quickly being co-opted and integrated into mainstream consciousness. In regional centres, at decompressions and via the Internet, Burning Man continues year round and far beyond the gates of Black Rock City.

The Future

What is the future of Burning Man? The future could go in a number of directions. One scenario is that the event continues to grow and Black Rock City expands to accommodate the growth. But unlimited growth will compromise the integrity of the event. Black Rock City could become like other retail entertainment districts, such as Disneyland or Las Vegas. The artists who imagined and built the event might no longer attend. Burning Man could become a big commercialized festival—a direction in which it is already heading. Another scenario is that Burning Man will get too large, spiral out of control, and, like Peter Schumann's Bread and Puppet 'Domestic Resurrection Circus' in Glover, Vermont, be forced by the authorities to shut down (Schumann's Circus ended after two deaths in 1998). In this scenario, Burning Man in the Nevada desert will cease while Burning Man culture continues to evolve through the Regional Network, possibly eventually manifesting as a large-scale event at another location. Or maybe Burning Man has reached its point of equilibrium and will simply go on as it has been.

Dubois is planning for a 10-year window for the event: 'Burning Man is not infinite, it isn't going to go on forever. That is why investing in the outreach is so important' (2008). In Goodell's opinion, in five years, the Burning Man event will still be around but not in 10:

> It has a shelf life. There is no way the six of us [LLC board members] will still be doing it in the same form. I don't think we can last 10 years together. We have to figure out how to change what we are doing. We have some stuff to go through. You might think it is just wonderful that the six of us are still together for 10 years but it has been really challenging recently because we all have different desires in the world (2008).

Mikel sees a significant transformation taking place:

> In a sense, Burning Man really grew up. Things are much different. We are a real operation and a real business that fits in the world. We are no longer the underground that we once were. Three years ago, Burning Man was listed in the travel guide that appears in every hotel room in Northern Nevada and Tahoe. And I thought, this is significant. We went from the bad rebellious group to a part of the tourist attraction for Nevada. Burning Man is starting to become a strong part of the economic culture. Now we are being courted by Nevada's tourist bureau as a

> main attraction. We were on the cover of Nevada Magazine, the tourist guide in August of 2007 (2008).

As a visionary, part of Mikel's role within the BMO is to follow trends and patterns within the community and the world at large in order to position it to take new steps towards the future:

> We have reached a point where the top-level management should not be involved with day-to-day management of the event in the desert. [. . .] In order for Burning Man to continue into the future, we need to cultivate new and young leadership and allow that leadership to take responsibility to run this organization. [. . .] Over the last few years, the LLC has become increasingly insular and is starting to exhibit signs of 'founders syndrome' as the organization grows beyond the ability of the founders to manage it. In time, we shall see how this plays out—that will be material for another book (ibid.).

One dominant trend, which Mikel is following closely, is the move towards the virtual world through sites such as Google Earth, Tribe.net and Second Life, where a virtual Burning Man world has been created, called 'Burning Life'. In 2008, Mikel organized an online Burn in Second Life, two weeks after the actual Burn, to be attended by online virtual avatars. Not only does Burning Man thrive as an active virtual community, the use of technology on the playa is also growing exponentially. Mikel envisions the next step as a two-way communication between a participant on the playa and someone in Australia in live time, so that the person in Australia can experience the event virtually. The key is the two-way interaction interface that will project virtual avatars on the playa. Efforts in this direction are already in place with Playa TV, which broadcasts the event live over the Internet in real time.

One of the allures of the desert event is the desire to be 'disconnected' from the world of cellphones, Internet, advertising and media. However, Internet connection and other modes of connectivity are becoming more accessible. For Mikel, there is no way to avoid connectivity on the playa; rather than fight it, he feels the BMO should embrace it: 'We will reach a point where our technology will become a part of us, like cyborgs. These tools are extensions of our central nervous system. It is the experience that counts' (ibid.). In Mikel's version of the future, participants at Burning Man could have cellphones to locate one another, Internet connection in their theme camps and virtual avatars wandering the playa. 'In the future,' Mikel prophesies, 'everything will be free, except your attention' (ibid.).

Daniel Pinchbeck, author of *2012: The Return of Quetzalcoatl* (2006), argues that Burning Man raises the possibility of creating a different kind of culture within a society, a culture with a completely different vision of the world. Our whole society, in Pinchbeck's estimation, is focused on a 'lock down mode of communication and consciousness with a narrow bandwidth that is completely ungenerous' (2004). Pinchbeck prophesies:

> We are in a period of rapid transformation, which could lead to an entirely different social structure. 2012: the end of the Mayan calendar. In 2013, the world will be like Burning Man, a world that recognizes the spirit and psyche as the essential realities. It would be based on generosity and compassion rather than insecurity and greed (ibid.).

In a transitional stage marked by the compression of time and space, a dimensional shift with a new way of thinking is taking place, what Pinchbeck calls a 'global awakening'—in which Burning Man plays a significant role (ibid.). For Pinchbeck, while art creates a transformative experience, Burning Man is not only an art movement but also a transformational and cultural shift towards a higher consciousness and a revitalized mode of being in the world.

One thing is clear: Burning Man has refined and capitalized on terms such as 'radical self-expression', 'transformational experience', 'participation', 'community' and 'radically inclusive'—catchphrases that have a marketable value in the 'experience economy'. Everyone wants to have a transformational experience, find community and feel included—and that is their strongest selling point. People will pay untold amounts of money to find those things and Burning Man fills that niche market. Burning Man offers a commodified ritual experience in 'participatory culture', mutating and transforming from community to community, yet also remaining recognizable as Burning Man—a brand as distinct as any other.

Burning Man continues to expand exponentially because many people are transformed and discover a community that exists beyond Black Rock City—both temporally and geographically. Their experiences are communicated through word of mouth, the most powerful form of viral marketing in existence. The desert is where the seeds for redefining community are planted, taking root in the consciousness and behaviour of those who have made the pilgrimage. Once people return to their home communities they manifest Burning Man ideals in their everyday lives, inspiring real life changes in themselves and in those they are in contact with.

For Harvey, Burning Man has already moved beyond the desert into the 'default' world, creating and transforming communities in significant ways through art and a renewed understanding of artistic community and collaboration. Harvey proclaimed, 'This is not just an event. This has become a movement' (1999). While Burning Man culture teeters on the edge between the counterculture and the mainstream, the vibrations of Black Rock City, while ephemeral, physically resonate throughout many levels of US culture, both consciously and unconsciously, creating new paradigms of performance, installation art, community and ritual—reawakening an avant-garde spirit in the twenty-first century.

SELECT BIBLIOGRAPHY

ABRAMOVIC, Marina, Chrissie Iles, Sean Kelly and Thomas Mcevilley. 2004. *Marina Abramovic: The House with an Ocean View*. Milan and New York: Charta.

ADAMS, G. B. and Alan Gailey. 1977. 'The Bonfire in North Irish Tradition'. *Folklore* 88: 3–38.

ADAMS, John W. 1973. *The Gitksan Potlatch: Population Flux, Resource Ownership and Reciprocity*. Toronto: Holt, Rinehart and Winston of Canada.

ALAN. 2004. Interview with author. Black Rock City, Nevada. 4 September.

ANDERSON, Lessley. 2004. 'The Great Blow Job Bust'. *Piss Clear* 24 (2 September): 3.

BABINSKI, Tony and Kristian Manchester. 2004. *Cirque Du Soleil: 20 Years Under the Sun. An Authorized History*. New York: Harry N. Abrams.

BACHELARD, Gaston. 1964. *The Psychoanalysis of Fire*. Boston: Beacon Press.

BACZKO, Bronislaw. 1989. *Utopian Lights: The Evolution of the Idea of Social Progress* (Judith L. Greenberg trans.). New York: Paragon House.

BAGSCHIK, Thorsten. 1996. *Utopias in the English-Speaking World and the Perception of Economic Reality*, VOL. 2. New York: P. Lang.

BAKHTIN, Mikhail 1984. *Rabelais and His World* (Hélène Iswolsky trans.). Bloomington: Indiana University Press.

BANES, Sally. 1993. *Greenwich Village 1963: Avant-Garde Performance and the Effervescent Body*. Durham: Duke University Press.

BAUDRILLARD, Jean. 1988. *America*. London/New York: Verso.

———. 1994. *Simulacra and Simulation*. Ann Arbor: University of Michigan Press.

BEAR CLAW MANUFACTURING. Available at: www.bearclawmfg.com/-images/fans. jpg (10 June 2006).

BERNEL, Suzanne. 2008. Telephone interview with author, 20 July.

BEST, David. 2005. Interview with author. Black Rock City, Nevada. 2 September.

BEY, Hakim. 1991 [1985]. *TAZ: The Temporary Autonomous Zone, Ontological Anarchy, Poetic Terrorism*. Brooklyn, NY: Autonomedia.

BLACK ROCK ARTS FOUNDATION (BRAF). 2008. Available at: www.black-rockarts.org (accessed 10 June 2008).

BLOCH, Ernst. 2000. *The Spirit of Utopia*. Stanford, CA: Stanford University Press.

BOURBOULE, Photeine P. 1964. *Ancient Festivals of 'Saturnalia' Type*. Thessalonika: Hetaireia Makedonikon Spoudon.

BOWDITCH, Rachel. 2007. 'Fire, Ritual, Play, and Profit: Rehearsing Utopian Performance at Burning Man'. Unpublished Ph.D. dissertation, New York University.

BOWMAN, Marion. 1993. 'Drawn to Glastonbury', in Ian Reader and Tony Walter (eds), *Pilgrimage in Popular Culture*. Basingstoke, Hampshire: Macmillan, p. 42.

BRAKE, Mike. 1985. *Comparative Youth Culture: The Sociology of Youth Cultures and Youth Subcultures in America, Britain, and Canada*. London/New York: Routledge and Kegan Paul.

BRECHT, Stefan and Peter Schumann. 1988. *Peter Schumann's Bread and Puppet Theatre*, VOL. 4. London/New York: Methuen/Routledge.

BRIGGEMAN, Jane. 2004. *Burlesque: Legendary Stars of the Stage*. Portland, OR: Collectors Press.

BRILL, Louis M. 1996. 'Saturday Night at the Opera'. *Black Rock Gazette* (31 August): 1.

———. 2006. 'The First Year in the Desert'. Available at: www.burningman.com/whatisburningman/1986_1996/firstyears.html (accessed 28 April).

Bureau of Land Management (BLM). 2000. *Black Rock Desert Visitors Guide*. Nevada: National Conservation Area and US Department of the Interior.

Burning Man Opera. 2008. Available at: www.burningmanopera.org (accessed 10 July 2008).

Burning Man Organization (BMO). 1997a. 'Performances'. See www.burningman.com/whatisburningman/1997/97_performances.html (accessed 28 April 2006).

———. 1997b. *Burning Man Summer Newsletter*. Available at: www.burningman.com/whatisburningman/1997/97n_letter_sum_2.html (accessed 1 December 2006).

———. 1999a. 'Art Installations'. Available at: www.burningman.com/1999/ 99_art.html (accessed 2 May 2006).

———. 1999b. *Black Rock Gazette*. Available at: www.burningman.com/ whatisburningman/1999/99_gazette.html (accessed 10 December 2006).

———. 2001. *Afterburn Report*. Available at: www.afterburn.burningman. com/02.html (accessed 28 April 2006).

———. 2002. *Afterburn Report*. Available at: www.afterburn.burningman. com/ 02.html (accessed 28 April 2006).

———. 2003a. *Afterburn Report*. See www.afterburn.burningman.com/ 03.html (accessed 28 April 2006).

———. 2003b. *Black Rock Gazette*. Available at: www.burningman.com/ whatisburningman/2003/03_gazette.html (accessed 1 December 2006).

———. 2004a. *Census*. Available at: afterburn.burningman.com/-04/census/census_voteact.html (accessed 10 December 2006).

———. 2004b. *Afterburn Report*. Available at: www.afterburn.burningman.com/ 04.html (accessed 28 April 2006).

———. 2004c. 'What? When? Where?' Official Burning Man Program for Vault of Heaven event guide. Nevada: Burning Man Organization.

———. 2004d. *Survival Guide*. Available at: www.burningman.com/-survivalguide.html (accessed 2 May 2006).

———. 2004e. 'Kids'. *Burning Man Journal* (Summer–Fall). Available at: www.burningman.com/whatisburningman/2004/04_news_sum-1.html (accessed 5 November 2008).

———. 2005a. *Afterburn Report*. Available at: www.afterburn.burningman.com/05.html (accessed 28 April 2006).

———. 2005b. 'What? When? Where? Official Burning Man Program'. Nevada: Burning Man Organization.

———. 2006a. 'Burning Man Infrastructure'. Available at: www.burningman.com/on_the_playa/infrastructure/dpw.html (accessed 2 May 2006).

———. 2006b. 'Black Rock City Growth'. Available at: www.burningman. com/whatisburningman/about_burningman/brc_growth.html (accessed 17 April 2006).

———. 2006c. *Afterburn Report*. Available at: www.afterburn.burningman.com/ 06.html (accessed 28 April 2006).

———. 2006d. 'History of Burning Man 1886–1996'. See www.burningman.com/whatisburningman/1986_1996/index.html (accessed 28 April 2006).

———. 2006e. 'Burning Man LLC Mission Statement'. Available at: www. burningman.com/whatisburningman/about_burningman/mission.html (accessed 28 April 2006)

———. 2006f. 'Burning Man Ten Principles'. Available at: www.burningman.com/whatisburningman/about_burningman/principles.html (accessed 17 April 2006).

———. 2006g. 'Theme Camps'. Available at: www.burningman.com/-themecamps.html (accessed 6 April 2006).

———. 2006h. 'Burning Man History and Timeline'. Available at: www.burningman.com/whatisburningman/about_bm/bm_timeline.ht ml (accessed 17 April 2006).

———. 2006i. 'Burning Man LLC'. Available at: www.burningman.com/people/project_bio.html (accessed 17 May 2006).

———. 2006j. 'Theme: Hope and Fear'. Available at: www.burningman.com/ 2005/06_theme.html (accessed 2 May 2006).

———. 2006k. 'Creating a Village'. Available at: www.burningman.com/themecamps/create_village.html (accessed 13 April 2006).

———. 2007a. *Afterburn Report*. Available at: www.afterburn.burningman.com/ 02.html (accessed 28 April 2006).

———. 2007b. '07 Burning Man Arsonist to be Arraigned in Pershing County'. Available at: www.burningman.com/-news/070925_arsonist.html (accessed 5 November 2008).

———. 2008a. 'Burning Man Official Website'. Available at: www.burningman.com (accessed 14 April 2004).

———. 2008b. 'Burning Man Senior Staff'. Available at: www.burningman.com/ people/senior_bio.html (accessed 17 May 2008).

———. 2008c. 'Burning Man Support Staff'. Available at: www.burningman.com/people/support_bio.html (accessed 15 November 2008).

———. 2008d. 'Regional Network History'. Available at: regionals.burningman. com/regionals_history.html (accessed 10 December 2008).

———. 2008e. 'Burners Without Borders'. Available at: www.burningman. com/blackrockcity_yearround/regionals/burners_borders.html (accessed 10 December 2008).

———. 2008f. *Afterburn Financial Report*. Available at: www.afterburn.burningman.com (accessed 9 September 2009).

CACOPHONY Society. 2008. Available at: www.cacophony.org (accessed 15 November 2008).

CAILLOIS, Roger. 1959. *Man and the Sacred* (Meyer Barash trans.). Glencoe, ILL: Free Press.

———. 1961. *Man, Play, and Games* (Meyer Barash trans.). Glencoe, ILL: Free Press.

CARSE, James P. 1986. *Finite and Infinite Games*. New York: Free Press.

CHEN, Katherine. 2005. 'Incendiary Incentives' in Lee Gilmore and Mark van Proyen (eds), *After Burn: Reflections on Burning Man*. Albuquerque: University of New Mexico Press, , pp. 109–30.

———. 2009. *Enabling Creative Chaos: The Organization Behind the Burning Man Event*. Chicago: University of Chicago Press.

CLUPPER, Wendy. 2007. 'The Performance Culture of Burning Man'. Unpublished Ph.D. dissertation, University of Maryland.

CODERE, Helen. 1950. *Fighting with Property: A Study of Kwakiutl Potlatching and Warfare, 1792–1930*, VOL. 18. New York: J. J. Augustin.

CORTEZ, Donn. 2005. *The Man Burns Tonight: A Black Rock City Mystery*. New York: Pocket Books.

COURTENEY, Steve (Malderor). 2004. 'Raise Your Own Damn Money!' *Piss Clear* 22 (31 August): 2.

———. 2005. 'I Don't Want Your Stupid Gifts!' *Piss Clear* 27 (31 August): 2.

CROYDEN, Margaret. 1993. *In the Shadow of the Flame: Three Journeys*. New York: Continuum.

CSIKSZENTMIHALYI, Mihaly. 1975. *Beyond Boredom and Anxiety*. San Francisco: Jossey-Bass Publishers.

DA MATTA, Roberto. 1991. *Carnivals, Rogues, and Heroes: An Interpretation of the Brazilian Dilemma* (John Drury trans.). Notre Dame: University of Notre Dame Press.

DAVIES, J. G. 1988. *Pilgrimage Yesterday and Today: Why? Where? How?* London: SCM Press.

DAVIS, Susan G. 1986. *Parades and Power: Street Theatre in Nineteenth Century Philadelphia*. Philadelphia: Temple University Press.

DE CERTEAU, Michel. 1984. *The Practice of Everyday Life*. Berkeley, CA: University of California Press.

DEBORD, Guy. 1977. *Society of the Spectacle*. Detroit: Black & Red.

DEWEY, John. 1958. *Art as Experience*. New York: Capricorn Books.

DOHERTY, Brian. 2004. *This is Burning Man: The Rise of a New American Underground*. New York: Little, Brown and Company.

DOLAN, Jill. 2005. *Utopia in Performance: Finding Hope at the Theatre*. Ann Arbor: University of Michigan Press.

DOWLEN, Matty. 2005. Interview with author. Black Rock City, Nevada. 1 September.

———. 2008. Email interview with author, 15 November.

DRUCKER, Philip and Robert Fleming Heizer. 1967. *To Make My Name Good: A Reexamination of the Southern Kwakiutl Potlatch*. Berkeley: University of California Press.

DUBOIS, Harley K. 2005. Interview with author, Black Rock City. 25 August.

———. 2008. Interview with author. San Francisco. 10 March.

DUNKLE, Daniel. 2004. 'Artist Statement'. Available at: www.burningman.com/art_of_burningman/bm04_theme.html (accessed 15 October 2004).

DURKHEIM, Emile. 1996. 'Ritual, Magic, and the Sacred' in Ronald L. Grimes (ed), *Readings in Ritual Studies*. Upper Saddle River, NJ: Prentice Hall, pp. 188–93.

EASON, Cassandra. 2008. *Fabulous Creatures, Mythical Monsters, and Animal Power Symbols: A Handbook*. London: Greenwood Press.

ECKLEY, Wilton. 1984. *The American Circus*. Boston: Twayne Publishers.

EMIGH, John. 1996. *Masked Performance: The Play of Self and Other in Ritual and Theatre*. Philadelphia: University of Pennsylvania Press.

EVERETT, Neal. 2005. Interview with author. Black Rock City, Nevada. 1 September.

———. 2008. Interview with author. Black Rock City, Nevada. 3 September.

FALASSI, Alessandro. 1987. *Time Out of Time: Essays on the Festival*. Albuquerque: University of New Mexico Press.

FENNER, Mildred Sandison and Wolcott Fenner. 1970. *The Circus: Lure and Legend*. Englewood Cliffs, NJ: Prentice-Hall.

FIRAT, A. Fuat and Nikhilesh Dholakia. 1998. *Consuming People: From Political Economy to Theaters of Consumption*. London, New York: Routledge.

FLAMING LOTUS GIRLS. 2008. Available at: www.flaminglotus.com (accessed 1 August 2008).

FOUCAULT, Michel. 1979. *Discipline and Punish: The Birth of the Prison*. New York: Vintage Books.

———. 1986 [1967]. 'Of Other Spaces'. *Diacritics* 16 (24): 22–7.

———. 1988. *History of Sexuality*. New York: Vintage Books.

———. 1999. *Abnormal*. New York: Picador.

FOX, Michael V. 1988. *Temple in Society*. Winona Lake: Eisenbrauns.

GAMELAN X. 2008. Available at: www.gamelanx.com (accessed 18 November 2008).

GAROFOLI, Joe. 2007. 'Sustaining the Flame/Burning Man Artists Battle Urban Constraints to Keep Spirit Alive.' *San Francisco Chronicle* (20

August). Available at: www.extra-action.com/press/sfgate.html (accessed 5 November 2008).

Gazette Staff. 1999. 'Spencer Tunick's *Krystl*'. *Black Rock Gazette* (2 September): 1.

———. 2000. 'Arrests'. *Black Rock Gazette* (30 August): 2.

Gerlach Resident. 2004. Interview with author. Gerlach, Nevada. 2 September.

Gilmore, Lee. 2005a. 'Fires of the Heart: Ritual, Pilgrimage, and Transformation at Burning Man' in Lee Gilmore and Mark van Proyen (eds), *After Burn: Reflections on Burning Man*. Albuquerque: University of New Mexico Press, pp. 43–64.

———. 2005b. 'Theatre in Crowded Fire: Spirituality, Ritualization and Cultural Performativity at the Burning Man Festival'. Unpublished Ph.D. dissertation, Graduate Theological Union.

—— and Mark van Proyen (eds). 2005. *AfterBurn: Reflections on Burning Man*. Albuquerque: University of New Mexico Press.

Glaser, Jim. 2006. Interview with author. Brooklyn, New York. 5 May.

Goffman, Erving. 1959. *The Presentation of Self in Everyday Life*. Garden City, New York: Doubleday.

Goodell, Marian. 2004. Interview with author. Black Rock City, Nevada. 1 September.

———. 2008. Interview with author. Burning Man headquarters, San Francisco. 10 March.

Goodwin, Lee. 1998. 'Zozobra: Heritage and Change Through Community Celebrations: A Photographic Essay'. *The Western Historical Quarterly* 29 (2): 215–23.

Grace, Andie. 2005. Interview with author. Black Rock City, Nevada. 1 September.

———. 2008. Interview with author. Burning Man Headquarters, San Francisco. 11 March.

Hale, Kristin and Leslie Pritchcett. 2005. 'A Foundation for Community'. *Burning Man Journal* (Summer). Available at: www.burningman.com/-preparation/newsletters/2005-summer/05_news_sum4.html (accessed 5 November 2008).

HARDT, Michael and Antonio Negri. 2000. *Empire*. Cambridge, MA.: Harvard University Press.

HARVEY, Larry. 1997a. 'Burning Man: What Is It?' *Burning Man Spring Newsletter*. Available at: www.burningman.com/whatisburningman/1997/-97n_letter_sprg_1.html (accessed 5 November 2008).

———. 1997b. Speech to Burning Man Community, Hualapai Playa (30 August). Available at: www.burningman.com/whatisburningman/1997/97-_speech_1.html (accessed 5 November 2008).

———. 1998a. Speech to the Burning Man Community at Center Camp, September. Available at: www.burningman.com/whatisburningman/1998/ 98_speech_1.html (accessed 13 April 2006).

———. 1998b. Speech to Burning Man community (5 September). Available at: http://www.burningman.com/whatisburningman/1998/-98_speech_1.html (accessed 5 November 2008).

———. 1999. 'Desert Civilization'. *Burning Man Summer Newsletter*. Available at: www.burningman.com/whatisburningman/1999/99n_letter_-sum_0.html (accessed 10 October 2008).

———. 2000a. 'La Vie Boheme'. Speech at Walker Art Center, Minneapolis. Available at: www.burningman.com/art_of_burningman/ la_vie_boheme.html (accessed 2 May 2006).

———. 2000b. 'The Meaning of Participation'. Available at: www.burningman.com/whatisburningman/2000/00n_letter_sum_0.html (accessed 2 May 2006).

———. 2001. 'Radical Ritual'. Available at: www.gracecathedral.org/enrichment/ forum/for_20010520.html (accessed 2 May 2006).

———. 2002. 'Viva Las Xmas'. Speech at Cooper Union (25 April). Available at: www.burningman.com/whatisburningman/lectures/-viva.html (accessed 20 September 2008).

———. 2003. Speech at San Francisco Civic Center, 7 December'. Avail-able at: www.burningman.com/whatisburningman/lectures/-2003_gonzalez. html (accessed 17 May 2006).

———. 2004a. Interview with author. Black Rock City, Nevada. 31 August.

———. 2004b. 'Regional Contract'. Available at: regionals.burningman. com/network_coverletter.html (accessed 10 December).

———. 2005. 'Media Mecca' panel with Larry Harvey, Marian Goodell, Tom Price, Andy Grace and Harley Dubois. Black Rock City, Nevada. 1 September.

———. 2006a. 'Postmodernism and the Primal World of Burning Man'. Available at: www.zpub.com/burn/larry4.html (accessed 2 May 2006).

———. 2006b. 'About Ritual, Community, and Burning Man'. Available at: www.zpub.com/burn/larry2.html (accessed 13 April 2006).

———. 2006c. 'The Road to U(Dys)topia'. Available at: www.burningman.com/whatisburningman/2006/06_theme.html (accessed 10 August 2008).

———. 2008a. 'Theme: The American Dream'. Available at: www.burningman. com/2005/08_theme.html (accessed 5 November 2008).

———. 2008b. Interview with author. Burning Man headquarters, San Francisco. 11 March.

HAWTHORNE, Dusty and Michael Mikel. 2003. Interview with Pepe Ozan. San Francisco. Unpublished.

HAYDEN, Dolores. 1976. *Seven American Utopias: The Architecture of Communitarian Socialism, 1790–1975*. Cambridge, MA: MIT Press.

HEACOCK, Robert. 2006. Telephone interview with author, 5 June.

HEATH, Joseph and Andrew Potter. 2004. *Nation of Rebels: Why Counterculture Became Consumer Culture*. New York: Harper Business.

HEMRICH, Colinne. 2004. Interview with author. Black Rock City, Nevada. 3 September.

HEESTERMAN, J. C. 1993. *The Broken World of Sacrifice: An Essay on Ancient Indian Ritual*. Chicago: University of Chicago Press.

HILL, Dee J. 2004. *Freaks and Fire: The Underground Reinvention of Circus*. Brooklyn, NY: Soft Skull Press.

HINE, Robert V. 1966. *California's Utopian Colonies*. New Haven: Yale University Press.

HOCKETT, Jeremy. 2004. 'Reckoning Ritual and Counter-culture in the Burning Man Community: Communication, Ethnography, and the

Self in Reflexive Modernism'. Unpublished Ph.D. dissertation, University of New Mexico.

HOFMANN, Shawna. 2008. Telephone interview with author, 12 October.

HOLDEN, Kalea. 2004. 'Confessions of an Eleven-Year-Old Burner'. *Piss Clear* 23 (1 September): 4.

HOLLAR, Julie. 2000. 'Real Hallucinations'. *Burning Man Summer Newsletter*. Available at: www.burningman.com/whatisburningman/2000/00n_letter_ sum_0.html (accessed 2 May 2006).

HUIZINGA, Johan. 1970. *Homo Ludens: A Study of the Play Element in Culture*. London: Paladin.

HYDE, Lewis. 1983. *The Gift: Imagination and the Erotic Life of Property*. New York: Random House.

JAKOBSEN, Janet R. and Ann Pellegrini. 2003. *Love the Sin: Sexual Regulation and the Limits of Religious Tolerance*. New York, London: New York University Press.

JENNINGS, Theodore. (1996). 'On Ritual Knowledge' in Ronald L. Grimes (ed.), *Readings in Ritual Studies*. Upper Saddle River, NJ: Prentice Hall, pp. 324–34.

KAMAKSHI. 2007. 'Invocation: Pepe Ozan'. *Gateless* (5 May). Available at: gatelessgate.wordpress.com/2007/05/05/invocation-pepe-ozan/ (accessed 15 November 2008).

KANTER, Rosabeth Moss. 1972. *Commitment and Community: Communes and Utopias in Sociological Perspective*. Cambridge, MA: Harvard University Press.

KAPROW, Allan. 2003 [1966]. *Essays on the Blurring of Art and Life*. Berkeley, CA: University of California Press.

——, Gutai Bijutsu Kyokai and Jean Jacques Lebel. 1966. *Assemblage, Environments & Happenings*. New York: H. N. Abrams.

KAUFMANN, Moritz. 1972. *Utopias: Or, Schemes of Social Improvement*. Folcroft, PA: Folcroft Library Editions.

KELLEY, Jeff. 2003. 'Introduction' in Allan Kaprow, *Essays on the Blurring of Art and Life*. Berkeley, CA: University of California Press, pp. i–xxvi.

KILE, Jessie. 2004. Interview with author. Black Rock City, Nevada. 4 September.

KIRBY, Michael. 1994 [1965]. 'Happenings: An Introduction' in Mariellen R. Sandford (ed.), *Happenings and Other Acts*. London: Routledge, pp. 1–38.

—— and Jim Dine. 1965. *Happenings, an Illustrated Anthology. Scripts and Productions by Jim Dine and Others*. New York: Dutton.

KOZINETS, Robert V. 2002. 'Can Consumers Escape the Market? Emancipatory Illuminations from Burning Man'. *Journal of Consumer Research* (29 June 2002): 20–38.

—— and John F. Sherry. 2005. 'Welcome to the Black Rock Café' in Lee Gilmore and Mark van Proyen (eds), *After Burn: Reflections on Burning Man*. Albuquerque: University of New Mexico Press, 87–108.

KRISTEN, Christine (Lady Bee). 2003. 'The Outsider Art of Burning Man' *Leonardo* 36(5): 343–8.

———. 2005. Interview with author. Black Rock City, Nevada. 1 September.F

LAMPLIGHTERS. 2004. Speech to the community.

LAWLOR, Anthony. 1994. *The Temple in the House: Finding the Sacred in Everyday Architecture*. New York: Putnam.

LEAVE NO TRACE INC. 2001. *Desert and Canyons: Leave no Trace Skills and Ethics*. Boulder, Colorado: Leave No Trace Inc.

LEVENTMAN, Seymour. 1982. *Counterculture and Social Transformation: Essays on Negativistic Themes in Sociological Theory*. Springfield, IL: Thomas.

LEVY, Laura M. 2004. Interview with author. Gerlach, Nevada. 2 September.

LUNDQUIST, John M. 1993. *The Temple: Meeting Place of Heaven and Earth*. London: Thames and Hudson.

MACLEISH, Archibald. 1939 *America Was Promises*. New York: Duell, Sloan & Pearce, Inc.

MADAGASCAR INSTITUTE. 2008. Available at: www.madagascarinstitute.com (accessed 12 November 2008).

MAGIVER (Black Rock Ranger). 2004. Interview with author. Black Rock Ranger Headquarters: Black Rock City, Nevada. 2 September.

MALAKAI. 2008. Telephone interview with author. El Circo, November 15.

MANGRUM, Stuart. 1998. 'What is Burning Man?' *Burning Man Summer*

Newsletter. Available at: www.burningman.com/whatisburningman/1998/-98n_letter_sum_1.html (accessed 10 October 2008).

MANN, A. T. 1993. *Sacred Architecture*. Rockport, MA: Element.

MANY MOUTHS ONE STOMACH. 2008. Available at: www.allsoulsprocession.org (accessed 11 November 2008).

MARIN, Louis. 1984. *Utopics: Spatial Play*. Atlantic Highlands, NJ/London: Humanities Press/Macmillan.

MARSHALL, Cassandra. 2004. Interview with author. New York City, New York. 4 March.

MAUSS, Marcel. 1967. *The Gift: Forms and Functions of Exchange in Archaic Societies*. New York: W. W. Norton.

McMAHON, Michael and Michael G. Morris. 2005. 'Battling with Demons: How Our Correspondent Gave Up Capitalism in the Desert'. *The Economist* (22 September). Available at: www.economist.com/search/-search.cfm?rv=2&qr=battling+with+demons%3A+how+our+correspondent+gave+up+capitalism+in+the+desert&area=1&x=5&y=9 (accessed 5 November 2008).

MELVILLE, Keith. 1972. *Communes in the Counter Culture: Origins, Theories, Styles of Life*. New York: William Morrow.

MERMELL, Dean. 2000. *Eye of Rudra*. Documentary.

MIKEL, Michael. 2001. 'Silver Seed Tour'. Available at: www.roadtrip.burningman.com/content/index.html (accessed 15 July 2006).

———. 2008. Interview with author. Burning Man headquarters, San Francisco. 12 March.

MINDBENDER. 2006. Interview with author. Brooklyn, New York. April 4.

MOORE, Sally Falk and Barbara G. Myerhoff. 1977. *Secular Ritual*. Assen: Van Gorcum.

MORE, Thomas. 1516. *Utopia*. Louvain: Thierry Martin.

MORGAN, Arthur Ernest. 1946. *Nowhere was Somewhere: How History Makes Utopias and How Utopias Make History*. Chapel Hill: The University of North Carolina Press.

MORRIS, William. 1890. *News from Nowhere: Or, an Epoch of Rest, Being Some Chapters from a Utopian Romance*. Hammersmith: Kelmscott Press.

MOSES, Tai. 2001. 'Some Like it Hot'. *Metro Santa Cruz* (22–29 August).

Available at: http //www.metroactive.com/papers/cruz/08.22.01/fire-0134.html (accessed 25 April 2005).

MULROY, Patrick. 2006. 'Achtung Hippie: Reflections on the Burning Man Scam' (9 September). Available at: blog.hisnameistimmy.com/?p=12 (accessed 1 October 2006).

NASH, Leo. 1995. 'Interview with Larry Harvey'. Available at: www.z-pub.com/burn/larry5.html (accessed 13 April 2006).

——— and Daniel Pinchbeck. 2007. *Burning Man: Art in the Desert*. New York: Harry N. Abrams, Inc

NEGLEY, Glenn Robert and J. Max Patrick. 1971 [1952]. *The Quest for Utopia*. College Park, MD: McGrath Pub. Co.

NEWTON, Eric. 2005. Interview with author. Black Rock City, Nevada. 1 September.

NIBLEY, Hugh and Don E. Norton. 1992. *Temple and Cosmos: Beyond this Ignorant Present*, VOL. 12. Salt Lake City, UT/Provo, UT: Deseret Book Co./Foundation for Ancient Research and Mormon Studies.

OHTAKE, Miyoko. 2007. 'A Fiery Q&A With the Prankster Accused of Burning the Man'. *San Francisco Chronicle* (1 September). Available at: www.sfgate.com/cgi-bin/article.cgi?f=/c/a/2007/09/01/MN8LRTBB-N.DTL (accessed 15 November 2008).

OLIVER, Anthony. 2001. 'Paper Offerings for the Dead'. *Eye* 58. Available at: www.eyemagazine.com/feature.php?id=126&fid=556 (accessed 2 June 2008).

PARRINGTON, Vernon Louis. 1964. *American Dreams: a Study of American Utopias*. New York: Russell & Russell.

PAIUTE Tribe. 2008. Available at: www.nativeamerican.com/paiute.htm (accessed 10 October 2008).

PAULINE, Mark. 2008. 'Survival Research Laboratories'. Available at: www.srl.org (accessed 10 November 2008).

PEARSON, Mike and Michael Shanks. 2001. *Theatre/Archaeology*. London, New York: Routledge.

PIKE, Sarah M. 2005. 'No Novenas for the Dead: Ritual Action and Communal Memory at the Temple of Tears' in Lee Gilmore and Mark van Proyen (eds), *After Burn: Reflections on Burning Man*. Albuquerque: University of New Mexico Press, pp. 195–210.

PINCHBECK, Daniel. 2002. *Breaking Open the Head: A Psychedelic Journey into the Heart of Contemporary Shamanism*. New York: Broadway Books.

———. 2004. Interview with author. New York. 1 April.

———. 2006. *2012: The Return of Quetzalcoatl*. New York: Jeremy Tarcher/ Penguin.

PINE, B. Joseph II and James H. Gilmore. 1999. *The Experience Economy: Work is Theatre and Every Business a Stage*. Boston: Harvard Business School Press.

PLATO. 1974. *Plato's Republic* (G.Ma. Grube trans.). Indianapolis: Hackett.

POLLACK, Paradox. 2008. Interview with author. The Merry-Go-Round, San Francisco. 12 March.

POST, Paulus, Johannes Gijsbertus, J. Pieper and Marinus Van Uden. 1998. *The Modern Pilgrim: Multidisciplinary Explorations of Christian Pilgrimage*. Leuven: Peeters.

PRADEAU, Jean-Francois. 2000. 'Plato's Atlantis: The True Utopia' in Schaer, Roland Claeys, Gregory Sargent, Lyman Tower (eds), Utopia: The Search for the Ideal Society in the Western World. New York: Oxford University Press and New York Public Library, pp. 83–94.

RAINBOW FAMILY. 2008. Available at: welcomehome.org (accessed 15 August 2008).

READER, Ian and Tony Walter. 1993. *Pilgrimage in Popular Culture*. Basingstoke, HA: Macmillan.

REGYNALONGLANK. 2004. 'Rape Does Occur At Burning Man' (blog on *eplaya*, 16 September). Available at: eplaya.burningman.com/viewtopic.php?t= 6937 (accessed 15 April 2006).

REID, Terry. 2003. 'Playa Community Policing'. *Black Rock Gazette* (29 August). Available at: www.burningman.com/media/doc/whatisburningman/2003/-brg03_partyline_fri.pdf (accessed 10 October 2009).

REYNA, Raquel. 2008a. Email interview with author. 15 November.

———. 2008b. Telephone interview with author. 20 November.

RICHTER, Hans. 1965. *Dada: Art and Anti-Art*. New York: McGraw-Hill.

RIDENOUR, Al. 2006. 'Experiences Beyond the Mainstream'. Available at: www.cacophony.org/primer.html (accessed 17 April 2006).

RINALDI, John (Chicken John). 2006. Interview with author. Brooklyn, New York. 30 April.

ROBERTS, Adrian. 2004a. 'Save the Children: Kids at Burning Man is This Year's Hot-Topic Topic'. *Piss Clear* 23 (1 September): 1–4.

———. 2004b. 'Do it for the Kids, Man!' *Piss Clear* 23 (1 September): 4.

———. 2007a. 'How to Dress Like a Burner'. *Piss Clear* 25 (2 September): 1.

———. 2007b. Telephone interview with author, 15 November.

ROGER, Will. 2005. Interview with author. Black Rock City, Nevada. 2 September.

ROMANO, Tricia. 2003. 'Disco Inferno'. *Village Voice* (26 February–4 March): Available at: www.villagevoice.com/2003-02-25/news/disco-inferno/ (accessed 15 October 2008).

ROSE, Crimson. 2004a. Interview with author. Black Rock City, Nevada. 1 September.

———. 2004b. Opening Fire Ceremony Speech. Black Rock City, Nevada. 30 August.

———. 2008. Interview with author. Burning Man headquarters, San Francisco. 11 March.

ROSENTHAL, Rebecca. 2004. Interview with author. Black Rock City, Nevada. 4 September.

ROSSOTTI, Hazel. 1993. *Fire*. Oxford; New York: Oxford University Press.

ROSZAK, Theodore. 1969. *The Making of a Counter Culture: Reflections on the Technocratic Society and Its Youthful Opposition*. Garden City, NY: Doubleday.

ROTH, Gabrielle. 2008. '5 Rhythms Waves' Available at: www.gabrielleroth. com (accessed 10 September 2008).

RUDNITSKY, K. 1981. *Meyerhold, the Director*. Ann Arbor: Ardis.

RUIZ, Don Miguel. 1997. *The Four Agreements: A Practical Guide to Personal Freedom*. San Rafael, CA: Amber-Allen Publishing.

———. 1999. *Mastery of Love: A Practical Guide to the Art of Relationship*. San Rafael, CA: Amber-Allen Publishing.

RYDELL, Robert W. 1984. *All the World's a Fair: Visions of Empire at American International Expositions, 1876-1916*. Chicago: University of Chicago Press.

SARGENT, Denny. 1993. *Global Ritualism: Myth and Magic Around the World*. St Paul, MN: Llewellyn.

SARGENT, Lyman Tower. 2000. 'Utopian Traditions: Themes and Variations' in Roland Claeys, Gregory Sargent, Lyman Tower Sargent (eds), *Utopia*. New York: Oxford University Press and New York Public Library, pp. 8–17.

SCHECHNER, Richard. 1973. *Environmental Theater*. New York: Hawthorn Books.

———. 1985. *Between Theater & Anthropology*. Philadelphia: University of Pennsylvania Press.

———. 1988. *Performance Theory*. New York: Routledge.

———. 1993. *The Future of Ritual: Writings on Culture and Performance*. London; New York: Routledge.

SCHOOP, Terry. 2004. Interview with author. Black Rock City, Nevada. 3 September.

SCHWARTZ, David and Richard 'Spark' Szpigiel. 1999. Programme for AWD's performance at the Eureka Theater.

SHARPE, James. 2005. *Remember, Remember: A Cultural History of Guy Fawkes Day*. Cambridge: Harvard University Press.

SHERRY. 2004. Interview with author. Gerlach, Nevada. 30 August.

SHIPWRECK. 2003. 'The Temple is Coming'. *Black Rock Gazette* (27 August): 1.

SIA, Chris. 2005. Interview with author. Black Rock City, Nevada. 1 September.

SIMS, Caitlyn. 2005. 'Extreme Dance'. *Dance Spirit* (January): 47–53.

SINGER, Milton B. 1972. *When a Great Tradition Modernizes: An Anthropological Approach to Indian Civilization*. New York: Praeger Publishers.

SKLAR, Deidre. 2001. *Dancing with the Virgin: Body and Faith in the Fiesta of Tortugas, New Mexico*. Berkeley: University of California Press.

SLATON, Joyce. 2000. ''Interview with David Mermell'. Available at: www.sfindie.com/archive-digital00/html/eye_rudra.html (accessed 11 October 2008).

SLOPPY (Black Rock Ranger). 2004. Interview with author. Black Rock Ranger Headquarters: Black Rock City, Nevada. 2 September.

STARZECKA, D. C. 1996. *Maori Art and Culture*. London: British Museum Press.

STATES, Bert O. 1981. 'Phenomenology of the Curtain Call'. *Hudson Review* 34:(3): 371–80.

STERLING, Bruce. 1996. 'Greetings from Burning Man! The New American Holiday'. *Wired* 4(11): 196.

STEVENS, Richard. 2003. Burning for the Other: Semiotics of a Levinasian Theological Aesthetics in the Light of Burning Man'. Unpublished Ph.D. dissertation, Graduate Theological Union.

SUTTON-SMITH, Brian. 1997. *The Ambiguity of Play*. Cambridge, MA: Harvard University Press.

SWATOS, William H. and Luigi Tomasi. 2002. *From Medieval Pilgrimage to Religious Tourism: The Social and Cultural Economics of Piety*. Westport, CO.: Praeger Publishers.

SZPIGIEL, Richard 'Spark'. 2006. Interview with author. Brooklyn, New York. 4 April.

———. 2008. Email interview with author. 12 November.

TAIBBI, Matt. 2005. 'White Madness'. *Rolling Stone* 983(49) (22 September): 49–52.

TAYLOR, Diana. 2003. *The Archive and the Repertoire: Performing Cultural Memory in the Americas*. Durham: Duke University Press.

TEDWARD. 2005. Interview with author. Fire Conclave: Black Rock City, Nevada. 2 September.

———. 2006. Telephone interview with author. July 10.

TERDIMAN, Daniel. 2005. 'Burning Man Mourns the Big Easy'. *Wired* (6 September). Available at: www.wired.com/culture/lifestyle/news/2005/-09/68765 (accessed 5 November 2008).

THE CRUCIBLE. 2008. Available at: www.thecrucible.org (10 August).

TOD, Ian and Michael Wheeler. 1978. *Utopia*. London: Orbis.

TISDALL, Caroline. 1974. *Art into Society: Society into Art*. London: ICA.

TURNER, Victor. 1969. *The Ritual Process: Structure and Anti-Structure* (The Lewis Henry Morgan Lectures) New York: Aldine de Gruyter.

—— and Edith Turner. 1978. *Image and Pilgrimage in Christian Culture: Anthropological Perspectives*. New York: Columbia University Press.

ULRICH, John M. and Andrea L. Harris. 2003. *GenXegesis: Essays on Alternative Youth (Sub) Culture*. Madison: University of Wisconsin Press/Popular Press.

VAN GENNEP, Arnold. 1960. *The Rites of Passage*. Chicago: University of Chicago Press.

———. 1996 [1909]. 'Territorial Passage and the Classification of Rites' in Ronald L. Grimes (ed.), *Readings in Ritual Studies*. Saddle River, New Jersey: Prentice Hall, pp. 529–35.

VAN RHEY, Darryl. 1997. 'Burning Man and the Art of the 1990s: A Conversation with Larry Harvey in 1997'. Available at: www.burningman. com/whatisburningman/lectures/90s_art.html (accessed 23 August 2004).

———. 1999. 'Postmodernism and the Primal World of Burning'. Available at: www.zpub.com/burn/larry4.html (accessed 15 December).

———. 2002. 'An Economy of Gifts: Interview with Larry Harvey'. Available at: www.burningman.com/whatisburningman/2002/02_-news_ sum_2.html (accessed 28 April 2006).

VAU DE VIRE SOCIETY. 2008. Available at: www.vaudeviresociety.com (accessed 1 December 2008).

VONARY, Sarah. 2004. Interview with author. REMSA: Black Rock City, Nevada. 2 September.

WOOLDRIDGE, Mike. 1996. 'Organizers Deny Takeover Rumors'. *Black Rock Gazette* (29 August): 2.

WOLFE, William Dire. 2005. Interview with author. Black Rock City, Nevada. 2 September.

YINGER, Milton J. 1982. *Countercultures: The Promise and the Peril of a World Turned Upside Down*. New York/London: Free Press/Collier Macmillan.

INDEX